NYC RESTAURANTS

Editor-in-Chief
André Gayot

Managing Editor
Sharon Boorstin

Chief Restaurant Critic
Edward Guiliano

Associate Editors
Margaret Clark
Catherine Jordan

Contributing Editors
Arlyn Blake, Louis Charles, Sallie Han,
Bob Lape, John Mariani, Jack Robertiello,
Daniel Rosenblatt, Sheila Silver, Cheryl Ursin,
Whitney Walker, Maja Wolff

Publisher
Alain Gayot

http://www.gayot.com

GAULT MILLAU

Paris ■ Los Angeles ■ New York
London ■ Munich ■ San Francisco ■ Vienna

GAYOT PUBLICATIONS

The Best of Beverly Hills
The Best of Chicago
The Best of Florida
The Best of France
The Best of Germany
The Best of Hawaii
The Best of Hong Kong
The Best of Italy
The Best of London
The Best of Los Angeles
The Best of New England
The Best of New Orleans
The Best of New York
The Best of Paris
Paris, Ile-de-France & The Loire Valley
Paris & Provence
The Best of San Francisco
The Best of Thailand
The Best of Toronto
The Best of Washington, D.C.
The Best Wineries of North America

LA Restaurants, NYC Restaurants, SF Restaurants
The Food Paper, Tastes Newsletter

http://www.gayot.com

Copyright © 1996, 1999 by GaultMillau, Inc.

Published by GaultMillau, Inc.
5900 Wilshire Blvd.
Los Angeles, CA 90036

Please address all comments regarding
NYC Restaurants to:
GaultMillau, Inc.
P.O. Box 361144
Los Angeles, CA 90036
E-mail: gayots@aol.com

Production: Walter Mladina
Page Layout and Design: Mad Macs Communications
Illustrations: Judy Seckler

ISSN 1523-4010

Printed in the United States of America

CONTENTS

INTRODUCTION

NEW YORK CITY MAP	5
EATING THE BIG APPLE	6
OUR RESTAURANT RATING SYSTEM	8
OUR PRICING SYSTEM	10
ADVICE & COMMENTS	11
TOP RESTAURANTS: *Food Rating*	13

MANHATTAN — 17

MAP	18
DINING/AND ALSO...	19
BELOW HOUSTON	19
GREENWICH VILLAGE & ENVIRONS	47
14TH STREET-42ND STREET	67
MIDTOWN EAST	89
MIDTOWN WEST	111
UPPER EAST SIDE	131
UPPER WEST SIDE	155
QUICK BITES	164
GOURMET MARKETS & MORE	219

THE BRONX — 231

MAP	232
DINING/AND ALSO...	233
QUICK BITES	235

BROOKLYN — 237

MAP	238
DINING/AND ALSO...	239
QUICK BITES	247

QUEENS — 257

MAP	258
DINING/AND ALSO...	259
QUICK BITES	264

STATEN ISLAND — 269

MAP	270
DINING/AND ALSO...	271

GLOSSARIES & RESTAURANT INDEXES — 273

MENU SAVVY	274
COFFEE SAVVY	283
WINE SAVVY	287
FOOD & WINE EVENTS	297
FOOD & WINE PAIRINGS	300
WATER SAVVY	304
RESTAURANT INDEXES	312
RESTAURANTS: *By Cuisine*	312
RESTAURANTS: *By Notable Features*	323
RESTAURANTS: *By Area*	328

INDEX — 336

NYCRESTAURANTS

RIGHTS

SPECIAL SALES

Gayot Publications are available at discounts for bulk purchases, direct sales or premiums.

- Makes a great gift that will put your name in front of important clients over and over again—and at a small cost.
- Links your firm with internationally respected publications.
- Orders over 1,000 can be customized with your logo on the cover at no extra charge.

Call our toll-free number for information and orders:

1 (800) 532-3781

OR WRITE US:
Gayot Publications
5900 Wilshire Blvd.
Los Angeles, CA 90036

www.gayot.com
E-mail: Gayots@aol.com

DISCLAIMER

NEW YORK CITY MAP

EATING THE BIG APPLE

The Big Apple's on a roll, a long roll that has transformed the city—and that includes the restaurant landscape as well as the menu mix. First take the hard-nosed mayor who made such quality-of-life issues as reducing crime, cleaning streets, and improving traffic flow and safety his mission. Second, take an eight-year-long bull market that pumped out tax revenues like a geyser and year-end bonuses to match. And what you've got is a thriving, vibrant upbeat New York City with 250 pizza joints named Ray's all doing good business. You've also got more quality restaurants than ever before. Each year more new restaurants open than close. Try to get into many of them without a reservation and you are in for a disappointment. The joints are jumpin', some way into the night.

Location, Location, Location

While new notables have opened all over town, the trend continues to point downtown. (Is that why Francis Ford Coppola is selling his condominium in the Sherry Netherlands and shopping in the Village and below?) A decade or so ago, SoHo arrived as a gastronomic destination, and it still is. Next came TriBeCa, which fully arrived in the mid-1990s. Then Chelsea was transformed into a restaurant haven, especially the stretch of Eighth Avenue between 14th and 23rd Streets, which is now a virtual restaurant row. As the Chelsea neighborhood continues to gentrify, the restaurant influx has spread east, filling in and around Seventh, Sixth and Fifth Avenues. Most recently **Tonic**, **Cafeteria** and **Shaefer City Oyster Bar and Grill** joined the ranks of the "it's better than eating home" restaurants—which some call BATH (better alternative to home).

Down a few blocks, the Village proper has enjoyed a resurgence, with **Babbo**, **EQ**, and **Moomba** heading the list of super newcomers with excellent food and the associated buzz on the people and palate fronts. **Clementine** continues to sizzle in its front bar and just as often on the plate. Further east in the NoHo (North of Houston) section of the East Village, **Bond St.** is the new leading light, and what a light.

While continuing to be big news economically with the arrival of stores such as a Virgin Megastore on Union Square (the opposite end from a huge Barnes & Noble Bookstore), the Flatiron-Union Square area may be an old news food neighborhood (though it barely existed gastronomically a decade ago). But it is still generating excitement, especially with the openings in the past year of **Cena** and **Union Pacific**, among others. What's the biggest news of the moment is the arrival of nearby Madison Square Park as a culinary oasis, thanks in part to Danny Meyer, the restaurateur with the Midas touch who opened **Union Square Café** in 1984 and **Gramercy Tavern** a decade later. He has just opened **Eleven Madison Park** and also **Tabla**. These join such welcome newcomers as **27 Standard**, **Mad 28**, **La Terrazza** and a relocated **Sign of the Dove** scheduled to open in 1999. In short, it's hard to find a neighborhood south of 23rd Street without a lot of restaurant excitement and choices.

Fusion Confusion

What we've seen is the proliferation of raw bars. It seems everyone is oyster and crab crazy. We certainly don't mind the choice of 6 or 12 or 18 or 24 varieties of oysters to choose from. But it does point to a depressing trend towards sameness. Then there are the entire strata of the casual, homey places (BATH) where the semi-New American offerings are carbon copies of one another. Every restaurant seems to offer its interpretation of the menu staples of half a dozen ethnic specialties. Who do we thank for this? The "international" kitchen staff or the twenty-something of a chef with a few weeks of training in culinary school for each of the major cuisines of the world? Even worse is when anxious owners or ambitious chefs make like they are Jean-Georges Vongerichten. In an attempt to distinguish a few of the culinary offerings they wind up with fusion confusion, all sorts of cross-cultural dressing and odd ingredients (nettles anyone?) that simply don't work.

On the other hand, the January, 1999 reopening of a grand **Restaurant Daniel** at Park and 65th Street provides a megadose of excitement at the culinary high-end to match the infusion of haute cuisine and fireworks provided late in 1997 by the openings of **Jean Georges** and **Le Cirque 2000**. What signals the health of New York's fine world of dining at any cost, is the addition in the past year to the ranks of **Chanterelle**, **Nobu**, **La Grenouille**, **Aureole**, **Le Bernardin**, **Lutèce** and the like, of **Union Pacific**, **Bouley Bakery**, **Estitorio Milos**, **Cena**, **Restaurant EQ**, **Babbo** and a half dozen other contenders for the crown. And we're eager to see what chef Jean-Louis Palladin, whose restaurant at the Watergate in Washington D.C. we rated a 19/20, brings to New York's culinary palate when he opens **Palladin at the Time**, and **Jean-Louis** this spring.

So, to borrow a phrase, it is the best of times and the worst of times in New York dining, and without question it is the busiest of times. Enjoy.

–Edward Guiliano
Chief Restaurant Critic

OUR RESTAURANT RATING SYSTEM

Clearly, a good many of our restaurants are well worth your hard-earned dollars, and our team of professional restaurant critics has canvassed New York City to steer you right. Some words of advice: when you find a restaurant whose cooking, atmosphere and price range suit you, patronize it regularly instead of continually dashing off to the latest spot where Leonardo, Donald or Claudia were reputedly seen. Being a "regular" at a restaurant—so that you know at least some of the staff and they know you—is the best way to get a good table, good service and extra effort from the chef. And be as adventurous as the city and its chefs—for if it's true that we are what we eat, opt for being exciting, progressive and exotic.

Restaurant Categories

Restaurants are categorized in three ways:

DINING

Fine-dining palaces, trendy trattorias, steakhouses, French bistros and restaurants serving every imaginable ethnic cuisine. We have rated each of them (see rating system below) and pointed out details about the decor, look and ambience. We've also recommended some of our favorite dishes.

AND ALSO...

Restaurants that we have not rated, but we want you to know about anyway. Some of these places are new; many have been around so long, they're too often overlooked.

QUICK BITES

Spots where you can stop for an informal meal, and/or get a meal for a bargain. Here we categorize the burger joints, diners, trendy cafés, noodle shops, happening bars, pizza parlors and ethnic eateries galore—from taco stands to terrific Cuban-Chinese, Indian and even Tibetan dives—where you can eat for $15 per person and under. There are literally thousands of such places in New York City, so we've included only the best. Forgive us if we've left out your favorite—for now, at least, your secret is safe!

Using Our Rating System

What decides the rating of a restaurant? What is on the plate is by far the most important factor. The quality of produce is among the most telling signs of a restaurant's culinary status. It requires a great deal of commitment and money to stock the finest grades and cuts of meat and the finest quality of fish. There is tuna, for example, and there's *tuna*. Ask any sushi chef. One extra-virgin olive oil is not the same, by far, as the next. Ditto for chocolates, pastas, spices and one thousand other ingredients. Quality restaurants also attune themselves to seasonal produce, whether it be local berries or truffles from Italy.

Freshness is all-important, too, and a telling indication of quality. This means not only using fresh rather than frozen fish, for example, but also preparing everything from scratch at the last possible moment, from appetizers through desserts.

What else do we look for? Details are telling: if all the sauces are the same, you know that the kitchen is taking shortcuts. The bread on the table is always a tip-off; similarly, the house wine can speak volumes about the culinary attitude and level of an establishment. Wine is food, and wine lists and offerings can be revealing. A list doesn't have to be long or expensive to show a commitment to quality.

Finally, among the very finest restaurants, creativity and innovation are often determining factors. These qualities, however, are relatively unimportant for simply good restaurants, where the quality and consistency of what appears on the plates is the central factor. A restaurant that serves grilled chicken well is to be admired more than a restaurant that attempts some failed marriage of chicken and exotic produce, or some complicated chicken preparation that requires a larger and more talented kitchen brigade than is on hand. Don't be taken in by attempted fireworks that are really feeble sideshows.

Our Rating System Works as Follows:

Restaurants are ranked in the same manner that French students are graded, on a scale of one to twenty. *The rankings reflect only our opinion of the food. The decor, service, ambience and wine list are commented upon within each review.*

Restaurants that are ranked 13/20 and above are distinguished with toques (chef's hats) according to the table below.

Exceptional *(4 Toques)*
(ratings of 19/20)

Excellent *(3 Toques)*
(ratings of 17/20 and 18/20)

Very good *(2 Toques)*
(ratings of 15/20 and 16/20)

Good *(1 Toque)*
(ratings of 13/20 and 14/20)

Keep in mind that we are comparing New York City's restaurants to the very best in the world. Also, these ranks are relative. A 13/20 (one toque) may not be a superlative ranking for a highly reputed (and very expensive) restaurant, but it is quite complimentary for a small place without much culinary pretension. We know that diners often choose a restaurant for reasons other than the quality of the food—because of its location, type of cuisine—or just because it's a fun place to spend an evening.

Our Pricing System

In our DINING and AND ALSO... reviews, we code restaurant prices using one to four dollar signs. **Prices reflect the average cost of dinner for one person including appetizer, entrée, dessert, coffee, tax and tip. Not included is wine or other beverages, which vary greatly in price.** Restaurants often change their menus—and their menu prices. Forgive us if a restaurant is more expensive when you visit it.

$ = under $20

$$ = under $35

$$$ = under $50

$$$$ = $50 & up

Symbols

All credit cards taken . . . . **A**

Visa . . . . **VISA**

MasterCard . . . . MasterCard

American Express . . . .

Diners Club . . . .

Discover . . . . DISCOVER

Reservations suggested . . . . ☎

Valet parking . . . . 🚗

Ties suggested . . . .

Romantic setting . . . .

Heart-healthy dishes . . . . ♥

View . . . .

Outdoor dining . . . .

Open After Midnight . . . .

Advice & Comments

FUSION OR CONFUSION?

Before Nouvelle Cuisine was introduced to New York City in the '70s, followed by California cuisine in the '80s and New American, Fusion, Pan-Asian, Mediterranean and Pacific Rim cuisine in the '90s, it was easy to classify restaurants by their cuisine—there was American, French, Italian, Continental, Chinese, Japanese, Greek etc. Period. Today, however, the lines between the cuisines have blurred, and chefs create their own style of cooking—which might combine elements of some—or all—of the above.

We find it hard to slap labels on the type of cuisine that a restaurant serves, yet we must for the sake of indexing—and so that readers will have some hint of what they'll be served when they dine there. In most cases, we have labeled a restaurant's cuisine according to what its owners and chefs call it. But that does not always make things easier. For we've found that though one restaurant may describe its cuisine as New American, another as Contemporary and another as Eclectic, their dishes may be quite similar—innovative takes on new and old themes, concocted of fresh regional ingredients and using a combination of elements from various ethnic-cooking styles. But in the long run, who cares what we label a restaurant's cuisine? After all, it's not what type of cuisine you're eating that's important—it's how it tastes. And we hope it tastes great.

JUST HOW DRESSY IS DRESSY?

Dressing up is relative in New York. Generally, if you're off to one of the city's better restaurants, it means at least a jacket and tie and usually a suit for men. At some downtown locations, say in SoHo, TriBeCa or Greenwich Village, formal attire isn't usually the norm, but diners nonetheless still tend to polish themselves up in a casual if finished manner. Black always looks chic.

CELEBRITIES IN THE KITCHEN

When you make reservations in a place with a famous chef, check to be sure he or she will be there and not traveling across the country demonstrating his or her cooking style. Also, all chefs have good days and bad, so don't be too put off if your experience is less stellar than was ours; with luck it will be better.

ON MENUS

Most restaurants change their menus regularly, sometimes as often as daily, sometimes seasonally. In our reviews, we've identified the dishes we enjoyed, those we found lacking, plus some that are typical of the restaurant. We can't, however, guarantee you'll find the same exact dishes when you go.

THAT'S MY CAR!

In most areas of the city, you can find public garages which are safe and convenient—if expensive. The best advice is to take a taxi to and from your destination. Most restaurants will call you a cab if you're worried about finding one.

SECOND-HAND SMOKE

Since 1995, smoking has been prohibited in the dining areas of all New York City restaurants seating more than 35 people, but it is allowed in their bar areas. How strictly this Smoke-Free Air Act is enforced, however, varies from restaurant to restaurant.

SUMMER IN THE CITY

It seems as if restaurants of all stripes are setting up outdoor cafés or opening gardens out back. Given New York's climate, however, access is limited usually from May to September.

SO FRESH, IT'S STILL SWIMMING

Increasingly, it's easier to find superbly fresh seafood from around the world in restaurants—Atlantic farm-raised salmon and Hawaiian ahi tuna are undoubtedly the most popular. For the best fresh fish, go to any of the city's highest-rated sushi restaurants, or those Honk-Kong-style Chinese seafood restaurants where the fish swim happily in their tank until moments before they're cooked.

HOW MUCH IS ENOUGH?

Leaving a tip equivalent to fifteen percent of your pretax bill (including drinks) is customary. If you feel the service was above and beyond the call of duty, or you're with a large party, you may wish to leave eighteen to twenty percent. Only a few restaurants handle tipping European-style, by adding fifteen percent to the bill. Some restaurants automatically add a gratuity only for large groups (which tend to undertip).

Sample Review

The following key explains the information provided in our reviews.

STREET ADDRESS & AREA OF TOWN

CUISINE TYPE

FOOD RATING

ESTABLISHMENT NAME

TOQUE AWARD

RESTAURANT DANIEL   FRENCH   19/20

60 E. 65th Street (Park & Madison Aves.), 10021
288-0033, *Lunch & Dinner, Mon.-Sat.,* $$$$

Who could have imagined it? Daniel Boulud rose to prominence as the chef of the venerable Le Cirque. Then Daniel left and Le Cirque moved its big top to Madison Avenue, becoming Le Cirque 2000. Five years later Daniel has returned to the original Le Cirque location, this time flying on his own wings and creating the gastronomic sensation of this end of the century. At his stunning new restaurant, Daniel tailored the state-of-the-art kitchen he always wanted, and expanded the dining space to three rooms: a Venetian ...

CREDIT CARD NFORMATION
& RESTAURANT FEATURES
(SEE SYMBOLS KEY ON PG. 10)

REVIEW

DAYS OPEN &
PRICE CATEGORY

PHONE NUMBER

TOQUE TALLY
TOP RESTAURANTS: FOOD RATING

19/20 ♟♟♟♟

Jean Georges
Le Cirque 2000
Restaurant Daniel

18/20 ♟♟♟

Chanterelle
Lespinasse
Nobu

17/20 ♟♟♟

Aureole
Gotham Bar & Grill
La Grenouille
Le Bernardin
Les Célébrités
Lutèce
Peacock Alley
Union Pacific

16/20 ♟♟

Bouley Bakery Restaurant
Café Boulud
Cena
Destinée
Eleven Madison Park
Felidia Ristorante
Gertrude's
Gramercy Tavern
Honmura An
Jo Jo
March Restaurant
Mark's Restaurant
Montrachet
Mr. K's
Picholine
Restaurant 222
San Domenico
Union Square Café
Veritas

THE TOQUE, CIRCA 1700

Have you ever wondered about the origin of that towering, billowy (and slightly ridiculous) white hat worn by chefs all over the world? Chefs have played an important role in society since the fifth century B.C., but the hats didn't begin to appear in kitchens until around the eighteenth century A.D. The toque is said to be of Greek origin; many famous Greek cooks, to escape persecution, sought refuge in monasteries and continued to practice their art. The chefs donned the tall hats traditionally worn by Orthodox priests, but to distinguish themselves from their fellows, they wore white hats instead of black. The custom eventually was adopted by chefs from Paris to Peking.

15/20 ♟♟

Alison On Dominick
Aquagrill
Babbo
Blue Ribbon Sushi
Bond Street
Clementine
Estiatorio Milos
Etats-Unis
Fifty Seven Fifty Seven
Four Seasons
Fresco by Scotto
Harry Cipriani
Hudson River Club
I Trulli
Inagiku
Judson Grill
La Caravelle
La Réserve
Le Madri
Le Périgord
Le Régence
Manhattan Ocean Club
Mercer Kitchen
Mesa Grill
Michael's
Monkey Bar
Moomba
Nino's
Nippon
Oceana
Osteria del Circo
Paggio
Palio
Parioli Romanissimo
Patria
Payard Patisserie & Bistro
Periyali
Petrossian
Restaurant EQ
The River Café *(Brooklyn)*
Scarabée
Sonia Rose
Sushisay
Tabla
Taliesin
Terrace
Trois Jean
'21' Club
Vong
Zenon *(Queens)*
Zoë

14/20 ♟

American Park
An American Place
Aquavit
Arqua
Balthazar
Bambou Restaurant & Bar
Basta Pasta
Bellini
Bice
Blue Ribbon
Bolo
Bouterin
Café des Artistes
Campagna
Can
The Carlyle Restaurant
Casa La Femme
Chateaubriand
Chelsea Bistro & Bar
Chikubu
Chin Chin
Churrascaria Plataforma
Cibo
Cipriani Wall Street
City Wine & Cigar Company
Coco Pazzo
Cucina *(Brooklyn)*
Dawat
Downtown
Duane Park Café
Fantino
F.illi Ponte Ristorante
Fino
Firebird
Flowers
Follonico
"44"
Gabriel's
Halcyon
Hatsuhana
Il Buco
Il Cantinori
Il Mulino
Il Nido
Kokachin
Kuruma Zushi
L'Absinthe
La Colombe d'Or
La Côte Basque
La Fourchette
Le Pescadou
Le Refuge
Le Zoo
Lenox Room

Les Halles
Liam
Limoncello
Maloney & Porcelli
Match Uptown
Matthew's
Maya
Mazzei
Michael Jordan's The Steak House NYC
Mirezi
Molyvos
Mono
Monzù
Morton's of Chicago
Naples 45
Novitá
Orso
Pamir
Paola's Restaurant
Park Avenue Café
Park Bistro
Park View at the Boathouse
Patroon
Pò
The Post House
Primavera
Quatorze Bis
Quilty's
Rao's
Raphaël
Remi
Rocking Horse Café
Ruth's Chris Steakhouse
Seryna
Shaan
Shaffer City Oyster Bar & Grill
Shun Lee Palace
Sistina
Sparks Steakhouse
Sushi Bar
Syrah
Tapika
The Tonic
Torre di Pisa
TriBeCa Grill
27 Standard
Verbena
Vince and Eddie's
Waterloo

13/20 ♕

Al Bustan
Asia de Cuba
Atlantic Grill
Au Troquet
Bar Cichetti
Bar Six
Barbetta
Barocco
Barolo
Ben Benson's Steak House
Blue Water Grill
Bolivar
Briscola
Butterfield 81
Café Centro
Café Luxembourg
Café Pierre
Caffè Rosso
Canton
Cellini
Cent' Anni
Chelsea Trattoria
Chez Jacqueline
China Grill
Christer's
Cité
City Hall
Cub Room
Cyclo
Da Silvano Restaurant
Demarchelier
Diva
Eli's
Erminia
Eros
Ferrier
The 14 Wall Street Restaurant
Frontière
Gage & Tollner (Brooklyn)
Gallagher's
Gasgogne
Gemelli
Goody's (Queens)
Hasaki
Heartbeat
Home
I Coppi
Il Bagatto
Indochine
Istana
Jean-Claude
Jerry's
Jewel of India

Keen's
KPNY
Kum Gang San
La Goulue
La Métairie
Layla
Le Colonial
Le Solex
Lola
L-Ray
Lucky Cheng
Lusardi's
Mad 28
Manducatis *(Queens)*
Mezzaluna
Mezzogiorno
Mi Cocina
Mie
Mingala West
Moreno Ristorante
The Nice Restaurant
Oriental Pearl
Oyster Bar & Restaurant
The Palm
Pearl Oyster Bar
Peter Luger *(Brooklyn)*
Piadina
Pig Heaven
Pravda
Primola
Provence

Raga
The Redeye Grill
René Pujol
Restaurant 147
Restivo Ristorante
Rosa Mexicano
Rosemarie's
San Giusto
Sardi's
Savoy
The SeaGrill
Siena
Smith & Wollensky
Tatou
Tommaso's *(Brooklyn)*
Trois Canards
Tupelo Grill
The Vinegar Factory
Water's Edge *(Queens)*
Wilkinson's Restaurant
Zarela

No Rating

The Park
Rainbow Room

MANHATTAN DINING

MAP	**18**
BELOW HOUSTON	**19**
DINING	19
AND ALSO...	44
GREENWICH VILLAGE & ENVIRONS	**47**
DINING	47
AND ALSO...	64
14TH STREET-42ND STREET	**67**
DINING	67
AND ALSO...	87
MIDTOWN EAST	**89**
DINING	89
AND ALSO...	109
MIDTOWN WEST	**111**
DINING	111
AND ALSO...	128
UPPER EAST SIDE	**131**
DINING	131
AND ALSO...	152
UPPER WEST SIDE	**155**
DINING	155
AND ALSO...	161
QUICK BITES	**163**
GOURMET FOOD SHOPS & MORE	**219**

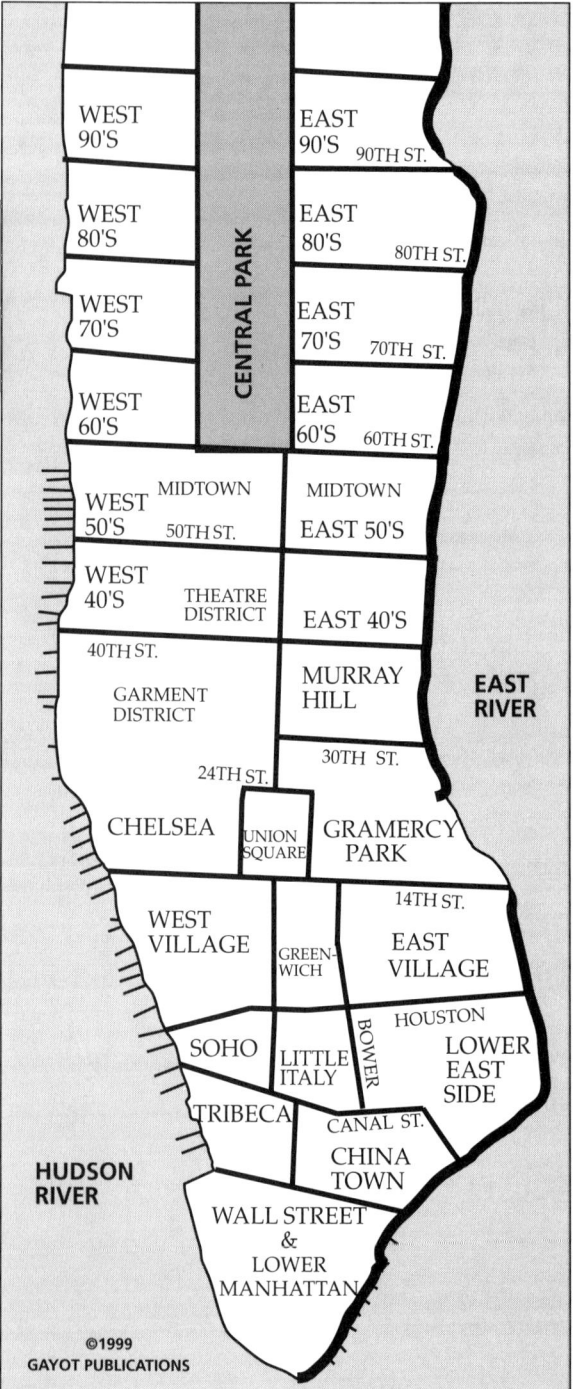

WEST 90'S

EAST 90'S   90TH ST.

WEST 80'S

EAST 80'S   80TH ST.

CENTRAL PARK

WEST 70'S

EAST 70'S   70TH ST.

WEST 60'S

EAST 60'S   60TH ST.

WEST 50'S   MIDTOWN   50TH ST.

MIDTOWN EAST 50'S

WEST 40'S   THEATRE DISTRICT

EAST 40'S

40TH ST.

GARMENT DISTRICT

MURRAY HILL

EAST RIVER

30TH ST.

24TH ST.

CHELSEA

UNION SQUARE

GRAMERCY PARK

14TH ST.

WEST VILLAGE

GREEN-WICH

EAST VILLAGE

HOUSTON

SOHO

LITTLE ITALY

BOWERY

LOWER EAST SIDE

TRIBECA

CANAL ST.

CHINA TOWN

HUDSON RIVER

WALL STREET & LOWER MANHATTAN

©1999
GAYOT PUBLICATIONS

18

BELOW HOUSTON

*Encompasses SoHo, TriBeCa, Little Italy, NoHo, Wall Street,
Chinatown and the Lower East Side*

DINING

All phone numbers are (212) unless otherwise indicated

ALISON ON DOMINICK   FRENCH   15/20

38 Dominick St. (Varick & Hudson Sts.), 10013
727-1188, *Dinner nightly,* **$$$$**

This tiny restaurant with its small bar and candlelit dining
room exudes the aroma of herbs and garlic, and the skillfully
prepared cuisine features inventive twists on French country
classics. The seasonally changing menu might include cold
poached foie gras in mulled apple consommé; creamless curry
bisque with green apples; roast duck with caramelized root vegetables, Armagnac-marinated prunes and candied walnuts; and
sautéed Maine salmon. The extensive wine list is mostly
French, and has a good selection of affordable finds. Since the
average price of an entrée is around $30, the $29.98 three-
course prix-fixe pre-theater menu is a good value.

AMERICAN PARK   SEAFOOD   14/20

Battery Park (off State St.), 10004
809-5508, *Lunch Mon.-Fri., Dinner Mon.-Sat.,* **$$$**

This upscale fish house in Battery Park is a fine addition to
the downtown scene. The handsome, glass-enclosed dining
room features an open kitchen, a raw bar, timbered beams
overhead and nautical accents, and the wind-swept terrace
makes a fine perch to admire Lady Liberty. The seafood prepa-
rations here are wonderfully buoyant, including sautéed
red snapper with white beans and spinach, grilled tuna with Greek
olives and whole roasted black bass. The menu also offers juicy
steaks with roasted potatoes.

AQUAGRILL   SEAFOOD/NEW AMERICAN   15/20

210 Spring St. (Sixth Ave.), 10013
274-0505, *Lunch Tues.-Fri., Dinner Tues.-Sun., Brunch Sat.-Sun.,* **$$**

A dependably good seafood restaurant, Aguagrill features a
formidable raw bar, a minimalist but comfortable setting (we
love the shell-covered light fixtures) and an intriguing international wine list. Appetizers include a luscious warm octopus
salad, supernal abalone sashimi with spicy eggplant, and crispy
salmon-skin salad with roasted garlic. Pay attention to the
chef's specialties, especially the grilled Atlantic salmon with a
falafel crust, and the plump seared sea scallops with crabmeat

polenta. If you don't appreciate exotic preparations (or you're on a diet), you can order just about anything grilled, poached or roasted. Desserts are rich and frivolous.

ARQUA   ITALIAN   14/20

281 Church St. (White St.), 10013
334-1888, *Lunch Mon.-Sat., Dinner nightly, $$$*

This out-of-the-way but hip Italian trattoria focuses on the food of the Veneto. Its hallmarks are seafood, fresh pasta and polenta, prepared simply with relatively little fat and the freshest of ingredients. In keeping with the cuisine, the decor is spare—there's little within the peach-colored walls to distract from the serious business of eating. Except the noise, which after 8:30 p.m. on a busy night can be deafening. However, lunch is a very civilized affair with City Hall officials and courthouse lawyers comprising most of the clientele. We recommend the grilled chicken-and-mushroom sausage and such fresh-made pastas as the pappardelle with duck.

BALTHAZAR RESTAURANT   FRENCH BISTRO   14/20

80 Spring St. (Crosby St.), 10012
965-1414, *Breakfast, Lunch & Dinner daily, $$$*

Arguably the trendiest of the trendy new restaurants of 1997/1998, this artfully recreated (leather banquettes, patinaed mirrors) traditional French brasserie is elbow-to-elbow with moguls, models, movers-and-shakers and wannabes. Its atmosphere has been compared to a bustling railway station. Perhaps—if the station is in St. Tropez in August. But it all works. The food is solid along classic bistro lines, with such dishes as whole roasted chicken with mashed potatoes, or striped bass over toasted bread infused with a tomato-Swiss chard broth. The sublime oyster and shellfish bar is one of the biggest around. The 200+ wines on the list wash down plenty of good eats. Baked in the adjacent **Balthazar Bakery**, the bread is superb. If you can't score a reservation, go for a post-midnight supper or a drink at the bar that winds down at 3 or 4 a.m.

BAR CICHETTI   ITALIAN   13/20

220 W. Houston St. (Seventh & Sixth Aves.), 10014
229-0314, *Lunch Mon.-Fri., Dinner nightly, $$$*

Manhattan's first bacaro—a Venetian-style wine bar—is not on a canal, but it isn't far from the Hudson River. Nearby advertising and publishing types are drawn to the easy informality of the place and its 200 wines, many by the glass and half-glass. (Cichetti are small, tapas-like plates for noshing.) Chef Dan Zwicke prepares a score of them, and his Venetian crabcakes and arancini (stuffed rice balls) are not to be missed. He also has a light touch in the impeccable execution of Italian classics. Pastas resonate with al dente goodness, fresh seafood and meats are simply and wisely handled, and rosemary-scented Friulian-bread pudding is a fine coda.

BAROCCO   ITALIAN   13/20

301 Church St. (Walker St.), 10013
431-1445, *Lunch Mon.-Fri., Dinner nightly*, $$$

A

A convivial trattoria in a former warehouse, Barocco has a simple decor, with high ceilings and tall, iron Corinthian columns. The food is simply prepared, and the appetizers and pastas are standouts: fettunta, grilled Tuscan bread dressed up with garlic and olive oil; ravioli stuffed with duck, spinach and sage in a light vegetable sauce. The entrées fare less well, but you won't go wrong with the simple grilled chicken or the grilled Norwegian salmon, especially with a side of roast potatoes. For dessert, we prefer the biscotti.

BAROLO   ITALIAN   13/20

398 W. Broadway (Spring & Broom Sts.), 10013
226-1102, *Lunch & Dinner daily*, $$$

A

If you're lucky enough to get a table in the back courtyard on a sunny day, you'll eat and drink well in one of the prettiest dining spots in the city. Don't despair if you dine inside; the setting is casual but elegant. If you order wisely, you can eat very well and authentically Italian. The menu is big, but the specials here are always best bets. The fail safe, though, is ravioli, especially the spinach-and-cheese version. We also recommend the quail salad with portobello mushrooms and lentils, the grilled calamari and the sea bass baked in salt. Trust the waiters' opinions to avoid the occasional misfire. With its savvy Italian selections, the wine list is exceptional.

BLUE RIBBON   ECLECTIC/FRENCH   14/20

97 Sullivan St. (Spring & Prince Sts.), 10012
274-0404, *Dinner Tues.-Sun.*, $$

This small and clubby storefront, which doesn't lock up 'til 4 a.m., has been a SoHo favorite with young, hip, food-loving night-owls since it opened in 1992. It was one of the first downtown spots with a raw bar, and the food and service have been admirably consistent. The rich and soothing bone marrow with oxtail and marmalade is a good starter, as is the platter of raw and cooked seafood served with a tangy celery-and-lemon mignonette. We've never been thrilled by the paella, but it remains a popular main course; try the shrimp Provencal. Still a top dessert is their rich cross between a flourless chocolate cake and chocolate mousse. The basically French and American wine list has grown considerably, and has plenty of inviting picks. If there's no room at Blue Ribbon, you may be able to squeeze into their **Blue Ribbon Sushi** next door—but don't count on it.

BLUE RIBBON SUSHI   SUSHI   15/20

119 Sullivan St. (Spring & Prince Sts.), 10012
343-0404, *Dinner Tues.-Sun.,* **$$$**

It's definitely hip, but it's not one of those warm-and-fuzzy sushi bars where the chefs laugh and drink beer, wielding their knives dramatically. The huge menu features all the usual sushi and sashimi possibilities and more, plus sushi rolls made with vegetables and filet mignon, all impeccably prepared. The wine list isn't much, but choose from a dozen or so sakés.

BOND STREET   JAPANESE/FUSION   15/20

6 Bond St. (Broadway & Lafayette Sts.), 10012
777-2500, *Dinner Mon.-Sat.,* **$$$$**

This townhouse triplex is a hot spot with attitude to match. Once past the door, however, the black-clad staff is as accommodating as anyone operating within a kettle drum could be. The candle-lit cocktail lounge on floor one is cozy and romantic. Upstairs is a cool and casual dining room, with a pandemoniacal sushi bar. (And yes, that IS Cindy Crawford.) Bond St. cuisine is Japanese with fusion touches, as in pan-seared foie gras with miso sauce and monkfish with spicy sauce. What to do with live scallops? "Pop 'em in your mouth." Desserts are a highlight: chocolate fondue for two, and an ice-cream assortment in a bento box with a chrysanthemum-petal cookie.

BOOM RESTAURANT   INTERNATIONAL   12/20

152 Spring St. (W. Broadway & Wooster St.), 10013
431-3663, *Lunch & Dinner daily,* **$$**

It's eclectic, different and fun, with monthly changing art shows, live music five nights a week and a DJ on the weekends. The menu is East meets West, with specialties including Vietnamese five-spiced grilled quail, Japanese-style spinach salad, pastas, sesame-seed-crusted tuna, grilled pork chops and a "Boom" burger with homemade ketchup. The novelty, crowd and the club are the attraction here, not the level of execution on the plate.

BOULEY BAKERY RESTAURANT   FRENCH   16/20

120 W. Broadway (Duane St.), 10013
964-2525, *Lunch & Dinner daily,* **$$$$**

Until David Bouley opens Danube, his Austrian restaurant, next door in the spring of '99, this tiny bakery/restaurant is the only spot to savor the chef's masterful culinary creations. In a serene setting with gauzy curtains and a vaulted ceiling, try not to overdose on the superb fresh-baked breads, and start with the likes of a salad of smoked bluefish with green apple and horseradish dressing, or phyllo-crusted shrimp with crabmeat and baby squid in an ocean-herbal broth. On the ever-changing menu, entrées might include salmon with braised endive, baby bok choy and clementine sauce, or breast of duck with red cabbage, pearl onions and Armagnac sauce, followed by a hot chocolate-brioche pudding with chocolate sorbet, and maple and prune-Armagnac ice cream. The small but well-chosen wine list includes some reasonably priced bottles.

BRIDGE CAFÉ   NEW AMERICAN   11/20

279 Water St. (Dover St.), 10038
227-3344, *Lunch Mon.-Fri., Dinner nightly, Brunch Sun.,* **$$$**

🅰 ☎

This cozy pub/café in a circa-1801 building is a stone's throw from the Brooklyn Bridge, but don't expect a great view: it's like looking at the bridge's ankles. Once the haunt of longshoremen, today the café is the watering hole of Wall Street executives. In season, soft-shell crabs in shallot butter is the best-selling dish, and for good reason. Fish dishes are quite good: seared yellowfin tuna; red snapper with vegetable risotto and oven-dried tomatoes. Try the salmon-and-corn chowder to start, and end with the chocolate indulgence cake. The all-American wine list has a range of good choices, and on Tuesdays, bottles are 30 percent off.

CAN   VIETNAMESE/FRENCH   14/20   👨‍🍳

482 W. Broadway (Houston St.), 10013
533-6333, *Lunch & Dinner daily,* **$$$**

[VISA] [MasterCard] [Diners Club] [💳]

The chefs and the dishes may change, but this attractive SoHo restaurant is consistently good. With its red carpeting, black chairs and walls missing a few bricks here and there, the sky-lit courtyard-like main dining room has somewhat of a faux Saigon-after-the-siege look. Among our favorite dishes: the crisp rice pancake topped with wild mushrooms and bean sprouts or stuffed with prawns, bean sprouts and mint; ginger-honey duck; wok-fried whole sea bass; pan-seared salmon with melon salsa and the rib-eye steak. Crème brûlée tops the dessert list. The short French-American wine list is a good one.

CANTON   CHINESE   13/20   👨‍🍳

45 Division St. (Market & Bowery Sts.), 10002
226-4441, 226-0921, *Lunch & Dinner Wed.-Sun., Closed mid-July through mid-Aug.,* **$$**
No cards

Ask Eileen Leong, who is a co-owner along with her chef-husband, Larry, to guide you through the menu of this Western-looking Chinatown restaurant. Larry prepares his specials from ingredients found at the market that morning, and stir-fried cooking is not the only rule. Good bets include the hand roll of lettuce stuffed with squab, chicken or vegetables, the steamed dumplings, chicken with ginger and scallions, and the simple roast duck. Call ahead to request his sublime stuffed duck or mousse of pike. Sea bass, one of the most popular choices here, is also tamed by the master in a number of impressive preparations.

CAPSOUTO FRÈRES   FRENCH   12/20

451 Washington St. (Watts St.), 10013
966-4900, *Lunch Tues.-Fri., Dinner nightly, Brunch Sat.-Sun., $$$*

Set in an out-of-the-way former warehouse, this spacious restaurant features a high-ceilinged, multi-leveled dining room with red brick walls, wooden floors, soaring columns and an antique wall mirror. Many find it romantic, but we think the place is showing its age. Still, it's fun for country-French staples and brunch near the river. You'll find good, spicy saucissons, smoked salmon, ravioli with scallops and mushrooms, steak frites and such specials as duckling with cassis and ginger. The soufflés are popular, but we're not crazy about them. The mostly French and American wine list is adequate.

CASA LA FEMME   EGYPTIAN   14/20

150 Wooster St. (Houston & Prince Sts.), 10012
505-0005, *Dinner nightly, $$$*

This romantic fantasy of a casbah is definitely theater-as-restaurant as opposed to restaurant-as-theater, with tented tables and, on Monday nights, belly dancers and tarot-card readers. It attracts black-lycra-clad hipsters until the wee hours, and they're not here for the food. Though, in fact, the food is surprisingly good—lots of eat-with-your-fingers and scoop-up-with-pita-bread appetizers, such as hummus and baba ghanouj. For $55, you can recline on pillows and indulge in a five-course Egyptian feast featuring such entrées as sugar-cane-marinated roasted squab, tahini-and-onion-crusted red snapper, or mint-roasted baby lamb shoulder with savory Egyptian bread pudding, topped off with a cup of strong, thick Turkish coffee.

CHANTERELLE   FRENCH/NEW AMERICAN   18/20

2 Harrison St. (Hudson St.), 10013
966-6960, *Lunch Tues.-Sat., Dinner Mon.-Sat., $$$$*

Civilized yet hip, bold and innovative yet solid and even conservative, Chanterelle has a personality all its own. You either love this place or you don't. We do. Chef David Waltuck and his wife, Karen, who runs the dining room, haven't changed their style much since they first opened Chanterelle in 1979 at another location. The minimalist, high-ceilinged dining room is adorned with some of the grandest flower arrangements in town and staffed by some of the most dedicated professionals. The dining room can be a quiet, almost religious temple of gastronomy or full of Wall Streeters high on a new high for the Dow. The $75 prix-fixe menu changes monthly and might include Waltuck's signature grilled seafood sausage, squab mousse flavored with juniper berries, wild striped bass with melted fennel, tuna with lemon fettuccini, and breast of moulard duck with bitter orange and chiles. For $15 extra, you'll be seduced by a fine assortment of French, Italian and American cheeses. The wine list is extraordinary; ask for sommelier Roger Dagorn's advice.

CIPRIANI WALL STREET   ITALIAN   14/20

55 Wall St. (Williams & Hanover Sts.), 10005
797-9255, Lunch & Dinner Mon.-Sat., $$$$

A beautiful new link in the Cipriani golden chain (how else to describe a chain of such expensive restaurants?), this very noisy Wall Street newcomer serves impeccable and oh-so-Italian dishes such as carpaccio, sautéed baby artichokes, pastas and veal chops. Tiny tables, high prices and an adjacent ball-room for gala private parties (in the former New York Custom House, which the Cipriani family is converting into a luxury hotel), means CWS will do well as well as the Dow stays high.

CITY HALL   AMERICAN   13/20

1131 Duane St.(Church St. & W. Broadway), 10013
227-7777, Lunch Mon.-Fri., Dinner Mon.-Sat., $$$$

A new restaurant with old-fashioned New York City fare has taken root in a cast-iron, landmark 1863 factory building with-in walking distance of its namesake, thanks to Henry Meer, whose Cub Room on Prince Street is also a winner. To spur conviviality, it has a big and bustling bar plus an oyster bar where shellfish stews and pan roasts are prepared before your eyes. There are broilings and roasts of meats in sizes for as many as six people, plus oysters Rockefeller, she-crab soup, time-honored hashes, steak tartare, hefty chops and shellfish fry-ups. The chefs buy vegetables from area greenmarkets, and encourage patrons to choose their own garnishes and sauces.

CITY WINE & CIGAR COMPANY   NEW AMERICAN   14/20

62 Laight St.(Hudson & Greenwich Sts.), 10013
334-2274, Lunch Thurs.-Fri., Dinner Mon.-Sat., $$$

You don't have to be an oenophile or cigar buff to love City Wine & Cigar Company in TriBeCa, but it doesn't hurt. Strikingly designed rooms celebrate cocktails, cigars, dining, and yes, even non-smokers. The 18-seat private dining room overlooks the busy kitchen of ballerina-turned-chef Patricia Williams. Her southwestern lineage makes it a natural to con-jure up tequila-cured salmon, chile rellenos with Oaxacan lamb and mango salsa, and pan-fried quail salad with toasted pecans and Maytag blue cheese. Thus, robust flavors go forth to wed big wines and costly smokes, both of which are dis-played in handsome wine rooms and humidors. One of Drew Nieporent's creations, City Wine has this trendsetting restaura-teur's characteristic bright, caring service team and an out-standing beverage program.

CUB ROOM   NEW AMERICAN   13/20

131 Sullivan St. (Prince St.), 10021
677-4100, *Dinner nightly, Brunch Sun.*, $$$

This trendy restaurant/bar/lounge extravaganza features eclectic, countryish antique furnishings. The main dining room is more upscale than the lounge or the café and certainly less noisy. You might begin a meal with a lobster salad with mango, duck confit, baby beets, grilled onions and frisée—delicious but characteristic of the menu's somewhat overly wrought dishes that sometimes don't work as well as this one. The pressed-vegetable terrine is also a popular starter. To follow, try the yellowfin tuna with a sesame-seed crust or the cherry-wood-smoked tenderloin of beef with polenta, and a peanut butter soufflé for dessert. In the café, there is a greater emphasis on salads, sandwiches and bakery items. The wine list is one of distinction with a bias towards small, independent growers.

DIVA   ITALIAN   13/20

341 W. Broadway (Grand & Broom Sts.), 10012
941-9024, *Lunch Tues.-Sun., Dinner nightly*, $$

This stylish SoHo-Italian opens up onto West Broadway in warm weather. Inside there's a huge old-looking bar, scarlet walls and a high wood-beamed ceiling—it's definitely a downtown look. The food is simple and pretty good: grilled baby octopus with mixed greens; salmon or beef carpaccio; various pastas including black lobster-stuffed ravioli with dill-perfumed vodka sauce; paella; seared beef in Cognac sauce. There's a good list of Italian wines. Don't let any empty places fool you in the daytime; this place booms late at night, and the kitchen generally stays open until 2 a.m.

DOWNTOWN   ITALIAN   14/20

376 W. Broadway (Broome St.), 10013
343-0999, *Lunch & Dinner daily*, $$$

This SoHo sibling of Harry Cipriani attracts tragically hip, Armani-clad Italians, leggy models and bridge-and-tunnel types who dream of blending in. The glittering Murano-glass chandelier is but one element of the white-on-white Venice-meets-SoHo décor. On a clear day, dine on the oh-so-chic rooftop patio, assuredly one of the few in the area, and pretend you're on the Lido. Simple and usually sublime pastas and the like are served to the devoted all day long.

DUANE PARK CAFÉ   NEW AMERICAN   14/20

157 Duane St. (W. Broadway & Hudson Sts.), 10013
732-5555, *Lunch Mon.-Fri., Dinner Mon.-Sat.*, $$$

Since 1989, this TriBeCa favorite has served dishes that blend Italian, Californian, Cajun and Japanese influences in a handsome yet subdued dining room with fabric and cherry-veneer walls in peach and salmon tones, wood floors and white sconces. Intriguing are the miso-marinated duck salad, the semolina-crusted oyster salad, the pappardelle with braised rabbit, and such entrées as pan-blackened salmon with ponzu dipping sauce, and crispy skate with roasted fennel, portobello mushrooms and cippollini onions. The sorbets burst with fruit flavors.

FÉLIX   FRENCH   12/20

340 W. Broadway (Grand St.), 10013
431-0021, *Lunch Tues.-Sun., Dinner nightly, Brunch Sat.-Sun., $$*

This lively corner bistro often overflows onto the streetside tables in nice weather. It draws not only shoppers and tourists, but also a very SoHo late-night, fun-loving Euro-crew with a heavy dose of French expats. (Can a French bistro be authentic without French regulars?) All the French-bistro classics, plus omelets, pastas, roasted salmon, roast chicken and a good French wine list.

F.ILLI PONTE RISTORANTE   ITALIAN   14/20

39 Desbrosses St. (West St.), 10013
226-4621, *Lunch Mon.-Fri, Dinner Mon.-Sat., $$$*

A former 1890s longshoremen's hotel has been turned into a tasteful showplace. Downstairs is a plush bar with overstuffed leather chairs, serving brick-oven pizza. Up an Italian-tile staircase is a cigar lounge and two handsome dining rooms with drop-dead views of the Hudson. The brick walls, high beamed ceiling and Persian carpets over wooden floors come together beautifully, and the service is first class. The food is pretty good, too: crispy zucchini blossoms and goat-cheese raviolini painted with beet reduction; orrechiette with hot-and-sweet sausage; "angry" lobster roasted with garlic and crushed pepper; and a 32-ounce T-bone Fiorentina. The wine list is excellent, as is the people-watching.

THE 14 WALL STREET RESTAURANT   FRENCH   13/20

114 Wall St., 31st Fl. (Broadway), 10005
233-2780, *Breakfast, Lunch & Dinner Mon.-Fri., $$$*

It's well worth meeting the challenge of two sets of elevators to reach this 31st-floor aerie for alimentation, the former home of legendary financier J. Pierpont Morgan. Modern money men and women gather amid turn-of-the-century opulence laid bare by owner Julian Davis, who stripped 50 coats of paint from the original mahogany moldings. Mr. Davis and chef Frederic Feufeu offer upscale bistro fare, and a view of Lady Liberty. Even salads sing a siren song with the likes of a mixed beans tossed with cured duck and walnut oil. Oxtail jelly and papaya provide counterpoint in chef Feufeu's suave foie gras "au torchon." Entrées are as light as fennel-smoked brook trout baked on a wooden plank, or as bracing as filet mignon with chanterelle cream and fingerling potatoes.

FRONTIÈRE   FRENCH/ITALIAN   13/20

199 Prince St. (MacDougal & Sullivan Sts.), 10012
387-0898, *Lunch & Dinner Mon.-Sat.,* $$$

This handsome little SoHo eatery delivers a warm and friendly dining experience. Certainly the vin du patron on the tables (pour your own—pay by consumption only) adds to the ambience, as do the exposed-brick walls, pressed-tin ceiling, the circa-1927 zinc bar and the candlelight. For starters, we've enjoyed the grilled wild mushroom salad with warm potatoes and goat cheese, and the grilled quail with balsamic-and-honey glaze. You can feast on a terrific côte de beouf for two ($58), lobster cassoulet or grilled Atlantic salmon.

GEMELLI   ITALIAN   13/20

4 World Trade Center, Plaza Level (Liberty & Vesey Sts.), 10048
488-2100, *Lunch & Dinner Mon.-Fri.,* $$$

Trail-blazing Italian restaurateur Tony May created more than "twins" in his innovative Gemelli under the Twin Towers of the World Trade Center. His multi-faceted complex celebrates rustic atmosphere and authentic, back-to-basics regional food of Italy, from leisurely to quick as a wink. Gemelli's main dining room draws the financial crowd and WTC occupants, who savor the sturdy Tuscan tomato-and-bread stew called pappa, or the bracing ribollita, a thick potage of cabbage, cheese, bread and borlotti beans. Farro, an ancient grain sometimes called spelt, is blended here with pesto and parsley-marinated lobster. **Pastabreak**, a quick and inexpensive pasta eat-in or take-out operation is downstairs. In the Spring of 1999, May will open **Gemelli Mare** here, featuring induction cooking of the best from the nearby Fulton Fish Market.

GHENET   ETHIOPIAN   12/20

284 Mulberry St. (Houston & Prince Sts.), 10002
343-1888, *Lunch & Dinner Tues.-Sun.,* $$

It's worth the effort to find this stylish, understated restaurant tucked away in the up-and-coming NoLiTa (short for North of Little Italy) neighborhood. To dine at Ghenet is to enjoy the taste of freedom—from utensils, that is. The kid in you will have fun eating with your hands, as is traditional in Ethiopian culture. Everything on the menu is served with injera, the spongy flat bread that's used as plate and wrapper for the thick, dark, spicy stews. The slow-cooked lentils and lamb stew will awaken sensations in your taste buds.

HONMURA AN   JAPANESE   16/20

170 Mercer St. (Houston & Prince Sts.), 10012
334-5253, *Lunch Wed.-Sat., Dinner Tues.-Sun., $$$*

On the Zen-like second floor of a nondescript SoHo build-
ing, this Japanese mecca sans sushi offers noodles and more
noodles, prepared better than you're likely to find anywhere
else in town. The crowd includes chairmen of top Japanese
corporations and trendy young Japanese expatriates blissfully
slurping (it's de rigeur) their noodles. This may be the only
place in New York where the soba (buckwheat) and udon
(white wheat) noodles are made daily. Try them cold at the
beginning of the meal, or hot in a bowl of rich benito-based
broth topped with tiny mushrooms as a main course. We also
enjoy the tori dango (chicken meatballs), the beef tataki
(Japanese carpaccio) and the giant prawn tempura.

HUDSON RIVER CLUB   NEW AMERICAN   15/20

4 World Financial Center, 250 Vesey St. (West St.), 10281
786-1500, *Lunch Mon.-Fri., Dinner Mon.-Sat., Brunch Sun., $$$$*

Talk about a spectacular setting: Facing New York Harbor,
the Statue of Liberty and Ellis Island, the Hudson River Club is
located in the World Financial Center across from the World
Trade Center. On entering, you will take in a long expanse of
windows with that gorgeous backdrop, in a three-level space.
Tables are well spaced, so conversations can be private. Chef
Matthew Maxwell prepares a seasonally changing menu, which
might include such specialties as potato-and-truffle ravioli, fen-
nel-and-coriander-crusted yellowfin tuna and Muscovy duck
breast with organic quinoa and wilted frisée. You can also get
such all-American favorites as a grilled 16-ounce sirloin steak
with macaroni and cheese. The selection of over 300 wines is
fairly priced and offers good picks from California and the
Hudson River Valley.

INDEPENDENT   AMERICAN   12/20

179 W. Broadway (Leonard St.), 10013
219-2010, *Lunch & Dinner daily, Brunch Sat. & Sun., $$*

This TriBeCa hot spot plays the artsy-bistro card and wins:
it's lighter and more comfortable than nearby Odeon, its inspiration. The menu features all the simple American basics with
an emphasis on the New American, from oysters and Caesar
salad, to roast garlic-lemon chicken, house-smoked pork ribs,
and baked lobster Thermidor, to bouillabaisse on Sundays. But
who cares about the food? This is one of those chicer-than-chic
places where it's who you see (and who sees you)—not what
you eat—that counts.

I TRE MERLI   ITALIAN   12/20

463 W. Broadway (Houston & Prince Sts.), 10012
254-8699, *Lunch & Dinner daily*, $$

Come for the homemade pastas; come for the SoHo scene.
You can always just sit at the shiny copper bar and contemplate
all those thousands of bottles of wine stacked along the brick
walls. The Italian food offerings are extensive, and when the
kitchen is doling out meals full throttle, don't expect sure-fire
accuracy. Tender homemade gnocchi come in a variety of
sauces, and the linguine al pesto is simple and balanced.
Among the best main courses is the filet mignon with a Barolo
wine sauce.

JEAN-CLAUDE   FRENCH   13/20

137 Sullivan St. (Houston & Prince Sts.), 10012
475-9232, *Dinner nightly*, $$
No cards

Owner Jean-Claude Iacovelli, formerly a captain at Bouley,
has created a cozy bistro that could have easily been transport-
ed—unfiltered cigarette smoke and all—from Paris' Left Bank.
The tables are wedged tightly together and the music and conversation reverberate off the original copper walls. The food is
prepared with the finesse of classical French training, and
often reflects ethnic influences. The daily-changing menu may
include roasted quail with glazed pears or seared scallops with
roasted beets to start, and such entrées as roasted monkfish
with savoy cabbage, olives and onions. The crème brûlée is
good and the wine list is very reasonably priced.

JERRY'S   NEW AMERICAN   13/20

101 Prince St. (Mercer & Greene Sts.), 10012
966-9464, *Breakfast & Lunch Mon.-Fri., Dinner Mon.-Sat., Brunch
Sat.-Sun.*, $

This brightly lit upscale diner, with its red-leatherette
booths, tile floor and zebra-print wall covering, is usually
bustling with SoHo neighbors and gallery-goers. At breakfast,
try the tomato-and-garlic-basted eggs, or a smoked salmon-and-
cream-cheese omelet. Daily market specials might include
roasted asparagus with shaved Parmesan, blackened tuna steak,
a grilled marinated lamb paillard with fried baby artichokes or
a spicy shrimp-salad sandwich on sourdough. If you love frites,
eat them here, and order the moist carrot cake for dessert.

KIN KHAO   THAI   11/20

171 Spring St. (Thompson St. & W. Broadway), 10013
966-3939, *Dinner nightly*, $$

This busy and terribly trendy SoHo spot features a food bar
perfect for single diners. The food is only standard, but the
crowd, neighborhood and reasonable prices make it worth the

stop. Tom yum kung, a clear, hot-and-sour soup with shrimp, straw mushrooms, lemon grass and chilies, isn't as intensely flavored as it should be. We prefer the tom kah kai, a rich soup of coconut milk and chicken. Pla kung, a hot-and-sour prawn salad with onions, chili, lemongrass and basil, is a delightful combination of spicy and refreshing. Entrées run the usual Thai gamut, including fried whole fish.

LAYLA   MIDDLE EASTERN   13/20

211 W. Broadway (Franklin St.), 10013
431-0700, *Lunch Fri., Dinner nightly*, $$

A mural of mosaic tiles and broken pottery swirls above the bar and snakes along the wall of Drew Nierporent's (and partners') 100-seat TriBeCa haunt, where the atmosphere is "It's midnight at the oasis— let's party!" You can make a meal of the small, appetizer-sized mezes: phyllo-dough-wrapped sardines; calamari stuffed with merguez sausage; and hummus, baba ghanouj and taramasalata scooped up with crisp and delicious homemade flatbreads. We like the moist Zaatar-spiced chicken with eggplant pancakes and the charmoula-marinated squab wrapped in grape leaves. You'll enjoy perusing the small and exotic wine list. And you'll either be beguiled or embarrassed by the occasional in-your-face belly dancer.

LE PESCADOU   FRENCH/SEAFOOD   14/20

18 King St. (Ave. of the Americas), 10014
924-3434, *Lunch Sun.-Fri., Dinner nightly*, $$

Provençal-style seafood is the thing at this bustling bistro, where everyone starts with a platter of fresh fruits de mer. Specialties include bouillabaisse, whole striped bass with fennel and anise-seed Pernod flambé, and thyme-misted crispy breast of duck atop a fennel-and-chive cream compote. Desserts include good seasonal fruit tarts, and there's a short French wine list.

LIAM   NEW AMERICAN   14/20

170 Thompson St. (Houston & Bleecker Sts.), 10012
387-0666, *Dinner Tues.-Sun.*, $$

Brothers William and Joe Prunty hit the bull's-eye with this tiny brick-walled NoHo pearl. The short but tantalizing menu features such contemporary dishes as potato-crusted salmon, arborio-crusted skatefish and herb-marinated pork loin with grilled peaches and white beans. The wine list, desserts, cordials and espresso exemplify the truly refined nature of this little spot.

L'ORANGE BLEUE   FRENCH BISTRO   11/20
430 Broome St. (Crosby St.), 10012
226-4999, *Lunch & Dinner daily, $$-$$$*

Around the corner from Balthazar on the expanding eastern edge of SoHo, this hip bistro—painted in oranges and
blues—is French with Moroccan overtones. It's the sort of
place that doesn't have a chef, just a cook. And that cook can
change by the hour. The food is as good as it needs to be—
poulet rôti, steak frites, couscous, cassoulet, fish of the day—
but pronounced and distinctive spicing gives it an identity.
People come to eat and hang out (and to speak French and
smoke Gauloises). There's live jazz on Wednesdays and outdoor sidewalk-style dining in good weather, but the bar is the
soul of this bistro that goes late into the night.

LUCKY STRIKE   NEW AMERICAN   12/20
59 Grand St. (Wooster St. & W. Broadway), 10013
941-0479, *Lunch & Dinner daily, $$*

A favorite with the leggy-model and black-leather crowd,
Lucky Strike also attracts collegiate types and working artists.
The floor is roughly hewn (its unevenness matches that of the
service), the tables are crowded, and the decaying silver mir-
rors on the walls display the short menu and wine list. Go at 2
p.m. or 2 a.m. for the hamburger, roast chicken or bistro steak,
and be sure to order the bread pudding for dessert. Caution: If
you hate dining in a haze of cigarette smoke, avoid Lucky
Strike.

MANDALAY KITCHEN   BURMESE   12/20
380 Broome St. (Mott & Mulberry Sts.), 10013
226-4218, *Lunch Sat.-Sun., Dinner nightly, $*

Similar to Thai cuisine but with Indian influences thrown
in, Burmese food is robust and features coconut milk, curry
spices and exotic produce. A Burmese meal traditionally
begins with soup or a selection of appetizers and/or noodles.
Here, the thick coconut-noodle soup is perfumed with kaffir-
lime leaves. The tastes here range from the somewhat bland
panthey egg noodles with tomatoes, cabbage, lime juice and a
sweet curry sauce to a Burmese salad of tea leaves and nuts
that has a strong flavor (it isn't to everyone's liking). Although
there are a handful of decent wines, your best bet is to order
Thai beer.

MATCH DOWNTOWN   INTERNATIONAL   12/20
60 Mercer St. (Houston & Prince Sts.), 10012
343-0830, 343-0181, *Brunch, Lunch & Dinner daily, $$*

This noisy restaurant-lounge is an eclectic mix that's all
over the place gastronomically and culturally, but it works.

Located in what was an old electrical company, the spacious interior is a mix of blond-wood paneling and old-world booths with industrial beams and fixtures—call it industrial chic as befits the neighborhood. The cuisine is wildly multicultural, ranging from dim sum to sushi to steak frites. If they have it, order the spit-roasted duck. The restaurant has its times of quiet and its dishes of high quality. The wines are from all over and are reasonably priced. The crowd here is hip and international, and sticks around until 4 a.m. on the weekends.

MERCER KITCHEN   NEW AMERICAN/FRENCH   15/20

The Mercer Hotel, 99 Prince St. (Mercer St.), 10012
966-5454, Breakfast & Lunch daily, Dinner Mon.-Sat., $$$-$$$$

The noise. That's what we remember even more than food at this underground restaurant complex from Jean-Georges Vongerichten. In the basement of the super-chic Mercer Hotel, down the stairs from one of the premier power bars and oh-so-sexy lounges of the upscale downtown world, lies an open kitchen (chefs communicating via headsets), a glassed-off area with high communal tables, another bar, and a dining area that extends to the turn-of-century brick walls and out under the sidewalk vault so you can see passers-by overhead through glass bubbles in the floor/ceiling. For a Vongerichten restaurant, the menu is relatively straightforward. Chef Richard Farnabe prepares a coriander-haunted black sea bass carpaccio that melts in your mouth, as well as an excellent roasted-beets-and-goat-cheese salad, and codfish roasted in a fig leaf with figs, eggplant and basmati rice. The pizza crusts are inconsistent, but the various toppings are very good (and right out of Wolfgang Puck). The glorious Alsatian tarte with fromage blanc reminds you of Jean-George's heritage, and the squab served with vegetables baked in a tagine reminds you this is his restaurant. The desserts are simple but rich and good.

MEZZOGIORNO   ITALIAN   13/20

195 Spring St. (Sullivan St.), 10012
334-2112, Lunch & Dinner daily, $$

More like a café than a full-blown restaurant, Mezzogiorno serves basically carpaccios, salads, pastas and pizzas. A large marble bar dominates the long, airy room, and a brick pizza oven burns brightly at noon and late into the evening. Small marble-topped tables are occupied by a mostly young, chic clientele. Start with beef carpaccio or a salad, then move on to pasta: thin spaghetti with shaved white truffles (in season) or squid-ink linguine bathed in a piquant, thick tomato sauce redolent of garlic. Lunchtime and a late supper (after 10 p.m.) bring individual pizzas with thin crusts and simple, fresh toppings like pancetta and onions.

MONTRACHET   FRENCH   16/20   ♔♔

239 W. Broadway (Walker & White Sts.), 10013
219-2777, *Lunch Fri., Dinner Mon.-Sat., $$$$*

Wall Street wear is just fine at this birthplace of the contemporary TriBeCa restaurant world. Wall Street salaries will help to sample some of the extraordinary wines. The food is good, very good, but since owner Drew Nieporent opened Montrachet with David Bouley as the first chef, a parade of men and women wearing the chef's toque, some better than others (like Traci des Jardins) but all good. The current chef is Remi Lauvand, who was promoted from sous-chef in early 1998. Lauvand is French and it shows on the plate, but his Gallic ways are also holding him back from generating the fusion cuisine that characterizes so many of New York's top restaurants. We're anxious to follow his development. In the three simple, tavern-like but elegant dining rooms here, we've enjoyed many meals and such dishes as the rabbit salad on frisée greens, sautéed black bass served on a green sauce made with nettles and garnished with artichokes, and always the superb crème brûlée. Try the goat cheese with fresh figs when they are available. Although prices can run high, Montrachet offers prix-fixed menus for $34 and $42.

MONZÙ   ITALIAN   14/20   ♔

The Guggenheim Museum, 142 Mercer St. (Prince St.), 10012
343-0333, *Lunch Mon.-Fri., Dinner nightly, Brunch Sat.-Sun., $$$*

The best of Sicily is the focus of peripatetic Mediterranean-flavor-meister Matthew Kenney's relaxed restaurant downstairs at the downtown Guggenheim Museum. Monzù, a term for chefs in noble homes of the Italian south, originated when Napoleon's invasion of Naples drove King Ferdinand and his French chefs, called "monsieurs," to Sicily. French technique with Sicilian ingredients and culinary traditions produced sophisticated a spin on rustic roots. Antipasti at Monzù are fine opportunities to savor Sicily's olives, smoked meats, fish, vegetables and cheese. Minestrone is a whole different experience here, with tiny farfalini and cauliflower pesto. Try the fettuccine with tuna bottarga, dried tuna roe with lemon and sea salt. Castelvetrano olives and caper vinaigrette bathe monkfish roasted in Monzù's bread oven. Three tasting menus tantalize: Your choice of three pastas in unlimited servings for $38; a five-course chef's tasting for $65; and an entire dinner of cheese, in three courses, for $38.

MORTON'S OF CHICAGO   STEAKHOUSE/AMERICAN   14/20   ♔

90 West St. (Albany & Cedar Sts.), 10006
732-5665, *Lunch Mon.-Fri., Dinner nightly, $$$$*

See review in "Midtown East"

THE NICE RESTAURANT   CHINESE/DIM SUM   13/20

35 E. Broadway (Catherine & Market Sts.), 10002
406-9776, *Breakfast, Lunch & Dinner daily*, $

A

A big, noisy Hong Kong-style restaurant, The Nice draws families from Chinatown and diners from all over the city. Admittedly, service can be uneven (and yes, not always nice), but the food is terrific: minced squab in lettuce leaves; roast suckling pig; seafood with fresh abalone, black mushrooms and moss; eggplant with cilantro and chopped pork. When it comes to the dim sum, prepare to be adventurous, as you're at the mercy of the waitstaff who hurriedly wheel the dim-sum-laden trolleys about, sometimes without having a clear idea of what's on them.

NOBU   JAPANESE   18/20

105 Hudson St. (Franklin St.), 10013
219-0500, *Lunch Mon.-Fri., Dinner nightly*, $$$$

Nobuyuki Matsuhisa is a busy man, jetting between his flag-ship restaurant in Los Angeles, his new restaurants in London and Tokyo, and this TriBeCa spot he opened with partners Robert DeNiro, Meir Teper and Drew Nieporent. When Nobu is not here, his chefs are capable of stunning gastronomic pyrotechnics, doing justice to his trend-setting New Age Japanese cuisine with its South American and Californian over-tones. And they usually pull it off, which is why Nobu main-tains its 18 rating. Nobu's ingredients are of the finest class, the crowd is a blend of see-and-be-seen downtowners and uptown power-brokers arriving by limo, and you can only get a reserva-tion if you call well in advance or know the restaurant's private number. But once you're in, you can have a great (and very expensive) meal: course after course of thrilling creations announcing pure and clean flavors amid elaborate prepara-tions. Try Nobu's new-style sashimi or the multi-course chef's choice ($40 per person and up—with an emphasis on the "up.") It may include such signature dishes as squid "pasta" (paper-thin shavings of squid) with a garlic sauce, sashimi salad and black cod with miso. There is a good selection of wine, Japanese beers and sakés. The desserts speak to a transcultural east-west schizophrenia—some would be at home at the TriBeCa Grill down the block. Nobu has a casual downtown feel while featuring flamboyant decor along a theme-park Japanese path: beechwood floors are stenciled with cherry blossoms; tall birch-tree columns rise to a high ceiling; the sushi bar is set with stools that have legs like chopsticks—mod-ern while country and very rococo.

If you can't get a reservation at Nobu, you may be able to squeeze into the new (no reservations) **Next Door Nobu** (105 Hudson St., 334-4455), which features a sleek, clean-lined décor, a raw bar, a sushi bar and a saké bar, plus a variety of noodles and tempura, and some of Nobu's signature dishes.

Unlike Nobu, they serve until midnight during the week and until 1 a.m. on Fridays and Saturdays.

THE ODÉON   NEW AMERICAN   12/20

145 W. Broadway (Thomas St.), 10007
233-0507, *Lunch Mon.-Fri., Dinner nightly, Brunch Sat.-Sun., $$*

Perhaps the first restaurant/bar to make the TriBeCa scene a scene, Odeon still draws the super-cool late-late-night fashion-and art-world crowd, along with smatterings of the bridge-and-tunnel set. It's dark, smoky and deliberately underdesigned with vinyl banquettes, Formica tables and linoleum floors. Expect a cocktail-party-like atmosphere (and noise level) and such just-okay bistro dishes as filet mignon, grilled tuna and braised lamb shank. You can also order an open-faced lamb sandwich or omelet from the Brasserie menu. Repeat: Odeon is not about the food.

OMEN   JAPANESE   12/20

113 Thompson St. (Prince & Spring Sts.), 10012
925-8923, *Dinner nightly, $$*

This rustic, Japanese-country-style dining room, up a flight of stairs from the street, is long and narrow, with brick walls and wood floors. As at its family-owned counterparts in Kyoto, people come to Omen for the specialty dish of the same name, an elaborate mating of assorted vegetables (spinach, scallions, burdock root, kelp) in a rich chicken broth with dried flakes of bonito, ginger, sesame seeds and udon noodles. But everything is tasty, from the tuna sashimi or salmon teriyaki, to the fried soba noodles. Four-course dinners run $39.95.

ORIENTAL PEARL   CHINESE/DIM SUM   13/20

103-105 Mott St. (Hester & Canal Sts.), 10013
219-8388, *Breakfast, Lunch & Dinner daily, $$*

This huge 200-seat eatery looks as if it were a sparkling 1930s cafeteria all dolled up with ceramic animals, colored lights and fiery-eyed dragons. Despite the clatter and decor, you can eat very well here, although it is best to know what to order. Some suggestions: deep-fried shrimp; crispy chicken; steamed sea bass in a soy-based, coriander-flecked broth; snow-pea leaves; and, if it's available, goose. Oriental Pearl also provides an excellent dim sum.

PAGGIO   ITALIAN   15/20

2223 W. Broadway (Franklin & White Sts.), 10013
334-8077, *Lunch Mon.-Fri., Dinner Mon.-Sat., $$$$*

In the heart of restaurant-rife TriBeCa, next to El Teddy's and a few steps from Montrachet, Paggio is a tall, cool and beautiful setting of glistening marble and graceful arches with a superb private function room. Chef Claudio Meneghini prepares classics superbly and innovates gently. Dinner may begin with an amuse bouche of black polenta, colored with cuttlefish ink and crowned with cod mousse. Butternut squash gnocchi are robed in an emulsion of butter and sage, and salmon filet is steamed in a cabbage envelope and napped in mustard-and-pink-peppercorn sauce. Paggio's risotto of the day might be made with a pesto of nettles. Expect meticulous service and a sensational flourless-chocolate cake.

PEARL OYSTER BAR   SEAFOOD   13/20

18 Cornelia St. (W. 4th & Bleecker Sts.), 10014
691-8211, *Lunch Mon.-Fri., Dinner Mon.-Sat.,* $

This place is so tiny, only 25 can eat at the bar and the one table—26 if someone perches on the window sill. But the buckets of steamer clams, the littlenecks on ice—and especially the meaty lobster rolls—are reason enough to wait for a chance to squeeze in.

PELIGRINOS   ITALIAN   11/20

138 Mulberry St. (Grand & Hester Sts.), 10013
226-3177, *Lunch & Dinner daily,* $$$

The flagship restaurant of owner Perry Criscitelli and one of the finer restaurants in New York's Little Italy, Peligrinos has rounded up all of the usual suspects to create one of the most well-balanced Italian menus south of Houston. The homemade gnocchi is always a favorite. During the summer weekends, Mulberry is closed to all but foot traffic, making this one of the best choices for al fresco dining.

PRAVDA   RUSSIAN/GOURMET BAR FOOD   13/20

281 Lafayette St. (Houston & Prince Sts.), 10012
226-4696, *Dinner nightly,* $$

No propaganda was necessary to make Pravda an instant scene, where young comrades salute glasnost with custom martinis, Dunhill cigars, and caviar wrapped in buckwheat blinis. Thirsty? Belt back signature infusions (horseradish vodka, anyone?) 24 single-malt scotches and 13 varieties of bourbon. Try the pirozki pastries stuffed with spinach and cheese, or the hearty rib-eye steak sandwich. French fries come wrapped in a Russian newspaper, and the smoked fish plate is just salty enough to keep the bar tab running. Take public transportation so you won't have to drive home, and wear black.

PROVENCE   FRENCH BISTRO   13/20

38 MacDougal St. (Houston & Prince Sts.), 10012
475-7500, *Lunch & Dinner daily,* $$$

This handsome Provençal bistro has been a crazy, wonderful success and slice of France since it opened in SoHo on

Bastille Day 1986. Its atmosphere and spirit are intoxicating. The blue-bordered French windows, big flower arrangements, country furniture, wood-paneled front room and handsome chandelier evoke images of sunny Provence. There is also a garden out back sitting 40 (with heaters for cool nights). Now add a new chef to the mix, Liz Arana, who brings added zest to the plates of this sunny, country outpost in a land of bistro, bistro, bistro. We recommend the bourride, a fish soup with aïoli, the pissaladière, with its evocative anchovies, the mussels gratinées seasoned with garlic and almonds and the grilled baby octopus with caramelized garlic, chickpeas and tapénade. The desserts are fine—such as the lemon-blueberry clafoutis— and the wines finer, but the feeling at Provence is the finest.

QUILTY'S   NEW AMERICAN   14/20

177 Prince St. (Sullivan & MacDougal Sts.), 10012
254-1260, *Lunch Mon.-Sat., Dinner nightly, Bunch Sun.,* $$$$

We find this SoHo dining room a welcome oasis for serious food but a bit pretentious. On the other hand, award-winning Chef Kathleen Sparks is very talented, and we respect her elaborate preparations. How about oysters in a Gewürztraminer cream for a starter? The salad with fennel and blood oranges is one of our favorites. Ditto the braised rabbit on pappardelle. Sparks is big on potatoes and potato preparations, so you can expect things like twice-baked or goat-cheese-filled potatoes. Fish and meat get equal treatment here, though on our last visit the fish and wine both came to the table lukewarm. Still, business is very good, and a meal can be too. The slim rectangular dining room with grayish walls, wood floors and framed insect gravures sometimes gets a bit noisy.

RAOUL'S   FRENCH   11/20

180 Prince St. (Sullivan & Thompson Sts.), 10012
966-3518, *Dinner nightly,* $$$

One of the first bistros to open in SoHo, Raoul's has always been popular with the local hip-artist and leggy-model set, and uptowners eager to hang with them. The decor is classic New York storefront: a long narrow room with an art-deco bar up front, black-tin ceilings, a collection of photos, prints and offbeat calendars as well as booth seating. Like most good bistros, the blackboard specials change daily, and may include pungent country pâté, fresh seafood, fresh oysters and steak au poivre with crispy french fries. A laid-back, friendly atmosphere (with a soupçon of attitude) prevails here, perhaps because locals still drop by and patrons seem to know each other.

RIALTO   NEW AMERICAN   12/20

265 Elizabeth St. (Houston & Prince Sts.), 10012
334-7900, *Lunch & Dinner daily, Brunch Sat.-Sun., $$*

Elizabeth, Mulberry and Mott Streets between Houston and Spring now house some of the city's most interesting boutiques, and the restaurant scene is catching up. At Rialto, choose from more than two dozen international wines at either the long, wooden bar in the front room or on a sofa in the lounge. Then, sink into the big red vinyl banquettes in the ivory-colored dining room, or seek an umbrella-covered table in the garden. On cold days, try the roasted garlic soup with candied cloves, or roast chicken with mashed potatoes. The marinated yellowfin tuna with wasabi-mashed potatoes goes over swimmingly.

ROSEMARIE'S   ITALIAN   13/20

145 Duane St. (W. Broadway & Church St.), 10007
285-2610, *Lunch Mon.-Fri., Dinner Mon.-Sat., $$$*

At this romantic little trattoria, the tables are set far enough apart to prevent eavesdropping, waiters are friendly, and the fare is simple yet original. Appetizers might include seared quail with pumpkin pancake and fig, or wild mushrooms with polenta. Pastas range from spaghetti with shrimp to butternut squash ravioli. Entrées include calf's lever with hot mustard, seared cod with a horseradish crust, and lamb shank with eggplant and white beans. A reasonably priced wine list offers decent California and Italian vintages.

SALIENT   FRENCH-INDIAN FUSION   11/20

337 W. Broadway (Grand St.), 10013
431-6222, *Dinner nightly, Brunch Sat.-Sun., $$*

The plain and simple new Salient calls itself French-American with an Indian twist. Most of the dishes have European names with exotic Indian add-ons. Case in point: Stuffed quail with black chickpeas and amchoor. The shrimp pakora was one large and flavorful batter-fried shrimp; the leek-and-potato terrine was a bit bland. We preferred the pan-roasted dorade with its garnish of crispy fried onions, to the roast chicken with a minted-lamb samosa. But most exciting was the dessert, a warm apple tart with a scoop of kulfi—delicately spiced Indian ice cream. Since our visit shortly after Salient's opening, they put in two clay tandoor ovens, for preparing Indian naan breads and tandoori specialties.

SAMMY'S ROUMANIAN STEAKHOUSE EASTERN EUROPEAN/JEWISH 11/20

157 Chrystie St. (Delancey St.), 10002
673-0330, *Dinner nightly, $$*

You can forget kosher here. You can forget Roumanian, too. The fare is quintessential Central European Jewish cooking with a large dollop of cholesterol and schmaltz. People flock to this noisy storefront restaurant in a run-down section of the Lower East Side for the chopped eggs and onions, the chicken soup and the chopped liver mixed tableside with grated radish, fried onions and fried chicken skin. There's also stuffed derma (kishka), sliced brains, Roumanian beef sausages (karnatzlach), grilled meats with chopped garlic and potato pancakes. The place has low ceilings, dark walls, a private party room where there always seems to be a Bar Mitzvah or wedding going on, and a backdrop of noise and music.

SAVOY   NEW AMERICAN   13/20

70 Prince St. (Crosby St.), 10012
219-8570, *Lunch Mon.-Sat., Dinner nightly, $$*

Savoy charms with its arts-and-crafts-inspired wood-paneled decor, complete with fireplace and museum-quality handicrafts. The service is friendly and efficient, the ambience, for SoHo, remarkably laid-back. The weekly changing menu might feature such dishes as grilled chile-pasted squid with wheatberries, green olives and tomato, potato ravioli with dried mushroom broth and brussel sprout leaves, and grilled calf's liver with bacon and artichokes. For dessert, try a fruit cobbler then move to the upstairs lounge.

SORRENTO   ITALIAN   12/20

132 Mulberry St. (Grand & Hester Sts.), 10013
219-8634, *Lunch & Dinner daily, $$$*

This Neapolitan restaurant appreciates the concept of simple pasta—go easy on the sauce. Hidden in the madness of New York's Little Italy, Sorrento could easily be mistaken for another tourist joint. But if it's Italian you desire, this is one of the best in the neighborhood.

S.P.Q.R.   ITALIAN   12/20

133 Mulberry St. (Grand & Hester Sts.), 10013
925-3120, *Lunch & Dinner daily, $$$$*

"Senatus popules que Romanus" translated loosely means, "the senate and the people of Rome." Any restaurant that wishes to associate itself with the once-great empire must be equally enduring. This member of the Sal Anthony family restaurants has been serving fine central-Italian cuisine in Little Italy for years. In the high-ceilinged, white-columned room, ease into comfy leather chairs and enjoy pastas and traditional Italian veal and beef dishes.

TAI HONG LAU   CHINESE/DIM SUM   12/20

70 Mott St. (Canal & Bayard Sts.), 10013
219-1431, *Lunch & Dinner daily, $$*

Long regarded by many as one of the best restaurants in
Chinatown, Tai Hong Lau doesn't always deliver. The dim sum,
however, is excellent, as are the soups and the succulent salt-
baked squab. There's a typically Chinatown wine list, which
means it's sometimes hit and mostly miss, with generic brands
or special bottles that don't quite marry with the food in an
exciting and complementary manner.

TALIESIN   NEW AMERICAN   15/20

The Millenium Hilton Hotel, 55 Church St.(Fulton & Dey Sts.), 10007
693-2001, *Breakfast, Lunch & Dinner Mon.-Fri., $$$*

The ambience in this art deco-style room is refined, the service is superb and the river views are sublime. Chef Mark
Breault's menu features refined contemporary American dishes such as lobster-and-shiitake tortelli with plum wine-soaked
vegetables and ginger consommé, whole roasted tomato
stuffed with charred rabbit loin or a mosaic of rosemary-
smoked salmon with Boursin cheese to start, and entrées
including hoisin-glazed game hen and blackened tuna steak
with corn-studded polenta. The wine offerings are extensive
with plenty of by-the-glass specials.

TAORMINA   ITALIAN   12/20

147 Mulberry St. (Grand & Hester Sts.), 10013
219-1007, *Lunch & dinner daily, $$$*

Hailed as one of the best on Mulberry Street, this Italian
restaurant keeps guests satisfied with all the usual Italian dish-
es—in big portions. The menu is traditional, the wine list a bit
upscale, and the service is always above average.

THAILAND RESTAURANT   THAI   12/20

106 Bayard St. (Baxter St.), 10013
349-3132, *Lunch & Dinner daily, $*

This Chinatown hole-in-the-wall is a good and inexpensive
Thai restaurant, but beware: it's not for the tender of palate, as
most of the seafood, beef and whole-fish courses are HOT. An
exception is tom kah kai, the classic chicken-coconut-milk
soup. The shrimp cooked in lime juice was so hot it brought
tears to our eyes as did a sautéed chicken with a good, thick
peanut sauce. At lunch, the place is packed with lawyers and
jurors from the nearby courthouses.

TRATTORIA VENTI TRÈ   ITALIAN   12/20

23 Cleveland Pl. (Lafayette & Spring Sts.), 10012
941-0286, *Lunch Mon.-Fri., Dinner nightly,* $

A comfortable SoHo Italian with friendly waiters, a lovely back garden and reasonable prices, Trattoria Venti Trè serves all the usual Italian suspects, from linguine with olive oil and garlic, to veal cooked every which way. The best choices are not on the menu, including seafood fra diavolo, a family-size portion of fresh clams, mussels, shrimp and calamari, served over pasta in a spicy tomato sauce. The wine list is small, reasonable and Italian, but you can bring your own bottle.

TRIBECA GRILL   NEW AMERICAN   14/20

375 Greenwich St. (Franklin St.), 10013
941-3900, *Lunch Mon.-Fri., Dinner nightly, Brunch Sun.,* $$$

Crowds of downtown New Yorkers, celebrities, tourists and out-of-towners have flocked here since Drew Nierporent (with partner Robert DeNiro) opened this place in 1990. They leave satisfied by the good food and their money's worth of atmosphere. The exterior and main dining area have an authentic TriBeCa look—loading platforms, metal stairs, exposed brick, barbershop tiles, ceiling tiles and other warehouse accoutrements—dressed up with carpeting and comfortable chairs, booths and a big four-sided art-deco (and legendary singles) bar. Count on good New American bistro fare, such as seared tuna with sesame noodles, crab-crusted sea bass with pine-nut polenta, barbecued breast of duck, and baby chicken with lemon-thyme risotto. The wine offerings, mostly American with lots of French and some Italian bottles too, are excellent.

20 MOTT STREET RESTAURANT   CHINESE/DIM SUM 12/20

20 Mott St. (Bowery & Pell Sts.), 10013
964-0380, *Breakfast, Lunch & Dinner daily,* $$

From 9 a.m. to 4 p.m., Chinese waitresses circle the floors of this three-tiered restaurant ablaze with bright lights and mirrors, pushing trolleys packed with inviting dishes. Some offerings are familiar, such as spring rolls or wonton soup. Be on the lookout for golden-fried crab claws, but skip the steamed beef. The food—be it dim sum or the more elaborate fare off the regular menu—is satisfying and arrives promptly. The lightly battered fried oysters reflect the kitchen's mastery of the ancient salt-cooking technique. Other best bets: shrimp in the shell, the seafood basket and "black fish" with black-pepper sauce.

VINCENT'S RESTAURANT ITALIAN 11/20

119 Mott St. (Hester St.), 10013
226-8133, *Lunch & Dinner daily,* $$$

On the corner of Mott and Hester since Little Italy was founded, Vincent's remains a premiere destination for the lover of southern Italian fish dishes. Scungilli, calamari, soft-shell crabs and gamberi all get the royal treatment from chefs. Order pasta dishes with "Vincent's famous sauce." The wine, too, is as unpretentious as the food. A fresh cannoli and a short espresso put the perfect finishing touch on an evening here.

WINDOWS ON THE WORLD CONTINENTAL/GLOBAL 12/20

1 World Trade Center, West Street (Liberty & Vesey Sts.) 10048
524-7000, *Lunch Mon.-Fri., Dinner nightly, Brunch Sun.,* $$$$

Long a "must visit" for the view alone, this two-acre drinking, dining and entertainment destination on the 107th floor of the World Trade Center features a sprawling bar that's a great place for a rendezvous, drink and nibble (and live entertainment), but the dining room is more a tourist attraction than a culinary destination. Still, the food is sound (though pricey), the wine list is impressive (and moderately priced), and the service is exemplary. Specialties include such dishes as seared scallops on potato pancakes with three-caviar sauce, duck prosciutto with roasted pear chutney, grilled venison chops with whisky-pecan yams and flash-cooked squab. Desserts won't make you forget the view. The $35 prix-fixe menu is near bargain here. As we went to press, the more intimate Cellar in the Sky was soon to re-open as **Wild Blue**.

WONG KEE CHINESE-AMERICAN 12/20

113 Mott St. (Canal & Hester Sts.), 10013
966-1160, *Lunch & Dinner daily,* $
No cards

One of our favorites in Chinatown for a quick in-and-out meal, Wong Kee has brisk yet efficient service and pretty good food. You will certainly get your money's worth. For appetizers we recommend the roast pork, barbecued spare ribs or dumplings. For a main course, try the chicken in sizzling platter, the Wong Kee spiced chicken or pork, crispy hong shiu chicken, and the Wong Kee sizzling steak.

ZOË NEW AMERICAN 15/20

90 Prince St. (Broadway & Mercer St.), 10012
966-6722, *Lunch Tues.-Fri., Dinner nightly, Brunch Sat.-Sun.,* $$$

We're big fans of this colorful but noisy SoHo eatery, with its dramatic yet comfortable design and inventive Asian-accented cuisine. A stool at the kitchen food counter in back is a great place to eat and take in the show if you're alone. Try the crispy calamari with Vietnamese dipping sauce, the spiced

43

salmon tartare or the mushroom risotto with sheep's milk Camembert and lemon-sage gremolata to start. Move on to, say, mustard-crusted tuna, grilled salmon with lobster couscous or sliced sirloin steak. You may also want a side of truffle-mashed potatoes. The all-American wine list is done superbly, and there is an ever-changing assortment of fine wines by the glass. If you are still thirsty, there is a long and outstanding list of international after-dinner drinks.

AND ALSO ...

ACQUARIO   SPANISH/ITALIAN
5 Bleecker St. (Elizabeth & Bowery Sts.), 10013
260-4666, *Dinner Mon.-Sat., $$*
No Cards

A simple but charming little new spot where you can share little plates of Spanish tapas—fresh grilled sardines, Spanish anchovies marinated in vinegar, grilled squid—or enjoy a three-course dinner featuring hearty pastas, Portuguese fish stew or even a good sliced sirloin steak. For dessert, try the crema Catalana, the Spanish version of crème brûlée.

B BAR   NEW AMERICAN
40 E. 4th St. (Bowery St.), 10003
475-2220, *Lunch Mon.-Fri., Dinner nightly, Brunch Sat.-Sun., $$*

If it's the scene more than the cuisine you're interested in, check out this celeb-and-supermodel-haunt in what was once a gas station, where a velvet rope keeps out the riff-raff and there's plenty of attitude. The fare runs from burgers with fries to sophisticated squid-ink fettuccine, along with grilled veggies, meats and fish. Don't even bother showing up before 10 p.m. for dinner, and wear something tight and black.

BAYARD'S   FRENCH/FUSION
1 Hanover Square (William & Pearl Sts.), 10004
514-9454, *Dinner nightly, $$$$*

What has for years been a private men's club in Wall Street's historic India House, is now open by night, at least, to the public. In a grand mahogany-and-brass setting, dine on chef Luc Dendievel's exotic elaborations on French cuisine: terrine of foie gras marinated in sweet Vouvray-onion marmalade and raisin-peppercorn brioche; open ravioli with sea scallops, goat-cheese fondant and lobster coulis; gnocchi with chicken livers and sweet garlic; salmon in a soft leek crust; and roasted duck with spices and honey, mousseline of dates, compote of apples and saffron.

THE BUBBLE LOUNGE   GOURMET BAR FOOD

228 W. Broadway (Franklin St.), 10013
431-3433, *Dinner Mon.-Sat.,* $$

A

Talk about lounging in the lap of luxury: This sophisticated 1930s-style spot features white-marble cocktail tables, red sofas, ceiling fans and eight posh salons, each named for a different Champagne house. It gets better: they serve 300 Champagnes and sparkling wines (30 by the glass) until four in the morning. To go with are (what else?) Petrossian caviar, smoked salmon and foie gras, oysters, sushi rolls and rich chocolate desserts. Occasional vertical tastings of rare vintages and music liven up the place even more than it already is.

CAVIARTERIA CHAMPAGNE CAVIAR BAR CAVIAR & GOURMET BAR FOOD

SoHo Grand Hotel, 310 W. Broadway (Canal St.), 10013
925-5515, *Lunch & Dinner,* $$$$

A

This venerable caviar retailer opened this posh spot to enjoy their wares—Caspian caviar, carpaccio made with hand-massaged Kobe beef, French foie gras, truffle soup and smoked Scottish salmon—while drinking what these gourmet treats should be served with: French Champagne. Come the revolution...

EL TEDDY'S   MEXICAN

219 W. Broadway (Franklin & White Sts.), 10013
941-7070, *Lunch Mon.-Fri., Dinner Mon.-Sat.,* $$

This energetic late-night TriBeCa haunt is a kitschy collection of narrow hallways, brightly tiled dining rooms, '50s-style booths, fish tanks and wild-and-crazy Mexican art. Though they serve Mexican food with flair (bay scallop ceviche, smoked chicken-and goat-cheese quesadillas, grilled wild striped bass with Tequila-honey glaze), but the big draws are the killer margaritas and party atmosphere.

PENANG SOHO   MALAYSIAN

109 Spring St. (Greene & Mercer Sts.), 10012
274-8883, *Lunch & Dinner daily,* $$

The decor is South Pacific meets SoHo—tropical foliage, stilt houses, a waterfall. Waitpersons wearing sarongs help you decipher the menu of Malayasian delicacies: crêpe-like roti dipped in chicken, potato and coconut curry; a fried taro basket filled with assorted seafood and vegetables; noodles with shrimp, eggs and chives; water spinach with shrimp paste; and peanut pancakes for dessert. **Also on the Upper East Side (83rd St. & Second Ave., 585-3838) and the Upper West Side (71st St. & Columbus Ave., 769-3988).**

RADIO MEXICO CAFÉ   MEXICAN/SOUTHWESTERN

259 Front St. (Brooklyn Bridge), 10038
791-5416, *Lunch & Dinner daily*, **$**

You can get burritos in Little Italy at this cute, cramped and noisy cantina with a cramped and noisy bar. The dishes are made with the kind of imported ingredients—anejo cheese and cactus—that show an authentic Mexican presence in the kitchen. Bar foods like buffalo wings and Yucatán potstickers, fajitas and enchiladas, along with more ambitious fare such as curried chicken and vegetable chimichangas.

THE SCREENING ROOM   NEW AMERICAN

54 Varick St. (Laight St.), 10013
334-2100, *Lunch Tues.-Fri, Dinner nightly, Brunch Sun.*, **$$**

Just like it says, this red-velvet-draped restaurant runs independent films in its adjoining screening room. The innovative fare might include the likes of pan-fried artichokes, fresh salmon and lemon-caramel icebox cake. After Sunday brunch, it has become somewhat of a neighborhood tradition to adjourn to the screening room to watch *Breakfast at Tiffany's*.

SOHO KITCHEN & BAR   AMERICAN

103 Greene St. (Prince & Spring Sts.), 10012
925-1866, *Lunch & Dinner daily*, **$$**

This place is definitely about scene, not cuisine. Over 100 wines by the glass, over 50 beers and just okay food in this typically trendy, high-ceilinged, brick-walled SoHo hangout. Oddly, if you want a table for a drink, not a meal too, you may be out of luck.

SPY   GOURMET BAR FOOD

101 Greene St. (Prince & Spring Sts.), 10012
343-9000, *Dinner nightly*, **$$$**

This very dark former cabaret theater is now a salon/bar with ornate crystal chandeliers, heavy velvet curtains draped over the brick walls, seating on old stuffed (and sometimes lumpy) armchairs and sofas that were once stage props, frayed oriental rugs on the worn-wood floor, and dramatic stage track-lighting. Sip Champagne and order from a pricey selection of such to-go-withs as caviar, oysters, mousse de foie de canard with figs and smoked trout. But Spy is a swank place that's all about posing (and drinking), not eating. The best time here is well past midnight, when there's a DJ or occasional live jazz, and dancing in the aisles. Earlier in the evening, the place is quiet (and gloomy) enough for a seance.

GREENWICH VILLAGE & ENVIRONS

DINING

All phone numbers are (212) unless otherwise indicated

ASTOR RESTAURANT & LOUNGE   CONTEMPORARY   12/20

316 Bowery (Bleecker St.), 10003
212-253-8644, *Dinner nightly, Brunch Sat.-Sun., $$*

Balthazar in the Bowery. More spacious than most trendy East Village hang outs, Astor Place boasts a hammered-tin-ceilinged bar, a very very dark, palm-fringed (and quite sexy) dining room, and a basement lounge where the tile-trimmed walls are reminiscent of Casablanca and the young and the restless lounge about on well-worn overstuffed sofas. It's hard to read the menu in the dim candlelight, but you'll find specialties that are more sophisticated than need be for this setting—grilled squid with red pepper, chili-rubbed shrimp, braised lamb shank, and seared coriander-crusted tuna—most prepared reasonably well.

AU TROQUET   FRENCH   13/20

328 W. 12th St. (Hudson & Washington Sts.), 10014
924-3413, *Dinner nightly, $$$*

The dull corner locale belies the romantic setting that lies behind the lace-curtained windows in this cozy room with antiques, flowers and oil paintings. The dishes are predictable though hearty and good, generally one step up from bistro fare. The handwritten menu changes periodically. Among the entrées, the chicken breast with mustard sauce is reliable, as are the rack of lamb, the monkfish, the roasted rabbit and the quail in Port sauce. For dessert, enjoy the daily tart. The wine list of mostly French and a few American wines could use some details and upgrading.

BABBO   ITALIAN   15/20

110 Waverly Pl (6th Ave. & Washington Sq.), 10012
777-0303, *Lunch Tues.-Sat. Dinner Tues.-Sun., $$$$*

New York is overflowing with Italian restaurants, but we still welcome the serious, pasta-wonderful new Babbo. Mario Batali, the chef/owner of Pó, and Joseph Bastianich, of Becco and Frico and son of Lidia Bastianich of Felidia fame, transformed

47

the Old Coach House, a New York restaurant landmark from the 1960s, into a warm and modern trattoria serving an impressive array of Italian foods and wines. The upstairs is the more sedate of the two dining rooms, but yellow walls, a sun-spraying skylight and beautiful flowers bring it to life. By all means, order the special pasta menu—five pastas followed by two desserts (talk about a winning formula)—which might include beef-cheek ravioli with squab liver. Other treats: spicy calamari; marinated fresh anchovies; wild striped bass in lemon broth; and grilled lamb chops. Consider a cheese course in addition to dessert, which might be an impressive saffron panna cotta with poached peaches.

BAR PITTI   ITALIAN   12/20

268 Sixth Ave. (Houston & Bleecker Sts.), 10014
982-3300, *Lunch & Dinner daily*, **$$**
No cards

This Tuscan-style bistro is warm and cozy in winter, and in summer when the windowed doors burst open it creates a delightful sidewalk café. One of our favorite appetizers is fettunta—grilled country bread redolent of garlic and olive oil. Another good choices are the white-bean salad with tuna, the chicken-liver pâté, the panzanella, a cold bread salad with roasted peppers. The pastas are classic and well presented. The entrées change daily; we recommend the sautéed calves liver with sage and the chicken Milanese. The short wine list features good Italian bottles at reasonable prices.

BAR SIX   FRENCH/MOROCCAN   13/20

502 Sixth Ave. (12th & 13th Sts.), 10011
691-1363, 645-2439, *Lunch & Dinner daily, Brunch Sat.-Sun.*, **$$**

Sip a beer at the bar or enjoy good food in the dining room. In fact, in fair weather, the scene at this cozy bistro flows out onto the sidewalk. The kitchen is open from noon until the wee hours, and it's a good one. We like the hummus, and white-bean brandade with pita bread, or the fried calamari with a spicy sauce, to start. As French bistro fare goes, the steak frites is fine, but we favor such exotic dishes as chicken tagine and lamb kebabs with lemon couscous. Expect good wines, good casual service and plenty of noise, including music—a DJ starts at 11 p.m. most nights.

BOCA CHICA   LATIN AMERICAN   10/20

13 First Ave. (1st St.), 10003
473-0108, *Dinner nightly*, **$$**

The name literally means "small mouth," but you'll want a big mouth—or at least a big appetite—to appreciate all the distinctive offerings on this pan-Latin menu. It's also a great restaurant for large parties and birthday celebrations, thanks to the festive atmosphere, booming salsa music, friendly waiters and killer margaritas. Even the finger food is fun. Share a plate of

ENHANCE

THE

Experience.

Vittel®

YOUR SOURCE *of* VITALITY.

Sacred Hill
New Zealand

1997

Whitecliff
HAWKES BAY
SAUVIGNON
BLANC

"Exceptional"
—Dan Berger

crispy coconut-coated shrimp or fried yucca, tostones (garlicky plantains) and maduros (sweet plantains). If you still have room, pass around a plate of chicharones de pollo, little nuggets of ultra-crispy fried chicken to gnaw straight off the bone. Next to mouthwatering ropa vieja (literally "old rags"), shredded beef in a savory tomato sauce, the vegetarian dishes seem pretty bland. But at least there's plenty of fish on the menu, including Bahian-style mixed seafood in a spicy coconut sauce.

BOP   KOREAN   12/20

325 Bowery (Second St.), 10012
254-7887, *Dinner nightly, $$$*

Seoul food made deliciously hip is what you'll find at this chic East Village eatery. Diners who are trying Korean cuisine for the first time can check their trepidation at the door. Upstairs, the small, select menu boasts crowd-pleasing Korean comfort foods like bi bim bop, a hearty rice bowl served with savory vegetables and beef, as well as more exotic specialties like yuk hwe, Korean-style beef tartare seasoned with sesame oil. The Korean barbecue is not to be missed. The bar-lounge serves Japanese saké and cool cocktails made with soju, a type of Korean vodka.

BRISCOLA   ITALIAN   13/20

65 Fourth Ave. (9th & 10th Sts.), 10003
254-1940, *Dinner nightly, $$$*

In front is a funky sitting room with a few café tables for espresso, gelato or drinks. The back dining room features a combination of soft colors and bizarre stalactite sconces and chandeliers. There's an informality to it all, thanks in part to the waiters wearing jeans with white aprons and shirts. Gino Cammarata's good Sicilian fare includes fish and meat dishes. If available, make sure you order the sweet baby clams from the Adriatic on a bed of spaghetti lightly tossed in a tomato-garlic sauce. Gino has a knack with fish, and if you don't go for the traditional Sicilian-style codfish, try the salmon. For dessert, the choice is homemade gelati. The wines are mostly Sicilian and Italian—and mostly expensive.

CAFÉ DE BRUXELLES   BELGIAN/FRENCH   12/20

118 Greenwich Ave. (13th St.), 10014
206-1830, *Lunch & Dinner daily, $$*

Located at an odd-shaped intersection, this triangular restaurant features white lace curtains and walls lacquered in essence-of-bistro beige. The menu includes Belgian-style french fries, rabbit with prunes, Belgian beer stew of beef, broiled salmon with shrimps and half-a-dozen variations on the theme of steamed mussels. The short wine list offers a superb assortment of Belgian and European beers.

CAFÉ LOUP   FRENCH   12/20

105 W. 13th St. (Sixth & Seventh Aves.), 10011
255-4746, *Lunch Mon.-Fri., Dinner nightly, Brunch Sun.,* $$

The large dining room features exposed-brick walls hung
with museum-quality photos and eclectic ceramics, and a long,
busy bar. The bistro fare is piled on the plate rather than sculp-
tured, and they're not stingy with vegetables and things to go
along with the standard old-style chicken, steak, calf's liver and
brains. We still like the escargots and mussels for starters. For
dessert, try the creamy rice pudding sandwiched between two
giant lace cookies. The international wine list offers plenty of
bottles in the teens and twenties.

CAFFÈ ROSSO   ITALIAN   13/20

284 W. 12th St. (W. 4th St.), 10014
633-9277, *Lunch & Dinner daily, Tues.-Sun., Dinner nightly,* $$

Some may call this quaint Greenwich Village storefront
restaurant romantic, with its wooden floors, oak bar, and
Venetian-orange walls. The back room and bar feature aged-
and-cracked banquettes to add to the 19th-century ambience.
The Northern Italian menu is seasonal, and select offerings
can be inspired. The grilled shrimp with arugula, and seared
scallops with portobello mushrooms and roasted beets, are
good openers. The pastas change daily, and if you like steak
tartare, enjoy it here as a main course. The reasonably priced
wine list offers selections from four continents.

CENT'ANNI   ITALIAN   13/20

50 Carmine St. (Bleecker & Bedford Sts.), 10014
989-9494, *Lunch Mon.-Sat., Dinner nightly,* $$

Good feelings abound in this bustling storefront restaurant,
featuring a blond-wood minimalist decor, an engaging staff
and enormous portions of lusty Florentine food. At Cent'Anni,
the little appetizer your waiter proposes invariably turns out to
be a generous assortment of offerings. We find it hard to pass
up the grilled portobello mushrooms, the grilled calamari or
the hefty double-cut veal chop with fresh sage. Among the out-
standing pastas are the capellini with lobster. If a bisteca
Fiorentina is on your culinary itinerary, make a stop here. The
mostly Italian wine list has plenty of picks in the $20-to-$30
range.

CHEZ ES SAADA   FRENCH/MOROCCAN   12/20

42 E. 1st St. (First & Second Aves.), 10003
777-5617, *Dinner nightly,* $$$

Stepping into Chez es Saada is like discovering a '90s-ver-
sion of Rick's Café. Candlelight flickers in the casual upstairs
bistro, while down below, a cavernous Moroccan salon awaits.

Of course, this environment attracts a beautiful crowd, who lounge around the low tables sipping cocktails that match the colorful tapestries. Snack on phyllo-wrapped braewats (a Middle Eastern appetizer of spinach and Fontina), a Marrakesh salad, b'stilla, or chicken marinated in an exotic spice blend of dried lime and allepo pepper. Cap off dinner with a pot of Moroccan mint tea and a plate of honey braewats. And if you're not ready to turn in yet, stick around for live music and a lighter, late-night menu served until 2 a.m.

CHEZ JACQUELINE   FRENCH   13/20

72 MacDougal St. (Houston St.), 10012
505-0727, *Lunch Mon.-Fri., Dinner nightly, $$$*

The culinary accent at this simple circa-1977 bistro is the South of France, particularly Nice, which is obvious in the fine rendition of escargots presented in a pastis-laced tomato sauce, and the fish soup. For us, the pièce de résistance remains the brandade de morue, an airy whip of salt cod, garlic, olive oil and potato purée. Among the entrées are a veal chop with braised vegetables, striped bass in a pink sauce, beef stew in red wine sauce and a straightforward rack of lamb. The French wines are relatively inexpensive.

CHEZ MA TANTE   FRENCH   11/20

189 W. 10th St. (Bleecker & W. 4th Sts.), 10014
620-0223, *Dinner nightly, Brunch Sun., $$*

This casual, wide-open storefront beckons passersby with its pretty interior and the heady smell of garlic. Inside you'll find off-white walls, French posters and wood floors. Be advised, it can be crowded and noisy. Perhaps that's because they sell a choice of pastas for $15.95 and an array of French bistro specialties—roast duck, leg of lamb, steak au poivre—for $19.95. The crème brûlée is a nice dessert, often served still warm with a properly crusty top. The wines remain predictable choices.

CLEMENTINE   NEW AMERICAN   15/20

1 Fifth Ave. (Eighth St.), 10003
253-0003, *Dinner nightly, $$*

With its long, curving brass-railed bar, porthole sconces and white-and-burgundy leather booths, the front lounge is the most appealing room in this hot spot. No surprise that it's packed with a hip young crowd until 4 a.m. on weekends. In the honey-colored dining room, an odd-looking (okay, ugly) sculptural rock fountain is supposed to be the focus, but we're more interested in what's on the plate. Co-owner/chef John Schenk does inventive, offbeat and full-flavored cuisine well here. We've enjoyed the merguez sausage-stuffed squid with couscous, the jumbo shrimp wrapped in strips of phyllo, the zesty chili-rubbed pork loin with cheddar-coriander custard, and the roast Long Island duck served with soft polenta, sugar snap peas, Madeira cherries and green peppercorns. We're absolutely crazy about such desserts as the moist lemon icebox cake that oozes caramel when you cut into it.

COUP   FRENCH/MEXICAN   12/20

509 E. Sixth Street (First Ave. & Avenue A), 10009
979-2815, *Dinner Mon.-Sat., Brunch Sat.-Sun.*, $$$

With no sign out front and a blank wall for a storefront, Coup could be taking a stab at cool anonymity, but after tasting the unexciting food we think they may be hiding. Sleek and modern, this newcomer stands apart from the usual East Village lair, though, and its minimalist design borders on sterile. Unfortunately, the fusion cooking also lacks fervor. Chef Karin Trouyet was raised in Mexico City by French parents, and she borrows from both cultures to create a provocative-sounding menu, but the execution is shaky. There's potential here, however, evidenced in a few winners like the fragrant and puffy apple-potato blini and the crisp-skinned roasted hen with dried cranberries.

CUISINE DE SAIGON   VIETNAMESE   11/20

154 W. 13th St. (Sixth & Seventh Aves.), 10011
255-6003, *Lunch Mon.-Fri., Dinner nightly*, $$

There may be more authentic Vietnamese restaurants in Manhattan, but Cuisine de Saigon remains a respectable choice. Skip the fried appetizers and go straight for the entrées: chao tom, broiled shrimp fixed to a sugar-cane stalk and served with rice paper, lettuce and vegetables; an intriguing noodle dish with minced pork and mushrooms; and lemon-grass beef in a peanut-curry sauce. Choose from a handful of beers, and a small selection of reasonably priced French wines.

CYCLO   VIETNAMESE   13/20

203 First Ave. (12th & 13th Sts.), 10003
673-3975, *Dinner nightly*, $$

The name "Cyclo" refers to the bicycle-powered Vietnamese rickshaw parked out front, but it's just for show—not delivery. In fact, Cyclo's sophisticated, complex cuisine draws diners from all over the city to this tiny East Village dining room, where miniature tea glasses full of wheat grass sit on each table, and map-covered sconces warm the seafoam green walls. Start with Vietnamese spring rolls, crispy egg rolls full of ground meat and bean sprouts which you wrap in lettuce leaves with sprigs of mint and basil, then dip in a piquant sauce fragrant with lemon grass and lime. Crispy snapper with chili-lime sauce boasts moist fish beneath a sweet crust, and ginger chicken comes in a clay pot brimming with rice and veggies. An order of nutty sticky rice will cool any excess spices.

DA SILVANO RESTAURANT   ITALIAN   13/20

260 Sixth Ave. (Bleecker & Houston Sts.), 10012
982-2343, Lunch Mon.-Sat., Dinner nightly, $$$

Since it opened in 1975, this trattoria has oozed rustic charm, thanks to the exposed-brick walls, antiques and ceramics. In warm weather the doors open wide onto a sidewalk café. Many of the rustic dishes are as good as those you'd get in Italy: marinated anchovies; crostini toscani; pasta with pesto and zucchini flowers; osso buco; and braised lamb shank. Desserts hold no surprises, but the Italian wine list is a good one.

DELÍCIA   BRAZILIAN   12/20

322 W. 11th St. (Greenwich & Washington Sts.), 10014
242-2002, Dinner Tues.-Sun. $$

If dinner at Delícia is indicative of how well one can eat in Brazil, start packing. True, the whitewashed walls and spare décor aren't much to look at, but it's a good place to go for tasty comfort food, Carioca-style. Jose Fonseca, the restaurant's affable owner, has put together a menu of his favorite foods from home: fresh, hot cheese rolls, crisp fried yucca and, of course, the Brazilian national dish, feijoada. Delícia serves a particularly delicious version of this stew of black beans and pork that's just melting off the bone, served with rice, collard greens, orange slices and farofa, a kind of Brazilian polenta made with yucca. The mango and passion fruit mousses are flavorful desserts.

EL FARO   SPANISH   10/20

823 Greenwich St. (Horatio St.), 10014
929-8210, Lunch & Dinner daily, $$

You can smell the garlic three doors away. But tiny El Faro, with its raffish decor, cozy booths and murals of flamenco dancers, is a Village institution—tourists have been flocking here since it opened in 1927. Expect a wait, as there are no reservations. Is this authentic Spanish food? It's definitely authentic Greenwich Village Spanish, from calamares fritos and mariscada (mixed seafood) with egg sauce, to steaks, chops and paella. Perhaps best is the side order of fried potatoes. Generous portions, good flan for dessert and sangria by the pitcher.

EL RINCON DE ESPAÑA   SPANISH   10/20

226 Thompson St. (Bleecker & W. 3rd Sts.), 10012
260-4950, Lunch & Dinner daily, $$

A village fixture since 1964, this colorful restaurant is owned by Carlos Ventoso, a Spanish chef who specializes in an octopus dish with a pungent taste of garlic. Start with the chorizo sausages or Spanish mountain ham with melon, then revel in one of the hearty paellas, chock full of fresh seafood (and chicken in the paella Valenciana). Also recommended are the arroz con pollo and the camarones à la Carlos. The best dessert is the homemade flan. The coffee tastes as it ought to: strong, robust, with a true Spanish spirit. The wine list has a decent selection of Spanish wines.

ENNIO & MICHAEL'S RESTAURANT   ITALIAN   12/20
539 LaGuardia Pl. (Bleecker & W. 3rd Sts.), 10012
677-8577, *Lunch & Dinner daily, $$*

This warm and friendly Village spot has a lovely front patio for fine-weather dining. Inside, the dining room is sleekly elegant with some art-deco overtones. Start with thin strips of fried zucchini or an assortment of antipasti, move on to such hearty pastas as rigatoni with onions and prosciutto or gnocchi. Main courses might include osso buco, various fresh fish, and such traditional veal specialties as scaloppine baked with eggplant and mozzarella. The wine list could still use some work, though most of Italy is represented. Try the cheesecake for dessert.

FLEA MARKET   FRENCH   11/20
131 Ave. A (8th & 9th Sts.), 10009
358-9280, *Lunch & Dinner daily, Brunch Sat.-Sun., $$*

The kitschy decor—Bakelite, 1960s lunchboxes and other goodies you find at a flea market—screams of a place trying too desperately to be hip. But the place becomes packed with people sipping wine and ducking outside for a cigarette, especially later in the evening. Located on Ave. A's burgeoning restaurant row, Flea Market is a friendly neighborhood bistro that serves reliable (as long as its simple) French fare. We recommend just about anything that comes with the crisp french fries—steak frites, moules marnieres and the hamburger on a baguette. During brunch on the weekends, kick back and enjoy the people-watching around Tompkins Square Park.

FLORENT   FRENCH   12/20
69 Gansevoort St. (Greenwich & Washington Sts.), 10014
989-5779, *Breakfast, Lunch & Dinner daily, Brunch Sat. & Sun., $*
No cards

This funky retro-1940s diner in the way-West Village is a beloved eatery to many, especially those looking for a place open 'til 5 a.m. on weekdays and 24 hours on weekends. The prices can't be beat, especially the $18.50 three-course prix-fixe menu with lots of choices, and the wine offerings at less than $15. The menu is enormous, but many regulars order the steamed mussels or the boudin noir, followed by the steak frites, fish of the day or roasted chicken. Evelyn's goat cheese salad is a winner, as is the chocolate-truffle cake for dessert.

GOTHAM BAR & GRILL   NEW AMERICAN   17/20

12 E. 12th St. (Fifth Ave. & University Pl.), 10013
620-4020, *Lunch Mon.-Fri., Dinner nightly, $$$$*

This big post-modern restaurant offers a terrific, fun, casu-ally elegant downtown dining experience of distinguished preparations and outstanding wines. Talented executive chef Alfred Portale has the kitchen well under control—in fact, we've never had a disappointing meal here. Among the appe-tizers on the seasonally changing menu you might find salmon carpaccio with cremini mushrooms, cauliflower vichyssoise with seared scallops, risotto with duck confit and roasted-pumpkin ravioli in duck broth with Mascarpone cheese. Among the entrées, we're partial to the striped bass with roast fennel, the ginger-and-juniper-marinated roast pheasant, and the squab with white polenta. The most popular dessert is the warm chocolate cake with espresso ice cream. The impressive wine list features over 200 selections from all over the map.

THE GRANGE HALL   AMERICAN/HEALTHY   10/20

50 Commerce St. (Barrow St.), 10014
924-5246, *Breakfast, Lunch & Dinner daily, $*

The trendy and busy Grange Hall serves "Food From the American Farm" and lots of drinks to go with. For breakfast, try the scallion-scrambled eggs with smoked trout. Lunch fea-tures sandwiches made with organic turkey and chicken. At dinner, stick with what's simple—cranberry-glazed pork chops or grilled lamb steak. Affordable wines by the bottle or glass, as well as beers on tap and small-batch bourbons. Desserts are of the all-American variety: snowy-white coconut cake, homemade fruit or berry pies, or iced devil's food layer cake.

HASAKI   JAPANESE   13/20

210 E. 9th St. (Second & Third Aves.), 10003
473-3327, *Dinner nightly, $$$*

With a saké bar, a soba noodle shop and a Japanese super-market all on the same block, locals have taken to calling 9th St. the Little Japan of the East Village. But it's easy to recognize Hasaki, the best of the sushi restaurants here. The tiny blonde-wood underground eatery doesn't take reservations, so there's always a long line out front. Luckily, the restaurant doesn't seat parties larger than four, so tables turn over pretty quickly. Besides, Hasaki's devotees seem to be willing to withstand any inconvenience for the buttery soft yellowtail, crispy salmon skin and succulent king crab. There are also plenty of extras, such as soba noodles and tempura. For dessert, spoon into creamy green tea ice cream topped with sticky red beans and order a pot of siphon coffee, brewed tableside in a futuristic beaker.

HOME   AMERICAN   13/20

20 Cornelia St. (Bleecker & W. Fourth Sts.), 10014
243-9579, *Breakfast & Lunch Mon.-Fri, Dinner nightly, Brunch Sat.-Sun.,*
$$

Co-owner/chef David Page brings a bit of the country to
this homey neighborhood restaurant with its intimate farm-
house setting and a heated year-round garden. On mismatched
china plates under handcrafted light fixtures, Page offers such
starters as homemade ginger-and-black-pepper salami or blue-
cheese fondue with caramelized shallots and rosemary toast. A
popular entrée is the roasted chicken piled with spicy onion
rings and served with homemade ketchup. The chocolate pud-
ding gets our first nod among desserts. If you can't get into this
tiny restaurant, try Home's new sister restaurant nearby:
Drovers Tap Room (9 Jones St., 627-1233).

I COPPI   ITALIAN   13/20

432 E. 9th St. (First Ave. & Ave. A), 10009
254-2263, *Dinner nightly, Brunch Sat.-Sun.,* **$$**

This cozy new place in Alphabet City draws an artsy crowd
who like the Tuscan-bistro look—exposed brick walls, beamed
ceilings, brick pizza oven, hand-crafted pine tables and
chairs—and the authentic Tuscan food. On the daily-changing
menu, expect fresh-baked breads and pizzas, hard-to-find
Italian wines and cheeses, pastas (try one with pesto blanco),
and such grilled entrées as salmon with artichokes and stewed
rabbit with black olives.

IL BAGATTO   ITALIAN   13/20

192 E. 2nd St. (Aves. A & B), 10009
228-0977, *Dinner Tues.-Sun.,* **$$**
No cards

A Roman holiday awaits those lucky enough to get a seat at
this charming homestyle trattoria, where rustic decor marries
authentic Italian cuisine. Begin the evening in the intimate
downstairs lounge, then dine upstairs on tuna carpaccio or
mushrooms stuffed with spinach and goat cheese, followed by
buttery-soft three-cheese gnocchi beef sauté, a Roman specialty
of meat slices thin enough to wrap around a steamy nugget of
garlic. If you want to keep coming back, don't break the rules:
cash or check only, smoking allowed, arrive on time (reserva-
tions are only held for 10 minutes), and don't ask for
Parmesan on the pasta with seafood sauce.

IL BUCO   ITALIAN   14/20

4 Bond St. (Bowery & Lafayette Sts.), 10012
533-1932, *Lunch Tues.-Sat., Dinner nightly,* **$$$**

Donna Lennard and Alberto Avalle originally opened this
hole in the wall as an antique store, then decided to sell wine

and food as well. Now, the place is more restaurant than antique store (though if you like that old chair you can buy it). In fact, with Jody William as chef, Il Buco has become so popular that reservations are a must. Il Buco's menu features such Italian-inspired dishes as grilled polenta with baby eels, crisp risotto cakes with wild mushrooms, several fresh pastas, seared tuna with white corona beans and grilled jumbo shrimp. The wine list is considerably longer, which is fitting since the wine cellar here is reputed to have been the inspiration for Edgar Allan Poe's classic short story, *The Cask of Amontillado.*

IL CANTINORI   ITALIAN   14/20   ♟

32 E. 10th St. (Broadway & University Pl.), 10003
673-6044, *Lunch Mon.-Fri., Dinner nightly,* $$$$

For over 15 years, Il Cantinori has served first-rate Italian food in a rustic setting that reminds us of Tuscany. In fact, this casually elegant restaurant always seems filled with tables of six or eight having a good time and a good meal. On the changing menu, starters might include filet mignon carpaccio or grilled squid. The tagliolini with crab, brandy and grilled radicchio is a sophisticated pasta. Plenty of good fresh fish dishes are offered along with such seasonal specialties as, in winter, Tuscan pot roast. Order biscotti to dip into vin santo at the close of your meal. The exclusively Italian wine list is well chosen, and the grappa selections invite tough decisions.

IL MULINO   ITALIAN   14/20   ♟

86 W. 3rd St. (Sullivan & Thompson Sts.), 10012
673-3783, *Lunch Mon.-Fri., Dinner Mon.-Sat.,* $$$$

Even with a reservation you may wind up waiting (and waiting) for your table at this popular—and very noisy—Village Italian. Once you're seated, however, flagging spirits are revived by wonderfully crisp fried zucchini or bruschetta. The cozy, dimly lit dining room is divided by a row of tall, stately plants. The food is full of flavor, and we're always pleased by the such pasta specials as pappardelle in a robust fresh tomato (or sometimes game) sauce, or classic spaghettini alla Bolognese. Another good appetizer is the addictive bocconcini, moist balls of buffalo mozzarella flecked with roasted sweet peppers. Some entrées come quite naked, so order a veggie or two. Fresh orange slices marinated in Grand Marnier and raspberries, are just right as a dessert.

INDOCHINE   VIETNAMESE   13/20   ♟

430 Lafayette St. (Astor Pl. & 4th St.), 10012
505-5111, *Dinner nightly,* $$$

This theatrically exotic (or perhaps exotically theatrical) setting features enough palm fronds—real, and painted on the walls—to thatch several tropical huts. The see-and-be-seen dining room features clubby, dark-green banquettes and colorful tropical flowers. We recommend the fish soup sweetened with coconut milk, the summer roll of shrimp wrapped in rice paper and, for those who like it hot, the beef salad. Highlights among the main courses are the crispy whole red snapper with a spicy sweet-and-sour pimento sauce and the grilled baby back ribs. A side order of sticky rice will offset the spicier dishes. Try the exotically flavored sorbets for dessert.

JULES   FRENCH   12/20

65 St. Mark's Pl. (First & Second Aves.), 10003
477-5560, *Lunch & Dinner daily*, $$$

This quintessential neighborhood bistro in the East Village consistently delivers home-style French cooking. Although one may find the wait staff a bit curt, the steak au poivre with mashed potatoes is the genuine article, the bar is boisterous, and the wine list features many affordable gems.

KPNY (KEN'S PLACE NEW YORK)   HEALTHY/AMERICAN   13/20

557 Hudson Street (Perry & W. 11th Sts.), 10011
627-3092, *Lunch & Dinner daily*, $$

Here's a spot where vegetarians and carnivores peacefully coexist thanks to a menu that offers tasty vegetable, grain and legume dishes as well as meats and fish. And while some health food restaurants are more about karma than cooking, we've found plenty to recommend here, like the assertively dressed salads and vegan plates that deftly mix grilled tofu with sundry veggies and herbs. Those who scoff at "rabbit food" have mainstream but healthy options such as skinless chicken, filet mignon and soy-glazed salmon.

LA MÉTAIRIE   FRENCH   13/20

189 W. 10th St., (W. 4th St.), 10014
989-0343, *Dinner nightly, Brunch Sat.-Sun.*, $$$

The look is rustic-country French—dark-wood beams, white-stuccoed walls, farmyard artifacts, dried flowers and Provençal paisleys. The food is southern French and satisfying. Good appetizers include the garlic mousse with sautéed wild mushrooms and the smoked-salmon cannoli. The rack of lamb served with a garlic and herbs is a solid entrée, as are the roast cod with olive-mashed potatoes, the seared tuna with quinoa and plum-wine sauce, and the lobster risotto. Desserts are serviceable as are the French (and some American) wines.

LA RIPAILLE   FRENCH   12/20

605 Hudson St. (12th & Bethune Sts.), 10014
255-4406, *Dinner nightly*, $$$

Who would predict back in 1979 when this little authentic taste of France opened that it would still attract a crowd in the late '90s? The romantic, inn-in-the-city decor remains unchanged: a tiny bar and a cozy room with huge cross beams overhead. Much of the French fare comes in the classic style without being old-fashioned: broccoli mousse with lemon butter; escargots; salmon with fennel and couscous; rack of lamb; roast duck. For dessert, go with the tarte tatin. We applaud the range of inexpensive regional French wines from Cahors, Buzet, Corbières, Ventoux and Gascogne.

LE TABLEAU FRENCH 12/20

511 E. 5th St. (Aves. A & B), 10009
260-1333, *Dinner nightly, $$*
No cards

The "tableau" here is ever-changing, and can focus on French roots one night, then play up inspirations from North Africa, Italy or Greece the next. Or it can spotlight some seasonal ingredient, like a bright-and-tangy blood-orange sauce on grilled salmon. The seafood pasta was super fresh, if a tad too al dente, but the crisp peppered duck was succulently braised. Of course, this wouldn't be a French bistro without escargot, cassoulet and peppery steak au poivre. On Mondays, Le Tableau features guest chefs. The solicitous staff blends friendly charm with just enough French attitude to feel authentic.

LE ZOO RESTAURANT FRENCH 14/20

314 W. 11th St. (Greenwich St.), 10014
620-0393, *Dinner nightly, Brunch Sun., $$*

This rustic spot with exposed-brick-and-wood walls, crowded tables and two walls of windows, looks like it belongs on the Left Bank, and it's always packed. No wonder: it offers inventive French bistro cooking at modest prices. (Some fans call it "Bouley Jr.") The small menu might include such appetizers as apple-perfumed smoked salmon and trout or soft-shell crab with seaweed salad, and such entrées as honey-glazed pork loin, a lamb T-bone steak or salmon with a fennel-and-mustard-seed crust. Beware, it's also hard to get in—especially on Sundays, when the neighborhood piles in for brunch.

L-RAY CAJUN/TEX-MEX 13/20

64 W. 10th St. (Fifth & Sixth Aves.), 10011
505-7777, *Dinner nightly, Brunch Sat.-Sun., $$*

With its bayou-style decor, animated scene and spicy fare, this new "Gulf Rim bistro" has been discovered by the neighborhood. Everything here plays against pretension, from the toothpicks and Tabasco bottles on every table to the printed sheet of yellow paper that serves as the menu. The cuisine—a sunny amalgam of Cajun, Tex-Mex and Cuban dishes—draws robust flavors from lime, garlic, coriander and chilies, and despite an occasional flat note, is uncomplicated and appealing. Iced oysters and lethal frozen margaritas make for an arresting starter, as does a platter of assorted grilled sausages. Favorite entrées include the pan-fried grouper in a green chili sauce and roasted duck breast.

LUCKY CHENG   PAN-ASIAN   13/20

24 First Ave. (1st & 2nd Sts.), 10009
473-0516, Dinner nightly, $$

A restaurant with a kitschy Oriental decor and Asian drag-queen waiters (or do we call them waitresses)? Okay, Lucky Cheng isn't a restaurant to which you'd take your grandmother (she'd go deaf from the high noise level, if she isn't already), but you can have a lot of fun here. In fact, many celebs do. Surprisingly, the food is better than just adequate: crackling-sesame calamari in a chick-pea crust; firecracker duck spring rolls; a salad of smoked duck and roasted pistachios. For a small fee, you can have your own private drag queen perform at your table.

MESOPOTAMIA   BELGIAN/MIDDLE EASTERN   10/20

98 Ave. B (6th & 7th Sts.), 10009
358-1166, Brunch Sat.-Sun., Dinner nightly, $$

Colorful mosaic wall tiles and etched-glass light fixtures make for a Middle Eastern art deco look, but the menu is even more surprising. Thanks to a Turkish owner and a Belgian chef, Mesopotamia's food is a little of both. That's why you can get smoked eggplant dip or honey-baked goat cheese salad, followed by grilled striped bass with Hoegarden beer sauce or steak au poivre with Belgian fries. The early bird special features soup or greens, an entrée, dessert and coffee for just $11.95. But if you'd rather come late (the kitchen serves until 1 a.m. every night except Sunday), try the grilled lamb. The wine list is as international as the menu, and includes some impressive choices for under $20.

MI COCINA   MEXICAN   13/20

57 Jane St. (Hudson St.), 10014
627-8273, Dinner nightly, Brunch Sun., $$

In a tiny dining room with little atmosphere, Mi Cocina serves serious regional Mexican food. Appetizers include beef-and-raisin empaniditas, shrimp in a spicy chile adobo sauce, fried Mexican beer-battered calamari as well as oregano-kissed guacamole. A list of specials changes daily, and entrées often include fettuccini with grilled breast of chicken and shrimp in a sauce of roasted tomato, chipotle and white wine. For the less adventurous, there are enchiladas de mole poblano and fajitas.

MIE   JAPANESE   13/20

196 Second Ave. (12th & 13th Sts.), 10003
674-7060, Dinner nightly, $$

As in many Tokyo restaurants, you enter this basement restaurant down a "landscaped" stone path, past rocks and a semblance of a garden. If you order à la carte rather than the set dinners, the chef will know you're serious. His sushi and sashimi are excellent, and if you sit at the sushi bar and befriend him, you'll be in for a treat. Yakiniku, thin slices of beef broiled with garlic and ancho peppers, come tender and rare, and will remind you of tuna. We've enjoyed the fish teriyaki, the udon-noodle dishes and chawan-mushi egg custard filled with tiny pieces of chicken, vegetables, shrimp and gingko nuts.

MIRACLE GRILL   SOUTHWESTERN   12/20

112 First Ave. (6th & 7th Sts.), 10003
254-2353, Dinner nightly, Brunch Sat.-Sun., $$

Popular with a hip downtown crowd, the Miracle Grill is always busy, so you may have to wait for a table; in summer, a table in the lovely back garden is much coveted. Starters include the likes of catfish tacos, chile-rubbed chicken satay, and tortilla soup chock-o-block with grilled chicken, chiles and avocado. We've enjoyed the grilled shrimp-and-wild-mushroom risotto, the grilled portobello fajitas and the barbecued salmon over a ragout of white beans and winter greens.

MONO   NEW AMERICAN   14/20

344 W. 11th St. (Washington St.), 10014
645-9009, Dinner Tues.-Sun., Brunch Sun., $$$

Mono (moe-know) is one of the most beguiling spots to open in the West Village in the past year. Working out of a kitchen not much bigger than a bus shelter, chef Pat Kotsonis turns out New American fare that's boldly seasoned and utterly delicious. The two small dining rooms have a spare, rustic feeling and the crowd—like the cooking—is hip but unpretentious. Standout dishes include foie-gras-and-apple terrine with reduced port sauce and Chilean sea bass with preserved lemon, fennel and tomato-pepper jus.

MOOMBA   NEW AMERICAN   15/20   ♟♟

133 Seventh Ave. South (Charles & W. 10th Sts.), 10014
989-1414, *Dinner nightly, $$$$*

A ☎

On the one hand, the limos outside, the velvet-rope entry and the likes of Leonardo Di Caprio regularly inside are enough to keep this trendy and chic spot, well, trendy and chic for quite a while. On the other hand, the ambitious kitchen, headed by chef and part-owner Frank Falcinelli, is wonderful and keeps us coming back. The space is narrow and multi-level, with some quiet tables in the front by the window (it's a noisy, club-like spot by design); beyond the bar there's a second level with seating. Foie gras is something of a specialty here, and you can find it inside ravioli, sautéed with tangerines and dates, or rubbed all over chicken. We also recommend the lamb shank osso buco. For dessert, the Moomba bar is just the sort of decadent candy cake the name conjures up.

PIADINA   ITALIAN   13/20   ♟

57 W. 10th St. (Fifth & Sixth Aves.), 10011
460-8017, *Dinner nightly, $$$*
No cards ☎ 🏃

This little basement restaurant has remained one of Manhattan's relatively undiscovered treasures. It's a hangout for the ultrahip, but ask Kiku for a table in the back and you'll discover its charm. Begin with the namesake Piadina sandwich and follow with the vongole in white wine and garlic. We recommend the seared ahi tuna, and for dessert, the panna cotta with a shot of espresso.

PÒ   ITALIAN   14/20   ♟

31 Cornelia St. (Bleecker & Sixth Ave.), 10014
645-2189, *Lunch Wed.-Sun., Dinner Tues.-Sun., $$*

☎

This tiny Village storefront restaurant with 12 tables is quite popular, so reserve ahead. It's the modern Italian food and modest prices that draws crowds. Co-owner Steve Crane works the front while co-owner and chef Mario Batali creates seasonal and innovative updated Bolognese and Tuscan classics. Start with grappa-cured salmon paired with crostini slathered with a lemony jam. Pastas might include tagliatelli with rabbit ragout and fettuccini with cayenne-scented walnuts. Among the winning entrées are the guinea hen with cranberry mustarda, escolar with lentils or perhaps braised duck and chorizo with leeks, olives, red potatoes and Cinzano. The warm apple tart makes for a fine ending, and the all-Italian wine list is replete with savvy selections.

RAGA   INDIAN   13/20

433 E. 6th Street (First Ave. & Avenue A), 10009
388-0957, *Dinner Tues.-Sun., $$*

The fusion cuisine rage has seen every divergent style from Mexican to Japanese combined, but, until recently, trailblazing chefs have largely ignored the sultry cooking and spices of India. At this East Village newcomer, classic French dishes such as braised lamb shank and bouillabaisse derive their flavors from bold Indian seasonings—cumin, cardamom, curry—which add a jolt of earthiness and depth. And typical Indian desserts like rice pudding, which are usually sugary and uninspired, are complex and minimally sweet.

RESTAURANT EQ   CONTEMPORARY AMERICAN   15/20

267 W. Fourth St. (at Perry St.), 10014
414-1961, *Dinner Mon.-Sat., $$$$*

This is a throwback—a small, intimate storefront with a simple but elegant décor, where food and service of the highest quality is the raison d'être. It has a calm feel—everything's done in beige and green with soft lighting. The steamed cockles with homemade noodles and slices of pink grapefruit is a winning combination that is becoming the restaurant's signature appetizers. Among the entrées we've enjoyed are various grilled and sautéed fish, including a salmon with candied fennel, and a superb saddle of rabbit. The wine list is relatively short but good, and the desserts are all inviting. It will be interesting to follow this newcomer to see if it moves up a notch. The arrows are pointing in that direction.

TREEHOUSE   NEW AMERICAN   12/20

436 Hudson. St. (Morton St.), 10014
989-1363, *Lunch Mon.-Fri., Dinner Mon.-Sat., $$*

They put a tree in the window, countrified the décor a bit and changed the name of the former Village Attelier. It's small and romantic, and filled with American country antiques (circa 1890) from owner/chef Craig Bero's family farm in northern Wisconsin. In keeping with the setting, the food is wholesome "farmhouse cooking" with updated twists. Start with the crabcakes with cracked-grain mustard, mushrooms in puff pastry or roasted garlic, then try grilled trout, roasted red snapper, medallions of pork or a steak. The wine list is carefully chosen, focusing on American wines from small vineyards as well as some French country wines.

WATERLOO   BELGIAN   14/40

145 Charles St. (Washington St.), 10014
352-1119, *Dinner Tues.-Sun., $$*

The hip folks from Le Zoo opened this hipper-than-hip spot in what was once an old garage. There's lots of posing (and smoking) at the bar, which serves over two-dozen beers (including Trappist, white and fruit beers, and Belgian ales) as well as the usual cocktails and wine. The Belgian food can either be terrific or terrible. Stick with the steamed mussels in herby white-wine sauce, served with crisp Belgian fries.

YE WAVERLY INN   AMERICAN   10/20

16 Bank St. (Waverly Pl.), 10014
929-4377, *Lunch Mon.-Fri., Dinner nightly, Brunch Sat.-Sun., $$*

Set in an old townhouse on one of the West Village's handsomest residential streets, this picturesque tavern which opened in 1920 has four cozy dining rooms just below street level which sport low ceilings, wooden booths and three working fireplaces. In summer, there are also tables in an outdoor garden. The fare is simple and honest American fare: chicken pot pie; meatloaf; Yankee pot roast; Southern fried chicken. Plenty of seafood specials are offered daily.

AND ALSO ...

DANAL   NEW AMERICAN/FRENCH

90 E. 10th St. (Third & Fourth Aves.), 10003
982-6930, *Lunch Mon.-Fri., Dinner nightly, High Tea Fri.-Sat., Brunch Sat.-Sun., $*

In this dining room filled with mismatched sofas and chairs, old lamps and knick-knacks gleaned from Paris fleamarkets, you might feel as if you're dining in an eccentric French auntie's house. Maybe that's why it's such a cozy spot for afternoon tea. The daily-changing dinner menu offers such French-inspired starters as a leek-and-goat-cheese tart, entrées that range from a grilled tuna salad to polenta-crusted salmon, usually accompanied by lentils or couscous, and perhaps croissant-bread pudding for dessert.

GARAGE   AMERICAN

99 Seventh Ave. (Barrow & Groves Sts.), 10014
645-0600, *Lunch Mon.-Fri., Dinner nightly, Brunch Sat.-Sun., $$*

🅰 ☎ 🖵

This theme-ish bar/restaurant/scene has giant Oldenberg-like sculptures of engine parts, mechanics' tools, but yes, also a knife, spoon and fork. There's a fireplace, a big bar, and food ranging from oysters, pizza and pastas, to steak. Lots of beers on tap, and on weekends, live jazz.

INDIGO   NEW AMERICAN

142 W. 10th St. (Greenwich Ave. & Waverly Pl.), 10014
691-7757, *Dinner nightly, $$*

🍴 ☎

Son of Luma (now renamed Siena). Scott Bryan opened this more casual, less expensive restaurant with a simple, ultra-modern decor and wonderfully flavorful food. Appealing dishes include the wild-mushroom strudel, brandade-and-lobster ravioli, the sage-roasted farm chicken and the port-wine-and-balsamic-braised pork.

LA BOHÈME   FRENCH/FUSION

24 Minetta Ln. (W. 3rd St. & Sixth Ave.), 10012
473-6447, *Lunch Tues.-Sun., Dinner nightly, $$$*

🍴 🖵 🎋

With its stacks of firewood, plank floors, white stucco walls and Provençal pottery, this quaint bistro would look quite at home in Nice. Many regulars subsist on the thin-crusted pizzas cooked in a wood-fired brick oven. Chef Larry Berson also offers fusion dishes like scallops with a mango-chile sauce and monkfish osso buco, as well as stuffed roasted leg of lamb. The reasonably priced French wine list is short but serviceable.

MEKKA   SOUL FOOD/CARIBBEAN

14 Ave. A (Houston & 2nd Sts.), 10009
475-8500, *Dinner nightly, Brunch Sun., $*

🅰 🖵

This place brings on da funk to the Alphabet City. Nouvelle Soul food means collards with smoked turkey wings instead of ham hocks, and mashed potatoes with a smattering of Cheddar cheese. You'll also find Southern fried chicken and barbecued ribs, along with spicy jerk fish that will remind you of Jamaica.

ONE IF BY LAND, TWO IF BY SEA   NEW AMERICAN

17 Barrow St. (Seventh Ave. South), 10014
228-0822, *Dinner nightly*, $$$$

Set in an 18th-century carriage house owned by Aaron Burr, this place is gorgeous and the service is cosseting. In fact, listening to the lilting piano music, gazing on the captivating flowers or the blazes in the fireplaces, you may be inspired romantically. We've never been crazy about the food, but now there's a new chef—David McInerney, who was at Raphael—and a new menu. We're eager to taste some of his specialties: seared tuna with wasabi, terrine of foie gras, lightly smoked and roasted rack of lamb, chicken breast with truffled-potato purée. The extensive French-American wine list is sound but hardly inspired.

SUD   FRENCH

210 W. 10th (Bleecker & W. 4th Sts.), 10014
255-3805, *Dinner nightly*, $$

The menu may make you think there's nothing exciting here—just the usual old French favorites—but North African spices (the owners are from Tunis) bring the food up several notches. In a spare and narrow room done in warm Mediterranean colors, try, perhaps, cumin-perfumed pumpkin soup, moist salmon, saffron-scented linguine with scallops, or couscous with veal meatballs and a fiery Tunisian harissa sauce.

SURYA   INDIAN/FUSION

302 Bleecker St. (Seventh Ave.), 10014
807-7770, *Dinner nightly, Brunch Sat.-Sun.*, $$

The service may not be too friendly at this new eatery in the West Village, but the room is attractive—burnt-orange walls and cozy sofas—and the cuisine—Southern Indian with French overtones—is intriguing. Among the best bets: sautéed scallops with chili and coriander; lentil cakes; cumin-perfumed rack of lamb; salmon in a sweet-and-sour-tinged sauce; and desserts including yogurt-like pudding.

14TH STREET TO 42ND STREET

DINING

All phone numbers are (212) unless otherwise indicated

AN AMERICAN PLACE   NEW AMERICAN   14/20   🍳

2 Park Ave. (32nd St.), 10016
684-2122, *Lunch Mon.-Fri., Dinner Mon.-Sat., $$$$*

🅰 ☎ ⚲

This friendly, all-American restaurant presents the ever-changing creations of chef Larry Forgione in a huge, high-ceilinged room decorated with slices of Americana, from Frank Lloyd Wright-inspired armchairs to art-deco columns and sconces. Starters might include a goat-cheese pancake with a warm salad of roasted beets and Black Mission figs, or charred buffalo carpaccio. Among the entrées are a wood-grilled breast of free-range chicken and black peppercorn-crusted Hudson Valley duck steak. For dessert, our favorite is the chocolate devil's food cake that is 50 percent fudge. You'll find mostly California wines, plus a few from New York and Washington State, with sound selections in the $20-to-$40 range.

ASIA DE CUBA   ASIAN/CUBAN   13/20   🍳

237 Madison Avenue (37th & 38th Sts.), 10016
726-7755, *Lunch Mon.-Fri., Dinner nightly, $$$*

💳 💳 ☎ ☎

This hotspot's landlord (but not owner) is hotelier Ian Schrager, whose cachet immediately made it a socially fervid scene when it opened in October 1997. Although the bi-level space suggests neither Asia nor Cuba, designer Philippe Starck's dining room has an ethereal, retro feel that's warm and appealing. The fusion fare embraces fresh and spicy flavors, but the execution is a bit slack, and waiters tend to dote over big spenders while ignoring others. The well-rounded wine list features quality selections but few bargains.

BAMBOU RESTAURANT & BAR   CARIBBEAN FUSION   14/20

243 E. 14th St. (Second & Third Aves.), 10003
358-0012, *Dinner nightly, $$$*

Gauzy white curtains frame the intimate white-on-white din-
ing room that looks right out of an *Architectural Digest*-ready
house in Jamaica, lazily spinning ceiling fans and all. Leggy
models sip martinis on chaise lounges in the candle-lit bar. The
limited menu offers contemporary dishes with a Caribbean
twist, some of which work better than others. Good bets
include steamed mussels, the grilled jerk-seasoned breast of
chicken, the Arawak-spiced shell steak, the whole snapper with
ginger, and for dessert, the coconut crème brûlée.

BASTA PASTA   ITALIAN   14/20

37 W. 17th St. (Fifth & Sixth Aves.), 10011
366-0888, *Lunch Mon.-Fri., Dinner nightly, $$$*

This is the sort of surprising, weird and wonderful restaurant that makes New York the restaurant town it is. The branch
of an Italian restaurant in Tokyo, and staffed with Japanese, it's
the match of any trattoria in New York staffed by native
Italians. To get to your table, you literally walk through the
kitchen—it's simply part of this storefront space, sinks, refrig-
erators, pastry station and all. The superb pastas include buckwheat tagliatelle with braised quail, linguini with fresh sea
urchin and spaghetti with flying-fish roe. We recommend the
grilled lamb chops as a main course.

BLUE WATER GRILL   SEAFOOD   13/20

31 Union Square West (16th St.), 10003
675-9500, *Lunch & Dinner nightly, Brunch Sun., $$*

This former bank building, with its Doric columns, marble
walls and vaulted ceilings, bustles with the tragically hip, who
come to hang out, hear live jazz (in the basement club) and
dine on fresh seafood. At the raw bar, you'll find over a dozen
varieties of oysters. There's also good grilled fresh fish and a
mighty Valhrona chocolate cake for dessert. On Sundays, the
jazz band plays in the main dining room near the bar, so you
can hear the music from anywhere you sit.

BOLO   SPANISH   14/20

23 E. 22nd St. (Broadway & Park Aves.), 10010
228-2200, *Lunch Mon.-Fri., Dinner nightly, $$$$*

At this post-modern high-energy restaurant, tables are set
with an eye to color and walls are decorated with Matisse- and
Braque-like collages. Chef/owner Bobby Flay uses Spanish

ingredients—olives, capers, pecans, chorizo, preserved lemons—creating such inventive dishes as piquillo peppers filled with salmon tartare, roasted beet-and-goat-cheese empanadillas, savory paellas, potato-horseradish-crusted red snapper, and roasted clams and hot Spanish sausage with sweet onion and grilled pepper relish. Desserts have their own whimsy, and there's a well-priced selection of Spanish and American wines, plus sangria by the glass or the pitcher.

BOTTINO — ITALIAN — 12/20

246 Tenth Ave. (24th & 25th Sts.), 10011
206-6766, *Lunch Tues.-Sun., Dinner nightly,* $$$

Tired of schlepping several blocks east for a decent bite to eat, the art gallery owners in this far-west Chelsea neighborhood pooled their resources to invest in a restaurant of their own. Unfortunately for the art dealers, Bottino has become so popular with fashion models and trend-setters that it's hardly a neighborhood artists' hang-out anymore. The converted hardware store retains the original wooden floors, shelving and skylight, and a sliding garage door opens onto a tranquil, plant-filled garden. We've enjoyed the grilled eggplant, the penne with tomato and smoky prosciutto and the New York strip steak. Bottino offers an impressive list of (mostly) Italian wines, with nearly a dozen selections by the glass for around $5. For dessert, the sweet, crusty bread pudding is a must.

BRYANT PARK GRILL — NEW AMERICAN — 12/20

25 W. 40th St., (Fifth & Sixth Aves.), 10018
840-6500, *Lunch Mon.-Fri., Dinner nightly,* Brunch Sat.-Sun., $$$

Tucked behind the New York Public Library, the Grill overlooks a splendid vista of shaded walkways, trees and wildflowers that feels more like Paris than Manhattan. It's all so picturesque that you can almost put up with the occasional lackluster food and attitude. Among the specialties: crabmeat spring rolls, confit-of-duck burritos and a crisp calamari salad to start, and such main dishes as penne with rock shrimp, Maine halibut with red lentils and grilled salmon. In season, the rooftop-garden **BP Café** serves salads & sandwiches.

CAFETERIA — NEW AMERICAN — 11/20

119 Seventh Ave. (17th St.), 10011
414-1717, *Breakfast, Lunch & Dinner daily,* $$

The school cafeteria was never like this, except maybe for the macaroni and cheese (salty). This happening, crowded Chelsea post-modern, white-on-white-with-aluminum cafeteria is high on style and more or less okay on the food—edible, big portions, good prices. Love the corn chowder with fresh clams. The short ribs have to be seen as do the musclemen eating them. Slim beauties of the opposite sex are readily on hand for viewing, too. Very late at night the small lounge downstairs is a place to sink into with a drink in hand.

CAL'S   MEDITERRANEAN   12/20
55 W. 21st St. (Fifth & Sixth Aves.), 10011
929-0740, *Lunch Mon.-Fri., Dinner nightly*, $$
A ☎

At this chic bistro, owner Khalil Ayoubi's huge modern paintings cover the walls, and the menu reads Mediterranean and beyond: smoked trout and couscous, seared sea scallops with potato crust, lobster ravioli in saffron beurre blanc, to start. Among the entrées, you'll find everything from risotto with spicy chicken livers and wild mushrooms, herb-crusted swordfish with potato-artichoke hash, to steak frites and a hamburger. The wine list may be unexciting, but it's decently priced.

CAMPAGNA   ITALIAN   14/20
24 E. 21st St. (Broadway & Park Ave.), 10010
460-0900, *Lunch Mon.-Fri., Dinner nightly*, $$$
A ☎

Mark Strausman's warm country-Italian eatery combines urban and rustic modalities with bravura, and serves earthy and robust—yet contemporary—Italian food. A classic antipasti table tempts with grilled and marinated vegetables, cured meats, salads and cheeses. Pastas might include fusilli with pesto, potatoes and green beans, and rigatoni with a spicy beef ragout. We recommend the grilled sliced tuna on a warm salad of three grains, cannellini beans and lentils, the wild striped bass with tomatoes, olives, raisins and potatoes, and the herb-roasted pork tenderloin with roasted fennel and figs. There is an extensive Italian and American wine list.

CEDARS OF LEBANON   MIDDLE EASTERN   11/20
8 W. 38th St. (Fifth & Sixth Aves.), 10018
391-1119, *Lunch & Dinner daily*, $$
A ☎

Once the only Middle Eastern restaurant in town, Cedars still offers presentable food, reasonable prices and an exotic atmosphere. All the usual scoop-up-with-pita-bread favorites, including creamy hummus and smoky baba ghanouj, plus falafel, shish kebab, sliced brains in a lemony sauce, fava beans with a lemon vinaigrette and tabouli.

CENA   NEW AMERICAN   16/20

12 E. 22nd St. (Broadway & Park Aves.), 10010
5050-1222, *Lunch & Dinner daily*, $$$$

This place feels cool and comfortable with its post-modern simplicity, a bar and café out front and a more formal dining area in the rear. Opened in 1998, it is the second restaurant of Thalia and Stephen Loffredo, whose Zoë in SoHo we admire. Chef Norman Laprise is behind such exemplary dishes as spice-lacquered smoked salmon with wasabi sauce, sweetbreads with white asparagus, seared foie gras with rhubarb compote, and wild red snapper with black bean, cumin and jalapeño compote. The lobster risotto is a feast for the eyes as well as the palate: the arborio rice is cooked with sun-dried tomatoes, baby yellow beets, sorrel and greens and packed back into the lobster shell, which is stood upright in a bowl and surrounded by cooked lobster. The venison is excellent, as is the roasted Barbarie duck breast with caramelized kumquats. The chocolate-pistachio-lemon cake is a winning dessert.

CHELSEA BISTRO & BAR   FRENCH   14/20

358 W. 23rd St. (Eighth & Ninth Aves.), 10011
727-2026, *Dinner nightly*, $$$

This rakish bistro exemplifies the best of its genre with rustic yet refined cooking, a knowledgeable staff and Parisian-style quarters complete with a working brick fireplace, velvet drapes, wooden floor, brass railings, candlelight, mahogany bar and Impressionist prints on the walls. The lusty fare is characterized by a sophisticated approach to bistro classics including a caramelized-onion-and-herbed-goat-cheese tart, roasted duck casserole, and a savory hanger steak in a dense red-wine sauce with crisp frites. Intelligently selected wines, an attractive crowd, and a candlelit, glass-wrapped terrace complement Chelsea's finest. The wine list merits high praise with many engaging French and American picks among the approximately 225 offerings.

CHELSEA TRATTORIA   ITALIAN   13/20

108 Eighth Ave. (16th St.), 10011
924-7786, *Lunch Mon.-Fri., Dinner nightly*, $$$

The Lattanzi family dishes out earthy, uncomplicated Northern Italian food in a warm, cozy dining room with brick and ochre walls. For appetizers, we like the salmon carpaccio and the artichoke hearts sautéed in oil and garlic. Pastas might include a lusty ravioli, linguine with clam sauce and black linguine in spicy tomato sauce. For something more substantial, go for one of the several veal dishes. The wine list features mostly Italian wines.

CIBO   NEW AMERICAN   14/20

767 Second Ave. (41st St.), 10017
681-6773, *Lunch Mon.-Fri., Dinner nightly, Brunch Sat.-Sun.,* **$$$**

You may recognize the art-deco building in which Cibo is located—it doubled as the *Daily Planet* Building in the *Superman* movies. Owner Ray Gilmore, a former NYPD undercover cop, plays host to swarms of suits from the nearby Flatiron district and foodies. The menu changes with the seasons, and might include starters such as a duo of yellowfin tuna and salmon tartares with pastrami salmon and flying-fish roe. Recommended entrées include Burgundy-braised short ribs with Vermont cheddar-cheese-mashed potatoes, sautéed lemon sole with portobello "grits" and maple-walnut-crusted tuna with spicy andouille-shrimp ragout. Take advantage of the $24.95 three-course prix-fixe dinner menu. For semi-privacy, reserve one of the four booths separated by wire-mesh curtains, in the slate-floored main dining room.

CITY CRAB & SEAFOOD COMPANY   SEAFOOD   12/20

235 Park Ave. South (19th St.), 10003
529-3800, *Lunch & Dinner daily, Brunch Sat.-Sun.,* **$$**

With its nautical decor and collection of fishing hats, this two-tiered Flatiron "fisheteria" could almost count as a "theme" restaurant. Don't expect speedy service, but do expect, in season, Florida stone crabs, Maryland blue crabs, soft-shell Crabs, Alaskan king crabs and Dungeness from British Columbia. Of the many regional American seafood dishes, stick with the simplest and you won't be disappointed.

DA UMBERTO   ITALIAN   12/20

107 W. 17th St. (Sixth Ave.), 10011
989-0303, *Lunch Mon.-Fri., Dinner Mon.-Sat.,* **$$$$**

Since 1988, Da Umberto has pleased customers with its satisfying Tuscan-style trattoria fare. Today the food in this fun and sometimes noisy spot can be uneven, but it's still worth a visit. The grilled and roasted vegetables on the antipasti tables are dripping with fruity olive oil. If available, try the stuffed eggplant. The Tuscan-style soup, rich with beans, bread and cheese, is also comforting. We've enjoyed the pastas, entrées ranging from the chicken paillard to the veal chop with Cognac, and the tiramisu.

EIGHTEENTH & EIGHTH   NEW AMERICAN   12/20

159 Eighth Ave. (18th St.) 10011
242-5000, *Breakfast, Lunch & Dinner daily,* $

At this delightful bistro du coin, the Chelsea community stops in for the cozy, attractive surroundings, friendly service and a diverse array of appealing, tasty and healthful dishes at modest prices. Specials might include fusilli with chicken sausage and black olives, ginger-perfumed chicken breast or fresh salmon. All entrées are served with a bountiful array of fresh vegetables and come with soup or salad. The short wine list is reasonably priced, with a dozen or so wines by the glass.

ELEVEN MADISON PARK   NEW AMERICAN   16/20

11 Madison Ave. (24th St.), 10010
889-0905, *Lunch Mon.-Fri., Dinner Mon.-Sat.,* $$$$

Danny Meyer, of Gramercy Park and Union Square Café fame, has another hit on his hands with this grand art-deco restaurant overlooking Madison Park. It's a festive, airy space, with 35-foot high windows, two mezzanine-level private-party rooms, and a cozy gold-leafed wine bar where three dozen or so wines are poured by the glass. Chef Kerry Heffernan, whose culinary credits include The Polo at The Westbury and Bouley, turns out such seasonally changing appetizers as terrine of beef shanks with foie gras and pigs' feet, and foie gras au torchon with pomegranate essence and toasted walnuts, though you can get the bountiful Atlantic shellfish assortment year-round. Main courses range from lobster pot au feu with sea-urchin toast, and roast chicken with potato-speck tart, to prime aged rib of beef for two with potato-fennel gratin. The extensive wine list is exclusively French, and there are many Cognac, Calvados and Armagnac choices as well.

FINO   ITALIAN   14/20

4 E. 36th St. (Fifth & Madison Aves.), 10016
689-8040, *Lunch & Dinner Mon.-Sat.,* $$

Popular with the garment-district execs and business types who work nearby, this well-run restaurant does a big lunch business but doesn't draw a broader audience at dinner. The Northern Italian cuisine is pretty good along conventional lines. The fettuccine is tossed with smoked salmon, vodka and Mascarpone, the ravioli is stuffed with lobster, and there are good fresh fish dishes, as well as nine preparations of veal, chicken and other classic New York Italian restaurant fare served in he-man portions. The wine list has some good Italian selections, and the service is fairly formal, old-style European.

FLOWERS   NEW AMERICAN   14/20

21 W. 17th St. (Fifth & Sixth Aves.), 10011
691-8888, Lunch Mon.-Fri., Dinner Mon.-Sat., Brunch Sun., $$$

Chef Miro Maran turns out very good contemporary food at this hip but schizophrenic sort of restaurant, with its two strikingly different looking (and feeling) dining rooms separated by a wide bar. The front is bistroish and noisy; the back is very country and warm with wood beams and a low ceiling. In season, the best place to sit is the rooftop garden. Recommended starters include the tuna-tartare napoleon and the crabcake with cucumber-and-avocado salsa. Good entrées include the duck breast with gingery bread pudding, the banana-leaf-wrapped wild striped bass with coconut-lemongrass infusion and the grilled sirloin steak with Gorgonzola.

FOLLONICO   ITALIAN   14/20

6 W. 24th St. (Fifth & Sixth Aves.), 10010
691-6359, Lunch Mon.-Fri., Dinner Mon.-Sat., $$

The hand-crafted quality about this cozy place more than recommends it. Situated in a 19th-century townhouse with yellow-stucco walls and terra-cotta floors, the restaurant has a glow that is both form and function—the wood-burning oven is the gastronomic and climatic core of the restaurant. From it come roasted fish, meat, game, pizzas and various vegetables and breads. The seasonally changing menu is often inspired. We recommend the whole roasted fish in a rock-salt crust and the game dishes in season. Good cheeses and excellent biscotti and cookies finish out a meal here. The wine list reflects a wide selection of small producers, from Italy and elsewhere.

FRANK'S RESTAURANT   ITALIAN/STEAKHOUSE   12/20

85 Tenth Ave. (15th St.), 10014
243-1349, Lunch Mon.-Fri., Dinner nightly, $$$

A

Founded in 1912 in the heart of the meat-packing district, Frank's recently moved to a new location. It remains an old-fashioned restaurant with a soul that remains pure, centering on pastas, steak, friendly service, good prices and food the way it used to taste. Pay attention to the catch of the day and the meat specials and other extensive offerings, but don't neglect the prime ribs or the skirt steak. Wine has long been a tradition at Frank's, and the markup on popular Italian and French wines (and a few familiar California ones) is low.

GASGOGNE   FRENCH   13/20

158 Eighth Ave. (17th & 18th Sts.), 10011
675-6564, Lunch Mon.- Fri., Dinner nightly, Brunch Sun., $$

With its rough sandstone walls and exposed brick, the setting is perfect for the lusty Gasgogne fare from the Southwest of France, and in summer the small outdoor garden is lovely. Consider the foie gras, a hearty cassoulet, wild baby boar (in season) in a Cahors wine sauce or a terrine of smoked salmon and potatoes. The frozen Armagnac soufflé ends the meal on the same Gallic theme. You'll find some impressive wines of the region plus a comprehensive collection of Armagnacs, another specialty of Gascony.

GRAMERCY TAVERN   NEW AMERICAN   16/20

42 E. 20th St. (Park Ave. South & Broadway), 10003
477-0777, Dining Room: Lunch Mon.-Fri., Dinner nightly; Tavern: Lunch & Dinner daily, $$$$

The brainchild of co-owners Danny Meyer and chef Tom Colicchio, this restaurant is dedicated to "a rediscovery of the classic American tavern offering extraordinary New American cuisine and hospitality in a historic landmark building." The American cooking here has heavy French and Mediterranean leanings, as does the decor. Seating over 200, the large, vaulted-ceilinged space is broken down into a stunning Tavern Room and bar, three dining areas plus an enclosed private dining room. Paintings and antique artifacts contribute to the ambience. Ever-changing specialties include seared tuna with white beans, braised rabbit, tuna tartare and sautéed foie gras. From the day the restaurant opened, we've loved the variations on fresh fish; the cheese board is exceptional as are the desserts. In the dining rooms, there is a three-course prix-fixe dinner for $62. The menu in the more casual Tavern is shorter, simpler—and less expensive. If all you can get is a seat at the bar, take it.

I TRULLI   ITALIAN   15/20

122 E. 27th St. (Park & Lexington Aves.), 10016
481-7372, Lunch Mon.-Fri., Dinner Mon.-Sat., $$$$

Southern Italian fare is served in a handsome and cozy country-restaurant-in-the-city setting, right down to the wood-burning oven, fireplace and pretty garden. Sample the wines of Southern Italy to go with, say, grilled stuffed squid, duck-filled pasta with braised baby artichokes and mint, chickpea fritters with goat cheese, medallions of wild boar with lemon-and-oregano sauce or wild striped bass with fennel, black olives and red wine. Don't miss the flour dumplings with broccoli rabe and roasted almonds. The earthy braised rabbit almost makes you feel you are out among the orchards of Apulia. Forgive the pun, but Trulli is truly fine.

KEEN'S   STEAKHOUSE/AMERICAN   13/20

72 W. 36th St. (Fifth & Sixth Aves.), 10018
947-3636, Lunch Mon.-Fri., Dinner Mon.-Sat., $$$$

In an historical-landmark building, Keen's is worth a visit just to taste the signature fist-sized mutton chop and to see the 90,000 pieces of memorabilia. Clay churchwarden pipes, theater posters and programs, photographs, early American prints and paintings, and period newspapers all help to give this restaurant an early 1900s air. Opened in 1885 as a clubby garment-center haunt, Keen's does a steady lunch-hour business (reservations are a must), as does the tap room. We start with the Maryland lump crabcakes, and whenever we pass up the famous chop it's for the aged prime porterhouse steak. For dessert, try the warm deep-dish apple pie. There are over 150 reasonably priced bottles on the wine list, and a large collection of single-malt Scotches.

KUM GANG SAN   KOREAN/JAPANESE   13/20

49 W. 32nd St. (Broadway & Fifth Ave.), 10001
967-0909, Open 24 hours daily, $$

When in Little Korea, follow the locals to Kum Gang San. Situated in a dressed-up, two-story space, the restaurant has been drawing enthusiastic crowds since the doors opened. We advise going with a group, since Korean cuisine lends itself to family-style sharing. Kum Gang San features a Japanese sushi bar as well a dining room serving traditional Korean favorites. Choose from marinated barbecues of beef, pork or chicken, and bubbling casseroles of seafood, vegetables or tofu. A welcoming touch are the complimentary dishes of kim chee and other Korean pickles and salads. **Also in Queens (138-28 Northern Blvd., Flushing, 718-461-0909).**

L'ACAJOU   FRENCH   12/20

53 W. 19th St. (Sixth Ave.), 10011
645-6658, Lunch Mon.-Fri., Dinner nightly, $$

There are those who think L'Acajou is one step up from a dowdy coffee shop, and then there are those who find it so charming they could eat here every week. We like to visit now and again. The regular menu offers all the regular French bistro standards. We like their three or four festivals a year, including their Alsace festival when choucroute turns up. The regular wine menu is exhaustive, with some excellent values.

LA COLOMBE D'OR   FRENCH   14/20

134 E. 26th St. (Lexington & Third Aves.), 10011
689-0666, Lunch & Dinner Mon.-Sat., $$$

This rustic Provençal restaurant opened in 1976, but is now owned by Michel Mastantvono. He has kept on Naj Zougari as chef, and the cooking philosophy remains firm. In addition, the wine list is exemplary, and the dining room is as romantic as ever. Comprising the ground floor of two brownstones, the restaurant features brick walls, tin ceilings, paintings and provincial-print banquettes. You'll find all the classic French favorites, from a vibrant ratatouille to bouillabaisse, cassoulet and chicken with roasted shallots and truffle-mashed potatoes. French wines are available by the glass for $6. There's also a casual, open-every-night café offering more modestly priced food, regional wines by the glass and cigars.

LA PIZZA FRESCA   ITALIAN   12/20

31 E. 20th St. (Park Ave. South & Broadway), 10003
598-0141, *Lunch Mon.-Sat., Dinner nightly, $$*

A

Don't let the name fool you—this isn't just a pizza joint. In fact, the restaurant is one of only two in the U.S. whose pizza has been certified by the Italian government as serving "vera pizza Napoletana," or true Neapolitan pizza. Each pizza is made by hand with tomatoes and mozzarella cheese flown in from Italy, then baked in a brick oven to delicious effect. They also serve such luscious non-pizza dishes as polenta con funghi and rigatoni quattro P, so named because the pasta is tossed with pesto, Parmigiano, pomodoro and panna (cream).

LE MADRI   ITALIAN   15/20

168 W. 18th St. (Seventh Ave.), 10011
727-8022, *Lunch & Dinner nightly, $$$$*

Though Le Madri has long been among the best Italian restaurants in New York, we've been less enthusiastic about it of late. The large main dining room with its vaulted ceiling, Tuscan-yellow walls, artsy black-and-white photos, tables set well apart and a wood-burning oven, attracts a fashionable clientele. Distinctive specialties include the thin-crusted pizzas, carpaccios, such pastas as artichoke ravioli, fettuccine with wild mushrooms and oven-dried cherry tomatoes, and spaghetti with lobster. The osso buco is a lusty main course; we also enjoy the wood-oven-roasted baby chicken or fish. Desserts are good and the Italian wine list with 200+ offerings is more than good.

LE SOLEX   FRENCH   13/20

470 W. 23rd St. (10th Ave.), 10011
627-1331, *Breakfast, Lunch & Dinner daily, $$$*

A resurgence in West Chelsea's art scene benefits this glass-enclosed bistro, which displays the canvases of up-and-coming artists on the walls. The restaurant borrows its name from a popular French motor bike, and parked by the front door are two vintage specimens. Neighborhood residents stumble in here at 8 a.m. for fluffy herb-filled omelets, chocolate croissants and frothy cups of cafe au lait, while the lunch crowd is mostly fast-talking art dealers and gallery-goers. At dinner, the sense of midday urgency disappears, and you can leisurely tuck into pleasing bistro fare such as steak frites, fricasseé of rabbit and daube, a classic, long-simmered dish of beef, red wine, vegetables and herbs.

LES HALLES   FRENCH   14/20

411 Park Ave. South (28th & 29th Sts.), 10016
679-4111, *Lunch & Dinner daily*, $$

This busy brasserie has a butcher shop selling French-cut entrecôtes, filets and the like, as well as boudins, andouillettes and tripe. In the dining room, the seating is tight, the noise level high, and the waitstaff is friendly and attentive, if harried. The food is as authentic as the atmosphere: boudin with caramelized apples, cassoulet, leg of lamb, and steak or poulet frites (the frites—burnished and lightly salted—are among the best in town). The hangar steak is meltingly tender, the filet mignon rich and buttery-soft. The wine list consists mostly of well-priced bottles, and the desserts are bistro standards: chocolate mousse, crème caramel and the like.

LEMON   NEW AMERICAN   12/20

230 Park Ave. South (18th & 19th Sts.), 10003
614-1200, *Lunch Mon.-Fri., Dinner nightly, Brunch Sun.*, $$

The look of this trendy bar/restaurant (with an emphasis on the bar) is post-garage "industrial": cement floors, exposed-brick walls, a balcony lounge where hipsters hang out 'til the wee hours and big front windows that open to the street in warm weather. Expect distracted service by waitpersons who look like models, and the kind of food that models eat: barely dressed salads, steamed mussels, crisp-crusted pizzas, and steaks and fish from the grill.

LOLA   SOUTHERN/CARIBBEAN   13/20

30 W. 22nd St. (Fifth & Sixth Aves.), 10011
675-6700, *Lunch Tues.-Fri, Dinner nightly, Brunch Sun.*, $$$

Lola long ago decamped, but the decor at this colorful, lively and inviting Chelsea restaurant hasn't changed: the small tables up front are great for drinks or bar food. You can still get Lola's 100-spices Caribbean fried chicken that packs some heat. The cuisine remains an idiosyncratic version of American Southern cooking with Caribbean and sometimes Asian highlights. Ultimately, there's nothing tame about the combinations and condiments. We like the fried calamari, fried shrimp or Asian baby-back ribs, and for dessert, the banana-bread pudding. A well-designed wine list features reasonably priced international wines, and there's a $29.75 Sunday gospel brunch. Lola Bowla next door serves Thai food during lunch.

MAD 28   ITALIAN   13/20

72 Madison Ave. (27th & 28th Sts.), 10010
689-2828, *Lunch Mon.-Fri., Dinner nightly*, $$$$

Don't look for this hip Italian restaurant at 28 Madison Ave. It's at 72 Madison Ave near 28th Street, but look for it as part of the influx of upscale dining establishments in the Gramercy/Madison Square Park food neighborhood. It's a big soaring, handsome space with windows onto the street and features a wood-burning pizza open that turns out reasonably good pizza. There are excellent pastas and good fish—you know the routine. Still, the potential is here.

MAVALLI PALACE   INDIAN/VEGETARIAN   12/20

46 E. 29th St. (Park & Madison Aves.), 10016
679-5535, *Lunch & Dinner Tues.-Sun.*, $

This Indian vegetarian restaurant differentiates itself from the others in an already crowded field. The food is fresh, prices are reasonable, and the service is warm and friendly. The decor is simple, the walls covered with Hindu carvings. Try the bosai, a crêpe made from lenti-and-rice flour, along with such specialties as aluchat, cold potato chunks in a spicy-sweet tamarind sauce peppered with hot chilies, and curries including palak paneer, cubes of cottage cheese in a fresh, spiced spinach sauce. The kitchen excels at unusual rice dishes, such as lemon rice with saffron, yogurt rice with mustard seeds and the daily rice special—tamarind, tomato and lemon.

MESA GRILL   SOUTHWESTERN   15/20

102 Fifth Ave. (15th & 16th Sts.), 10011
807 7400, *Lunch Mon.-Fri , Dinner nightly, Brunch Sat.-Sun.*, $$$$

This Southwestern extravaganza is a huge, high-ceilinged (and yes, noisy) affair with soaring columns, a narrow balcony, cowboy-lassos-horse banquettes, plus a big bar. The vibes here are terrific, and chef Bobby Flay's counterpoints of hot against sweet get better all the time. Dazzling starters include cornmeal-crusted oysters and a Parmesan-crusted wild mushroom quesadilla, and we're wild for the shrimp-and-roasted-garlic tamales. Try on the Black Angus steak for size, served with kickass steak sauce plus a double-baked horseradish potato. Desserts are fine (anyone for the pecan-chocolate-graham cake with roasted marshmallows?) For brunch, try scrambled eggs enchiladas with grilled chorizo and nibble the corn muffins. The wine list is good, as is the extensive Margarita menu.

MORENO RISTORANTE   ITALIAN   13/20

65 Irving Pl. (18th St.), 10003
673-3939, *Lunch Mon.-Fri., Dinner nightly, Brunch Sun., $$$*

At this friendly restaurant just off Gramercy Square, the bright, yellow-colored dining room is welcoming, as are, in good weather, the outside tables. The Gramercy Park crowd comes primarily for the homemade pastas—farfalle with fresh salmon and asparagus, fettuccine with lobster, penne with fresh mozzarella cheese. If available, try the meaty portobello mushroom in garlic oil, or the pan-roasted chicken with rosemary and garlic. Sundays, there's a prix-fixe dinner menu for $19.95 from noon on.

NOVITÁ   ITALIAN   14/20

102 E. 22nd St. (Lexington & Park Aves.), 10010
677-2222, *Lunch Mon.-Fri., Dinner nightly, $$$*

Some pretty innovative and delicious food is served at this comfortable Gramercy Park restaurant run by chef Marco Fregonese and family. It's a soothing, refined, minimalist setting: Venetian-style stucco; walls painted saffron yellow; Murano glass sconces; cherry-wood banquettes and Etro woven-paisley upholstery. Chef Fregonese's specialties include a warm calamari salad, such pastas as tagliatelle with shrimp and artichokes, entrées including pan-roasted branzino, grilled salmon, and a surprisingly light breast of duck with Barolo sauce, raspberries and pine nuts. For dessert, try the tortino di cioccolato, an individual warm chocolate tart with pistachio sauce and white-chocolate gelato.

OLD HOMESTEAD RESTAURANT   STEAKHOUSE/AMERICAN   11/20

56 Ninth Ave. (W. 14th & 15th Sts.), 10011
242-9040, *Lunch Mon.-Fri., Dinner nightly, $$$$*

Established in 1868, one of the oldest continuously operating restaurants in the city serves generous portions: from a whale-sized lobster (that's how it's listed on the menu) to a porterhouse steak for two weighing about the size and thickness of a standard dictionary. Vegetables, desserts, wines and service are somewhat incidental, except in the broad context of a nostalgic visit to an old-time restaurant that continues to attract visitors from out-of-town to an out-of-the-way location. Weekend dinner here begins at 1 p.m., just like in the old days. Order two weeks in advance, and you can get a Kobe beef steak (for $110.)

PARK AVALON   NEW AMERICAN   12/20

225 Park Ave. (18th & 19th Sts), 10003
533-2500, *Lunch Mon.-Fri., Dinner nightly, Brunch Sun.,* **$$**

The too-cool-for-words crowd comes more for the scene—
or to celebrate—than to eat. So the fare, while it includes all
the trendy New-American ingredients and combinations, does-
n't always excite us. Pizzas have nice thin crusts and come with
creative if not always fresh toppings. You can also get a few
sushi items, a chopped salad, pepper-crusted tuna and pastas.

PARK BISTRO   FRENCH   14/20

414 Park Ave. South (28th & 29th Sts.), 10016
689-1360, *Lunch Mon.-Fri., Dinner nightly,* **$$$**

Close your eyes and you're in a 1950s Parisian bistro: burgundy leather banquettes, French film posters and a small window that looks into the busy kitchen. We like any of their "classics," such as warm potato salad topped with grilled goat cheese,
sautéed skate with aged vinegar-and-port sauce and the hanger
steak with sautéed potatoes. Other possibilities include slow-
roasted-and-caramelized shoulder of pork and daube of beef.
For dessert, go for apple tart with Armagnac. The short wine list
features reasonably priced wines from small producers.

PATRIA   NUEVO LATINO/CUBAN   15/20

250 Park Ave. South (20th St.), 10003
777-6211, *Lunch Mon.-Fri. Dinner nightly,* **$$$$**

Think South America-meets-chic-New York at this funky,
colorful and lively restaurant. Save for an occasional menu or
service miss, Douglas Rodriguez's inspired, nouvelle-Latin
American spot really delivers—right down to the presentations
on beautiful glass plates. Have an exotic Latin American cocktail and start with, say, Peruvian ceviche blackened with squid
ink. For entrées, don't miss the fried whole-boned snapper on
a bed of coconut rice, the smoky rib-eye steak or the
Guatemalan chicken. Among our favorite sides are the yellow
corncakes and the cumin-spiked black beans and rice. The
flans are creamy, but just for fun, if they have it the night
you're there, order the chocolate Cuban cigar with a book of
sugar matches for dessert. The wine list is short, but includes
an intriguing selection of South American and Spanish wines.

PERIYALI   GREEK   15/20

35 W. 20th St. (Fifth & Sixth Aves.), 10011
463-7890, *Lunch Mon.-Fri., Dinner Mon.-Sat.,* **$$$**

Manhattan foodniks, corporate entertainers and people of
Greek heritage flock to this gentrified taverna for good food

and a good time. The theatrical setting features white walls, tiled floor, dark beams and a tented ceiling of billowing white cloth. Many of the dishes have Greek names but translate into straightforward charcoal-grilled items, such as the grilled octopus and rosemary-scented lamb chops. Other favorites: the phyllo-wrapped cheese-and-spinach pies, the grilled whole sea bass, the hearty moussaka and for dessert, the rice pudding. The wine list features a page of Greek wines along with a satisfying selection of French, Italian and American offerings.

RESTAURANT 147   NEW AMERICAN   13/20

147 W. 15th St. (Sixth & Seventh Aves.), 10011
929-5000, *Dinner nightly, Brunch Sun.*, $$$$

The bar here is as long as a hook-and-ladder truck, and it's not unusual to see it lined with hipsters and wannabes from end to end. This former firehouse, redecorated in a sleekly sophisticated style with high white ceilings and hardwood floors, boasts one of the hottest scenes in Chelsea, with frequent celebrity sightings reported. But what attracts the beautiful people—and the rest of us—is the tasteful menu. For starters, try duck carpaccio or tuna tartare with wasabi and watercress purée. The savory crabcake is all crab, no cake. The decadent diner might want to sup on truffled-Champagne risotto while the traditionalist indulges in a steak frites. On top of that, the staff here is as nice as they are good looking. There's live jazz during the week, and the restaurant is open past midnight on weekends, making this a prime destination for a celebration.

RESTIVO RISTORANTE   ITALIAN   13/20

209 Seventh Ave. (22nd St.), 10011
366-4133, *Lunch Mon.-Fri., Dinner nightly, Brunch Sat.-Sun.*, $$

Set on the ground floor a 19th-century brownstone building, this narrow, intimate—and reasonably priced—restaurant features a small bar and tables in the front room, and cozy tables in the back room. The filet mignon carpaccio, with or without hearts of palm, is a winning appetizer. Rigatoni Restivo is tossed with eggplant, capers, oregano and ricotta cheese, while the pollo Restivo is chicken breast sautéed with Cognac. There's a $7.95 lunch and a $9.95 brunch.

ROCKING HORSE CAFÉ MEXICANO   MEXICAN   14/20

182 Eighth Ave. (19th & 20th Sts.), 10011
243-9511, *Lunch & Dinner daily*, $$$

At this Chelsea spot, the walls display a revolving selection of Mexican-inspired art works, the glass front wall opens onto the sidewalk and the menu gets revamped every season. But while the dishes may change, the contemporary Mexican cuisine remains consistently good. Fresh tortillas are made by hand and the staff often travels to Mexico to pick up new ideas. Case in point, the nixtamal, a special corn dough that chef Sue Torres grinds into tamales and gorditas. Other appealing dishes include crepas de huitlacoche and Mascarpone cheese and tiny tamales filled with duck confit and habañero-pear jus. Rocking Horse's bar boasts 40 tequilas and 20 wines, but the margaritas are popular. Try peach or raspberry and you'll see why.

SHAFFER CITY OYSTER BAR & GRILL   SEAFOOD   14/20

5 W. 21st St. (Fifth & Sixth Aves.), 10010
255-9827, Lunch Mon.-Fri., Dinner Mon.-Sat., $$$$

A

The name suggests it all: oysters and grilled fish in a old-style oyster saloon, though newly minted, and all courtesy of owner and executive chef A. Jay Shaffer. He's a gracious host and eager owner. This is a casual and appealing place with a contemporary retro feel where beer is the beverage of choice. Besides oysters—raw, poached or fried—try the lobster cocktail with mango slaw for a starter. Fish is the main draw here, and we like the roasted halibut with a spicy turnip purée.

SIENA   ITALIAN   13/20

200 Ninth Ave. (22nd & 23rd Sts.), 10011
633-8033, Dinner nightly, $$$

What does it mean when a restaurant that started out as a vegetarian/health food restaurant, then introduced beef, butter and crème brûlée, has now transformed itself into an Italian restaurant? Maybe only that owners Scott Bryan and Gino Diaferia wanted a change. The point is, that most everything on the short menu is quite delicious: warm dandelion greens tossed with crisp pancetta; avant-garde pasta dishes like tagliatelle with dried tuna roe; and entrées like Barolo-braised pork with Mascarpone polenta. The wine list continues to be excellent here with many choices under $25.

SONIA ROSE   FRENCH/ECLECTIC   15/20

150 E. 34th St. (Lexington & Third Aves.), 10016
545-1777, Lunch & Dinner daily, $$$

Sonia Rose always manages to be extremely charming. Service is friendly and professional, prices are reasonable and the food is rendered with authority. We always overdose on the warm brioche bread. On the oft-changing menu, you might find breast of quail en croûte or luscious oysters in cornmeal. The meal abounds in true flavors and comes with plenty of vegetables. Expect veal, ostrich, chicken and usually steak au poivre. The shrewdly compiled wine list includes French and American wines priced in the $20s and $30s per bottle.

STEAK FRITES   FRENCH   12/20

9 E. 16th St. (Fifth Ave. & Union Square), 10003
463-7101, *Lunch & Dinner daily, Brunch Sat.-Sun.*, $$$

The room resembles a faux garage gallery with a big old bar, and in good weather the tables overflow out to the sidewalk. Late at night a youngish and more European crew replace some of the casual and artsy regulars. Appetizers include moules marinières, frisée salad with Roquefort and perhaps a grilled vegetable terrine. But this is the place for steak and poulet frites, or perhaps garlic-crusted rack of lamb. The desserts are laudable, and though the wine list is okay, the wines by the glass offer good choices and values.

TABLA   NEW AMERICAN/INDIAN   15/20

11 Madison Ave. (25th St.), 10010
889-0667, *Lunch Mon.-Fri., Dinner Mon.-Sat.*, $$$

Danny Meyer's new exciting Tabla, with its Indian-inspired architectural touches, features a no-reservations "Bread Bar" where you can sample an array of puffy Indian breads hot from the clay tandoor oven—rosemary naan with tandoori lamb sauce, for example—and a more formal upstairs dining room where tasting menus include the likes of coriander-and-mustard-crusted strip loin of beef, rice-flake-crisped black bass and fricassée of cockle clams, mussels and baby octopus. The exotic desserts include ambrosial anise-cranberry and caramel-coriarder ice creams, and green-tea-orange sorbet.

THE TONIC   NEW AMERICAN   14/20

108 W. 18th St. (Sixth & Seventh Aves.), 10011
929-9744, *Lunch & Dinner Mon.-Sat.*, $$$

No fewer than eight staff members said "Good-bye and thank you for coming," on our way out of this split-personality restaurant that opened in the late fall of 1998, the creation of Scott Carney, ex-GM of the Gotham Bar & Grill, and Chris Gesulaldi, ex-chef of Montrachet. The warm, dark-wood-paneled, tile-floored Tavern has a wonderful bistro menu: endive salad with duck prosciutto; fish and chips; roast chicken—even Yankee pot roast—and for dessert, a warm chocolate-brioche pudding. Beyond the Tavern is the dining room, all light colors, blond woods and clean lines. Here, the menu is far more ambitious, starting with the cod tart with ragout of shrimp, and continuing with the rack of lamb. The wine list is big but still needs work in its infant days.

TROIS CANARDS   FRENCH   13/20

184 Eighth Ave. (19th & 20th Sts.), 10011
929-4320, *Lunch Mon.-Fri., Dinner nightly, Brunch Sat.-Sun., $$*

The duck motif is played up at this attractive, comfortable, polished-wood-and-mirror-paneled neighborhood bistro. All the French-bistro regulars appear on the menu, from escargots and onion soup to grilled lamb chops and roast chicken. There are also pastas, cassoulet, beef bouguignon, and roast duck with seasonal fruit sauce.

TUPELO GRILL   STEAKHOUSE/AMERICAN   13/20

One Penn Plaza (33rd St. & Eighth Ave.), 10019
760-2700, *Lunch & Dinner Daily, $$$*

Finally, a quality dining establishment near Madison Square Garden—and one with a dramatic design. The menu holds no surprises: chilled shellfish, oversized salads, grilled meats, creme brulée. The decor, however, forgoes the usual mahogany and leather in favor of an airy space with light woods, hard-edged surfaces and soaring windows. Though the restaurant's prices are high for the neighborhood, they're no problem for the Armani-clad executives and Garden sky-box holders who swarm here.

TURKISH KITCHEN   TURKISH   12/20

386 Third Ave. (27th & 28th Sts.), 10016
679-1810, *Lunch & Dinner daily, $$*

Dazzlingly painted in red, gold, blue and violet, and decorated with lavish kilim rugs and brass objects, Turkish Kitchen is a sexy setting for an exotic dining experience. An entire meal could be made from the starters and a crusty loaf of pide, an oversized sesame flatbread. The sigara boregi, pan-fried cigar-shaped rolls of phyllo stuffed with feta cheese, are cooked until crisp and golden. Main courses inevitably revolve around lamb, but also consider the chicken stuffed with green peppers, tomatoes and cheese. A side of the homemade yogurt will help ease the garlic-and-pepper overload. Try one of the tart Turkish kavaklidere wines with dinner, and thick Turkish coffee with a dessert of honey-drenched baklava.

27 STANDARD/THE JAZZ STANDARD   NEW AMERICAN   14/20

116 E. 27th St. (Park Avenue South & Lexington), 10016
447-7733, *Lunch Mon.-Fri., Dinner nightly, $$$*

A restaurant-cum-jazz club swings into this neighborhood just north of the Flatiron district, where the seasonal American fare is as appealing as the bang-up jazz. The dining room is a claustrophobe's dream, with generously spaced tables and high ceilings. The cuisine features cleanly orchestrated flavors evidenced in dishes such as grilled tuna with minted couscous and figs, scallops with Swiss chard, pepper-crusted lamb chops and filet of beef with truffled potatoes. The subterranean nightclub suggests a modern-day speakeasy. Serving less serious fare like burgers, gourmet pizza and chicken, it's the perfect spot for jazz lovers to woo a date.

UNION PACIFIC   NEW AMERICAN   17/20   ♟♟♟

11 E. 22nd St. (Park Ave. South & Lexington Ave.), 10010
995-8500, *Lunch Mon.-Fri., Dinner Mon.-Sat.*, $$$$

Easily one of the most exciting culinary openings in the past couple of years, Union Pacific is a serious and sophisticated dining room replete with a curtain of falling water near the entrance. The pro staff is excited about the intricate offerings fron chef Rocco DiSpirito's kitchen. His signature is original flavor pairings along the French-Asian axis. So for a little tease he may offer you yellowtail wrapped around tuna tartar or maybe wild strawberries with foie gras cru. His halibut is brilliant, poached in goose fat and topped with cracklings made of shallots. We adored the sea bass with figs and sunflower seeds, as well as the slow-poached chicken. Desserts, like everything, are market sensitive and reflect several flavor layers—perhaps a raspberry tart with lavender. The wine list includes some unusual offerings, including a host of German and Austrian selections.

UNION SQUARE CAFÉ   NEW AMERICAN   16/20   ♟♟

21 E. 16th St. (Fifth Ave. & Union Square West), 10003
243-4020, *Lunch Mon.-Sat., Dinner nightly*, $$$$

We've been fans of Danny Meyer's USC since it opened in 1985. It's a restaurant fully under control, from the greeting to the checkroom to the bar to the waitstaff to the kitchen to the wines. The American food with rustic Italian accents is rock solid—even the hamburger and tuna burger. We also recommend the lobster salad, the seductive shell steak, the seared salmon with balsamic-butter sauce, and such sides as the hot garlic-potato chips. Every night, there's a different, homey special such as, in winter, lobster shepherd's pie. The three dining areas have wood floors, green wainscoting and ample space between tables. Or you can eat at the bar, sampling wines by the glass while enjoying a casual meal. A long list of dessert wines accompanies the mostly American-style desserts, such as the signature warm banana tart with macadamia nut brittle. Wines are something of a signature as well. The impressive— and fairly priced—international list is organized by varietal and "flavor" rather than by country or region, which may help you deal with the over 200 choices.

VERBENA   NEW AMERICAN   14/20   ♟

54 Irving Pl. (17th St.), 10003
260-5454, *Dinner nightly, Brunch Sat.-Sun.*, $$$

Set in an historic townhouse, Verbena offers a soothing respite from the bustle of the city. Two working fireplaces, potted plants, warm woods and mirrored partitions highlight the decor. The courtyard garden seems to be an inspiration for chef-owner Diane Forley's refined cuisine. On her seasonally changing menu, are such dishes as the parsley-root custard with a stew of fava beans, or the orange-scented butternut-squash ravioli, wild Columbia River sturgeon in a green peppercorn vinaigrette and saddle of rabbit. Consider the prix-fixe menus, the inviting wine list and the handsome converted carriage house for private parties.

VERITAS   NEW AMERICAN   16/20

43 E. 20th St. (Park & Broadway), 10003
353-3700, *Lunch & Dinner daily*, $$$

No need to be a Roman to state that the very veritas of Veritas is in its vino. Come early to read the incredible 1300-bottle wine list featuring many rarities. Whether it's $18 or $25,000 you want to shell out for your bottle, it's easy to find the perfect match for the sophisticated modern cuisine of Scott Bryan. Subtle Asian touches dot his French foundation, as in the seared crisp-skinned salmon with a curried nage. Scott signs his menu with his warm oyster stew and his squab in a creamy foie gras emulsion.

WOO CHON   KOREAN   12/20

8-10 W. 36th St., (Fifth Ave.), 10018
695-0676, *Open 24 hours daily*, $$

Korean barbecue is the draw at this elegant wood-paneled restaurant, where service can sometimes be rushed. Watch the parade of small salads arrive, ranging from fish cakes to kim chi, followed by beef, lamb, pork or seafood, which you grill at your table. There is sushi, for those desiring a smoke-free meal.

AND ALSO...

HANGAWI   KOREAN/VEGETARIAN

12 E. 32nd St. (Fifth & Madison Aves.), 10016
213-0077, *Lunch & Dinner daily*, $$$

Talk about an exotic New York experience: Slip off your shoes and step into this serene, Zen-like setting, which serves the temple food of Buddhist monks—all vegetarian, all simply and beautifully prepared.

PITCHOUNE   FRENCH

226 Third Ave. (19th St.,) 10003
614-8641, *Dinner nightly*, $$

This cozy neighborhood restaurant is oh-so-French, with tightly packed tables, good bread and tapenade, and inventive versions of old favorites: roasted squash soup; grilled octopus; monkfish casserole; and pork loin with caramelized onions.

As a member of The James Beard Foundation you don't need a special occasion to treat yourself to a unique gastronomic experience.

You're invited to one almost every night of the week.

Founded in 1986 by the late Peter Kump and Julia Child, The James Beard Foundation is a not-for-profit organization dedicated to preserving the country's culinary heritage. Based in James Beard's Greenwich Village brownstone—the nation's only historic culinary landmark—the Foundation's mission is to foster the appreciation and development of gastronomy by recognizing and promoting excellence in all aspects of the culinary arts.

The Foundation accomplishes this mission through a full calendar of events at the Beard House, the annual James Beard Foundation Awards, a growing Scholarship and grant program, an extensive library and archive, and publications including the monthly "Calendar and Newsletter," and the quarterly *Beard House* magazine.

James Beard Foundation members enjoy advance notice of events, reduced prices, and restaurant and food-world information that only real insiders ever know. Memberships begin at $125. Call for details.

Every great House is built on a strong Foundation.

MIDTOWN EAST

DINING

All phone numbers are (212) unless otherwise indicated

AKBAR   INDIAN   12/20

475 Park Ave. (57th & 58th Sts.), 10022
838-1717, *Lunch Mon.-Fri., Dinner nightly, $$*

The stately dining room beckons with its stained-glass ceiling, well-spaced tables and alcoves along the wall. Service can be casual, but the well-spiced food makes up for it. Meats, poultry and seafood are succulent when marinated and roasted in the clay tandoor oven; try the ginger-marinated chicken kebab. In addition to a myriad of curries, you'll find a lengthy list of vegetarian specialties, which are good with a selection of Indian breads. The $18 and $21 "Executive Lunch" menus offer five and six courses. New is the **Chai Salon**, a sumptuous lounge for cocktails, tea and Indian hors d'ouvres.

AL BUSTAN   LEBANESE   13/20

827 Third Ave. (50th & 51st Sts.), 10022
759-8439, *Lunch & Dinner daily, $$*

If you must satisfy a passion for lamb, falafel, tabbouleh and all the superb dips, salads and tangy cheeses of the Middle East, this premier Lebanese restaurant is the place to go. The lavish grazing appetizer, the Royal Meze, is more than a dozen small plates, a meal for three or four tasters. From there, move on to a mixed grill of lamb, lamb sausage and chicken, or simply grilled fish. Al Bustan's Lebanese desserts are among the city's most unusual and will recall the time when Beirut was the Paris of the Middle East.

BELLINI   ITALIAN   14/20

208 E. 52nd St. (Second & Third Aves.), 10022
308-0830, *Lunch Mon.-Fri., Dinner Mon.-Sat., $$$*

Lello Arpaia, one of New York's premier Italian restaurateurs for the past 25 years, is strictly in the background of sleek new Bellini. His daughter, Donatella, runs the restaurant. The setting is rich in blonde good looks with white brick arches and unglazed tile floors. Guests are well-cared for and Bellini's taste-focused menu of northern Italian inspiration will please anyone. Chestnut gnocchi in Fontina cheese sauce is a show-

89

stopper. Desserts shine, whether tiramisu enclosed in slabs of dark chocolate streaked with white chocolate, or moist Amaretto cake on a white plate with a knife and fork image outlined in cocoa. Many winning small touches reveal the Arpaia family's practiced hospitality skill.

BICE   ITALIAN   14/20

7 E. 54th St. (Madison & Fifth Aves.), 10022
688-1999, *Lunch & Dinner daily, $$$$*

Like a sleek Armani suit, Bice endures season after season. It is all about style—a stylish interior, stylish patrons and stylish food. The best dishes on the daily-changing menu are the simplest, such as carpaccio with hearts of palm, grilled chicken and a grilled veal chop. The selection of freshly made pastas runs from the exotic to such basics as spaghetti with meat sauce. The adequate wine list includes many Italian and California offerings. At lunch, there may be a line of diners snaking through the bar—and those are the people with reservations.

BOUTERIN   FRENCH   14/20

420 E. 59th St. (First Ave. & York), 10022
758-0323, *Dinner nightly, $$*

We're charmed by this lovely, antique- and flower-filled Provençal restaurant, where, on warm nights, you can dine on a terrace with a partial view of the East River bridges. Antoine Bouterin's menu offers homey Provençal dishes from pistou soup, country pâté and eggplant caviar on parsley pancakes, to daube of beef, sea bass in bouillabaisse sauce and herb-crusted rack of lamb. We keep coming back for such soul-warming standards as seven-hour lamb stew, followed by the wondrous chocolate soufflé or floating island.

CAFÉ CENTRO   FRENCH   13/20

200 Park Ave. (Vanderbilt Ave. & 45th St.), 10166
818-1222, *Lunch Mon.-Fri., Dinner Mon.-Sat., $$$*

This Americanized French brasserie in the MetLife Building gets high marks for looks—brass railings, art-deco details—and solid marks for eats. There's a wood-burning rotisserie in the dining room and the stainless-steel kitchen is visible beyond a glass wall. While basically French, the fare displays plenty of Moroccan highlights, starting with fragrant b'stilla. We like the steamed mussels, Provençal fish soup and choices from the raw bar. At lunch and during Happy Hour, the power-suit crowd jams the adjoining **Beer Bar**, which has its own menu and extended hours—and is very noisy.

CELLINI ITALIAN 13/20

65 E. 54th St. (Madison & Park Aves.), 10022
751-1555, *Lunch Mon.-Fri., Dinner Mon.-Sat.,* $$$

A fine location to talk business or promote a romance, Cellini has the aura of an upscale Tuscan farmhouse with warm hospitality that begins at the door and never stops. The centerpiece: thoughtful and well-made food with special emphasis on stuffed pastas, grilled meats and whole fish baked in foil. Chef Dino Arpaia's inbustata is a #10 envelope-shaped pasta filled with minced chicken, veal, mozzarella, shiitake mushrooms and spinach, and sealed with a dab of fresh tomato sauce. One night, his ravioli might be stuffed with beets and herbs and napped with light Gorgonzola sauce. "Cellini's Closet" is a closet holding anything a guest might suddenly need such as make-up, sewing kits, nylon stockings or rain hats (but not cash)—compliments of the management.

CHIKUBU JAPANESE 14/20

12 E. 44th St. (Fifth & Madison Aves.), 10017
818-0715, *Lunch Mon.-Fri., Dinner Mon.-Sat.,* $$$$

The specialty here is the cuisine of Kyoto, served in the four tatami rooms upstairs or in the long, sleek dining room. Among the surprises that might appear when you say "omakase" (chef's choice—$80-$120 per person) are a delicious whole raw fish, its flesh chopped tartare-fashion with scallions and horseradish, re-assembled minus the skin; miso soup with bits of poached chicken; morsels of octopus; an exquisite steamed dish of freshwater eel with burdock; beef filets served on a hot stone; a small, grilled whole river fish with a green-vinegar sauce; a tempura dish of shrimp balls and lotus root with mysterious and delicious batter-dipped flowers; fried bean curd in mirin broth; and a windup of delicious rice steamed with seafood and pickled vegetables.

CHIN CHIN CHINESE 14/20

216 E. 49th St. (Second & Third Aves.), 10017
888 4555, *Lunch Mon.-Fri., Dinner nightly,* $$

This new-wave Chinese restaurant looks like a Californian bistro and serves some of the best Chinese food in town. Sepia-tone photo portraits of the extended Chin family provide the unifying decorative theme in the two art-deco-inspired dining rooms. The imaginative fare respects the traditional dishes yet often yields unexpected flavors—snails with coriander in garlic broth, for example, or sautéed leg of lamb with leeks. We love the shrimp dumplings and duck salad for starters, and the $28.50 Peking duck dinner. Unlike most Chinese restaurants, Chin Chin has an excellent, well-priced wine list.

CIGAR ROOM AT TRUMPETS   AMERICAN   12/20

Grand Hyatt New York, 2 Park Ave. & Grand Central, 10017
850-5999, *Dinner Mon.-Sat., $$*

At this clubby dining room and cocktail lounge adjacent to
Trumpets Restaurant in the Grand Hyatt, cigar aficionados will
find a vast selection of the best puros. Non-smokers will appre-
ciate the cool ambience, elegant decor and, yes, (almost)
smoke-free air thanks to a state-of-the-art air-conditioning sys-
tem. All the usual bar snacks, from buffalo wings to quesadillas,
plus filet mignon wraps and lamb chops. The service is smooth
and professional; the wine list has a serious tone, good choices
and wallet-friendly prices.

DAWAT   INDIAN   14/20

210 E. 58th St. (Second & Third Aves.), 10022
355-7555, *Lunch Mon.-Sat., Dinner nightly, $$$*

For those in search of arguably the best Indian food in New
York, Dawat is Nirvana. This elegant establishment, which has
chef/cookbook author/TV personality and actress Madhur
Jaffrey as a consultant, features many seasonally changing specialties. Flavors sing in the Bombay dhansak, an earthy veg-
etable-and-goat stew, and crusty scallops with a green corian-
der-chili sauce, a specialty of Goa. Other favorites are saag
paneer, homemade pressed-curd cheese topped with a gingery
salad of diced cucumbers and tomatoes, and succulent chick-
en, lamb, fish and giant shrimp, along with puffy breads, from
the tandoor clay oven.

EROS   GREEK   13/20

1076 First Ave. (58th & 59th Sts.), 10022
223-2322, *Dinner nightly, $$*

Lighted nearly entirely with candles, this taverna with slip-
covered loveseats and a gold ceiling is definitely romantic. The
only problem is that the low lighting doesn't do the food jus-
tice. Everything on the mezze plate—almost a meal in itself—is
tasty, and there are such unexpected selections as lentil-olive
purée. The chopped lamb patties are offset by cold garlic-and-
walnut-mashed potatoes and lightly sugared beets. Steamed
mussels are accented by a white-wine-and-oregano broth stud-
ded with tomatoes, capers and haloumi (the Greek version of
Parmesan cheese). There are generous portions of all the
usual Greek entrées from lamb kababs to moussaka. Try the
cherry-filled baklava for dessert.

FELIDIA RISTORANTE   ITALIAN   16/20   🍴🍴

243 E. 58th St. (Second & Third Aves.), 10022
758-1479, Lunch Mon.-Fri., Dinner Mon.-Sat., $$$$
🅐 ☎ 🕴

Set in an elegantly restored townhouse, this flower-filled
split-level restaurant exudes the love of food and wine, and is
the flagship of Lidia Bastianich, a cookbook author and the co-
owner of Frico and Becco. Busy as she is, Lidia manages to
remain Felidia's executive chef, delivering a consistently distinctive gastronomic experience notable for its nod to Istria,
near the Italian and former-Yugoslavian border. Start with the
grilled calamari, or the lobster-shrimp-chickpea salad, then try
such pastas as Istrian wedding pillows filled with Italian cheese,
citrus rind, raisins and rum-savory reduction. The balsamic-lac-
quered wild salmon or warm calf's tongue are hearty entrées,
and, in season, try the wild-game specialties. The enormous
wine list is justly famous, especially for its Italian wines. And if
you want to taste grappa, this is the place. The $32 lunch spe-
cial is a good value.

FIFTY SEVEN FIFTY SEVEN   NEW AMERICAN   15/20   🍴🍴

Four Seasons Hotel, 57 E. 57th St. (Park & Madison Aves.), 10022
758-5757, Breakfast, Lunch & Dinner daily, Brunch Sat.-Sun., $$$$
🅐 ☎ ❤

This I.M. Pei-designed hotel is a city landmark, and its high
style heightens the drama of dining here. The restaurant is a
grand interpretation of a classic brasserie, with 22-foot-high
coffered ceilings, maple floors and sleekly modern brass-and-
onyx chandeliers. The food is consistently well-prepared, with
an emphasis on fresh ingredients and heart-healthy dishes.
Starters might include a squab-and-arugula salad or Hudson
Valley foie gras with gingered fig chutney. Entrées range from
shrimp-and-crabmeat risotto with sweet corn and peas, and
seared Atlantic salmon, to a thyme-roasted veal chop.

FOUR SEASONS   NEW AMERICAN/CONTINENTAL   15/20   🍴🍴

99 E. 52nd St. (Park & Lexington Aves.), 10022
754-9494, Lunch Mon.-Fri., Dinner Mon.-Sat., $$$$
🅐 ☎ ❤ 🍴 🕴

A New York institution, like Macy's or Rockefeller Center,
the dignified Four Seasons is increasingly like a museum. The
1959 Miles van der Rohe building and Philip Johnson interior
design are worth seeing if only to appreciate their place in
post-modern architecture. But as a restaurant, the Four
Seasons is no longer so distinguished. The food is good, but
not as good as in years gone by; ditto the service, which a
decade ago reigned as the finest in the city. On top of that,
today you risk getting a truly failed dish—at ultra-high prices.
The famed Grill Room that was once the most august power-
lunch spot outside the Oval Office, chugs along. No doubt
David Rockefeller and Henry Kissinger still stop by, but excitement and innovation seem to us missing. There's comfort,
though, in the soothing and soaring Pool Room that is thirty

years old and has a Continental menu with items that are easily recognized without listing the six main components. So, the Four Seasons has a secure place in the New York restaurant alignment, just not among the leading lights.

FRESCO BY SCOTTO — ITALIAN — 15/20

34 E. 52nd St. (Park & Madison Aves.), 10022
935-3434, *Lunch Mon.-Fri., Dinner Mon.-Sat.,* $$$$

The Scotto family's immensely popular and whimsically decorated Tuscan restaurant has a good new chef, Stefano Battistini, whose new dishes range from sevruga caviar spooned over mashed potatoes laced with Mascarpone cheese, to almond-crusted crabcakes. Still available: diabolically delicious zucchini and potato chips sprinkled with Gorgonzola cheese, and the grilled pizza Margherita. Now there is delicious braised, stuffed rabbit, basil-mashed potatoes and the Fresco prime steak, 32-ounces of juicy goodness plated with garlic-mashed potatoes and spinach. While matriarch Marion Scotto and daughters Elaina and Rosanna spread the welcome mat, son Anthony, Jr., guides guests' selections among almost 400 wines.

HATSUHANA — JAPANESE — 14/20

17 E. 48th St. (Madison & Fifth Aves.), 10017
355-3345, *Lunch Mon.-Fri., Dinner Mon.-Sat.,* $$$

For years the sushi here has been considered among the finest in the city, and even with lots of new competition, it still is. Hatsuhana is busiest at lunch and reservations are recommended, but if you are alone you can usually grab a seat at one of the two long sushi bars. You'll find the fish always fresh and the futomaki (a vegetable roll with pickled vegetables and egg) savory. We also like the mackerel with pickled ginger in a white radish wrapping, the buttery fluke and the chopped yellowtail flounder dotted with scallions. Ultimately, the restaurant is no longer on the cutting edge, but it remains a reliable and reasonably priced choice for mid-town diners. **Also at 237 Park Ave. (46th St.), 661-3400.**

HEARTBEAT — HEALTHY/ORGANIC — 13/20

W New York Hotel, 541 Lexington (49th & 50th Sts.,), 10022
407-2900, *Breakfast, Lunch & Dinner daily,* $$$

Balance and well-being are the themes of the new W New York Hotel, so it's only natural that its restaurant, Heartbeat, a Drew Nieporent production directed by chef Michel Nischan, serves dishes stressing the natural flavors of fresh seasonal organic food—no butter, cream or saturated oils allowed (except in certain "indulgences" as a chocolate mousse for dessert). In a stunning dining room designed by David Rockwell using natural fibers, wheatstraw tabletops and earthy hues of green, brown and blue, feel healthy eating the likes of roasted quail with fig-and-mushroom hash, coriander-seared duck with parsnip-and-sweet-potato sauce, and grilled paillard of salmon with caramelized cauliflower. With coffee come candried oranges and fresh made carmel squares.

IL NIDO   ITALIAN   14/20

251 E. 53rd St. (Second & Third Aves.), 10022
753-8450, *Lunch & Dinner Mon.-Sat., $$$*

For nearly 20 years, Il Nido has been serving serious northern Italian cuisine in a serious (and quiet) setting. In a Tuscanish setting of plaster walls and half timbering, there are comfortable, well-spaced leather banquettes and thick carpeting. Try the superb ravioli malfatti, which are basically ravioli without the wrapping—feather-light dumplings of cheese and spinach in a fresh tomato sauce. Risottos are cooked to perfection—creamy with just the right degree of crunchiness—and you can rely on any of the fish dishes or the veal chop. For dessert, there are excellent homemade gelati. The 250-item wine list still excites, especially the Italian wine selections.

INAGIKU   JAPANESE   15/20

The Waldorf-Astoria Hotel, 111 E. 49th St.
(Park & Lexington Aves.), 10022
355-0440, *Lunch Mon.-Fri., Dinner nightly, $$$$*

There's a lot to like about the modernized signature Japanese restaurant in the Waldorf-Astoria. Adam Tihany's multi-million-dollar rejuvenation pumped a full measure of fun into the equation, lightening and brightening the various components, from the five tatami rooms to the exciting Shabu Shabu Bar. Chef Ohbu scoured the home islands to arrive at a free-form "New Style Japanese" cuisine. Think Nobu in terms of creative vigor. There are splendid sushi and sashimi presentations and elaborate omakase tasting dinners. Some standouts: sea urchin roe on uni toast, tempura eel and salmon baked in rock salt. If you're flush, try wagyu beef, Kobe beef served sliced on a wood-framed hot stone—you do the cooking. A sommelier pitches in with a good wine list.

ISTANA   MEDITERRANEAN 13/20

The New York Palace Hotel, Entrance on E. 51st St.
(Madison & Park Aves.), 10022
303-6032, *Breakfast, Lunch & Dinner daily, $$$*

Istana straddles the lobby of the New York Palace Hotel with graceful arches and easy chairs, friendly service and a plethora of olives, sherries, tapas and teas. Its olive bar and sherry collection are New York's best—about three dozen of each. Chef Vincent Hodgins does not stop there. His menus are full of flavors and harmonious pairings: grilled flatbreads with hummus, eggplant and goat cheese, and charred lamb with marinated Tuscan white beans, for example. Elderflower vinaigrette accents a heart-healthy salad of tiny lettuces with ripe peaches. Instana's staff will lay on tasting flights of sherries to complement paella-style seafood with chorizo and assorted shellfish.

KOKACHIN NEW AMERICAN 14/20

Omni Berkshire Place Hotel, 21 E. 52nd St. (Madison Ave.), 10022
355-9300, *Breakfast daily, Lunch Mon.-Fri., Dinner nightly, $$$$*

Opened in late '95 as part of the $65 million renovation of the Omni Berkshire Place, Kokachin embodies the rarified atmosphere not uncommon in fine hotel restaurants. Among the inventive dishes are seared scallops with truffles, potato fondants and thyme, grilled foie gras with pear chutney and glazed figs, pan-roasted lobster flamed with bourbon, filet mignon of buffalo and lemon-thyme-mashed potatoes.

KURUMA ZUSHI JAPANESE 14/20

7 E. 47th St., Second Fl. (Madison & Fifth Aves.) 10017
317-2802, *Lunch & Dinner Mon.-Sat., $$$$*

Now in a new location, with a sushi bar and two private tatami rooms, Kuruma Zushi continues to serve some of the finest sushi and sashimi in the city. In addition are such Japanese specialties as chicken or beef teriyaki or broiled fish. Other than the food, perhaps the liveliest part of the dining experience here comes from the chefs, who call out greetings, farewells and requests for the bill.

LA GRENOUILLE FRENCH 17/20

3 E. 52nd St. (Fifth & Madison Aves.), 10023
752-1495, *Lunch & Dinner Tues.-Sat., $$$$*

Vive La Grenouille, so beautiful, so elegant, so reminiscent of the French-restaurant romance of the 1960s. The dining room is still renowned for its sensational flower arrangements, golden light and superb service. The menu of classics is superbly executed, and holds an occasional modern surprise or two. We recommend the restaurant's namesake, sautéed frogs infused with browned butter and garlic, and quenelles de brochet, pike dumplings that are firm but light. Other dishes might include duck with chestnuts, curried lobster, smoked-trout soufflé with truffles, and lamb served rare with crisp, seared edges. Classic-dessert lovers will delight in the airy soufflés. The wine list is impressive, and the prix-fixe menus start at $45 for lunch and $80 for dinner.

de Ladoucette Pouilly-Fumé: "Subtle green plum, mineral and herb with notes that carry through from start to the long, mouthwatering finish. Appealing for its subtlety and grace." - *Wine Spectator*

SETTING THE STANDARD FOR THE WORLD'S WHITE WINES.

de Ladoucette

Pouilly-Fumé
France

LE CIRQUE 2000   FRENCH   19/20

New York Palace Hotel, 455 Madison Ave. (50th & 51st Sts), 10022
303-7788, Lunch Mon.-Sat., Dinner nightly, $$$$

This 25 year-old legend—the ne plus ultra of New York soci-ety dining and fine cuisine—could have coasted, but in 1997 famed restaurateur Sirio Maccioni moved out of his East 65th Street digs into the landmark Villard House at the Palace Hotel. Sirio, as everyone calls him, wanted to rebuild Le Cirque into Le Cirque 2000, and meet the challenge of staying on the cutting edge. In his most prescient move, he anointed the brilliant chef Sottha Khunn as Executive Chef. The shy, French-trained Cambodian had long been the number 2 in the kitchen and had done much of the cooking that earned Le Cirque its critical raves. When Khunn stepped forward, the gas-tronomic constellations shifted, for though he has a reverence for classic French cooking, he brings to it his inherent feel for Asian ingredients and flavors. The old signature dishes are still there, but so are Khunn's inspired new creations. Long-time GM Benito Sevarin has things well under control, as does cele-brated pastry chef Jacques Torres, who builds whimsical edi-bles out of spun sugar and chocolate, and makes arguably the best crème brûlée in the city. On top of that, the wine list is extraordinary for its tremendous depth and quality.

The bright, bold and playful design of Le Cirque 2000 embodies the circus in its name. Famed architect-designer Adam Tihany took this opulent neo-classical mansion, built in 1882-84, and, in effect drove a Ferrari up the grand marble staircase, overlaying the stately elements with freestanding con-temporary design statements in the circus motif. Carpets in the dining rooms shout geometric designs in purples, greens and red. The surrealistic-feeling bar features high-contrast colors and parabolic-neon lines, and a large clock that moves across the room on a high wire. In good weather, the courtyard—for-merly the mansion's carriage courtyard—is packed. If you are celebrating a mega-deal or some other special occasion, head for Le Cirque. If you are looking for a gastronomic tour-de-force, don't even look at a menu: tell them how many courses you want and have the chef strut his stuff. If you are looking for the Le Cirque experience at a budget price, however, dream on.

LE COLONIAL   VIETNAMESE   13/20

149 E. 57th St. (Lexington & Third Aves.), 10022
752-0808, Lunch Mon.-Fri., Dinner nightly, $$$

A nostalgic recreation of a glamorous French-Vietnamese club in '30s Saigon, Le Colonial is like a stage set of Asian tiles, rattan chairs, hammered-tin ceilings, potted palms and lazily spinning ceiling fans. The delicate cuisine is full of surprising contrasts of salty, sweet and spicy. Try the spring rolls, the seafood steamed in a banana leaf with lemon grass, the buttery filet mignon, and, to start with cocktails in the sexy upstairs lounge, the light-as-air shrimp chips.

LE PÉRIGORD   FRENCH   15/20   ♟♟

405 E. 52nd St. (First Ave), 10022
755-6244, *Lunch Mon.-Fri., Dinner nightly, $$$$*

🅰 ☎ ▮

Open since 1964, this serious French restaurant caters to a
UN and neighborhood crowd, is about to be remodeled. Chef
Pascal Coudouy prepares Périgord classics just the way his regulars like them: smoked salmon; a croustillant of goat cheese,
prunes and smoked duck; warm duck foie gras with apples and
port-wine sauce. Dover sole meunière, roast duck with orange
sauce, calf's liver, veal kidneys and roasted veal chop are
among the popular entrées, and wonderful made-to-order
soufflés are best bets for dessert. The big, French-dominated
wine list is decent, though the prices make you blink.

LESPINASSE   FRENCH   18/20   ♟♟♟

St. Regis Hotel, 2 E. 55th St., 10022
339-6719, *Breakfast, Lunch & Dinner Tues.-Sat., $$$$*

🅰 ☎

Say goodbye to ex-Chef Gray Kunz's striking French fare
with Asian influences and hello to (ex-Célébrités) Christian
Delouvrier's solid, classic French cuisine with occasional
thrusts into updated and adventuresome dishes. If Kunz was
like no one else, Delouvrier, at least, is right on day after day,
so it is hard to experience a flawed meal here. And since he
took over this $2 million kitchen the second half of 1998, he
has been emboldened to the point of some surprisingly complex and contemporary dishes. Butternut-squash soup, for
example, comes with pieces of duck breast and bits of sautéed
foie gras. Still, meats and butter-based sauces are the standards
at Lespinasse, and the portions are generous, the prices high.
How about a tasting menu at dinner for $135 per person? The
re-opening saw little change in the décor (new paintings, different flowers) so the setting remains ultra-deluxe with splendid Louis something-or-other high ceilings, gilded columns,
oversized chairs, and a certain dullness reserved for hotel dining rooms, which this is.

LUTÈCE   FRENCH   17/20   ♟♟♟

249 E. 50th St. (Second & Third Aves.), 10022
752-2225, *Lunch Tues.-Fri., Dinner Mon.-Sat., $$$$*

🅰 ☎ ▮ 🏃

Since chef (and part owner, with Ark Restaurants)
Eberhard Müller took over this venerable French restaurant in
1995, he has worked hard to maintain its stellar reputation
while infusing the cuisine and ambience with his own personality. Along with refreshing the décor, Müller has won over old
regulars with his cooking. Though different from Soltner's traditional approach, it is sublime nonetheless. German-born
Müller is best known for his artistry with seafood, as in such

appetizers as lobster medallions and quince braised in Madeira, crabmeat-and-potato salad with black-truffle vinaigrette, and warm oysters and stewed leeks in Champagne sauce, and in such entrées as steamed grouper and cockles in a saffron broth, crisp black bass with lobster sauce and whole roasted lobster with Cognac butter. Of course there are distinctive non-seafood dishes as well, including roasted duck with baked lemon and rack of lamb with a mustard-honey glaze. There are over 300 selections on the wine list, including, mon Dieu, American wines. Order a soufflé for dessert.

MALONEY & PORCELLI   STEAKHOUSE/AMERICAN   14/20

37 E. 50th St. (Madison & Park Aves.) 10022
750-2233, *Lunch & Dinner daily*, $$$$

Part of Alan Stillman's NY Restaurant Group, Maloney & Porcelli takes its name from Stillman's lawyers, and it's the kind of guy place lawyers and other suits love: there's a big bar and the menu is dedicated to "classic American cuisine from the '30s through the millennium." Order an aged steak and it comes huge, perfectly cooked, delicious—and naked. (Don't forget to order potatoes and vegetables.) The seafood is okay, and you can start with oysters or the distinctive salmon pastrami or thin-crusted pizza. Calorie-rich desserts include a luscious chocolate-mousse layer cake. The wine offerings are strong.

MARCH RESTAURANT   NEW AMERICAN   16/20

405 E. 58th St. (First Ave. & Sutton Pl.), 10022
754-6272, *Dinner nightly*, $$$$

March marches on with its appealing combination of compelling cross-cultural fare in an attractive setting. The narrow dining room opens into a pair of small back rooms, one overlooking a pretty garden. With a fireplace and woodsy, cozy appointments, the interior feels almost like that of a private home. Wayne Nish's distinctive West-East-fusion food has risen to new levels of sophistication and is offered via various prix-fixe menus that range from $68 to $125. Appetizers might include lobster carpaccio, ravioli of sweet garlic and baby leeks, and a salad of fifty herbs with Ligurian olive oil. Entrées range from an exotic mixed grill of quail and squab with sautéed hen-of-the-woods mushrooms to hot smoked salmon with sauerkraut, Irish bacon and juniper berries. Desserts are stellar, especially the Provençal sparkling-wine sorbet with pink grapefruit in Tanquerary gin and coriander-seed syrup. The wine list is one of the best in town.

MICHAEL JORDAN'S THE STEAK HOUSE NYC STEAKHOUSE 14/20

Grand Central Terminal, 23 Vanderbilt Ave. (47th St.), 10017
655-2300, *Lunch & Dinner daily, $$$$*

Don't plan on wearing your Bulls T-shirt when dining at this sophisticated new restaurant on the balcony of the gloriously restored Grand Central Station. The theme here is great trains, not great basketball (except in the gift shop), with plush lounge chairs and tables set with crisp white linens, like those on yesteryear's 20th Century Limited. The oversized crystal and silverware are big enough for #23's grip, and the portions of chef David Walzog's refined-macho cuisine would definitely fuel His Airness before a game: feisty garlic bread with Gorgonzola fondue, creamy corn soup boasting a pepper-pumped crabcake and a half-dozen varieties of prime dry-aged red meat. Definitely worth a stop before you catch your train.

MONKEY BAR   NEW AMERICAN   15/20

60 E. 54th St. (Madison & Park Aves.), 10022
838-2600, *Lunch Mon.-Fri., Dinner nightly, $$$$*

A swank watering hole for New York's high-society set in the '30s and '40s, the Monkey Bar was refurbished to its former splendor in 1994 by designer David Rockwell. The famous murals of frolicking monkeys may draw you to the dark-wooded bar, but don't overlook the glamorous back dining room, with its velvet-swathed columns, see-and-be-seen booths and etched-glass room dividers. The seasonally changing menu might include such appetizers as linguine with blue cheese and basil, chestnut soup hiding Armagnac-soaked prunes, or oysters topped with yellowfin tuna tartare. Entrées range from silken roast chicken in wine sauce to crispy shrimp with a tropical-fruit sauce. To see whose company you would have been keeping if you'd come here in the good old days, check out the Abe Hirschfeld caricatures of past celebrity regulars.

MORTON'S OF CHICAGO   STEAKHOUSE/AMERICAN   14/20

551 Fifth Ave. (45th St.), 10017
972-3315, *Lunch Mon.-Fri., Dinner nightly, $$$$*

In this clubby, comfortable—and masculine—setting, the waitpersons present the menu in a flashy, show-and-tell recitation, holding up various hunks of meat (wrapped in plastic), giant lobsters, and potatoes the size of footballs to make their point. The basics are this upscale steakhouse chain's strength. Starters include shrimp cocktail, raw oysters and smoked salmon. Here, juicy steaks star: a New York strip, an enormous double porterhouse and a double filet mignon. There are also good prime rib, lamb chops, Maine lobster, grilled salmon and lemon-oregano chicken. For sides, we recommend the potatoes Lyonnaise. The wine list is adequate.

MR. K'S   CHINESE   16/20

570 Lexington Ave. (51st St.), 10022
583-1668, *Lunch & Dinner daily*, $$$$

One year and $5+ million in the making, Mr. K's is New York's most elegant Chinese restaurant, perfect for the conduct of business or romance. A former bank has become an art-deco dining palace with graceful banquettes and easy chairs, museum-grade jade artifacts, glass cases of celebrity chopsticks and built-in lazy susans lit from below. Johnny Kao, whose Washington Mr. K's has thrived for 15 years, offers a slightly westernized menu of dishes presented with great style and gorgeous table appointments. The five-course prix-fixe dinner, including Peking Duck, is a good deal. Soup and coffee courses should not be missed for the sheer fun of their delivery systems. If you want to really impress guests, arrange for their own personalized chopsticks before taking them here.

NAPLES 45   ITALIAN   14/20

MetLife Building, 200 Park Ave.
(45th St., Lexington & Vanderbilt Aves.), 10166
972-7001, *Breakfast Mon.-Fri., Lunch & Dinner Mon.-Sat.*, $$

This vast—260 seats—busy and noisy slice of Neapolitan food and hospitality offers a take so faithful that not just the ovens (named Etna, Vesuvio and Stromboli) and the flour, but the very composition of its water is replicated in the pizza preparation. There are also more than 20 small plates akin to tapas. Baked pasta dishes join others as intriguing as spaghetti with swordfish, olives, capers, tomatoes and olive oil. The bustling kitchen also taps southern Italy's seaside inspiration for the likes of wood-oven-baked black sea bass filled with garlic, rosemary and orange segments. The 75-foot-long Wine Bar offers more than 70 vino variations and other first-rate potables.

NIPPON   JAPANESE   15/20

155 E. 52nd St. (Third & Lexington Aves.), 10022
758-0226, *Lunch Mon.-Fri., Dinner Mon.-Sat.*, $$$

One of the first authentic Japanese restaurants in the U.S., Nippon is still a trailblazer after 35 years. For example, from October to March it features fugu, the famed blowfish that can kill if improperly prepared. Not to worry. Owner/founder Nobuyoshi Kuraoka imports the finest sushi and sashimi chefs from Japan. (On the other hand, the $170 tab for the seven-course fugu fish dinner may give you a heart attack.) The split-level dining room is surrounded by several private tatami rooms where whispering waitresses in traditional kimonos minister to your needs. Among the hot appetizers, we adore the shishamo (small broiled smelts) and the smoked salmon skin soaked in saké then broiled until delicately crisp. The chefs grind their own imported-from-Japan buckwheat for the delicious, freshly rolled and cut soba noodles, which come with a variety of toppings. Mr. Kuraoka also introduced New York to the kobachi: six small dishes to eat while drinking saké.

OCEANA   SEAFOOD   15/20

55 E. 54th St. (Madison & Park Aves.), 10022
759-5941, *Lunch Mon.-Fri., Dinner Mon.-Sat.,* $$$$

Refurbished a couple of years ago, this contemporary seafood restaurant features nautical accents and an upstairs bar. The service and ambience are refined, and chef Rick Moonen plays with colors and flavors on the plate and almost always wins. The $65 three-course prix-fixe dinner menu includes such appetizers as grilled baby octopus, salmon tart wrapped with smoked salmon and a jumbo lump crabcake. The entrées are prepared simply, many with Asian or Mediterranean twists: bouillabaisse, "everything"-crusted yellowfin tuna, miso-glazed Chilean sea bass. The dozen desserts range from a luscious coffee-Mascarpone-mousse cake to a raspberry-chocolate napoleon. The wine list is excellent.

OYSTER BAR & RESTAURANT   SEAFOOD/AMERICAN   13/20

Grand Central Terminal lower level, (42nd St. & Vanderbilt Ave.), 10017
490-6650, *Lunch & Dinner Mon.-Fri.,* $$$

This place has to be seen to be believed: The cavernous main dining room in Grand Central Station boasts acres of tables under a colossal vaulted ceiling, where a couple of thousand meals are served here each weekday. The daily menu reflects the day's catch, and usually includes about 30 types of seafood, from grouper to wolf fish. We prefer fish here cooked simply—grilled, fried, meunière—and the fresh oysters. Consider the broiled extra-large Maine sea scallops or the bouillabaisse. The desserts include apple pies, cheesecake and rice pudding. The all-American list of 150 wines offers plenty of nicely priced choices, and there are a dozen beers on draught. As odd as it may sound for a place of this size, reservations are a necessity for lunch.

THE PALM   STEAKHOUSE/AMERICAN   13/20

837 Second Ave. (44th St.), 10017
687-2953, *Lunch Mon.-Fri., Dinner Mon.-Sat.,* $$$$

This no-frills steakhouse with sawdust on the floors and caricatures of famous faces on the walls, opened in 1926 and is still going strong. The waiters have a no-nonsense approach, and the menu covers the basics such as jumbo lobsters (boiled, broiled), the double New York strip steak, lamb chops, pork chops and the occasional chicken dish. If ordered broiled, the four-pound lobsters can be dry; boiled, they are a moist, fresh sea feast. The rib roast, about three inches thick, is magnificent. A heap of crisp-fried potatoes-and-onions is the signature side order here, but skip the oil-drenched iceberg lettuce and tomato salad. For dessert (if you have room), the cheesecake has just the right creamy texture and the chocolate mousse cake is sinfully rich. There is a full bar, and the wine list has been greatly improved and expanded. Across the street, **Palm Two** is a faithful replica.

PAMIR   AFGHAN   14/20

1065 First Ave., (58th St), 10022
644-9258, *Dinner Tues.-Sun.*, $$

See review in "Upper East Side."

PAPER MOON   ITALIAN   12/20

39 E. 58th St. (Park & Madison Aves.), 10022
758-8600, *Lunch Mon.-Sat., Dinner nightly*, $

Black-and-white photos adorn the walls of this chic, contemporary spot, a branch of the trendy Paper Moon in Milan. Come here to people-watch or to snack on thin-crusted pizzas with toppings such as bresaola and arugula, Italian sandwiches in all shapes and sizes, salads and pastas. Dessert offerings include a light tiramisu, gelati drenched in liqueur and several pastries. **Paper Moon Express** (54 E. 59th St., 688-5500) does delivery and take-out.

THE PARK   ITALIAN/CONTEMPORARY   NO RATING

Lombardy Hotel, 109 E. 56th St. (Park & Lexington), 10022
750-5656, *Lunch Mon.-Fri., Dinner Mon.-Sat.*, $$$

What a sexy place to meet your lover—or your spouse. John Scotto (his family owns Fresco) re-created the decadent Baccarat-chandelier-and-velvet-sofa look that William Randolph Hearst envisioned when he built the Lombardy as a residential hotel back in 1926. We could spend hours in one of the plush swivel chairs in the lounge, but the dining room with its Florentine-patterned carpets, faux windows and gold-leafed wood moldings—beckons. The service is close to fawning, and as we went to press, Scotto had brought in a new chef, Brian Bennington, whose specialties include: pear, watercress and Pecorino salad with toasted pine nuts; crisp pizzettes with, say, roasted baby artichokes, goat cheese and broccoli rabe; gossamer ravioli stuffed with striped bass and spinach; farfalle with braised rabbit; crispy skinned bass with sun-dried tomato risotto; and osso buco. There are several grand rooms for private parties.

PATROON   NEW AMERICAN   14/20

160 E. 46th St. (Third & Lexington Aves.), 10017
883-7373, *Lunch Mon.-Fri., Dinner Mon.-Sat., $$$$*

Ken Aretsky's new-but-old-fashioned restaurant boasts an upstairs cigar lounge where men (and, yes, women) sit back in oversized leather club chairs to smoke and schmooze. Everything about this macho place is big, from the menus themselves to the portions to the prices—$28 for spit-roasted organic chicken, $38 for the prime rib. In the rather sedate dining room, you're likely to see power-mongers discussing mega-mergers while savoring the buttery foie-gras terrine and other hearty dishes that may inspire extra minutes on the treadmill the morning after. The menu has ventured into more sophisticated territory in the past year or so, with the addition of such specialties as pistachio-truffle-crusted sea bass and guinea hen with leek-and-squash cannelloni. The wine list is formidable in scope, and, like the food here, pricey.

PEACOCK ALLEY   FRENCH   17/20

The Waldorf-Astoria Hotel, 301 Park Ave. (49th & 50th Sts.), 10022
872-4895, *Lunch Mon.-Fri., Dinner Tues.-Sat., Brunch Sun., $$$$*

The Waldorf-Astoria made a wise investment recently by hiring hard-driving chef Laurent Gras, the former chef de cuisine to Alain Ducasse in France. Thus New York landed a true tastemaker, an innovator whose short menus explode with exciting, harmonious flavors. No one but Gras would dare wed seared blue-fin tuna with a medley of seaweed, peanuts and tabbouleh, or see roast veal loin's possibilities when pickled with plums and plated with green-tomato chutney and romaine lettuce. Nor would any other kitchen commander figure Dover sole makes a great salad when combined with romaine, sea urchins and grapefruit. The Peacock Alley brigade seizes every seasonal moment, such as the arrival of fresh truffles, which are luxuriously showered over many dishes. Peacock Alley's look has been lightened, its harp deleted, and new service leadership results in crisp, discreet, silver-domed service.

ROSA MEXICANO   MEXICAN   13/20

1063 First Ave. (58th St.), 10022
753-7407, *Dinner nightly, $$*

A

The upscale regional-Mexican fare is consistently good at this festive restaurant, with its pretty-in-stucco south-of-the-border setting and warm service. You're greeted outside by six large metal gods and fitting idols—pine, corn, pomegranate, beans, chile and tomato. Just inside, the bar does a big business in margaritas. For appetizers, try the oysters, sautéed and served chilled in a marinade of chilies and spices, or the tortillas filled with shredded pork and smoked chili chipotle. But the guacamole, made tableside to your heat specificity, wins the popularity contest. Main courses range from grilled whole red snapper and skewered marinated shrimp to filet mignon.

RUTH'S CHRIS STEAKHOUSE   STEAKHOUSE/AMERICAN   14/20

148 W. 51st St. (Sixth & Seventh Aves.), 10022
245-9600, *Lunch Mon.-Fri., Dinner nightly, $$$$*

A ☎

Just when you thought New York had enough steakhouses, Ruth's Chris, a New Orleans-based chain, opened a branch in the city. Those who swear by the Ruth's Chris-formula are rejoicing—they love the tender steaks dripping in melted butter, just the way Ruth's makes them. The sides and fish dishes are just okay here; it's the butter-basted cuts of meat that set this place apart.

SAN GIUSTO   ITALIAN   13/20

935 Second Ave. (49th & 50th Sts.), 10022
319-0900, *Lunch Mon.-Fri., Dinner Mon.-Sat., $$$*

VISA ☎

Elegant San Giusto is the creation of two Italians who come from the same Italian enclave in Yugoslavia: chef Gino Martincich, and host Bruno Viscovich. Jovial Bruno seems everywhere at once. The best way to order is to put yourself in his hands. Perhaps you'll start with delicious clams with sweet-pepper dressing and pancetta, or house-cured prosciutto with cheese. The homemade pastas are all good—you pick the noodle and match it with a sauce. Among the fish and seafood dishes, standouts include the grilled calamari, the broiled jump shrimp in sherry-haunted garlic butter, and poached salmon.

SCARABÉE   FRENCH-MEDITERRANEAN   16/20

230 E. 51st St. (Second & Third Aves.), 10022
758-6644, *Lunch Mon.-Fri., Dinner nightly, Brunch Sun., $$$*

A ☎

In the ancient Egyptian pantheon, the scarab was the symbol of longevity. We wish a long life for Karim El Sherrif's elegant but unpretentious restaurant with its blue and beige tones and black and white rings borrowed from Tutankhamen's scepter. With solid experience acquired in the best restaurants in New York (Le Bernardin, Daniel), Karim has put together the elements required for success—including chef Joseph Fortunato (late of Layla), whose mission it is to seduce palates with his Mediterranean-accented revisited French fare. (After all, Egypt also belongs to the Mediterranean.) Among Furtunato's original dishes are seared scallops in a piquant vinaigrette au poivre, truffle-marinated squab and pomegranate-glazed salmon. Daily-changing classics include couscous royal and fricassée of rabbit. Pastry chef Dalia Jurgensen adds her own exotic touch with such desserts as a pyramid of chocolate and bittersweet chocolate mousse. Having composed his own cellar over the years, Karim can offer good value for unusual wines.

SERYNA   JAPANESE   14/20

I I E. 53rd St. (Madison & Fifth Aves.), 10022
980-9393, *Lunch Mon.-Fri., Dinner Mon.-Sat., $$$*

Japanese businessmen pack this formal but comfortable restaurant on the ground floor of a Madison Avenue high-rise. Its forte is ishiyaki steak, tender filet mignon sizzled on a hot stone that absorbs all the fat. The shabu-shabu, a beef-and-vegetable self-cooked stew, has panache here. In addition, there are well-prepared versions of beef sashimi, shu-mai, sashimi, tempura and teriyaki dishes, and some sushi. A delicious side dish is steamed rice which has been spiced with salted Japanese plums, sesame seeds, crushed bonito and chopped shiso leaves (a fragrant member of the mint family).

SHUN LEE PALACE   CHINESE   14/20

155 E. 55th St. (Third & Lexington Aves.), 10022
371-8844, *Lunch & Dinner daily, $$$*

Shun Lee Palace has been a best bet for excellent Cantonese and Szechuan cuisine in mid-town (at mid-town prices) for nearly three decades. In the spacious dining room remodeled by Adam Tihany, the tables are set European-style and the maitre d' wears a tux. Start with crispy shrimp balls and dumplings, followed by slices of lean-and-smoky cold duck served with a pungent Hunan sauce. Next, order wontons floating in a rich duck broth. You can get all the usual pork, chicken and noodle standbys—done expertly—plus such unusual dishes as sweetbreads in a peppery Szechuan sauce and prawns coated with water-chestnut flour and sautéed in a Grand-Marnier sauce. The first-rate Peking duck is worth ordering for the high-speed, knife-flashing presentation alone. The service can be slow, but the food is worth the wait.

SMITH & WOLLENSKY   STEAKHOUSE/AMERICAN   13/20

201 E. 49th St. (Third Ave.), 10017
753-1530, *Lunch Mon.-Fri., Dinner nightly, $$$$*

This clubby wood-and-brass steakhouse can feed about 500 carnivores (mostly males) daily in its two dining rooms, saloon and outdoor café. Americana abounds here: ornithological prints, duck decoys and weather vanes set the tone. Most popular are the sliced steak, sirloin, filet mignon, prime rib, triple lamb chops or veal chop, with hash browns on the side. If you're off of red meat, try one of the humongous lobsters. In addition to cheesecake for dessert, there's terrific deep-dish apple pie. The wine list distinguishes S&W, which boasts a 50,000 bottle cellar, and from the prices, it seems that people who order expensive steaks drink expensive wines. There are great old vintages of Bordeaux and Californian Cabernets and plenty of oversize bottles as well.

SPARKS STEAKHOUSE   STEAKHOUSE/AMERICAN   14/20

210 E. 46th St. (Second & Third Aves.), 10017
687-4855, *Lunch Mon.-Fri., Dinner Mon.-Sat., $$$$*

Sparks recently expanded into the space next door, which means your wait for a table may be shorter than it used to be at this mahogany-paneled steak institution. We can't fault the tender prime sirloin or juicy filet mignon, the lamb chops (three doubles), or the charred veal chop and the broiled lobsters. The meats come unadorned, so order a side of buttery spinach or a baked potato. Desserts are just okay, but there's a good dessert-wine list. In fact, Sparks has one of the best overall wine cellars in the city—and some of the fairest wine prices.

SUSHI BAR   SUSHI   14/20

256 E. 49th St. (Second & Third Aves.)
644-8750, *Lunch Mon.-Fri., Dinner nightly, $$*

What's behind the simple name? A cave-like below-street-level space where the decor is industrial-chic, the rock music is loud, a TV shows sports events and young sushi chefs craft sushi—all the usual versions done extremely well—at the mirror-backed blond wood sushi bar. Upstairs, you'll find an even hipper and louder bar/lounge and a karaoke studio that rocks.

SUSHISAY   JAPANESE   15/20

38 E. 51st St. (Madison & Park Aves.), 10022
755-1780, *Lunch Mon.-Fri., Dinner Mon.-Sat., $$$*

Don't even think about getting into Sushisay without a reservation. This midtown Japanese restaurant serves some of the finest sushi and sashimi in the city and seats here are always in demand. You won't find tempura or teriyaki. The focus is on raw and marinated dishes, which allows the Tokyo-trained chefs to devote their full attention to creating fresh and eclectic preparations like vegetable hand rolls of radish sprout or burdock. If it's available, try the salmon roe over grated Japanese white radish or the yellowtail with scallion and wasabi. Given the emphasis on quality, you'd probably never guess that Sushisay is part of a 32-restaurant Tokyo chain.

TATOU   FRENCH/NEW AMERICAN   13/20

151 E. 50th St. (Lexington & Third Aves.), 10022
753-1144, Lunch Mon.-Fri., Dinner Mon.-Sat., $$$

This sexy supper club is set in a building that was meant to be a small opera house in the 1920s but never opened because of the Depression. Faded draperies adorn an overhead balcony, while a giant chandelier hangs from the 30-foot-high ceiling. On the small curtained stage, a pianist plays during lunch and various musical groups liven up most evenings. Dining is on two tiers; ask for a table on the second level so that you can survey the crowd. Chef Neill Becker prepares such contemporary dishes as tuna tartare, a mosaic of smoked salmon, potato and goat cheese, Moroccan-spiced wild salmon, adobo-style breast of chicken and cherry-wood smoked breast of squab. The mostly American wine list has some fairly priced selections.

VONG   THAI/FRENCH   15/20

200 E. 54th St. (Third Ave.), 10022
486-9592, Lunch Mon.-Fri., Dinner nightly, $$$

Jean-George Vongerichten's drop-dead-beautiful Southeast Asian restaurant has packed them in since it opened in '92, and it has cloned itself in Hong Kong, among other places. David Rockwell's decor is strictly the stuff of a movie set: burnt orange and salmon colors, collaged walls with faux decay and faded newspapers, potted palms, recessed booths, louvered-wooden shades, spice displays, gold leaf details. You won't find a menu like this in Thailand, where Vongerichten was once a chef. The crab spring roll with outer crunch and inner delicacy, and the silken sautéed foie gras with mango and ginger, are the best starters (pass on the grilled squid salad). Main courses of note: rabbit curry, crisp squab with an egg-noodle pancake, and spiced cod with curried artichokes. For dessert, how about baked banana with poppy seed-honey ice cream and warm chocolate on phyllo.

ZARELA   MEXICAN   13/20

953 Second Ave. (50th & 51st Sts.), 10022
644-6740, Lunch Mon.-Fri., Dinner nightly, $$

There's always a party mood (or so it seems) at this colorful restaurant and bar, decorated with Mexican handicrafts, piñatas and all. Zarela Martinez pointedly avoids serving such common items as tacos and burritos, and instead features the more flavorful cuisine of Mexico's coastal regions. Enchiladas and tamales are served along with such intriguing starters as snapper hash and a poblano chile stuffed with chicken and dried-fruit picadillo. Seafood specialties might include tuna in mole sauce, grilled salmon with chipotle mayonnaise and delicious spicy shrimp. Desserts are extravagant, perhaps bread pudding with applejack-brandy-butter sauce and dried fruits. Mexican beer goes well with this food.

AND ALSO...

THE BARCLAY BAR & GRILL   NEW AMERICAN

Hotel Inter-Continental, 111 E. 48th St. (Park & Lexington Aves.), 10017
421-0836, *Breakfast, Lunch & Dinner daily, Brunch Sun.*, $$$

Overlooking the handsome lobby of the Hotel Inter-Continental, this is a comfortable spot for a lavish buffet breakfast or a quiet business lunch or dinner. Appetizers include a warm langoustine salad and sea-bass carpaccio, while entrées range from fresh pastas to a hefty Black Angus steak. The $42 Sunday brunch includes tastings of California sparkling wines and Champagne. The wine list is extensive.

BOBBY VAN'S STEAKHOUSE   STEAKHOUSE/AMERICAN

230 Park Ave. (46th St.), 10169
867-5490, *Lunch Mon.-Fri., Dinner Mon.-Sat.*, $$$$

As if Peter Luger, the Palm and Morton's weren't enough, here's another he-man steakhouse where you should throw all cholesterol-caution to the wind. In addition to juicy and delicious cuts of red meat, you'll find gigantic Maine lobsters and lemon-pepper shrimp, and all-American desserts (chocolate mud cake, pecan pie) that require more than one hungry eater to finish them off.

THE BOX TREE   FRENCH

250 E. 49th St. (Second & Third Aves.), 10017
758-8320, *Lunch Mon.-Fri., Dinner nightly*, $$$

Pretentious? Precious? Overpriced? Perhaps. But the Box Tree is one of Manhattan's most beautiful and romantic restaurants, a jewel of a townhouse filled with antiques, fine art and three working fireplaces. A perfect place to propose over a five-course $86 dinner with such classic dishes as escargots, pecan-nut-crusted red snapper, roast venison, veal medallions and French pastries.

CAFÉ ADRIANA   FRENCH

The Galleria, 115 E. 57th St. (Fifth Ave.), 10022
829-8180, *Lunch Mon.-Fri.*, $

Philippe Feret, who cooked at Taillevent in France and Windows on the World, now has his own cozy bistro in the arcade of this glitzy shopping emporium. In addition to such classics as frisée au lardons with poached eggs, you'll find chicken b'stilla, a buffalo burger, and braised short ribs.

CAVIAR RUSSE   CAVIAR/FRENCH

538 Madison Ave. (54th St.), 10022
980-5908, *Lunch & Dinner daily, Tea Mon-Fri., $$$$*

A former furniture showroom has been converted into a luxurious and romantic little spot—glittering chandeliers, a robin's-egg-blue ceiling and Russian murals—where guests indulge in caviar, caviar and more caviar, along with other such decadent celebratory fare as smoked salmon and blini, duck confit with foie gras, Maine lobster and tartare of sirloin of steak—each with a dollop or two of caviar upon request. Lots of vodkas and Champagnes to wash it all down. Caspian caviar—and all the accoutrements—are available to go as well.

SAKAGURA   JAPANESE

211 E. 43rd St. (Second & Third Aves.), 10017
953-7253, *Dinner nightly, $$*

Hidden away in a basement, this beautiful little enclave of soft golden light is a favorite with Japanese businessmen, and offers more than 200 types of saké, along with such non-sushi Japanese items as sashimi, teriyaki chicken and steak.

TROPICA   SEAFOOD/FUSION

The MetLife Building, 200 Park Ave. (45th St.), 10128
867-6767, *Lunch & Dinner Mon.-Fri., $$$*

This businesspeople magnet is en route to Grand Central Station, so if you phone during Happy Hour it's likely to be so loud in the restaurant, the hostess won't be able to hear your request for a reservation. The large airy dining room has a bit of a tropical-club feel to it, with fish motifs here and there in the décor. The chunky ginger-haunted tuna tartare and crab-cakes are good to start, but if there's a special of sea urchin in a piquant tomato water, try it. Other recommended dishes: mussels in a spicy Thai-curry broth; Chilean sea bass with whipped taro root; and yes, among all the seafood offerings, even a good grilled sirloin steak.

TYPHOON BREWERY   THAI/BREWPUB

22 E. 54th St. (Madison & Fifth Ave.), 10022
754-9006, *Lunch & Dinner Mon.-Sat., $$*

This two-level, wide-open industrial space with a 60-foot bar has huge tanks on display and more in the basement, which brew the six beers they have on tap. In addition, you can get at least 15 bottled microbrews, three dozen wines by the glass and dozens of single-malt scotches and tequilas. There's Thai food too—curries, noodle dishes and dumplings—and a humidor.

MIDTOWN WEST

DINING

All phone numbers are (212) unless otherwise indicated

AQUAVIT   SCANDINAVIAN   14/20

13 W. 54th St. (Fifth & Sixth Aves.), 10019
307-7311, *Lunch Mon.-Fri., Dinner nightly, Brunch Sun. Sept.-May, $$$$*

Once the home of Nelson Rockefeller, today this town-house is a strikingly modern restaurant: Upstairs is a bar and café; downstairs is an eight-story atrium where kite-like mobiles hang from the glass ceiling, and one wall is a waterfall. On the $64 four-course dinner menu, Chef Marcus Samuelsson, a native of Ethiopia, starts you off with such Scandinavian standards as pickled herring, gravlax, smoked salmon, caviar and cured foie gras. Entrées range from lotus-crusted char with black tagliarini and anchovy soufflé to balsamic-poached rack of lamb with grilled vegetable panini and sunchoke purée. What to drink with all of this? To start, a shot of one of the eight varieties of flavored aquavits; to finish, a Finnish liqueur.

B. SMITH'S   SOUTHERN/AMERICAN   11/20

771 Eighth Ave. (47th St.), 10036
247-2222, *Lunch & Dinner daily, $*

A high-energy spot in the theater district, B. Smith's is known for American fare that tends towards the down-home Southern. Specialties include gulf shrimp steeped in Chardonnay; a potato-and-leek pancake with roast tomato, smoked salmon and a dollop of crème fraîche; hot grilled salmon salad with wild mushrooms, roast potato and greens; and whiting dipped in cornmeal and lightly fried, served with cole slaw, potato straws and tartar sauce. For dessert, try the sweet-potato pie with pecans.

BARBETTA   ITALIAN   13/20

321 W. 46th St. (Eighth & Ninth Aves.), 10036
246-9171, *Lunch & Dinner Mon.-Sat., $$$$*

The oldest Italian restaurant in the city, Barbetta occupies two elegant town houses on the theater district's "Restaurant Row." The dining room is filled with antiques and crystal chandeliers; upstairs are private dining rooms complete with fire-places and beautiful original woodwork; the inner garden sports a bubbling fountain and is brightened by flowering

bushes. We have enjoyed Barbetta's risottos, and we also recommend the grilled squab, foie gras and succulent beef
braised in red wine and served with polenta. The dessert trol-
ley features dozens of luxurious confections, and the wine list
includes 300 labels. Prices are steep, but there is a reasonably
priced prix-fixe pre-theater dinner menu.

BECCO   ITALIAN   11/20

355 W. 46th St. (Eighth & Ninth Aves.), 10036
397-7597, *Lunch & Dinner daily*, $$

A ☎

Opened in 1992 by Joe Bastianich and his mother Lidia,
who owns Felidia, Becco has a lot going for it: The portions are
enormous and prices are modest. You can also find more than
50 red and white Italian wines by the bottle—all priced $15.
Bravo. For $21.95, you get an assortment of grilled marinated
vegetables or Caesar salad, plus unlimited servings of three of
the daily-changing pastas. For up to $15 more, add such
entrées as seared loin of tuna over baby arugula salad or lamb
chops with limas beans and spinach with a cherry sauce.

BEN BENSON'S STEAK HOUSE   STEAKHOUSE/AMERICAN   13/20   ♀

123 W. 52nd St. (Sixth & Seventh Aves.), 10019
581-8888, *Lunch Mon-Thurs., Dinner nightly*, $$$$

A ☎

Thick plates, wood floors, dim lights and cigar smoke make
this an authentic old-world steakhouse. Waiters wear butchers'
smocks while waitresses are noticeably absent. Simply put, Ben
Benson's is a New York steakhouse and a good one. Good fresh
fish too.

CABANA CARIOCA   BRAZILIAN   12/20

123 W. 45th St. (Sixth Ave. & Broadway), 10036
581-8088, *Lunch & Dinner daily*, $

A ☎

This colorful Brazilian restaurant in the theater district has
been delivering hearty fare—and lots of it—at bargain-base-
ment prices for 25 years. The small bar is lined with regulars
downing massive portions of feijoada, Brazil's national dish—
$15.95 except when it's a $12.95 special on some nights—a
substantial black-bean stew filled with rich sausage, beef ribs,
pork and whatever other meat comes up in the ladle. Lots of
seafood dishes, as well as fried chicken with potatoes, plus a
salad bar and a dessert table, where just a taste of the Brazilian
flan might be all you have room for after dinner.

CAFÉ NICOLE   FRENCH/AMERICAN   11/20

Novotel New York, 226 W. 52nd St. (Broadway), 10019
315-0100 ext. 7120, *Breakfast, Lunch & Dinner daily*, $$

A 📷

With its panoramic view of Broadway, Café Nicole is a perfect place for a breakfast buffet that offers choices of tradition-

al favorites and a fine selection of croissants and assorted pastries. The location—right off Times Square—also makes it a good stop for a light lunch or perhaps dinner before the theater. The fare is straightforward: onion soup, steak sandwich, pasta with vegetables and lamb chops sautéed with roasted garlic and thyme.

CHATEAUBRIAND   FRENCH   14/20

68 W. 58th (Fifth & Sixth Aves.), 10019
751-2323, Lunch Mon.-Fri., Dinner nightly, $$

A longtime French-bistro fixture in mid-town, Jean Lafitte underwent a freshening up in early 1998, making the setting—dark-wood booths, gold tiles, palms and French film posters—look and feel even more like one on the Left Bank. They also changed the name. French-style steaks are the thing here, from filet mignon to chateaubriand for two. We're impressed that at lunch or dinner, you can get a rib-eye steak, salad and frites for only $19.98.

CHINA GRILL   PAN ASIAN   13/20

52 W. 53rd St. (Fifth and Sixth Aves.), 10019
333-7788, Lunch Mon.-Fri., Dinner nightly, $$$$

This beautiful, hip—and NOISY—space features soaring ceilings, a black-and-white color scheme, an open kitchen and two very busy bars. The menu focuses on the cuisines of Asia, and dishes might include sashimi tuna wrapped in seaweed, quickly battered and deep fried, sizzling whole fish with black-bean sauce, grilled Szechwan beef or sensational Shanghai lobster in a ginger-curry sauce. The not-so-Asian desserts include cream-cheese mousse and pumpkin cheesecake. The wine list is too small for our liking, but includes some top European and California vintages.

CHRISTER'S   SCANDINAVIAN   13/20

145 W. 55th St. (Sixth & Seventh Aves.), 10019
9/4-7224, Lunch Mon.-Fri., Dinner Mon.-Sat., $$$$

At Christer's, Scandinavian meets Southwest and points beyond. The eclectic decor includes a middle room with blue-checked banquettes and a gas fireplace, and a back room with skylights and a blue-stained wood floor decorated with fish. Choose from a selection of assorted gravlax, herring and smoked fish. Christer Larsson's main courses include juniper-smoked salmon with hazelnut crust, salmon baked on an oak board, the intriguing "rhapsody of lamb" featuring lamb shank, lamb chop and lamb sausage and, in season, venison and wood pigeon. The wine list includes good beer and aquavit choices.

CHURRASCARIA PLATAFORMA   BRAZILIAN   14/20

316 W. 49th St. (Eighth & Ninth Aves.), 10019
245-0505, *Lunch & Dinner daily*, $$$

A

For a festive and formidable feed, try a no-holds-barred visit to Churrascaria Plataforma, the gold standard of Brazilian rodizio restaurants. A top-quality salad bar festooned with quail eggs, risotto, bacalao, octopus in tomato sauce and much more is but prelude to a carnival for carnivores. Friendly waiters bring more than a dozen spit-roasted meats, poultry and seafood items to each table. You may have as much—or as little—as you wish of each. Roast suckling pig, lamb, pork, salmon, spare ribs, turkey wrapped in bacon, chicken hearts and thighs—on and on it goes until guests stop the parade by turning up the red side of a small plastic counter on the table. Such appetite-quashing adventures are usually accompanied by Brazilian cocktails made with the sugar-cane spirit cachaca.

CITÉ   FRENCH   13/20

120 W. 51st St. (Sixth & Seventh Aves.), 10019
956-7100, *Lunch & Dinner daily*, $$$$

A

This Americanized interpretation of a lively Parisian brasserie is great fun. All done in cream and yellow, Cité is a rococo, art-deco extravaganza with a bi-level dining room great for business lunching and people-watching. The fare is classic French bistro: straightforward fish, chops and steak frites—with an emphasis on the frites—plus herb-crusted salmon steak and spit-roasted chicken. The French and American desserts are standard. The extensive wine list has selections from all over the map, many at very reasonable prices. There's a pre-theater menu for $39.50, and after 8 p.m. Monday through Saturday, the $59.50 prix-fixe dinner includes tastes of four wines—in unlimited quantities. The more casual **Cité Grill** adjoining the restaurant features a less expensive menu (956-7262).

DELTA GRILL   CAJUN   12/20

700 Ninth Avenue (48th St.), 10036
956-0934, *Lunch & Dinner daily*, $$

Ninth Avenue has become a Restaurant Row for the budget-conscious, and this down-home spot—with faded wood floors, a fireplace and barn-style murals—fits right in. While the food never strays from familiar territory, there are plenty of dishes that will set off your personal smoke detector, particularly the blackened dishes. The gumbos and the jambalaya, on the other hand, are rather one-dimensional. Adventurous appetites might consider the stewed alligator, which tastes like—what else?—chicken. Lowbrow charm and a charged atmosphere make this newcomer a popular after-hours post.

ESTIATORIO MILOS   GREEK/SEAFOOD   15/20

125 W. 55th St. (Sixth & Seventh Aves.), 10019
245-7400, Lunch Mon.-Fri., Dinner nightly, $$$$

Your waiter may whisk you on a tour of this stunning restaurant: past the fresh seafood display where fish from all over the world lounge atop mounds of shimmering shaved ice...past the wood-burning oven, where the fish are whole-roasted with oregano and a touch of fragrant Greek olive oil...past the open kitchen where chefs grill yellow Holland peppers and giant Polish mushrooms to serve as a first course. The look of this imported-from-Greece-via-Montreal seafood restaurant is high-tech-meets-theatrical: blond woods, high ceilings, gauzy white curtains and a raised dining area. The star of the show is fresh seafood, done simply, everything from Moroccan pageot to wild North Carolina sea bass. End your meal with a dish of refreshing homemade yogurt and what could be the city's best baklava.

FANTINO   ITALIAN/MEDITERRANEAN   14/20

The Westin Hotel, 112 Central Park South (Sixth & Seventh Aves.), 10019
757-1900, Lunch daily, Dinner Tues.-Sun., Brunch Sat.-Sun., $$$$

The former Jockey Club, Fantino has crystal chandeliers, spectacular floral arrangements, gilt-framed paintings—all very old-world luxurious. The fare, however, prepared by chef Michael Walsh, is contemporary Italian with tastes of other Mediterranean cuisines as well. Start with beef carpaccio with hearts of palm or seared scallops with caviar. Pastas include pappardelle with grilled shrimp and wild mushroom-truffle ravioli, and main courses run from roasted baby chicken to herb-seared salmon with sweet garlic purée under a dome of Parmesan. The comprehensive international wine list contains some good bets.

FIREBIRD   RUSSIAN   14/20

365 W. 46th St. (Eighth & Ninth Aves.), 10036
586-0244, Lunch Mon.-Sat., Dinner nightly, $$$$

In this age of restaurants as theater, this theater-district Russian wins an award. The stage is two brownstones turned into colorful art-and-artifact-filled dining rooms reminiscent of a St. Petersburg mansion before the Russian Revolution. The waiters wear Cossack uniform-like costumes and serve classically haute Russian cuisine. Perhaps surprisingly, it all works. Of course, it's hard to go wrong with caviar and Champagne, but we have been repeatedly pleased with such starters as smoked sturgeon, herring, roasted beets and walnuts, and steamed dumplings with minted sour cream. The borscht is uncommonly good, as are the skewered quail and lamb shashlik. Next door is **Café Firebird**, a Cabaret with quality singers and vodka.

"44"   NEW AMERICAN   14/20

Royalton Hotel, 44 W. 44th St. (Fifth & Sixth Aves.), 10036
944-9414, Breakfast, Lunch & Dinner daily, $$$$

Known at lunchtime as the Condé Nast cafeteria, the bar and restaurant of this sleek hotel attracts publishing and fashion types. (We've even spotted a chain-smoking, Bordeaux-drinking Hollywood-screenwriter-wannabe creating away at his laptop.) A $43 prix-fixe pre-theater menu is available in addition to à la carte selections that usually include simply grilled steaks, chicken and fish such as Atlantic salmon or Maine cod. The medium-priced wines come from all over the globe, as do the guests. In fact, if you miss your curtain, you can always enjoy the lobby show.

GALLAGHER'S   STEAKHOUSE/AMERICAN   13/20

228 W. 52nd St. (Broadway & Eighth Ave.), 10019
245-5336, Lunch & Dinner daily, $$$

Since 1927, this former speakeasy-turned-steakhouse has packed in businesspeople at lunch, and the Broadway crowd at night. The bustling wood-paneled dining room with its red-checked tablecloths and photos of famous New York politicians, athletes and actors is inviting. Most people come here for the steaks, grilled over hickory logs, but the roast prime rib of beef and lamb chops are safe bets, and you can't go wrong with the clams, oysters or oxtail soup. The grilled lobster is also good, and the french fries are fine. The cheesecake—which can be easily shared—lives up to expectations. The wine list is small and limited to mostly expensive Californian wines.

HALCYON   NEW AMERICAN   14/20

Rihga Royal Hotel, 151 W. 54th St. (Sixth & Seventh Aves.), 10019
468-8888, Breakfast, Lunch & Dinner daily, $$$

Halcyon is a tranquil haven within the spacious and comfortable Rihga Royal hotel. Dine on innovative dishes from a warm duck confit salad and sweet-pea blinis with smoked salmon, to medallions of Axis venison with Parmesan-roasted new potatoes and smoked-and-roasted rack of lamb with rosemary-Mascarpone risotto. The wines are affordable here, especially considering the luxurious surroundings. Halcyon offers pre-theater dining, along with a $45.98 three-course prix-fixe menu.

JEWEL OF INDIA   INDIAN   13/20

15 W. 44th St. (Fifth & Sixth Aves.), 10036
869-5544, *Lunch & Dinner daily, $$$*

Jewel of India and its younger sibling, Shaan, are lavish
Indian sanctuaries. Jewel of India fulfills its name with glisten-
ing mother-of-pearl-mosaic walls and elaborate ethnic trap-
pings. From the clay tandoor ovens come barbecued prawns
blushing with spices, and boneless chicken marinated in yogurt
and ginger. Many Indian families dine together here on fierce
vindaloo curries, many-flavored vegetable biryanis and a wide
array of breads, filled, puffed or plain. In addition to the oblig-
atory all-you-can-eat lunch buffet, there are a number of com-
plete meals for dieters or vegetarians.

JEZEBEL   SOUL FOOD/SOUTHERN   11/20

630 Ninth Ave. (W. 45th St.), 10036
582-1045, *Dinner Mon.-Sat., $$$*

The decor is something out of the New Orleans French
Quarter, with seven-foot-high palms, white wicker furniture,
crystal chandeliers and antique shawls draped from the ceiling.
Seatings are at 6 p.m. and 8:30 p.m. on weekdays, with a third,
10:30 p.m. seating on Fridays and Saturdays (but regulars
arrive whenever). The crowd is dominated by actors, directors
and acting students who take turns in the lawn swings, table-
hop, and, on weekends, sing along to the blues being ham-
mered out at the piano. The scene is worth the price of a meal:
soul food in portions fit for construction workers—spicy rib
bits, crispy chicken livers, she crab soup, and fried chicken,
smothered with gravy or not.

JUDSON GRILL   NEW AMERICAN   15/20

152 W. 52nd St. (Sixth & Seventh Aves.), 10019
582-5252, *Lunch Mon.-Fri., Dinner Mon.-Sat., $$$*

This dramatic high-ceilinged restaurant with an upstairs
balcony and a classy bar, is the quintessential high-energy mid-
town New York restaurant—good for business lunches, chic
dinners and pre-theater dining. Chef since early 1998, William
Telepan serves innovative, stunningly presented dishes that
change with the seasons, and might include such dishes as
peekytoe crab cocktail with sevruga caviar and avocado, bacon-
wrapped monkfish, duck breast with blood orange sauce and
golden beets and wild striped bass with canellini beans and

oregano-mint pesto. After your entrée, end with a selection of handcrafted domestic cheeses, or a Jack Daniels-punched ice cream soda.

LA CARAVELLE   FRENCH   15/20

33 W. 55th St. (Fifth & Sixth Aves.), 10021
586-4252, *Lunch Mon.-Fri., Dinner Mon.-Sat., $$$$*

A French dining institution in New York since 1960, La Caravelle still appeals with its serious European waiters, dim lighting, fine china, glimmering silverware and signature post-war murals of Paris. But the cuisine, by executive chef Cyril Renaud, delights with its exotic and innovative touches. In addition to such La Caravelle classics as mussel-cream soup, roasted duck with cranberries and apple confit, and a sublime chocolate soufflé, Renaud prepares goat-cheese-and-artichoke ravioli with beet juice and mustard, roasted lobster and squash with walnut-wine sauce and a veal chop with confit of citrus. The mostly French wine list is huge, and the prix-fixe menus range from $44 to $90.

LA CÔTE BASQUE   FRENCH   14/20

60 W. 55th St. (Fifth & Sixth Aves.), 10019
688-6525, *Lunch Mon.-Sat., Dinner nightly, $$$$*

Wear Chanel when you dine at this French restaurant land-mark, in New York (at other locations) since 1941. Stunning Lamotte murals set the festive yet formal mood—trompe l'oeil shutters opening onto sunny Mediterranean seascapes. So does the pampering old-guard service. Jean-Jacques Rachou turns out fare that tends towards lighter versions of the French clas-sics, all beautifully presented and served. On the $63 prix-fixe dinner menu, choose among such appetizers as goat cheese with artichoke hearts, snails in casserole or a silken lobster ter-rine, then move on to simply grilled red snapper, roast duck-ling, or the signature cassoulet. Pastry chef Andrew Shotts, a consultant to Valrhona Chocolate company, creates such astounding grande finales as a chocolate-and-caramel-mousse pyramid with a crème brûlée center. The wine list is big, French and pricey.

LA RÉSERVE   FRENCH   15/20

4 W. 49th St. (Fifth Ave.), 10019
247-2993, *Lunch Mon.- Fri., Dinner Mon.-Sat., $$$$*

Jean-Louis Missud opened this impressive salon in 1983, and with Dominique Payraudeau as chef since 1990, things run very smoothly indeed. Two dining rooms featuring attractive fabric-covered banquettes, paintings of waterfowl and beautiful chandeliers, set the stage for a pleasant and serious dining experience. Starters might include a mousse of smoked salmon and caviar or a grilled quail salad. The fish are perfectly cooked, and we've always enjoyed the roast duck with a fruity sauce. Remember those dessert carts in big hotels and grand French restaurants? You can still see one in action here, though you'll probably commit beforehand to a classic soufflé. The wine list features a couple hundred French and American wines and is good though not distinguished. The service, however, is excellent.

LE BERNARDIN   FRENCH/SEAFOOD   17/20

155 W. 51st St. (Sixth & Seventh Aves.), 10019
489-1515, Lunch Mon.-Fri., Dinner Mon.-Sat., $$$$

Praise be to the great Le Bernardin, which since it opened in 1986 has been a long-running top-end gastronomic destination. It's understandable that Le Bernardin strives for thrilling culinary epiphanies of the sort the late chef Gilbert Le Coze brought to American cuisine. Le Coze's successor, Chef Eric Ripert, has a repertoire that includes what he absorbed from his mentor, but also his menu is becoming more complex and reflects fusion elements, particularly from South America and the Mediterranean. Ripert's flavors are less pronounced than those that were shouted from the plate in Le Bernardin's early days. To experience Ripert's cuisine at its best, order the $120 tasting menu. At our most recent visit it started with a progressive tasting of simply adorned oysters, littleneck clams and baby scallops on the half-shell, followed by a warm lobster timbale topped with cucumbers and avocado and served with a spicy lobster sauce. Next came a sautéed red snapper over pickled celery, carrot and fennel in a sweet-and-sour tumeric-mustard-seed broth. This was followed by barely cooked salmon with melted lettuce and truffle sauce. Braised halibut served in casserole with asparagus and seasonal wild mushrooms concluded the fish offerings, and dessert was a sublime frozen raspberry and meringue concoction with a port-raspberry sauce. The dining room is a very large, rectangular corporate setting, lacking in intimacy. It works in its way, and a bit of French attitude by the staff and the driving co-owner Maguy Le Coze gives it personality.

LE MARAIS   FRENCH/KOSHER   12/20

150 W. 46th St. (Sixth & Seventh Aves.), 10036
869-0900, Lunch Sun.-Fri., Dinner Sat.-Thurs., $$

This restaurant in New York's "Diamond District" reminds us of a bistro in its namesake Paris neighborhood, Le Marais—except that in addition, the food and wine here are Kosher. As at Le Marais' sister restaurant, Les Halles, (which is not Kosher), the spit-roasted chicken and grilled steaks (hanger, rib-eye and tournedos) are served with perfect frites. There is a private smoking room and bar, and a butcher's case in the front where you can buy kosher meats and poultry to go.

LES CÉLÉBRITÉS   FRENCH   17/20

The Essex House, 155 W. 58th St. (Sixth & Seventh Aves.), 10019
484-5113, Dinner Tues.-Sat., $$$$

The great Christian Delouvrier is gone (to Lespinasse in the St. Regis Hotel, who had lost their great chef, Gary Kunz). But vive Luc Dimnet! The Alsace-born right hand to Delouvrier was quickly absorbed at Les Célébrités, overcoming the turbulence of the musical-chefs game. Dimnet presents the kind of extraordinary menu you expect to find in one of the most refined restaurants in town. Your wallet allowing, it's hard to make a choice among delicate lobster medallions with fennel-and-celery confit in a star anise sabayon, truffled-showered sautéed foie gras paired with French prunes and a scintillating ginger-chestnut sauce, whole roasted baby pig with truffle sauce and spit-roasted baby lamb with fresh rosemary jus, all followed by a dark Venezuelan chocolate mousse encasing violet crème brûlée. Maitre d' Ciro Santoro's formally clad staff sees to every nuance of want or need. As one of New York's most costly dinners, available only five nights a week, it must be extraordinary on every count, and it is.

LIMONCELLO   ITALIAN   14/20

777 Seventh Ave. (50th & 51st. Sts.), 10019
582-7932, Breakfast & Dinner daily, Lunch Mon.-Fri., $$$$

This very civilized restaurant, with its fin-de-siecle wall murals, modern Italian light fixtures and windows overlooking Seventh Avenue, soothes with its attentive service and updated versions of Italian classics. Start with grilled baby octopus napping sautéed potatoes in truffle oil, or a selection from the display of fresh oysters. They bake their own breads and pastries and make their own pastas, such as refreshingly light spaghetti tossed with garlic, olive oil, pepperoncino and lemon zest. Entrées on the seasonally changing menu might include seared tuna with green olives, roasted peppers and anchovy sauce, or roasted baby chicken with caramelized shallots and balsamic tarragon sauce. Follow dessert with a glass of homemade limoncello liqueur, then descend to the **Grotto Bar** for a cigar.

MANGIA   ITALIAN   11/20

50 W. 57th St. (Fifth & Sixth Aves.), 10019
582-5554, Lunch Mon.-Sat., $

A favorite quick-but-chic lunch spot for young hip professionals, Mangia offers a collection of pastas, pizzettes and an all-you-can-eat Mediterranean antipasto selection for $13.95, featuring everything from grilled vegetables to paella. The store, with some café seating, is open for dining and take-out until 8 p.m. on weekdays. **Also at 16 E. 48th St. (Fifth & Madison Aves.) 754-7600, & 40 Wall St. (Broad & William Sts.) 425-4040.**

MANHATTAN OCEAN CLUB   AMERICAN/SEAFOOD 15/20

57 W. 58th St. (Fifth & Sixth Aves.), 10019
371-7777, Lunch Mon.-Fri., Dinner daily, $$$$

A handsome two-floor restaurant with soft colorings on the walls, tranquil lighting and inviting chairs and tables, Manhattan Ocean Club is the place for fresh fish—broiled, roasted or sautéed. Start with marinated smoked salmon or gravlax, fresh oysters and clams—even sea urchins or crab in season. We've enjoyed the spicy and moist crabcakes, and the swordfish au poivre. You can get salmon plain or grilled with tandoori spices, and such sides as terrific shoestring potatoes. The computerized wine list contains some good California wines and some fairly good French ones.

MICHAEL'S   NEW AMERICAN   15/20

24 W. 55th St. (Fifth & Sixth Aves.), 10019
767-0555, Breakfast & Lunch, Mon.-Fri., Dinner Mon.-Sat., $$$

Like the Royalton Hotel's "44," Michael's is a power-lunch spot for the New York magazine-publishing set. Owner/host Michael McCarty, whose original Michael's is still going strong in Santa Monica, wins customer loyalty with the restaurant's professional service and style, and simple yet high-quality cuisine. Striking modern art hangs on the restaurant's walls, and the atrium dining area feels like one in Southern California. Those California credos of wood grilling, minimal saucing and lots of flavorful vegetables and greens are omnipresent on the menu. Expect to see precise and lengthy descriptions of dishes such as Canadian salmon with golden caviar, California squab with perhaps a Pinot Noir reduction and lamb with Cabernet Sauvignon, black currants and thyme. Michael's pastas are light and flavorful, and the wine list entices with a superb collection of California bottlings, especially older Cabernets.

MOLYVOS   GREEK   14/20

871 Seventh Ave. (55th & 56th Sts.), 10019
582-7500, Lunch & Dinner daily, $$

With its nooks, family pictures and wood paneling, Molyvos looks like a taverna on its namesake island, the home of its owners, the Livanos family, operators of the seafood restaurant Oceana. The kitchen brings new lightness to Greek classics with no flavor loss: tiny lamb meatballs in egg-lemon sauce; terrific cabbage dolmades; boldly cinnamoned moussaka; whole plank-grilled fish; octopus salad; lamb shanks baked in a clay pot. This is a fail-safe menu—order anything and be prepared for a thrill. The service is attentive, the ambience lively, and there's an impressive collection of Greek wines.

ORSO   ITALIAN   14/20   ♟

322 W. 46th St. (Eighth & Ninth Aves.), 10036
489-7212, *Lunch & Dinner daily,* $$

Since 1985, this rustic two-level trattoria has been one of the most popular spots to eat in the theater district, so don't be surprised if you encounter some attitude. A hangout for actors, critics and producers, its walls are cluttered with photos of the known and the unknown. We could easily fill up on the rosemary-and-olive-oil-haunted pizza bread, and we advise that with any entrée, from the grilled tuna to the braised lamb shank, you order a side of white beans with garlic, rosemary and oil. The pizzas are crisp crusted, and the daily-changing pastas are hearty, such as matriciani with braised calamari, tomatoes, onions and spicy red peppers.

OSTERIA DEL CIRCO   ITALIAN   15/20   ♟♟

120 W. 55th St. (Sixth & Seventh Aves.), 10019
265-3636, *Lunch Mon.-Sat., Dinner nightly,* $$$

At this colorful and fun son-of-Le-Cirque, designer Adam Tihany played the circus theme to the hilt: panels of red-and-yellow cloth evoke a circus tent; Calder-like metal monkeys and clowns gambol overhead; an aerialist's ladder swoops over the bar. Brothers Mario, Marco and Mauro Maccioni learned how to run a tight ship from their father, Le Cirque 2000 owner Sirio Maccioni. But it's Sirio's wife, Egidiana, who influenced such dishes as "ravioli di mamma Egi" ravioli (spinach and sheep's-milk ricotta in a butter-sage sauce). In addition to homemade pastas, you can start with a thin-crusted pizza or such appetizers as beef carpaccio with an aromatic herb crust. Entrées range from a rich Tuscan fish soup and savory herb-and-pepper-crusted tuna to a lamb T-bone steak. Almost as show-stopping as the multimillion-dollar decor are the desserts.

PALIO   ITALIAN   15/20   ♟♟

151 W. 51st (Sixth & Seventh Aves.), 10019
245-4850, *Lunch Mon.-Fri., Dinner Mon.-Sat.,* $$$$

If you want to impress business clients, start in the bar, where there's a huge mural depicting the famous Siennese racing festival painted by Sandro Chia, a Florentine artist whose work hangs in the Museum of Modern Art. This dramatic two-level restaurant in the Equitable Center serves the simple yet superb cuisine from the northeast of Italy. The breadsticks are fabulous, as are the homemade pastas—pumpkin-stuffed tortelloni tossed in melted butter and sprinkled with grated Parmesan and crumbled amaretti, lobster ravioli or seafood ragout with garlic-kissed potatoes. The pre-theater menu is a reasonable—for this stunning setting—$45 per person.

PATSY'S   ITALIAN   12/20

236 W. 56th St. (Broadway & Eighth Ave.), 10019
247-3491, *Lunch & Dinner daily, $$$$*

🅰 ☎

In the heart of the theater district, this respected old-world
Italian may be showing its age. Still, it's fed everyone from
Sinatra to Limbaugh, and serves steaks, pastas and all the old-
Italian favorites for the pre- and post-theater crowd.

PETROSSIAN   CAVIAR/FRENCH   15/20

182 W. 58th St. (Seventh Ave.), 10019
245-2214, *Lunch & Dinner daily, Brunch Sat.-Sun., $$$$*

💳 💳 💳 💳 ☎ 🍴

Celebrating? Petrossian serves caviar, foie gras and smoked
salmon in this small art-deco dining room decorated with
etched Erté mirrors and Lalique appointments. True aficionados of those fragile fish eggs enjoy them au naturel, without
chopped onions, eggs or sour cream. The same goes for the
salmon and the foie gras. You can order a $35 three-course
menu or splurge on a $165 tasting that can keep two people
happy with not only caviar, but such Petrossian delicacies as
smoked eel, smoked sturgeon, smoked-salmon beggar's purses
filled with salmon tartare, and foie gras in pastry. Other dishes
are French with Russian touches: borscht with and pirozkis,
baked monkfish wrapped in bacon and sautéed loin of Arctic
venison with wild mushrooms and juniper berry sauce.

THE RAINBOW ROOM   NO RATING

30 Rockefeller Plaza, 65th Fl. (49th & 50th Sts.), 100209
632-5100

As we went to press, this fabulous 1930s art-deco penthouse
palace with its fabulous city-skyline views, had been restored to
its former splendor but was about to close, having been sold to
the Cipriani family of Harry's Bar, Cipriani Downtown and
Cipriani Wall Street fame. Rumor has it that they're going to
open a Harry's Bar-type restaurant where the supper club once
was, and use the former cabaret for private parties. Stay tuned.

RAPHAËL   FRENCH   14/20

33 W. 54th St. (Fifth & Sixth Aves.), 10019
582-8993, *Lunch Mon.-Fri., Dinner Mon.-Sat., $$$$*

💳 💳 💳 💳 ☎ 🍴 🚶 🖥

With its lovely garden and exposed wood beams, this
romantic little hideaway resembles more a French country
home than a restaurant. One wall is brick with a cozy fireplace,
while the other has a mural of vineyards. Chef Gavin Citrone
fine-tunes French classics with exotic touches. Consider roasted foie gras with pineapple-tomato jam and carrot bouillon,
wild striped bass with mussels, clams and burnt orange saffron
nage and crackling breast of duck with lentils, walnuts and
oven-roasted pears. There are several prix-fixe menus, includ-

ing a pre-theater offering for a reasonable $32, and an extensive—mostly French—wine list.

THE REDEYE GRILL   SEAFOOD/NEW AMERICAN   13/20

890 Seventh Ave. (56th St.), 10019
541-9000, *Lunch & Dinner daily, Brunch Sat.-Sun., $$$*

Across the street from Carnegie Hall, this restaurant may be called the "Home of the Dancing Shrimp," but the "dancing shrimp"—two slowly revolving six-foot bronze-colored statues—are the least whimsical aspect of David Rockwell's campy design. You're more likely to notice the murals of frolicky nudes which wrap the 15-foot-high columns, or the lavish display of smoked fish—from tequila-, jalapeño- and orange-flavored smoked salmon, to smoked sable and chub. We like the accompanying cold salads—eggplant and peppers, celery root remoulade, orange and fennel—the grilled shrimp Louis and the luscious banana-cream pie. There's live jazz most evenings and during Sunday brunch.

REMI   ITALIAN   14/20

145 W. 53rd St. (Sixth & Seventh Aves.), 10019
581-4242, *Lunch Mon.-Fri., Dinner nightly, $$$*

The very model of a modern Italian restaurant thanks to a look created by co-owner (and architect/designer) Adam Tihany. The gorgeous covered-atrium dining room is a favorite with the power-lunch bunch (celebs included). There is also solid, mostly modern Venetian cuisine prepared by co-owner and chef Francesco Antonnuci. Good bets: ravioli Marco Polo filled with fresh tuna and ginger served in a light tomato sauce; fusilli with capers, olives, tomatoes and hot peppers; garganelli with balsamic sauce and Coho salmon; seared tuna served over oven-dried tomatoes and spinach; and calf's liver sautéed with sweet-and-sour white onions and polenta. Gather a party of 16 and dine at the chef's table in the kitchen.

RENÉ PUJOL   FRENCH   13/20

321 W. 51st St. (Eighth & Ninth Aves.), 10019
246-3023, *Lunch & Dinner Mon.-Sat., $$$*

For nearly 30 years, this small, charming family-run bistro has attracted hordes of theatergoers looking for not-too-too-expensive, authentic French food. Chef Claude Franques (husband of Pujol's daughter, Nicole, who presides over the dining room) has lightened the menu. The $38 prix-fixe dinner offers many choices (some at additional cost) including such starters as warm lobster salad and garlic sausage with diced potatoes, entrées such as Dover sole or herb-crusted chicken, and finishing with desserts including a caramelized coconut custard with coconut sorbet. The wine list has a comprehensive French assortment at reasonable prices.

RUSSIAN SAMOVAR   RUSSIAN   12/20

256 W. 52nd St. (Broadway & Eighth Ave.), 10019
757-0168, Lunch Tues-.Sat., Dinner nightly, $$

If you speak Russian, you'll fit right in at this rowdy haunt of New York's Russian-émigré elite. The decor has a few old-country touches, a pianist plays nightly, and the Russian food from borscht, smoked salmon with CD-sized blinis and zakuski, to shashlik is pretty good. But the raison d'être here is the party atmosphere. After a few vodkas, you'll understand.

SAN DOMENICO   ITALIAN   16/20

240 Central Park South (Columbus Circle), 10019
265-5959, Lunch Mon.-Fri., Dinner nightly, $$$

Since 1988, San Domenico has been an upscale spot with aristocratic cooking and a refined ambience. Chef Odette Fada, who trained under Gianfranco Vissani in Italy, does justice to the restaurant's old favorites. For example, a soft egg yolk nestled inside a pasta casing with hazelnut butter—one incision and the yolk infuses the entire dish. Other laudable choices include her braised octopus with tomatoes and peppers, raviolini filled with sea urchin, veal medallions with sweetbreads and lamb chops with a mushroom-and-potato napoleon. On the seasonal truffle menu, you pay for your truffles by the gram ($5 a gram at last count). The wine list includes some superb (but not inexpensive) out-of-the-way Italian wines.

SARDI'S   CONTINENTAL   13/20

234 W 44th St. (Broadway & Eighth St.), 10036
221-8444, Lunch & Dinner Tues.-Sun., $$

A theater-district legend for 73 years, Sardi's honors its Broadway clientele in the over 1000 caricatures covering the walls. The main dining room, done in dark burgundy with glittering chandeliers, is comfortable; the upstairs rooms are open to actors (just show your equity card). The updated Continental fare includes everything from a tasting of fresh oysters, clams and shrimp, and sautéed salmon with spinach to juicy prime rib. Thursdays and Fridays, there are jazz and cabaret performances. Call Ticketmaster and you can book a $41.50 prix-fixe dinner at Sardi's along with theater tickets.

THE SEAGRILL   SEAFOOD/NEW AMERICAN   13/20

19 W. 49th St. (Rockefeller Center), 10020
332-7610, Lunch Mon.-Fri., Dinner Mon.-Sat., $$$

This elegant Rockefeller Center restaurant boasts a perfect view of the ice-skaters in winter; in summer, when the ice rink gives way to a garden, guests can dine al fresco. Chef Edward Brown zests the daily-changing menu with such specialties as grilled fresh sardines with red onion confit and sherry vinegar glaze, scallops with truffle-mashed potatoes and wild chervil, and grilled Arctic char with sautéed foie gras, purple potato purée and apple juice broth. Meat-eaters can get a hefty sirloin steak with a side of portobello "fries." There is a reasonably priced all-American wine list, a $39 pre-theater prix-fixe dinner, and a $15 discount on parking after 5 p.m. in the Rockefeller Center garage, good for seven hours.

SHAAN   INDIAN   14/20

57 W. 48th St. (Fifth & Sixth Aves.), 10036
977-8400, *Lunch & Dinner daily, $$$*

Shirtsleeves may be today's dining attire for business nabobs, especially at steakhouses, but Shaan, the Indian word for pride, feels a bit grand for such informality. Luxurious banquettes, striking ethnic tapestries, romantic lighting and well-spaced tables argue for a jacket if management does not. Shaan's kitchen, which produces a generous all-you-can-eat luncheon buffet, is capable of uncommon refinement at dinner. Clay-oven tandoors send forth lobster, rack and whole leg of lamb, and one of the most savory quail dishes of our time. If asked, solicitous servers may indicate a few "grandmother" dishes such as flour puffs stuffed with potatoes, chickpeas, and sprouted beans, topped with tamarind and mint sauce, or potato patties stuffed with minced lamb.

TAPIKA   SOUTHWESTERN   14/20

950 Eighth Ave. (56th St.), 10019
397-3737, *Lunch Mon.-Fri., Dinner nightly, $$$*

The design is David Rockwell's homage to cowboy culture: rusted-steel light fixtures with cut-out talismans hang from the ceiling; a stylized picket fence frames the windows; and a "picture" of woven wheat backed by cobalt blue glass dominates the far wall. Chef David Walzog's rendition of Southwestern cuisine is equally artistic, and includes such dishes as a pulled-chicken burrito with lime-cabbage slaw, roasted lemon-marinated shrimp with a tomato-Mascarpone chalupa and fresh corn sauce, a roasted venison chop with chayote salsa, and pan-roasted Atlantic salmon with whole wheat noodles.

TORRE DI PISA   ITALIAN   14/20

19 W. 44th St. (Fifth & Sixth Aves.), 10036
398-4400, *Lunch Mon.-Fri., Dinner Mon.-Sat., $$$*

We love the whimsical David Rockwell design: a giant clock face in the colorful dining room, and a receding row of columns that evoke De Chirico. To start, nibble on deep fried artichoke hearts and cardoons with a generous shaving of Parmesan. Move on to spaghetti with broccoli rabe, roasted garlic and pancetta, or chicken-and-sundried-tomato ravioli. Other stand-outs include grilled beef paillard brushed with

Dijon mustard, sautéed chicken breast with roasted potatoes and calf's liver grilled with caramelized onions and soft polenta. The chocolate-mousse tower is served slightly at an angle, like the restaurant's leaning-tower namesake.

'21' CLUB   AMERICAN   15/20

21 W. 52nd St. (Fifth & Sixth Aves.), 10019
582-7200, *Lunch Mon.-Fri., Dinner Mon.-Sat., $$$$*

After an $8-million burnishing, this 76-old hospitality showplace can knock anyone's socks off. The storied setting, A-list patrons, warm and cosseting service, long wine list and a great blend of '21' classic dishes with creative contemporary cuisine make this a must-experience stop in New York. Most fun of all, and most expensive ($400 per person), is the Chef's Table Tasting, a candlelit dinner in the historic wine cellar that repeatedly eluded government raiders during Prohibition. However, '21' has excellent value (under $30) prix-fixe menus at lunch and before and after the theater. The à la carte menu embraces vintage favorites newly restored to their original recipes, from chicken hash to grilled Dover sole and the '21' burger. Along with heating up such retro practices as the flambé, '21 is snaring a new generation clientele with the likes of seared peppered tuna with a shrimp-and-avocado roll. There is also a Lounge menu for those seeking a snack with their cocktail or a post-prandial cigar and brandy. Say hello to "The Rev," perhaps Manhattan's most amusing men's room attendant.

ZEN PALATE   VEGETARIAN   10/20

663 Ninth Ave. (46th St.), 10036
582-1669, *Lunch Mon.-Sat., Dinner nightly, $*

The New Age atmosphere at these sleek, serene vegetarian gourmet shop/restaurants make you feel as if you've entered another reality. But no dish is as weird as it may sound, and most taste just fine. The scallion pancakes are less greasy than in ordinary Chinese restaurants. Entrées have such exotic names as "Shredded Melody" (shredded soy gluten sautéed with celery, carrots and pine nuts in a spicy-and-sweet sauce) and "Rose Petals" (soy pasta in a sweet rice-ginger sauce with vegetables). The noodle and rice dishes are exemplary, and the non-dairy banana pie tastes surprisingly rich. **Also at 34 E. Union Square (16th St.) 614-9345.**

AND ALSO...

ADRIENNE   NEW AMERICAN

The Peninsula Hotel, 700 Fifth Ave. (55th St.), 10019
903-3918, *Breakfast, Lunch & Dinner daily, Brunch Sun.,* $$$$

As we went to press, the posh Peninsula Hotel had just
reopened after a complete renovation. So did the Peninsula's
sophisticated restaurant overlooking Fifth Avenue. Using
organic and locally farmed ingredients, chef John Rees prepares such seasonally changing specialties as Hudson Valley
foie gras on duck hash, salmon cannelloni on sugar snap peas
with ginger-Champagne sauce, seared squab with char-siu glaze
and crispy ahi tuna in rice paper with seaweed salad and chive-
potato purée.

AMERICAN FESTIVAL CAFÉ   AMERICAN

20 W. 50th St. (Rockefeller Center), 10020
246-6699, *Breakfast, Lunch & Dinner daily,* $$$

Sit out in the garden in the summer, watch the skaters in
winter; you can even have "breakfast with Santa" during the
holidays at this Rockefeller tourist spot. The fare is strictly for
the tourists too: steaks and hamburgers, bountiful salads and
daily-changing regional specialties. Lots of microbrews and
wines by the glass to enjoy while writing that postcard home.

BAY LEAF BRASSERIE   INDIAN

49 W. 56th St. (Fifth & Sixth Aves.), 10019
957-1818, *Lunch & Dinner daily,* $$

This handsome midtown spot looks like a brasserie but
smells like an Indian restaurant—which it is. The décor and
service are better than you'll find in most of the Indian restaurants that line Sixth Street. Lunch is the best meal here, when
the $13.95 buffet offers a dozen dishes, from salads to tandoori
chicken. The Bay Leaf does particularly well with vegetables—
puréed eggplant and onions, cauliflower with spinach and ginger, and kidney beans with tomatoes.

FLUTE   CHAMPAGNE BAR/GOURMET BAR FOOD

205 W. 54th St. (Broadway & Seventh Ave.), 10019
265-5169, *Dinner Mon.-Sat., $$$$*

Yes another new Champagne bar, this time in a sexy antique-filled art-deco subterranean spot that was once a speakeasy. To go with the over 100 different Champagnes (many by the glass) are caviar, of course, plus Scottish smoked salmon, foie gras, a variety of Vietnamese spring rolls and Maison du Chocolat bonbons.

FRICO BAR RESTAURANT   ITALIAN

402 W. 43rd St. (Ninth Ave), 10036
564-7272, *Lunch Mon.-Fri., Dinner nightly, $$$*

Joe Bastianich, son of Felidia's Lidia Bastianich, runs this casual theater-district Italian, where you can snack pre-theater on fricos, crisp little cheese pancakes folded around potatoes and onions, or dine leisurely on the likes of herb-cured seared tuna, Istrian pasta pillows stuffed with cheese, raisins and citrus, or sautéed veal with wild mushrooms and white wine. The patio is lovely in good weather.

LA VINERIA   ITALIAN

19 W. 55th St. (Fifth & Sixth Aves.), 10019
247-3400, *Lunch Mon.-Sat., Dinner nightly, $$*

They've brought in a pizza "maestro" from Sorrento to man the brick oven at this casual Italian restaurant. In addition to crisp-crusted pizzas, are such pastas as penne with wild mushrooms and garlic and pappardelle with duck ragout, and entrées including pistachio-herb-crusted rack of lamb and seafood stew. They bake their own breads and pastries, which are also available throughout the day at the adjoining **Caffé del Corso**.

SAM'S   AMERICAN

263 W. 45th St. (Broadway & Eighth Ave.), 10045
719-5416, *Lunch & Dinner daily, Brunch Sun., $*

Broadway stars may dine further uptown, but members of the chorus come to this long-running (since 1920) theater district favorite. The food is straightforward—everything from a burger to linguini Sinatra to Danish baby back ribs to grilled tuna or a T-bone steak—and the prices are right. Plus, you can't beat the energy, especially when there's live music late in the evenings.

UPPER EAST SIDE

DINING

All phone numbers are (212) unless otherwise indicated

ATLANTIC GRILL   SEAFOOD   13/20

1341 Third Ave. (76th & 77th Sts.), 10021
988-9200, *Lunch Mon.-Sat., Dinner nightly, Brunch Sun., $$$*

Atlantic Grill follows the identical formula as its sibling restaurants, Blue Water Grill and Ocean Grill: fashionable settings, au courant crowds and simply prepared fruits of the sea. This new spot has made quite a splash in the neighborhood, and reservations are hard to get. The kitchen is especially adept at frying, evidenced by the superbly crisp lobster spring roll. While the grilled fish menu is largely conventional, the kitchen's execution is solid, and the wood-burning grill imparts a wonderful—almost meaty—flavor. You can also order a finely grilled filet mignon and a textbook rendition of roasted chicken.

AUREOLE   NEW AMERICAN   17/20

34 E. 61st St. (Madison & Park Aves.), 10021
319-1660, *Lunch Mon.-Fri, Dinner Mon.-Sat., $$$$*

Chef/owner Charlie Palmer's New American cuisine continues to dazzle at this gorgeous restaurant. Set on two floors of an elegantly converted brownstone, the flower-filled dining room is decorated with a stunning bas-relief frieze of birds flying; seating upstairs affords an atrium-like view of the action below. We find Palmer's fare inspired and quite lusty, with such inviting starters as spiced shrimp and sweet-pea risotto, oak-smoked salmon with "velvet blini" and sautéed foie gras with roasted apples. Entrées range from caramelized pheasant with chanterelles, and wood-grilled lobster and citrus salad, to simple oak-grilled meats, fish and poultry. And as our rating suggests, the list of can't-miss dishes goes on and on, right down to the desserts—toasted almond galette with double-roasted anjou pear—which can be dauntingly architectural. The distinguished wine list is a mix of American and European vintages in all price ranges. Relatively speaking, the $19.99 prix-fixe lunch available after 2 p.m. is a bargain.

BOLIVAR   LATIN AMERICAN   13/20

206 E. 60th St. (Second & Third Aves.), 10022
838-0440, *Lunch & Dinner Daily, $$*

Those who remember Arizona 206 and its kinetic Southwestern fare might be disappointed to learn it has been converted to a South American grill, but fans of greater value will appreciate Bolivar. Like the previous restaurant, the dining room suggests an adobe with cave-like stucco walls, tile floors, desert tones and bleached wood tables. What has changed is the food—now, a mix of refreshing ceviches and char-grilled meats. Inattention to seasonings debases some otherwise good preparations, but most of the fare is straightforward and flavorful. Skip the bland piqueos (tapas-style appetizers) and head for the assertively dressed salads, restorative soups and such entrées as pepper-dusted chicken, boneless trout, calf's liver and double cut pork chops, all $15 and under.

BUSBY'S   NEW AMERICAN   11/20

45 E. 92nd St. (Madison Ave.), 10128
360-7373, *Lunch & Dinner daily, Brunch Sun.*, $$

The neighbors in Carnegie Hill depend on this casual, American-style bistro with a turn-of-the-century feel. Stick with the specials: a grilled half-chicken with Pommery mustard sauce and straw potatoes, a grilled turkey breast sandwich on toasted Tuscan bread with sun-dried tomato mayonnaise, and curried lentils.

BUTTERFIELD 81   NEW AMERICAN   13/20   ♟

168-170 E. 81st St., (Third & Lexington Aves.), 10028
288-2700, *Dinner nightly, Brunch Sat.-Sun.*, $$$$

Casual elegance greets you at this neighborhoody (in a very expensive neighborhood) "Old New York" bistro. The tables are tightly packed, the décor a soothing combination of dark-wood paneling and deep burgundy. The dishes are elaborate and many are grilled over a wood fire, while some are prepared with meat-stock- or cream-based sauces. The overall effect is fare that is flavorful and light (though sometimes a bit salty). The butternut squash agnolotti with smoked duck and sage in a Parmesan broth was delicate and savory, as was the crispy-skinned roasted sea bass with red-lentil mash. Creamy polenta was a soft cushion for the braised lamb shank. Among the desserts, the fig tart is a must. The extensive wine list begins at $38. Look hard in the dark dining room and you may glimpse some faces you recognize from the society page.

CAFÉ BOULUD   FRENCH   16/20   ♟♟

20 E. 76th St. (Madison & Fifth Aves.), 10021
772-2600, *Lunch Tues.-Sat., Dinner nightly*, $$$$

We admire Daniel Boulud and his prodigious talent, but his notion of a café is akin to Stephen Sondheim's notion of a Sunday in the park. No, Café Boulud doesn't fit any acceptable definition of a café and the sensational food has little to do with bistro fare. It starts with the freshest and finest ingredients and involves labor-intensive precision in preparation, as in the "simple" appetizer of a dozen exceptional garden vegetables, sliced and diced and infused with basil, ginger and olive oil. Chef Boulud's notion of café mostly has to do with nostalgia and décor. With the move of his flagship Daniel to Le Cirque's old digs on East 65th Street, Daniel quickly remodeled this dining room, bringing the bar into the room, opening up the partitions and toning down the look with lots of beige, browns and grays. (It's not really cheerful, nor is it helped by the mahogany bar and wall.) He named it after a turn-of-the-century café his family owned on the outskirts of Lyon, but the Old-World menu there surely had nothing to do with this brilliant tour-de-force menu. Organized in four sections ("muses"), it features classic French dishes, seasonal dishes, vegetarian dishes and specialties from different parts of the world. Included are some of Boulud's signature dishes such as paupiette of sea bass in a crisp potato shell with red wine. What makes Café Boulud even more attractive, is that the food-and-wine prices are about a third that of those at his flagship restaurant.

CAFÉ CROCODILE   MEDITERRANEAN   12/20

354 E. 74th St. (First & Second Aves.), 10021
249-6619, Dinner Mon.-Sat., $$

A

This neighborhood bistro on the ground floor of an Upper East Side townhouse, run by Andrée and Charlie Abramoff, who both grew up in Egypt, serves up dishes from nearly every country that borders the Mediterranean. Dried flowers, large mirrors with antique frames and a trompe l'oeil scene of Provence contribute to the cozy, laid-back atmosphere. The menu changes monthly, save for a few staple dishes such as the cassoulet, tuna steak and the Moroccan couscous. Popular dishes include rack of lamb, smoked haddock and crème brûlée.

CAFÉ PIERRE   FRENCH/NEW AMERICAN   13/20

Hotel Pierre, 2 E. 61st St. (Fifth Ave.), 10021
940-8185, Breakfast, Lunch & Dinner daily, Brunch Sun., $$$$

A ☎ ♥ ▮ ⚘

The gilt trim is dazzling in this plush, baroque spot set in one of New York's landmark (and best) hotels. The room is long and sleek, with beige, gold-trimmed walls, attentive waiters gliding among the elegantly set tables and piano music in the evenings. Lunch is more popular than dinner, when local power moguls drop in. The seasonally changing menu features a few heart-healthy "alternative cuisine" selections, along with such standards as lobster bisque, chicken pot pie, Dover sole and tiramisu wrapped in a chocolate wafer. The excellent wine list features more than 350 well-chosen wines. The less formal **Rotunda** serves a lighter menu and high tea.

THE CARLYLE RESTAURANT   FRENCH/CONTINENTAL   14/20

The Carlyle Hotel, 35 E. 76th St. (Madison Ave.), 10021
744-1600, *Breakfast, Lunch & Dinner daily, $$$$*

This is perhaps what everyone thinks of in terms of elegant hotel dining: rich and refined decor and very professional and efficient service. It is, after all, part of a hotel that caters to the rich and famous. It is also not just a place for dinner. The morning buffet is laden with fruit, all kinds of breads, muffins, rolls, scrambled eggs and so on, and there's a luncheon buffet as well. Starters might include a rich terrine of fresh foie gras, a variety of salads, rack of lamb, roast half chicken with herbed mashed potatoes, or a grilled veal tenderloin with wild mushrooms. We love the chocolate soufflé. The extensive wine list has mostly French and American selections; prices range from moderate to expensive.

COCO PAZZO   ITALIAN   14/20

23 E. 74th St. (Madison & Fifth Aves.), 10021
794-0205, *Lunch & Dinner daily, Brunch Sun., $$$*

With all the Coco Pazzos Pino Luongo keeps adding to his restaurant plate (Chicago among them), it's a wonder that the original runs so smoothly. Yet this handsome restaurant continues to provide the très trendy East Side clientele with good Tuscan fare. The emphasis is on simply prepared dishes: grilled portobello mushroom caps; spaghetti with clams; grilled rib-eye steak; whole fish; roasted with fresh herbs and lemon. The portions here are large, and there is a $24.50 Sunday brunch. Choose from lots of Italian wine selections, but few bargains.

CONTRAPUNTO   ITALIAN   12/20

200 E. 60th St. (Third Ave.), 10022
751-8616, *Lunch & Dinner daily, $$*

Contrapunto is always crowded with Bloomies shoppers and Third Avenue moviegoers. The pace in this white-on-white space with its open kitchen can get hectic, but it is still comfortable. Simpler is better here. Try the grilled coriander-crusted quail to start, or such pastas as angel hair with sun-dried tomatoes and jalapeños or spinach pappardelle with chicken. Also find roasted, grilled and sautéed meats and fish, including mint-infused grilled leg of lamb.

DEMARCHELIER   FRENCH   13/20

50 E. 86th (Madison & Park Aves.), 10028
249-6300, *Lunch & Dinner daily, $$$*

A cozy French bistro on the Upper East Side, authentic right down to the lace curtains, tightly spaced tables and tilted-down mirrors so that people facing the wall won't miss the action—and the occasional attitude. Start with onion soup or a salad dressed with a bracing French vinaigrette made with grainy Dijon mustard, then move on to steak frites, roasted duck, rack of lamb, or, on Fridays, choucroute.

DESTINEÉ   FRENCH   16/20 ♔♔

134 E. 61st St.(Lexington & Park Aves.), 10021
888-1220, *Lunch & Dinner Mon.-Sat.*, $$$$
A ☎ 🕏

Some popular restaurants are so quiet about it that they are almost stealth stops, filling daily with regulars who try to keep them for themselves. Such a restaurant is this polished performer with a soft, romantic look, a discerning clientele and prix-fixed meals of significant value. Chef/partner Jean-Yves Schillinger keeps flavors coming in creative new combinations. Hand-cut, herbed-salmon tartare is surrounded by sculpted cucumbers and garnished with a quail egg and caviar. Cucumber, apple and curry star in a marinade for herring chartreuse, presented with horseradish cream. One of New York's largest crème brûlées has lime and honey accents, and Destinee's potential to surprise is evident in the carpaccio of pineapple with Szechwan pepper, lemon sorbet and mint.

ELI'S   ITALIAN   13/20 ♔

1621 Second Ave. (84th & 5th Sts.), 10028
772-2242, *Dinner nightly*, $$$
A ☎

Noisy but fun, this neighborhood gathering spot (in a very upscale neighborhood) is great for people watching. Eli's gets its fair share of celebrities, especially the big-name television types. The wait for a table can be endless, but the room is animated and welcoming, encircled by globe lights, wood paneling and wainscoting—quintessential Upper East Side chic. Think of Eli's as an Elaine's with good food: shrimp-and-white-bean salad; spaghetti and veal every which way. The fish varies from day to day, and is cooked with respect, especially the simple Dover sole. Desserts fare better than in the usual Italian restaurant; if they've baked a lemon tart that day, go for it.

EMILY'S   SOUL FOOD/SOUTHERN   12/20

1325 Fifth Ave. (111th St.), 10029
996-1212, *Breakfast & Lunch Mon.-Fri., Dinner nightly, Brunch Sat.-Sun.*, $
A

Emily's is a place for hungry New Yorkers looking for either a satisfying breakfast or a real, rib-sticking dinner. How about starting the day with thick homemade waffles topped with maple syrup and Southern-fried chicken? While breakfasts are good, dinner is king here: juicy fried chicken; tangy barbecued chicken; barbecued baby back ribs; pan-fried catfish with zesty okra. The side dishes are good here also, including crunchy fried plantains, black-eyed peas, cheesy macaroni and coleslaw. Save room for the luscious sweet-potato pie. There is a full bar and live music Thursday and Saturday nights.

ERMINIA   ITALIAN   13/20

250 E. 83rd St. (Second & Third Aves.), 10028
879-4284, Dinner Mon.-Sat. (check for summer closing), $$$

Restaurants don't come much more romantic: a candlelit room with a dozen tables, walls of exposed brick and a wood fire. The specialties are pastas and grilled foods: fresh-made mozzarella with roasted peppers and basil; orecchiette with a savory mix of sausage and broccoli; pappardelle wrapped in a buttery ricotta-cheese sauce; vermicelli pizzaiola bursting with the flavors of garlic, capers, tomato and olives. Various skewers—meat, poultry, shellfish—are carefully mesquite-grilled. For dessert, consider the tartufo, the chocolate mousse or the luscious deep-fried apples. Jackets are required.

ETATS-UNIS   FRENCH/NEW AMERICAN   15/20

242 E. 81st St. (Second Ave.), 10028
517-8826, Dinner Mon.-Sat., $$$

The setting may be plain—a storefront with white plaster walls—but the kitchen consistently delivers cuisine as fine as what's served in some of the most celebrated places in town. Owners Tom and Jonathan Rapp call themselves "cooks" rather than "chefs," but they come up with such innovative dishes as baked oysters with leeks purée or seared scallops with poached quince and roasted pumpkin to start, and pork or turkey cooked with apples, cabbage and smoked chili, and roasted wild-striped bass with long-cooked peppers, onions and eggplant as main courses. The fresh fruit cobblers and crisps are homey desserts. The mostly French wine list is well chosen and moderately priced, the service friendly and efficient. Since this place is a real "find," make reservations long in advance.

FERRIER   FRENCH   13/20

29 E. 65th St. (Madison & Park Aves.), 10021
772-9000, Lunch & Dinner daily, $$$

This casual but oh-so-chic bistro, always packed with a young, hip crowd, emphasizes substance over style, though it handles both well. The service is straightforward, not florid, and the tables crowded together seem intimate, not intimidating. Familiar dishes are prepared with élan: leeks vinaigrette, rich leek-and-potato soup, chunky pork terrine, steak frites and rack of lamb. Desserts are what you might expect: tarte tatin, crème brûlée and profiteroles. At lunchtime, Park Avenue executives vie for tables with Madison Avenue shoppers, and in summer, the outdoor tables are much in demand.

GERTRUDE'S   NEW AMERICAN   16/20   ♟♟

33 E. 61st. St. (Madison & Park Aves.), 10022
888-9127, *Lunch Mon.-Sat., Dinner nightly, $$$$*

A ⫯ 🏃

Named for Gertrude Stein, this chic Upper East Sider with its conservative English decor, features the earthy French cuisine of Laurent Manrique, the Gascon native who last wowed us at the Waldorf's Peacock Alley. His terrine is as lusty as they come, with tastes of foie gras, cured duck and white beans. Even more intense are the foie-gras-filled ravioli. Other delights on the seasonally changing menu might include grilled quail and roasted monkfish on the bone in the summer, and in winter, such specials as seared tuna with truffle vinaigrette and monkfish with seffron sauce.

HARRY CIPRIANI   ITALIAN   15/20   ♟♟

Sherry Netherland Hotel, 781 Fifth Ave. (59th & 60th Sts.), 10022
753-5566, *Breakfast, Lunch & Dinner daily, $$$$*

A ☎ ⫯

The Ciprianis have opened restaurants in SoHo and Wall Street, with more on the way, but this elegant setting is favored by society dames and Italian Italians—which is appropriate for this Hemingway-esque kin to the famed Harry's Bar in Venice. The cuisine remains some of the most authentically Italian in New York, especially the fine pastas (green tagliolini baked with ham) and the myriad risotti. Most of the fish and meat offerings (calf's liver Venetian-style) lead up nicely to some outstanding desserts. For starters order a peach-and-Champagne Bellini—it was invented in Harry's Bar in Venice. Service is grand European and prices are otherworldly.

HYOTAN-NIPPON   JAPANESE   11/20

119 E. 59th St. (Park & Lexington Aves.), 10022
751-7690, *Lunch Mon.-Fri., Dinner Sun.-Fri., $$*

[VISA] [MasterCard] [Diner's Club] [💳] ❤

They cater to American tastes—which means they offer low-cal and broiled dishes along with performing chefs. Like Kabuki actors in the throes of a colorful dance, the chefs are always busy cooking, broiling, tempura-frying or cutting sashimi. An enormous, amoebae-shaped wooden counter dominates the dining room, along with a large tank of lobsters. The freshly rolled-and-cut soba noodles are a must; in fact, Hyotan was one of the first authentic soba restaurants in New York. Order sushi, or start with chicken yakitori or char-grilled eggplant, then move on to teriyaki, sukiyaki or don-buri dishes, steaming rice with, say, chicken, egg and vegetables.

IL VALLETTO   ITALIAN   11/20

133 E. 61st St. (Lexington & Park Aves.), 10021
838-3939, *Lunch Mon.-Fri., Dinner Mon.-Sat., $$$*

A

Sit in the elegant little dining room just beyond the bar; it's cozier than the larger front room which can be a bit noisy. The bruschetta piled with garlicky diced tomatoes, basil and herbs, remains one of the best starters. Order pasta tossed with diced tomatoes, zucchini, eggplant and fresh basil or with garlicky white-clam sauce. While not every entrée is a winner (choose from the usual veal, chicken and fish dishes), the sautéed zucchini that accompanies them is first-rate. Desserts include the likes of berries in season and zabaglione. The Italian and French wine list is a bit on the expensive side.

JO JO   FRENCH   16/20   🍴🍴

160 E. 64th St. (Lexington & Third Aves.), 10021
223-5656, *Lunch Mon.-Fri., Dinner Mon.-Sat., $$$$*

Expect a wait at the tiny, cramped bar at this first restaurant in superchef Jean-Georges Vongerichten's growing culinary empire (which includes multiple Vongs, and Jean Georges). The native of Alsace is a master of cooking with Asian spices, infused oils, vegetable juices and exotic vinaigrettes. Using a minimum of butter, cream and flour, he creates the most vivid food you will ever find in a place that is supposedly nothing more than a simple bistro. The peripatetic Vongerichten rarely cooks here, but the dishes remain of his style and up to his standards. Start with such transcendent offerings as a goat-cheese-and-potato terrine or porcini grilled with thyme and eggplant caviar. Entrées might include slowly-baked salmon with truffle-mashed potatoes, duck roasted with figs, port wine and glazed turnips, and steamed black bass with cumin-scented carrot confit. Desserts include a rich Valrhona chocolate cake. Book downstairs to experience the bustle, upstairs for some degree of calm.

L'ABSINTHE   FRENCH   14/20   🍴

227 E. 67th St. (Second & Third Aves.), 10021
794-4950, *Lunch & Dinner daily, Brunch Sat.-Sun., $$$*

A

You could be in a turn-of-the-century Parisian brasserie when you enter this quasi-art-deco setting with its zinc bar, etched glass, old chandeliers, wainscoting and gilt-framed mirrors. Chef/co-owner Jean-Michel Bergougnoux prepares classic French cuisine bourgeoise—Beaujolais-style warm poached sausage with potatoes and lentils, slow-braised lean beef and cassoulet—along with such contemporary dishes as pan-seared yellowfin tuna steak in a crispy potato galette. The shellfish tray fit for three or four people is a good starter. The thin, crusty apple tart is glorious, and the sound French-American wine list is reasonably priced.

LA FOURCHETTE   FRENCH   14/20   🍴

1608 First Ave. (83rd & 84th Sts.) 10128
249-5924, *Dinner nightly, Brunch Sat.-Sun., $$$$*

We like young chefs who clearly display their ambitions. In exchange, we expect them to fulfill our expectations sooner or later. Still in his twenties, the Franco-American Marc Murphy does not want to wait to fly First Class on his own. To showcase his talents, he has established this sumptuous tiered dining room with a dream garden in the back. The well-polished patrons appreciating the sheer elegance of La Fourchette contribute to the refined atmosphere. But though Murphy is not stingy with rich ingredients, and his concepts are often brilliant, he sometimes falls a tad short of delivering the gastronomic Nirvana one is expecting. A few too many seconds of cooking time for the scallops, for example, and they lose something in their combination with bone marrow. The Chilean sea bass—already rich—is not necessarily enhanced by its pairing with foie gras. On the other hand, the cabbage-leaf-swathed squab is well-matched with its truffle sauce, and the compote of onion fares well with the roasted chicken. We predict that with a bit more experience, Murphy may well move into the circle of New York's top chefs. A six course tasting menu is offered for $75. The sommelier Kim Anderson will help you with the good wine list.

LA GOULUE   FRENCH   13/20

746 Madison Ave. (64th & 65th Sts.), 10021
988-8169, *Lunch & Dinner daily, Brunch Sun., $$$*

This turn-of-the-century-looking spot has been serving French bistro fare to a French-cigarette-inhaling, air-kissing crowd since it opened (in another spot) in 1972. The service remains faithfully aloof, and the fare ranges from creamy salt-cod brandade and salmon-tartare appetizers, to Dover sole, steak frites and the signature double-cheese soufflé.

LE REFUGE   FRENCH   14/20

166 E. 82nd St. (Lexington & Third Aves.), 10028
861-4505, *Lunch & Dinner daily, $$$$*

If you are going to the Metropolitan Museum of Art and are thinking about lunch or dinner, reserve here. The food and setting virtually guarantee a pleasant experience, so much so that every time we visit, we ask ourselves why we don't come more often. Situated in an 1868 townhouse with three small flower-and-antique-filled, wood-beam-ceilinged dining rooms, plus a garden patio, the place is indeed a refuge offering country-French charm on the Upper East Side. Chef-owner Pierre Saint-Denis has done a consistently good job since he opened in 1977, and has slowly evolved his cooking. Look for such specials as sea bass with endive and cardomom-citrus broth, leg of lamb with mushrooms, duck or bouillabaisse. If you like chocolate, order the chocolate soufflé cake.

LE RÉGENCE   FRENCH   15/20

Hotel Plaza Athénée, 37 E. 64th St. (Madison & Park Aves.), 10021
606-4647, 734-9100, *Breakfast, Lunch & Dinner daily, $$$$*

This room is indeed fit for a Regent with its glittering crystal chandeliers, gilt-encrusted mirrors and trompe l'oeil sky on the ceiling. Yet as regal as the setting is, it's not intimidating; rather, it is gently tempered to human dimensions "à la Francaise." The food, as well, is princely and served in grand style. Chef Robert Feenie follows the strong tradition of his seasoned French predecessors, and adds his own enlightening preparations. In these surroundings, the $36 three-course prix-fixe lunch is a steal: a velvety celery-root velouté with roasted-garlic froth and shaved truffles; roasted sea bass with a fondue of leeks, baby spinach and a warm balsamic reduction; and a heavenly Valrhona chocolate mousse. For dinner, start with sweet breads and fresh water prawn in a curry caper vinaigrette. The poached Arctic Char in a beurre blanc with artichokes is a delicate preparation cooked rightly. Desserts include a warm bittersweet chocolate tart or the Tahitian vanilla-bean panna cota with saffron infused winter fruits. Composed of seven courses, a tasting menu is offered for $85. The extensive wine list does not neglect affordable wines.

LE VEAU D'OR   FRENCH   11/20

129 E. 60th St. (Park & Lexington Aves.), 10022
838-8133, *Lunch & Dinner Mon.-Sat., Closed Sat. in June & Aug., $$*

This outpost of Paris, opened in 1937, has become an institution, celebrating "la bonne cuisine bourgeoise." A small restaurant, Le Veau d'Or is a complex of alcoves in which every centimeter counts. The current chef continues the restaurant's tradition of pure culinary nostalgia—down-home Parisian cooking from escargots in garlic butter to cassoulet and leg of lamb. If you like tripe and sweetbreads, this is the place to have them. Textbook, too, are the desserts, including a somewhat chalky chocolate mousse. The French and American wines are reasonably priced.

LENOX ROOM   NEW AMERICAN   14/20

1278 Third Ave. (73rd St.) 10021
772-0404, *Dinner nightly, Brunch Sun., $$$$*

The Lenox Room is neither trendsetting nor daring; it's a solid model of a lively and contemporary Upper East Side restaurant catering to sophisticated (and upscale) New Yorkers who dine out regularly. There arc raw bar offerings, such pastas as risotto with goat cheese and pea shoots, and fresh fish including salmon, mahi mahi and tuna. When available, the Asian-style noodles and double-lemon tart are best bets. The somewhat pricey French-American wine list fits the neighborhood and has some good choices as well as some puzzlers.

THE LOBSTER CLUB

NEW AMERICAN   12/20

24 E. 80th St. (Fifth & Madison Aves.) 10021
249-6500, *Lunch & Dinner daily*, $$

If your notion of the perfect Upper East Side afternoon includes a stroll through the Met, you might want to dine at this rustically appointed spin-off of chef/owner Anne Rosenzweig (now defunct) Arcadia. In a cozy former townhouse dominated by low-hanging exposed beams and a fireplace, order Rosenzweig's signature $24.50 lobster club sandwich, which defines her culinary aesthetic: tall on the plate, meticulously assembled between skinny layers of toasted brioche, a bit whimsical in concept, with a studied "lightness" that falls a little light on flavor as well. There are other dishes, including creative renditions of meatloaf and roast chicken, and an affordable wine list. Ask for a table upstairs, where the cathedral ceiling lends the space grandeur and airiness.

LUSARDI'S

ITALIAN   13/20

1494 Second Ave. (77th & 78th Sts.), 10021
249-2020, *Lunch Mon.- Fri., Dinner nightly*, $$$

This sophisticated but friendly neighborhood trattoria produces first-rate Northern Italian fare for a casual but usually well-dressed clientele and the occasional celeb. Good bets: the warm seafood salad, beef carpaccio or eggplant cannelloni. You can count on the pasta and risotto; favorite specials have included fusilli with pesto and risotto with porcini mushrooms. Lusardi's gets top marks for its chicken dishes, and the wine list is impressive for its assortment of luscious Italian dessert wines and fire-like grappas.

MARK'S RESTAURANT

NEW AMERICAN   16/20

The Mark Hotel, 25 E. 77th St. (Madison & Fifth Aves.), 10021
879-1864, *Breakfast, Lunch, Afternoon Tea & Dinner daily, Brunch Sun.*, $$$$

The intimate Mark Hotel features cosseting service and a luxurious restaurant reminiscent of a private London dinner club. Chef David Paulstich prepares a weekly changing menu of straightforward New American dishes with hints of Mediterranean and Asian influences. Start dinner with fresh oysters, a warm lobster-and-mushroom salad, or seared Hudson Valley foie gras, then continue with whole roasted black sea bass wrapped in sage and pancetta, medallions of veal with fettuccini and chanterelles or roasted chicken for two with sweet garlic-mashed potatoes. For dessert, indulge in the restaurant's signature white-chocolate-macadamia-nut cheesecake. There is a $19.99 prix-fixe lunch menu, a $29 pre-theater dinner menu, and an excellent wine selection overseen by Master Sommelier Richard Dean.

MATCH UPTOWN   NEW AMERICAN   14/20

33 E. 60th St. (Park & Madison Aves.), 10025
906-9177, *Lunch Mon.-Sat., Dinner nightly, $$$$*

Cool and handsome in woods and stone, Match Uptown sports sofas and easy chairs in a sunken lounge and plush banquettes in a back room—perfect for posing. The Pan-Asian influence is apparent from the sushi bar and dim-sum offerings, and such dishes as spicy tuna tartare in rice cakes, grilled rack of lamb with taro-root purée, sautéed mahi mahi with shrimp rolls, ginger-soy-glazed salmon with saké-steamed cockles, and roasted monkfish with lobster-tamarind broth and wild-mushroom dumplings. A late-night menu is served Tuesdays through Saturdays to a trendy and chic crowd until 2 a.m.

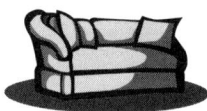

MATTHEW'S   MEDITERRANEAN   14/20

1030 Third Ave. (61st St.), 10021
838-4343, *Lunch Mon.-Fri., Dinner nightly, Brunch Sat.-Sun., $$$*

Chef Matthew Kenny has something of a Mediterranean, North African muse, captured in part from trips to Egypt and Morocco. This spacious restaurant near Bloomingdale's has a touch of the Banana Republic/Casablanca look with its rotating paddle fans, rattan chairs, wooden jalousies and palm plants. The menu covers a lot of the basics—risotto and such seafood dishes as grilled salmon, spice-crusted tuna, coriander-crusted cod and pignoli-crusted sea bass. The specialty ice creams are a good dessert pick, and there's a sound wine list.

MAYA   MEXICAN   14/20

1191 First Ave. (64th & 65th Sts.), 10021
585-1818, *Dinner nightly, $$$*

Maya is pretty and original—and popular and lively to the edge of distraction. Owner/chef Richard Sandoval tapped into his roots in a prominent Acapulco restaurant family to create an atmospheric setting to showcase "the gourmet side of Mexican food." Mayan masks and mirrors framed in ornately carved wood adorn coral-hued walls. But bring a flashlight—most menu descriptions run to three lines, and are difficult to read in the dim lighting. Start with spiced-to-your-taste guacamole or ceviche of mahi mahi. The chile relleno is a roasted poblano pepper stuffed with shrimp, scallops, calamari and Manchego cheese, posed on black-bean purée. Pairing warm lobster with tortilla crisps and roasted habañero chile salsa may ignite the digestive engine. Try the grilled pork tenderloin served with roasted corn purée and pumpkin-seed sauce.

MAZZEI   ITALIAN   14/20

1564 Second Ave. (81st & 82nd Sts.), 10028
628-3131, Dinner nightly, $$$

The freshness of Puglia's ingredients and the warmth of its people are evident in the elegant yet traditional cuisine at Mazzei. Strong in its seafood offerings, this warm softly lit restaurant, with a wood-burning oven, serves crunchy bruschetta piled high with ripe tomatoes, and cuttlefish baked in a traditional Pugliese terra-cotta pot. First courses like orecchiette with broccoli and sausage, and spicy Barese rigatoni with eggplant and pine nuts lead to main dishes such as the lightly breaded oven-baked monkfish.

MEZZALUNA   ITALIAN   13/20

1295 Third Ave. (74th & 75th Sts.), 10021
535-9600, Lunch & Dinner daily, $$

One of the first pasta and pizza trattorias in New York, Mezzaluna hasn't changed its menu much since it opened in 1984, and the marble-topped tables are tightly packed every night. The narrow storefront has a split-level dining area, one wall completely obscured by drawings, paintings and collages from students in a Florentine art school who'd been asked to create a "work" exploring the theme of Mezzaluna ("half-moon" in Italian.) At the rear, a wood-fired pizza oven turns out thin-crusted pizzas. In addition, there are numerous carpaccios and such pastas as cuttlefish-ink linguini. The wine list is short but serviceable.

NINO'S   ITALIAN   15/20

1354 First Ave. (72nd & 73rd Sts.), 10021
988-0002, Lunch Mon.-Fri., Dinner nightly, $$$$

Handsome is as handsome does. The dapper gentleman at the door is Nino Selimaj, and his quiet pride in the attractive crowd filling his good-looking restaurant is evident. The attractions here are engaging surroundings, suave and caring service, and superb food: The chef is from Aureole, the pastry chef from Picholine, and it shows. Shreds of veal dot rich lentil soup; prosciutto wraps a "Sicilian salad" with goat cheese and marinated artichokes; duck risotto gets its own wrap—a radicchio leaf—and it contains a whole leg of confit duck; warm puff pastry girds a medley of smoked salmon and fresh asparagus. Smokers often repair to Nino's comfortable cocktail lounge.

PAMIR   AFGHAN   14/20

1437 Second Ave. (74th & 75th Sts.), 10021
734-3791, *Dinner Tues.-Sun.*, *$$*

Afghan rugs hang from the walls, Eastern music plays softly in the background and exotic spices perfume the air of this enchanting candlelit oasis. Afghan cooking is earthier than its Indian counterparts, and the best bet here is to order a combination dinner. It may include such dishes as a scallion turnover with yogurt (bulanee gandana), a ground beef-and-potato turnover (bulanee kachalou) and scallion dumplings (aushak). Our favorite entrée is the orange palaw, seasoned lamb under a mound of saffron rice, topped with almonds, pistachios, orange strips, rosewater and cardamom. The marinated kebabs are also worth trying as are the spinach stew with spicy sauce and sautéed eggplant with yogurt. Stick with Afghan tea for a finisher; the three desserts are heavy, very sweet and dominated by pistachios. **Also at 1065 First Ave. (58th St.), 644-9258.**

PAOLA'S RESTAURANT   ITALIAN   14/20

343 E. 85th St. (First & Second Aves.), 10028
794-1890, *Dinner nightly*, *$$$*

Chef/owner Paola Marracino prepares simple, authentic Italian fare in this intimate—okay, tiny—restaurant that caters to women in elegant clothes and men in Brooks Brothers suits who look like they run the company that owns the company you work for. Start with the homemade fresh mozzarella, the spinach dumplings or the steamed mussels and clams. Pastas include the assertive fettuccine puttanesca and asparagus ravioli with wild mushrooms. Among the entrées, try the veal chop, veal scaloppine or the fish of the day, which might be red snapper in a light and lemony sauce. Desserts, like the seasonal menu, change regularly, and the wines off the short Italian list are sound but expensive.

PARIOLI ROMANISSIMO   ITALIAN   15/20

24 E. 81st St. (Fifth & Madison Aves.), 10028
288-2391, *Dinner Mon.-Sat., Closed for 2 wks. in Aug.*, *$$$$*

A truly elegant restaurant with an attentive staff, Parioli occupies a townhouse on an inviting tree-lined street, and offers two dining rooms which set different moods: one resembles an Italian banker's salon; the second is situated in a glass-enclosed courtyard with a gurgling fountain and a street lantern. The monthly changing menu might include baby artichokes filled with minced vegetables, baby clams in a curry-scented broth or pepper-crusted yellowfin tuna. The pastas and risottos are well prepared, especially, in season, the spaghetti with fresh white truffles, as are such entrées as the crispy

Stay at The Mark.
Stay Real.

THE MARK

N E W   Y O R K

Why stay in a posh uptown hotel with attitude, when you could stay at The Mark? We're posh, (even more so with our new rooms). The difference is you can relax, let loose, be yourself here. We have everything you need to make your business life easy—a prime location, a great restaurant, computer and fax capabilities, telephone voice mail plus a new world-class wellness suite with sauna to release some stress. And because after business we want you to be as comfortable as possible, we'd like you to wear what makes you happy. A T-shirt, perhaps. In fact, we like T-shirts so much, we have one with our name on it. **The Mark, Madison Ave. at E. 77th St., New York. Reservation, call 212-744-4300 or 1-800-843-6275.**

grilled whole Dover sole, the roasted rack of herb-marinated baby lamb and the succulent veal chop. The selection of 40 to 50 cheeses is impressive. Parioli's wine list is extensive and ranges from the affordable to the expensive.

PARK AVENUE CAFÉ   NEW AMERICAN   14/20

100 E. 63rd St. (Park & Lexington Aves.), 10021
644-1900, Lunch Mon.-Fri., Dinner nightly, Brunch Sat.-Sun., $$$$

New York restaurateur Alan Stillman and chef David Burke turn out all sorts of innovative dishes at this chic restaurant. Starters range from the divine "pastrami salmon" with warm corn blini, southern fried quail with greens, huckleberries, pecans and blue cheese, and cavatelli with wild mushrooms. Entrées reflect inspirations from all over the map: onion-crusted roast organic chicken; "Duck Duck Duck!" (duck breast, duck meatloaf and duck foie-gras dumplings; fresh prawns with mango spring rolls and pea shoots; and mustard-crusted tuna teriyaki. The mostly American wine list is in tune with the '90s and reasonably priced for this neighborhood. For a real culinary adventure, book a table for up to twelve in the kitchen.

PARK VIEW AT THE BOATHOUSE   NEW AMERICAN   14/20

Central Park (Park Drive North near E. 72nd St.), 10021
988-0575, Lunch Mon.-Fri. (May-October only), Dinner Tues.-Sat., Brunch Sat.-Sun., $$$

Overlooking the still waters of the park's lake, Park View's mood is low-key and casual, while the food raises the bar for open-air dining. Rising star chef John Villa, who made his name during a four-year run at Judson Grill, is a high volume specialist with a knack for aggressively seasoned modern food. Service can be inattentive, but the idyllic surroundings—a serene oasis of water, trees, and winding paths—transports you far from the city. Many of Villa's trademarks are reborn here, including oysters capped with iced saké and pickled plum, and chilled shrimp wrapped in rice paper. The entrées are inconsistent, but we've had great success with the rack of lamb, grilled seafood and pastas.

PAYARD PATISSERIE & BISTRO   FRENCH   15/20

1032 Lexington Ave. (73rd & 74th Sts.), 10021
717-5252, Café: Breakfast Mon.-Sat., Bistro: Lunch, Tea & Dinner Mon.-Fri., $$$$

Payard Patisserie's splendid desserts are found in many New York restaurants, but here they take second billing to expertly prepared bistro cuisine. The collaboration of Francois Payard, a third-generation pastry chef who won a huge following at Restaurant Daniel, his former boss Daniel Boulud, and Mr. Payard's wife Alexandra, the gracious hostess, Payard is a booming bistro with a wood-paneled, lived-in look ("boom" applies to noise-level as well as business). Executive chef

Philippe Bertineau prepares a memorable terrine of foie gras with pickled pearl onions and toasted country bread. Sturdy bouillabaisse features Chilean sea bass, mussels, clams and squid; and melt-in-the-mouth crisp skinned duck leg confit rides atop a seasonal bean fricassee and Black Mission figs. It's difficult to save room for dessert, but at Payard it is essential.

PETALUMA   ITALIAN   10/20

1356 First Ave. (73rd St.), 10021
772-8800, *Lunch & Dinner daily,* $$$

🄰 ☎ 🖥

The brainchild of Elio Guaitolini (owner of the popular Elio's), Petaluma is a modern-day, pastel-toned Left Bank-style café serving decent (although uneven) grilled fish and meats, brick-oven pizza and homemade pastas. You can order home-smoked salmon, or grilled chicken skewers to start, and many people come for the individual dinner-plate-size pizzas with a crispy thin crust. Many just come for the social scene.

PIG HEAVEN   CHINESE   13/20   ♟

1540 Second Ave. (80th & 81st Sts.), 10028
744-4333, *Lunch & Dinner daily, Brunch Sat.-Sun.,* $$

🄰

Pigs proliferate in the decor of this cutesy Upper East Side Chinese restaurant where the walls feature 150 little pink dancing pigs overlooking a large yellow moon. As its name implies, Pig Heaven serves up great Cantonese-style suckling pig and roast pork. Tender and sweet, with crackling skin, both dishes will have you licking your fingers. The menu also features several Szechuan dishes, such as pork with garlic sauce and braised pigs' feet. Spicy, tangy shredded pigs' ears make a crunchy appetizer, followed by delicate steamed dumplings. Main courses of note include the three-glass chicken or the crisp whole sea bass. On weekends, Pig Heaven offers a Chinese brunch of dumplings, congee and suckling pig.

PORTICO   ITALIAN   12/20

1431 Second Ave. (74th & 75th Sts.), 10021
794-1032, *Lunch Fri.-Sun., Dinner nightly,* $$$

💳 💳 💳 🄵 ☎ 🖥

This rustic trattoria recreates the feeling of a Tuscan farm-house, but the regional dishes hail from all over Italy present and past. If available, try a little-known specialty from Emilia Romagna: the fagottino, a giant beggar's purse of pasta filled with vegetables in a rich pesto sauce, or the tortelloni con la coda ("with tail"), which dates from the Renaissance, an elongated pasta with an nutmeg-kissed spinach-and-onion stuffing. Good main courses include the monkfish with artichokes, the chicken sautéed with sun-dried tomatoes and pine nuts and for dessert, try the hearty Sicilian bread pudding.

THE POST HOUSE   AMERICAN   14/20

The Lowell Hotel, 28 E. 63rd St. (Park & Madison Aves.) 10021
935-2888, *Lunch Mon.-Fri., Dinner nightly, $$$$*

A bastion of genteel power-dining, this Upper East Side
steakhouse is housed in the Lowell Hotel and is more elegant
than your typical steakhouse. In fact, the gilt-framed paintings
interspersed with the chalkboard menus, the leather banquettes and armchairs and the long, polished bar, lend the dining room the look and ambience of a private gentlemen's club.
The offerings include all the American classics: crabcakes,
Caesar salad, enormous and juicy steaks, along with mammoth
Maine lobsters. Daily specials might include beef Wellington or
roasted duck with maple-sweet-potato mash. The glass wine
cases hold some of the Post House's extensive collection of
boutique California and rare French wines, showcasing proprietor Alan Stillman's dedication to a serious wine program.

PRIMAVERA   ITALIAN   14/20

1578 First Ave. (82nd St.), 10028
861-8608, *Dinner nightly, $$$$*

Jacket and tie are de rigueur at this posh Italian spot, but
that's just fine with the ultra-chic patrons who keep their limos
waiting while they dine in style. The setting is romantic: a clubby, wood-paneled, carpeted dining room with marbled
columns and tulip sconces. Upon arrival, every party is served
a plate of fried zucchini or bruschetta, compliments of the
chef. Regulars let proprietor Nicola Civetta order for them.
Choices include such pastas as tortellini with prosciutto and
peas or capellini primavera, and succulent roasted marinated
kid. A silken ricotta cheesecake or tiramisu are fine desserts. In
keeping with the food, the wine selections here are extensive
but pricey.

PRIMOLA   ITALIAN   13/20

1226 Second Ave. (64th & 65th Sts.), 10021
758-1775, *Lunch Mon.-Fri., Dinner nightly, $$$*

This is just the place for a leisurely lunch, although at night
it bustles with high-powered East Side regulars. The decor is
spare —wood floors, some watercolors—but there is a welcom-
ing bar (which can be a bit raucous on crowded nights) and an
appealing display of hors d'oeuvres and desserts. In addition to
the menu are lots of specials, such as swordfish carpaccio,
homemade pastas, fresh seafood and perhaps charcoal-grilled
lamb chops or succulent boneless quail. Desserts include
homemade gelati; the wine list is 90 per cent Italian.

147

QUATORZE BIS   FRENCH   14/20

323 E. 79th St. (First & Second Aves.), 19921
535-1414, *Lunch Tues.-Sun., Dinner nightly, Brunch Sat.-Sun., $$$*

Quatorze Bis continues to deliver Parisian bistro fare and ambience (with some Alsatian highlights) to throngs of satisfied customers. The formula is simple: no attitude, simple dishes, very good preparation, large portions, and fine and well-priced wines. The rectangular dining room with a bar up front, banquette along the walls and French posters, makes for an inviting setting. The menu changes slightly with the season—the boeuf bourguignon and cassoulet come off in the summer; cold sliced steak goes on. The chicory with bacon and hot vinaigrette or the choucroute garnie are good, as is the steak with pommes frites. The signature hot apple tart is sublime.

RAO'S   ITALIAN   14/20

455 E. 114th St. (Pleasant Ave.), 10029
212-722-6709, *Dinner Mon.-Fri., $$$*
No cards

On any given night, you could be dining next to Woody Allen, Sophia Lauren or Anthony Quinn. That is, if you can get in. The reservations books are permanently closed at Rao's (pronounced RAY-oze), an 102-year-old Italian restaurant in East Harlem, where New York's elite and Hollywood's hip go to dine—or try to. Problem is, there's simply no vacancy in this cozy dining room with the blaring jukebox, perennial Christmas lights and steaming plates of pasta. Tradition mandates that there's only one seating a night at just ten tables. If, by some stroke of luck you do get in, plan on a tableside visit from one of the owners, Frank Pellegrino and Ron Straci, and since there's no written menu, trust Pellegrino's son, Frank Jr., to advise you on the night's selections—southern Italian staples like spaghetti with broccoli sauce, twice-broiled lemon chicken, roasted peppers with raisins and pine nuts, and deliciously fresh seafood salad. If you're lucky, Pellegrino, an actor and a singer on the side, will croon along with the jukebox.

RESTAURANT DANIEL   FRENCH   19/20

60 E. 65th St. (Park & Madison Aves.), 10021
288-0033, *Lunch & Dinner, Mon.-Sat., $$$$*

Who could have imagined it? Daniel Boulud rose to prominence as the chef of the venerable Le Cirque. Then Daniel left and Le Cirque moved its big top to Madison Avenue, becoming Le Cirque 2000. Five years later Daniel has returned to the original Le Cirque location, this time flying on his own wings and creating the gastronomic sensation of this end of the century. At his stunning new restaurant, Daniel tailored the state-of-the-art kitchen he always wanted, and expanded the dining space to three rooms: a Venetian Renaissance-inspired dining room seating 120 guests, a bar and lounge, and a private room. This entrepreneurial energy is not the sole reason of our admiration for Chef Boulud. He is arguably the finest and most inspired chef working today in New York. His impeccable technique allows him to play freely with his imagination. Merely reading his menu whips our curiosity and triggers our salivary glands. Who would not want to try the Nantucket Bay scallops with caperberries, crushed cauliflower and sweet and sour kumquats; the penne with shaved black truffles and baby artichokes; the lobster perfumed with licorice root? Many chefs preach the gospel of devotion to the freshest and finest ingredients and of precision in their preparation, but here the word is made flesh hundreds of times each day. Boulud's cooking is far, far from simple, but what appears on the plate is fresh, uncluttered, harmonious and bursting with the flavors of the two or three prime items. He layers taste upon taste to produce a combination that resonates without diminishing the dominant flavors. He is a marvel with vegetables. His signature sea bass wrapped in a crisp potato shell has been imitated a million times. Before we even settle into a meal, little finger foods and tiny soups and infusions tantalize us. Mind you, the menu changes frequently for Daniel and his executive chef, Alex Lee, translate the season to your plate. For serious gastronomes, the summit is the eight-course tasting menu, a discovery of the planet Tastes. Moderation? The three-course prix fixe is a good value for its superb quality. Sommelier Jean-Luc Le Du, who is also a poet, will find you a wine or two from an increasingly distinctive list, notable for its vintage runs from great houses as well as its organic producers. Count Restaurant Daniel as one of those places where trophy wines can be had for grand occasions at a range of high and higher prices. Why not? Where else?

SANT AMBROEUS   ITALIAN   12/20

1000 Madison Ave. (77th & 78th Sts.), 10021
570-2211, Breakfast, Lunch & Dinner daily, Brunch Sun., $$$

This little jewel box of a dining spot is nestled far in the back, past the stunning pastries and gelati of this sleek shop where well-dressed East Siders eat in great style. Sant Ambroeus is expensive, but it is an ultra-chic spot to have Continental breakfast, lunch, tea or dinner, or to relax after you've done the nearby gallery circuit. The antipasti and pastas are good, as are the grilled salmon, veal picatta and lamb chops with rosemary. Deserts are culled from the excellent gelati and pastries for which Sant Ambroeus is renowned.

SISTINA   ITALIAN   14/20

555 Second Ave. (80th & 81st Sts.), 10028
861-7660, Lunch & Dinner daily, $$$

This expensive, polished restaurant with its unstained-oak walls is one of the best places for Northern Italian food on the Upper East Side. The Italian waiters are fine, as are such dishes as gossamer duck or beef carpaccio, grilled shrimp and scallops with potatoes, pappardelle with tomatoes, veal and wild mushrooms and a hefty veal chop or roasted with wild mushrooms and white wine. Leave room for the homemade gelati. Unfortunately, the mostly Italian wine list is expensive.

SYLVIA'S RESTAURANT   SOUL FOOD/SOUTHERN   10/20

328 Lenox Ave. (126th & 127th Sts.), 10027
996-0660, *Breakfast & Lunch Mon.-Sat., Dinner nightly, Brunch Sun.,* **$**

Sylvia Woods moved north from South Carolina and started out with a tiny place with a few stools, but her soul-food mecca has grown to feed neighborhood residents, other New Yorkers and tourists, often by the busload. No matter the crowd, Sylvia's feels homey and warm. Tuck into some of the city's finest ribs, spicy and a little hot, or Southern fried chicken, served as a meal or with hot cakes at breakfast and brunch. The collard greens, stewed with smoked turkey are blissful. Other tempting specialties include smothered chicken, salmon croquettes, pork chops and short ribs of beef. The biscuits or cornbread start the meal. In fact, you can't lose at this Harlem institution if you stick to the standards. Lines can be long for the Sunday gospel brunch, but it's worth the wait. Wednesdays through Saturdays, there's live jazz.

SYRAH   NEW AMERICAN   14/20

1400 Second Ave. (73rd St.), 10021
327-1780, *Dinner nightly, Brunch Sat.-Sun.,* **$$**

Every neighborhood deserves a restaurant as appealing as this one, with a warm bistro ambience, an attractive decor (green granite bar, oak floors, comfy banquettes), reasonable prices (dinner entrées stay below $20), innovative food and a terrific, well-priced wine list (30 of the 50 offerings are examples of co-owner/manager James Broude's favorite Syrah grape. Co-owner/chef Ahmed El Sheikh, who was born in Sudan and trained in French cuisine, incorporates Middle Eastern touches in his dishes, starting off with the house-made flatbreads dipped into baba ghanouj. On the seasonally changing menu, you might find salads topped with sautéed wild mushrooms and goat cheese, orecchiette with a lamb-thyme Bolognese sauce, and chipotle-spiced halibut over couscous-stuffed grape leaves. Indulge in down-home comfort food with the spicy swordfish burger and crispy frites, followed by the hot-fudge-brownie sundae.

TROIS JEAN   FRENCH   15/20

154 E. 79th St. (Lexington & Third Aves.), 10021
988-4858, *Lunch & Dinner daily, Brunch Sun.,* **$$$**

This charming lace-curtained bistro doubles as a tea room and pastry shop, but most of the dinner action takes place upstairs. The menu offers straightforward bistro fare in unfussy presentations, and little toque icons mark the owners' favorite dishes. The house-smoked salmon is sublimely silky; sweet-bread lovers will enjoy the sautéed, cumin-scented preparation. For main courses, the cassoulet is one of the best in town, plus you can order steak tartare, fine roasted chicken with sage, rack of lamb and a hefty 13-ounce veal chop. The signature desserts are the chocolate-ganache pyramid or an assortment of miniature pastries. The prix-fixe menus run $19.99 for lunch and $39.50 for dinner.

THE VINEGAR FACTORY   NEW AMERICAN   13/20

431 E. 91st St. (York Ave.), 10128
987-0885, Breakfast & Brunch daily, $

Eli Zabar's specialty-food warehouse (where vinegar was once made) opens its huge upstairs loft space for brunch. Other times of day, customers can buy take out and eat it across the street at Across The Street, which serves only dinner (see And Also...) The food is top notch, the service seamless, the prices affordable. Tables are covered in white butcher paper and stocked with an array of the store's own preserves (which are so good you can't wait to buy them downstairs) and a basket brimming with fresh Eli's breads. Specialties range from omelets and roast beef hash with fried eggs, to pizzas, sandwiches and salads. During peak times, expect to browse among the gourmet delicacies downstairs while waiting for a table.

WILKINSON'S RESTAURANT   NEW AMERICAN/SEAFOOD   13/20

1573 York Ave. (83rd & 84th Sts.), 10028
535-5454, Dinner nightly, $$$

Some of the best seafood on the Upper East Side is served here. Simple brick walls, smoked-glass lamps, and trompe l'oeil flower niches make for a warm, cozy feel, which is only magnified by the long mahogany bar with its impressive selection of ports and brandies. Start with fresh oysters, or house-cured salmon with black beans and chipotle aïoli. Soups are flavorful, and entrées offer new twists on traditional fish house special-ties: coriander-dusted salmon on black-eyed pea-andouille ragout; blackened tuna on white bean-frisée salad; horseradish-crusted Chilean sea bass with multi-grains, wilted cabbage and red-wine-beet sauce; and pecan-crusted rainbow trout with wild rice and baby artichokes. Meat-lovers can get a filet mignon or chicken. Desserts are irresistible, especially the warm chocolate mousse cake.

AND ALSO...

ACROSS THE STREET   NEW AMERICAN
444 E. 91st St. (York Ave.), 10128
722-4000, *Dinner nightly, $$$$*

A fine-dining extension of Eli Zabar's Vinegar Factory across the street, this plain but high-style spot serves the homey, seasonally changing fare of chef Allan Schanbacher. Some of his autumn specialties, for example, include osso buco, venison with a port-and-roasted garlic sauce, spit-roasted goose, braised short ribs and traditional roast duck.

CAFÉ M   MEDITERRANEAN
Stanhope Hotel, 995 Fifth Ave. (81st St.), 10028
713-0303, *Breakfast, Lunch & Dinner daily, $$$*

M stands for Metropolitan Museum (which is across the street), chef Matthew Kenney, the managing partner, and Mediterranean, the type of cuisine served in this handsome earth-toned restaurant at the Stanhope Hotel. Among the signature dishes are mussels steamed with chili, parsley and garlic, fennel tart with char-grilled calamari, fresh oysters, macaroni with walnut-herb pesto, and such entrées as brick-grilled baby chicken and rabbit stew. There is an awesome selection of cheeses as well, with wines to go with them, and the $19.95 weekend brunch is a good deal before visiting the Met.

ELAINE'S   AMERICAN
1703 Second Ave. (88th & 89th Sts.), 10128
534-8103, *Dinner nightly, $$$$*

It's Woody Allen's favorite. It's also the favorite of a lot of other famous folks. Which is why, unless you know Elaine, you may not feel at home (or be welcomed) here. Homey cooking—steaks, chicken, pastas—for those who care more about the scene than the food.

FRED'S   NEW AMERICAN/ITALIAN
Barneys New York, 10 E. 61st St. (Madison Ave.), 10022
579-3076, *Lunch daily, Dinner Mon.-Sat., $$$*

Downstairs at Barneys, you'll find Mark Strausman's (Campagna) dining and gourmet-shopping emporium, with a wine bar and coffee bar too, named after the late owner of this chic department store. Chic customers dine on an eclectic array of dishes, from crabcakes to veal Milanese, yet somehow manage to keep their figures for the high-style fashions upstairs.

ISLAND   ECLECTIC

1305 Madison Ave. (92nd & 93rd Sts.), 10128
996-1200, *Lunch & Dinner daily, Brunch Sat.-Sun., $$*

Under new ownership, this is the sort of place where the hip meet the preppy in something like a year-round version of the Hamptons summer scene. But that doesn't take anything away from the food, which may include tuna carpaccio or smoked trout salad to start, and entrées ranging from saffron lasagna with spinach to crispy skate with spaghetti-squash cake. Dinner can be noisy, but this is the place to linger over a late lunch and pretend you are on the Côte d'Azur.

THE LIBRARY   GOURMET BAR FOOD

Regency Hotel, 540 Park Ave. (61st St.), 10021
759-4100, *Lunch & Dinner daily, $$*

You'd think Ralph Lauren, not David Rockwell (Tapika, Torri di Pisa) designed this clubby lounge/restaurant in the Regency Hotel that has real books on the shelves. Sink into an armchair and order a smoked-salmon omelet, with or without egg yolks, a warming cup of soup or a light but high-style snack. If you don't like dining on a coffee table, sit at one of the polished dining tables fit for a Park Avenue duplex.

LUCA   ITALIAN

1712 First Ave. (89th St.), 10128
987-9260, *Dinner nightly, $$*

At this spare but comfortable Yorkville Italian, you can make a meal of the bounteous antipasto platter for two, which includes sautéed radicchio, glazed chicken livers, grilled mushrooms, grilled squid and seared scallops, not to mention Italian cold cuts and grilled vegetables. But there are other specialties worth trying: round Venetian pasta with, say, a lusty lamb sauce; pumpkin-stuffed ravioli; potato-crusted salmon; and to finish, almond or grapefruit granita.

THE PEMBROKE ROOM   CONTINENTAL

The Lowell Hotel
28 E. 63rd St. (Park & Madison Aves.), 10021
838-1400, *Breakfast & Tea daily, Brunch Sat.-Sun., $$$*

You don't have to be a guest at this elegant hotel to enjoy the serenity of its sophisticated dining room tucked away on the second floor which serves on hand-painted Washington Pickard china. The $39 weekend brunch offers everything from classic English breakfast items, to spinach quiche and warm grilled chicken to smoked Scottish salmon with toasted bagels and cream cheese.

SERAFINA FABULOUS GRILL   ITALIAN

29 E. 61st St., (Madison & Park Aves.), 10022
702-9898, *Lunch & Dinner daily, $$$*
A 🦉

Formerly called Sofia Fabulous Grill, this spin-off of Sofia's Fabulous Pizza—now also renamed Serafina's—is a neighborhood favorite. In fact, Ivana Trump pulled the new name from a jar out of the many names submitted by local fans. As you expect in this Park Avenue-adjacent neighborhood, the menu features refined Italian salads, antipasti and pastas, plus entrées from the cherry-wood grill including calamari, lobster, Argentinean organic-sirloin steak and even Kobe filet mignon.

STEAK AU POIVRE   FRENCH BISTRO

1160 First Ave. (63rd & 64th Sts.), 10021
758-3518, *Dinner nightly, $*
No Cards 🦉

From the owner of Uzie & Marco's comes this new French bistro with very reasonable prices—especially for this neighborhood. Start with a garlic baguette with melted Roquefort, or onion soup, along with a bottle of wine from their under-$30 list. You can get a steak frites for $14.95, mussels, salmon or coq au vin for $12.95. They don't take plastic, but at these prices, you won't need much cash to have a great time here.

UZIE & MARCO'S   ITALIAN

1162 First Ave. (63rd. & 64th Sts.), 10021
758-0880, *Dinner Mon.-Sat., $$*
A ☎ 🚶

This romantic neighborhood restaurant—there's a fireplace in the bar, lush floral arrangements, warm mahogany furniture and piano music—offers friendly service and good contemporary Italian cuisine at good prices.

UPPER WEST SIDE

DINING

All phone numbers are (212) unless otherwise indicated

BACI   ITALIAN   12/20

412 Amsterdam Ave. (79th & 80th Sts.), 10024
496-1550, *Lunch & Dinner daily*, $$

A

Usually crowded and noisy, this upbeat Italian restaurant has exposed brick walls, Roman pillars and a wood-burning pizza oven turning crisp-crusted pizzas. We also like their pastas, perhaps linguine in a tuna-and-tomato sauce or with an intriguing blend of fresh sardines, fennel, pinoli nuts and raisins. The flavorful caponata goes well with the crusty bread.

BLUE NILE   ETHIOPIAN   10/20

103 W. 77th St. (Columbus Ave.), 10024
580-3232, *Lunch Sat.-Sun., Dinner Tues.-Sun.*, $$

If you like eating with your fingers and sitting on three-legged stools, this is a good place to experience Ethiopian cuisine. Use folded sheets of injera, a spongy white-flour pancake that's the national staple, to scoop up spicy beef tartare (kitfo), beef simmered in fenugreek and garlic (tibs wot), kale and potatoes with spices (yegomen wot), the hottest chicken in town (doro wot) or chickpea purée (shu ro wot). Avoid the Western desserts. Sample the Ethiopian wines by the glass.

CAFÉ DES ARTISTES   FRENCH/CONTINENTAL   14/20

1 W. 67th St. (Central Park West & Columbus Ave.), 10023
877-3500, *Lunch Mon.-Fri., Dinner nightly, Brunch Sat.-Sun.*, $$$

A

With its lush Howard Chandler Christie murals of cavorting nymphs, opulent floral arrangements and lavish display of pastries (owner George Lang is proudly Hungarian), Café des Artistes is one of New York's most beautiful restaurants, perfect for a special celebration. Among the specialties; salmon four ways—smoked, poached, dill-marinated and tartare; asparagus wrapped in gravlax; smoked salmon; sturgeon schnitzel; and Austrian beef goulash. We like the wine list, which features "basket wines" for $22 a bottle. If you can't decide among the multitude of pastries, share the voluptuous $25 "Great Dessert Plate."

CAFÉ LUXEMBOURG   FRENCH BISTRO   13/20

200 W. 70th St. (Amsterdam & West End Aves.), 10023
873-7411, *Lunch Mon.-Fri., Dinner nightly, Brunch Sat.-Sun., $$*

This tightly packed art-deco bistro, with its zinc-topped bar, cream-colored walls, antique silver mirrors—and occasional attitude—is a Lincoln Center-adjacent dining institution. Start with the likes of salt cod croquettes or the port-poached pear salad with melted Gorgonzola. Entrées range from grilled yellowfin tuna with lentil ragout to daube of beef short ribs with chive-mashed potatoes. There are three-course prix-fixe lunch and weekend brunch menus for $19.95, a $34.50 pre-theater menu, and for after theater, a supper menu offering omelets and sandwiches.

CITRUS BAR & GRILL   SOUTHWESTERN   12/20

320 Amsterdam Ave. (75th St.), 10023
595-0500, *Dinner nightly, Brunch Sun., $$$*

Though the Southwestern fare is sometimes flat, sometimes fabulous, khaki-clad upper West Siders keep lining up for Citrus' iron-branded tables. Perhaps they're drawn by yet-another success from the family famous for Josie's, Josephina and Blue Star. Or maybe they just like to sip margaritas at the retro-Western bar before checking out the live entertainment downstairs in the **Squeeze Lounge**. Sure, this kind of crowd gets noisy, but the dining room's waterfall and tall cacti help provide some intimacy. Best bets: queso fundido; lime-marinated salmon with a crunchy pine nut-studded skin; lean skirt steak in a coffee-barbecue sauce; and the turkey fajitas with cranberry sauce. The large desserts are meant to be shared, but you might want your own toasted tortilla filled with malted ice cream.

GABRIEL'S   ITALIAN   14/20

11 W. 60th St. (Broadway & Ninth Ave.), 10023
956-4600, *Lunch Mon.-Fri., Dinner Mon.-Sat., $$$$*

It isn't Le Cirque, '21' or Balthazar, but Gabriel's is a low-key but high-grade place for bi-coastal celebrity-spotting and excellent contemporary Italian food. The dining room is adorned with contemporary paintings by owner Gabriel Aiellos' artist wife, Christine Keefe. Plates are adorned with chef/partner Ralph Perrotti's antipasto of pulpo "inferno," a melange of braised calamari, poached shrimp with salsa verde, marinated mussels and fresh crabmeat. We recommend the baby chicken marinated in buttermilk and rosemary and served with garlic-mashed potatoes, roasted onions and hot peppers. The desserts are flat-out addictive.

JEAN GEORGES   FRENCH   19/20   ♟♟♟
Trump International Hotel, 1 Central Park West
(Columbus Circle), 10023
299-3000, Dining Room: Lunch Mon.-Fri., Dinner Mon.-Sat., $$$$
Nougatine Café: Breakfast, Lunch & Dinner daily, $$$

🅰 🏠 🍴 ⚥ 🖥

40ish Jean-Georges Vongerichten is New York's longest-reigning über chef and no doubt the most influential. When he was 29, and chef of the now defunct Restaurant Lafayette in the Drake Hotel, he rose to the top ranks and was showered with admiration. He responded to the recession by opening up Jo-Jo, which brought bistro to New York like never before and is still thriving. Next he added Vong, the brilliant Asian-fusion yet European restaurant that he and his partners have franchised with great success in London and Hong Kong. But Jean Georges is the flagship of his restaurant empire, the reference point for his cuisine. It is a cuisine that is anchored in the classic French and has nouvelle-cuisine tendencies, yet reveals plenty of Asian influences, assimilated, perhaps, from his years working in the Far East. Vongerichten influences not only the kitchens and chefs under his employ, but what diners experience as haute cuisine in 1999. Among the first in America to introduce Asian overtones, he was the first to introduce our palates to oils infused with herbs and spices. At Jean Georges, his relentless search for new flavors and vibrant, simple cuisine led him to introduce a range of wild edible plants. If you haven't tasted wood sorrel, yarrow, dandelions, garlic mustard, lamb's quarters, chicory, yellow dock, chickweed, miner's lettuce or lemon balm, you haven't been to Jean Georges.

At Jean Georges, expect three flavors on a plate, the highest quality ingredients and dishes that cannot be found elsewhere—for example, garlic soup with lemon thyme served with three tiny but plump sautéed frogs' legs, or Muscovy duck steak roasted with Asian spices, sweet-and-sour jus, wilted celery leaves and glazed vegetables. Expect a wine list that marries well with the cuisine, and European-style service from a bygone era. The expert waitstaff often finishes off dishes at tableside—cracking lobster, slicing meat, or even placing a garnish—adding to the intensity of the gastronomic experience. Architect-designer-restaurateur Adam Tihany designed Jean Georges as a cool Calvin Klein-meets-Donald Trump space with a hand-laid mosaic floor of white marble and terrazzo, warm woods, soothing taupes and high ceilings. The restaurant has three areas: the dining room, which seats 64 and is what all the fuss is about, the **Nougatine Café** bar-lounge dining area, and in good weather the no-reservations outdoor **Mistral Terrace**. Book the dining room well in advance for a singular experience.

LA BOÎTE EN BOIS   FRENCH   12/20

75 W. 68th St. (Central Park West & Columbus Ave.), 10023
874-2705, *Lunch Mon.-Sat., Dinner nightly, Brunch Sun., $$*
No cards

This tiny room with plank-wood walls adorned with farm implements and landscape paintings, has served substantial French provincial cooking since 1985, with such specialties as smoked salmon, a ragout of snails with Roquefort and angel-hair pasta and a Marseilles-style fish soup. Entrées might include grilled salmon with anchovy butter, grilled quails on a bed of cranberry beans or filet of red snapper baked in parchment paper. In addition to ordering à la carte, you can choose the $29 pre-theater or $32 prix-fixe dinner menu.

LA MIRABELLE   FRENCH   11/20

102 W. 86th St. (Columbus & Amsterdam Aves.), 10024
496-0458, *Dinner nightly, Brunch Sun., $$*

A

Now in a new location, this unpretentious French bistro serves such classics as coquilles St. Jacques, veal kidneys with mustard sauce, veal chop in an apple-Calvados sauce and herb-crusted rack of lamb. The bouillabaisse (on Friday) and couscous (on Saturday) all have their neighborhood devotees. Crème brûlée is the recommended dessert.

MERCHANT'S NY   NEW AMERICAN   12/20

521 Columbus Ave. (85th & 86th Sts.), 10024
721-3689, *Lunch & Dinner daily, $$*

Is it a bar with great food or a restaurant with great drinks? Either way, sip a Negroni martini served tableside in a chrome shaker or choose a glass from the wine bar, paired with a seared tuna sandwich or a late-night snack of steamed vegetable dumplings. A hopping place after midnight, when everyone wants to pose on the comfy lounge sofas. **Also at 1125 First Ave. (62nd St.) 832-1551, & 112 Seventh Ave. (16th & 17th Sts.) 366-7267.**

MINGALA WEST   BURMESE   13/20

325 Amsterdam Ave. (75th & 76th Sts.), 10023
873-0787, *Lunch Mon.-Fri., Dinner nightly, $*

Sample exotic Burmese cuisine in this softly lit, flower-laden dining room. The unusual salad of pickled green-tea leaves with toasted garlic, prawns and crunchy peanuts blends a variety of contrasting flavors, preparing the palate for good things to come. The chewy thousand-layer bread is a rich complement to such dishes as "Rangoon night market" noodles with hunks of duck, or sweet slices of pork with shallots in a brown sauce.

PICHOLINE   FRENCH/MEDITERRANEAN   16/20

35 W. 64th St. (Broadway & Central Park West), 10023
724-8585, *Lunch Tues.-Sat., Dinner nightly, $$$*

At chef/owner Terrance Brennan's Picholine, great things—culinarily-speaking—are happening. For one, he offers over 30 varieties of cheese, all maintained at perfect temperature and ripeness. In the beautiful dining room with cozy banquettes, French country antiques and Limoges china, sample such seasonally changing dishes as scallop tartare with caviar and potato wafers, fresh grilled octopus, roasted tenderloin of venison with pumpkin-prune pancakes, horseradish-crusted tournedos of salmon, and wild mushroom-and-duck risotto with butternut squash and white-truffle essence. The desserts are excellent, and there are several tasting menus that range from $35 to $85 per person. Of the over 200 wines, about 30 are priced at $35 or less, and at least 12 are offered by the glass. Be forewarned: the terrific house-made breadsticks and foccacia and the bowls of picholine olives that arrive at the start of a meal can make a serious dent in your appetite.

RESTAURANT 222   ECLECTIC   16/20

222 W. 79th St.(Amsterdam Ave. & Broadway), 10024
799-0400, *Lunch Tues.-Fri., Dinner nightly, $$$$*

This idiosyncratic restaurant is blazing brave new marks in taste and price. Marlies and Frank Valenza's superb kitchen makes the term extraordinary commonplace. It must. The appetizers range in price from $15 to $59, entrées from $32 to $120. Mr. Valenza, whose landmark price-buster The Palace stood the country on its ear in the '70's, claims that the ingredients he uses are simply the best in the world. That means white truffles, Israeli-goose foie gras, sushi-grade tuna, colossal shrimp, triple-O beluga caviar and Kobe steak. In counterpoint to the articulated avalanche of excess in the kitchen, 222 is a cozy paneled setting straight out of a London townhouse. Artfully rustic decorative touches abound, and the staff is helpful and engaging. Some dishes, Provençal-style fish soup teeming with tuna, lobster, salmon, tarragon broth and melted leeks, for example, with rouille and foccacia on the side, are a virtual meal. There's also a $35 prix-fixe lunch menu.

TAVERN ON THE GREEN   NEW AMERICAN   11/20

Central Park West & 67th St., 10023
873-3200, *Lunch Mon.-Fri., Dinner nightly, Brunch Sat.-Sun.,* $$$$

With its twinkling pin lights, glittering chandeliers, party atmosphere—and spectacular views of Central Park—Manhattan's biggest (and the nation's largest-grossing independently owned) dining extravaganza is a popular place for celebrations. In fact, they serve up to 2000 meals a day. As a result, the food can be uneven (or downright bad) and the service slow (not to mention rude). When you book (reservations are recommended, but walk-in seating is often available), specify the cozier **Chestnut Room** which has live entertainment, or the glass-enclosed **Crystal Room**. In fine weather, it's lovely to dine on the terrace. The seasonally changing menu might include house-cured salmon, baby back ribs and jumbo crabcakes to start, and such entrées as grilled Atlantic salmon with tomato salsa, prime Porterhouse steak for two with onion rings and rack of lamb with white bean purée.

TERRACE   NEW AMERICAN   15/20

Butler Hall, Columbia University, 400 W. 119th St.
(Amsterdam & Morningside Aves.), 10027
666-9490, *Lunch Tues.-Fri., Dinner Tues.-Sat.,* $$$$

The penthouse restaurant atop Columbia University's Butler Hall has long featured jaw-dropping views of northern Manhattan with necklaces of light gracing its bridges. Now there are flavor fireworks here too. In the main dining room, where sparkling crystal, red roses and a harpist set the stage for celebratory dining and romance, chef Kenneth Johnson has moved the cuisine from old-fashioned French to modern American, adding inspirations from around the globe: Moroccan-spiced jumbo prawns with red-lentil falafel, tomato chutney and harissa oil in chickpea vinaigrette; an arugula-and-ruby-grapefruit salad topped with grilled sweetbreads, asparagus and walnut-citrus vinaigrette. Terrace has 150 wines and efficient valet parking. The new **Sky Grille** offers the same awesome panorama to those who drop up for drinks and perhaps a bracing nosh, such as smoked-duck quesadilla with wicked habanero-mango catsup.

BRING THE LEVEL OF YOUR
NEXT MEETING
TO NEW
HEIGHTS

You get a different perspective from up here, high in the Southern Rockies of Colorado. You're in the midst of 250 magnificent square miles known as Forbes Trinchera - the perfect getaway from the stresses of the corporate world.

Your accommodations, which include an experienced professional staff of fifty, fit perfectly into the natural setting of this property.

Here, you're surrounded by majestic beauty. Lofty peaks scrape the blue Colorado sky - the highest reaching 14,345 feet. the air is so clear, fresh and clean that you feel invigorated, revitalized and re-generated. You will accomplish much more at your meetings.

And after work, there's play. More than forty miles of trout filled streams. Miles of trails to hike on and discover. Skeet shooting. Horseback riding. And you're not that far from a challenging golf course. Let our altitude give your next meeting a fresher attitude. If you'd like a closer look, **call 1-800-FORBES-5, or email us at tryland@forbes.com**

FORBES TRINCHERA RANCH:

A Forbes Executive Retreat

DOMAINES SCHLUMBERGER
ALSACE GRANDS CRUS-WINES

Gewürztraminer
Riesling
Pinot Blanc
Pinot Gris
Sylvaner

"A superb firm which produces
some of the most extraordinary
wines of France."

– Robert Parker
The Wine Advocate

TASTE THE HEART OF THE

SANTA MARIA BENCH

1996

Cambria

ESTATE BOTTLED

KATHERINE'S VINEYARD
Chardonnay
SANTA MARIA VALLEY, CALIFORNIA

TASTING ROOM OPEN
SATURDAY & SUNDAY 10 AM - 5 PM
5475 CHARDONNAY LANE
SANTA MARIA, CALIFORNIA 93454
888-339-9463

VINCE AND EDDIE'S   AMERICAN   14/20

70 W. 68th St. (Columbus Ave. & Central Park West), 10023
721-0068, *Lunch & Dinner daily*, $$$

With its fireplace, low ceilings, bare-wood floors, oil-cloth-covered tables and country antiques, this little hideaway around the corner from Lincoln Center could pass for a cozy country inn. The fare is comfort food; Maryland-style crab-cakes spiked with spicy corn relish, roasted chicken with lentils and garlic-scented spinach, Cornish game hen with cornbread stuffing, braised lamb shank and crumbly fruit cobblers for dessert. If whipped potatoes don't come with your dish, order them on the side. At lunch, go for an overstuffed grilled-tuna sandwich with house-made chips.

AND ALSO...

JOSIE'S   ORGANIC

300 Amsterdam Ave. (74th St.), 10023
769-1212, *Dinner nightly*, $$

Organic fruits and vegies, mostly free-range beef and poultry and filtered water are used in the preparation of the dishes listed on the recycled-paper menu—most of which are also dairy free—at this ecologically correct dining spot. You'll find grilled, not fried, calamari, homemade pastas, organic hot dogs and such good seafood offerings as herb-and-garlic-crusted St. Peter fish and the popular tuna burger. To drink—a selection of organic beers and wines along with fresh-squeezed juices.

MERLOT BAR & GRILL   NEW AMERICAN

48 W. 63rd St. (Broadway), 10023
3-MERLOT, *Lunch & Dinner daily*, $$$

Across the street from Lincoln Center and upstairs from **Iridium Jazz Club**, Merlot has a far-out design (lots of colors, musical motifs and undulating shapes), a 600-bottle wine cellar and such dishes as wild-mushroom strudel, crabcakes and osso buco of monkfish. Call about special vintner's dinners.

METISSE   FRENCH

239 W. 105th St. (Broadway & Amsterdam Ave.), 10025
666-8825, *Dinner nightly*, $$

This friendly neighborhood restaurant near Columbia serves French cuisine that's a blend of the classic with the nouvelle. Owner Claude Waryniak, who worked in dining rooms associated with Jean-Georges Vongerichten, is French-Dominican. The seasonally changing menu offers such starters as tuna carpaccio, escargots and warm goat cheese salad. Entrées range from a simple grilled veal chop and monkfish with couscous, to salmon in a white-wine sauce. In addition to a such French staples as vanilla mousse, they sometimes serve Caribbean sweet-plantain dumplings for dessert.

PENANG WEST   MALAYSIAN

240 Columbus Ave. (71st St.), 10023
769-3988, *Lunch & Dinner daily*, $$

This uptown version of the SoHo eatery lacks its waterfall, but makes up for that in light from a wall of French doors that open to the sidewalk café in warm weather. For more on the food, see review under "Below Houston—And Also.."

RAIN   PAN-ASIAN

100 W. 82nd St. (Columbus & Amsterdam Aves.), 10024
501-0776, *Lunch & Dinner daily*, $$

This hip & noisy neighborhood restaurant serves Vietnamese, Thai and Malaysian food—generally in small portions. You'll find a basket of crisp shrimp chips on your table, and a menu that offers everything from Malaysian chicken satay, Thai fried calamari and tuna-sushi rolls, to fiery jumbo shrimp, pan-seared mako shark with basil and Chinese eggplant, and Thai-style duck fajitas with moo-shu pancakes. The place is usually crowded, but if you're lucky, you'll be able to grab one of the wicker chairs in the lounge while you're waiting for a table. Few wines but lots of beers to choose from.

MANHATTAN QUICK BITES

CONTENTS

INTRODUCTION. 164
BAKERY/CAFÉS. 164
BARBECUE 167
BARS, SALOONS & TAVERNS 169
BREWPUBS 170
BURGERS, DOGS & CHILI 171
CAFÉS & COFFEEHOUSES. 175
COFFEE SHOPS & DINERS 179
DELIS & BAGEL SHOPS 183
ETHNIC FLAIR 186
        AFGHAN 186
        AMERICAN SOUTHWEST. 187
        ARGENTINEAN 187
        BELGIAN 188
        BRITISH 188
        CAJUN 189
        CARIBBEAN 189
        CHINESE/DIM SUM. 190
        CUBAN-CHINESE. 193
        GREEK 193
        INDIAN 194
        ITALIAN 195
        JAPANESE. 197
        KOREAN 198
        KOSHER 199
        MALAYSIAN. 200
        MEXICAN/LATIN AMERICAN 200
        MIDDLE EASTERN 203
        MOROCCAN 204
        PAN-ASIAN 204
        POLISH. 205
        SOUL FOOD/SOUTHERN 205
        SPANISH. 206
        THAI. 206
        TIBETAN 207
        VIETNAMESE. 207
ICE CREAM & MORE 208
PIZZA 211
SOUP 213
TEA ROOMS & PÂTISSERIES 213
THEME RESTAURANTS 214
VEGGIE/ORGANIC. 217

THE BIG NOSH

Got a yen to nosh? One of the great pleasures of New York is that you need never step foot in an assembly-line-style fast-food restaurant, even if you don't have much money to spend. Every neighborhood has casual, low-cost but satisfying dining choices: there are Asian restaurants of every variety in Chinatown and a United Nations of ethnic restaurants throughout the city; there are cafés in Greenwich Village, the East Village, the West Village, Chelsea and everywhere else; you'll find delis on the Lower East Side and Upper West Side, and pizza—and trendy coffee bars—on most every corner.

Midtown office workers have their favorite hot dog vendors or street carts; every neighborhood has its coffee shop, bar or saloon, and new, pure-entertainment "theme" restaurants—designed around everything from Harleys to the Red Planet — line 57th Street, Times Square and beyond.

Following are some of our favorites of the hundreds upon hundreds of New York's casual eateries. You can eat well (and have fun) in these **QUICK BITES** for $15; if you have a beer with your hot dog or a margarita with your enchiladas, expect to pay a little more.

We have categorized the following **QUICK BITES** according to their most noteworthy feature. However, many could easily be listed in more than one category: What makes a "Café" a "Bakery/Café" may only be its plethora of pastries or its shelves of fresh-baked bread for sale; most "Delis" could have been called "Eastern European" in the "Ethnic Flair" section as well; and you can get good burgers at most of the "Theme" restaurants. Looking for a bite to eat that will leave enough cash for a cab ride home? This is the place:

BAKERY-CAFÉS

All phone numbers are (212) unless otherwise indicated

BLEECKER STREET PASTRY & CAFÉ

245 Bleecker St. (Sixth & Seventh Aves.), 10014
242-4959, *Breakfast & Lunch daily*
No cards

This neighborhood bakery in the West Village bakes all the favorite Italian pastries: biscotti, panettone Genovese with fennel seeds, cannoli and zeppole during the holidays. It's hard to choose from among the vast selection of buttery cookies and meringues. Luscious cakes come with or without decorations. There are a few tiny tables where you can enjoy an espresso and a pastry—or in warm weather, a dish of gelato.

CUPCAKE CAFÉ

522 Ninth Ave. (39th St.), 10018
465-1530, *Breakfast & Lunch daily*
No cards

Okay, so the neighborhood near the Port Authority Bus Terminal isn't the best, but this little café oozes charm.

(Imagine that your down-at-the-heels auntie opened a little restaurant in her sitting room, and you've got the ambience down.) On top of that, their doughnuts are the best we've eaten: sweet potato, buttermilk, raspberry, orange-whole wheat, and whole wheat with walnuts and wheat germ. Their coffee cake and waffles are just as good. This is also a fine place for a lunch of soup and a sandwich or a pizza with smoked mozzarella cheese. The Cupcake's dense, flavorful cupcakes and cakes frosted with rich buttercream rival those at New York's best bakeries. Buy some to go.

E.A.T.

1064 Madison Ave. (80th & 81st Sts.), 10028
772-0022, *Breakfast, Lunch & Dinner daily*

Yes, it's very pricey, but the quality at Eli Zabar's Upper East Side is top-notch. E.A.T.'s excellent breads and baked goods are sold throughout the city, but one of the best selections is here. The prepared sandwiches are made on E.A.T.'s crusty baguettes or its dense rye bread, and there are usually at least 40-50 salads and antipasti from which to choose.

EATZI'S MARKET & BAKERY

Macy's Herald Square, 151 W. 34th St. (Sixth & Seventh Aves.), 10001
216-9660, *Breakfast, Lunch & Dinner daily*

A

French or Italian, soup or sandwich, sushi or sashimi, eat in or take out. There are a mind-boggling number of choices, and they are all yours to make at EatZi's. Located in the basement of Macy's is what could best be described as a mini-department store of food. Up to 1,800 different items are offered daily, and you can watch as chefs bake, roast, grill and fry everything in the open kitchens. Convenience is what this place is all about, although the crowds at lunch and dinner reminds you of midtown traffic.

EDGAR'S

255 W. 84th St. (Broadway & West End Ave.), 10024
496-6126, *Lunch & Dinner daily*
No cards

Edgar Allen Poe—who once lived on this Upper West Side block—would hardly recognize this place named after him, with its modern design and yuppie clientele. You can't miss the desert case, where each of the more than 40 pies and cakes looks better than the next. The three-berry and apple-crumb pies, for example, taste fresh and are a perfect match for the excellent coffee. Cakes range from Southern pecan and choco-late-cookie cheesecake to European classics. Their soups, sand-wiches and pizzas are also good.

FRIEND OF A FARMER

77 Irving Pl. (18th & 19th Sts.), 10003
477-2188, *Breakfast, Lunch & Dinner daily, Brunch Sat.-Sun.*
A

Friend of a Farmer has a lot more going for it than the faux-farmhouse décor. The baked goods are uniformly top-notch, and the sandwiches made with homemade white, wheat or other breads are sensational. The menu changes with the seasons, as does the selection of pastries, muffins, strudels, cakes and pies, depending on how many hungry Manhattanites got here before you. Friend of a Farmer does superb French toast at breakfast, and is quite busy with the overflow from the nearby Union Square Greenmarket for weekend brunches.

LA BOULANGÈRE

49 E. 21st St. (Park Ave. South & Broadway), 10010
475-8772, *Breakfast, Lunch & Dinner daily*
A

Linda Blankenhorn, a former psychologist, has turned her love of baking into an ever-expanding restaurant-cum-French bakery. She bakes and sells great croissants, Danish pastries, pain au chocolat, brioche, as well as more contemporary multi-grained breads. Lunch and dinner are casual affairs; best bets are the salads, quiches and any of the rotating selection of entrées.

PANYA

10 Stuyvestant St. (Third Ave. & E. 9th St.), 10003
777-1930, *Breakfast, Lunch & Dinner daily*
No cards

Blink and you will miss this slip of a place, squeezed as it is between a sushi restaurant and a Japanese supermarket. But is a good pit stop during an afternoon of prowling around the shops of terminally hip E. 9th St. Try the savory—if a bit unusual—Japanese-style buns filled with sweet red beans or octopus, or sandwiches made with spaghetti or potato salad, which are surprisingly satisfying. Panya (which means bakery in Japanese) also boasts some of the tastiest almond croissants you will find this side of Tokyo—or Paris, for that matter.

ROCCO PASTRY SHOP

243 Bleecker St. (Sixth & Seventh Aves.), 10014
242-6031, *Breakfast & Lunch daily*
No cards

You'll most likely have to wait in line to get into Rocco's, for its selection of almondy pignoli cookies, potent babas au rhum, crunchy anise biscotti and freshly-piped cannoli are scrumptious. In addition to traditional Italian pastries, you'll find mile-high napoleons. Villagers and shoppers like to sit at the tiny tables and enjoy cappuccinos with their treats.

SARABETH'S

423 Amsterdam Ave. (80th & 81st Sts.), 10023
496-6280, *Breakfast, Lunch, Tea & Dinner daily*

A

Sarabeth's has become somewhat of a New York institution, offering homey cakes, scones, brownies, jams and decadently rich-and-sweet sticky buns. The restaurants labor in the bakery's shadow, but they are good spots for hearty breakfasts of french toast, pancakes and such specialties as "Goldielox"—scrambled eggs with cream cheese and smoked salmon. The chicken pot pie is a seasonal dinner treat. **Also at 1295 Madison Ave. (92nd St.) 410-7335, and in the Whitney Museum, 570-3600, ext. 1670, open Breakfast & Lunch Tues.-Sun.**

TRIBAKERY

186 Franklin St. (Greenwich & Hudson Sts.), 10013
431-1114, *Breakfast & Lunch Mon.-Sat.*

Restaurateur Drew Nieporent's friendly neighborhood spot is good for homemade pastries and a caffè latte in the morning. In addition to the salads and sandwiches, such as roasted portabello and goat cheese, the lunch menu features such comfort foods as shepherd's pie, cabbage soup and chocolate-marble cheesecake.

VENIERO'S

342 E. 11th St. (First Ave.), 10003
674-7264, *Breakfast & Lunch daily*

It's not unusual to see limos parked in front of this unpretentious café and bakery, an East Village fixture since 1894. Rain or shine, the crowds waiting for tables spill out into the street, and around the holidays, orders for pies and cakes must be made weeks in advance. They make everything from Italian tiramisu to Viennese Sachertorte, as well as Danish pastries, fruit tarts and butter cookies. Even after cappuccino and a rich dessert, stop at the bakery counter. You'll regret it the next morning if you leave empty-handed.

BARBECUE

BROTHERS BAR-B-QUE

225 Varick (W. Houston & Sixth Ave.), 10014
777-2775, *Lunch & Dinner daily*

This funky dive serves up what may well be the best Texas- and North Carolina-style barbecue in New York. Brothers smokes its meats over hickory for 10 to 18 hours, and the result is hog heaven. Try the pork ribs, the tender pulled pork or the "pig-out," a mound of barbecued chicken, ribs, pork, beef and sausage. On Monday nights, the "all-you-can-eat" barbecue goes for a reasonable $13.95. You'll find other Southern dishes on the menu, along with such specials as mozzarella-spinach-and-ham-stuffed chicken fried steak, but barbecue is clearly the top priority. Certainly more so than the decor—which is license plates tacked on the wall along with photos of barbecue joints.

DALLAS B-B-Q

27 W. 72nd St. (Central Park West & Columbus Ave.), 10023
873-2004, *Lunch & Dinner daily*

If you don't mind eating cattle-car style with a few hundred other diners, you can share in a bargain-basement deal. The early-bird special makes up for shortcomings in atmosphere and graciousness: Before 6:30 p.m. Monday through Friday, or before 5 p.m. on the weekend, two can feast on chicken soup, half a barbecued chicken, cornbread and potatoes for just $7.95. The regular menu also offers baby back ribs, beef ribs, a "loaf" of deep-fried onions and hefty half-pound burgers. Don't expect down-home authenticity here, but the portions are big and kids are welcome. **Also at 1265 Third Ave. (72nd & 73rd Sts) 772-9393, 21 University Place (8th St.) 674-4450, and 132 Second Ave. (Eighth St.) 777-5574.**

DUKE'S

99 E. 19th St. (Park Ave. South & Irving Pl.) 10003
260-2922, *Lunch & Dinner daily, Brunch Sun.*

We almost categorized Duke's as a "Theme" restaurant, for with its Southern roadside dive decor—and old 45 rpm records plastered to the ceiling—it could definitely qualify. But since they slow-smoke their beef brisket, chicken and ribs over hickory, apple and mesquite hardwood, we thought they belonged here. You can also get a crabcake burger, macaroni and cheese as gooey as ice cream, Carolina pulled-pork sandwiches, buttermilk-fried chicken and "Aunt Mae's" meatloaf with gravy. Duke's is a hoot, and kids love it.

VIRGIL'S REAL BARBECUE

152 W. 44th St. (Broadway), 10036
921-9494, *Lunch & Dinner daily*

With its faux-roadhouse setting, Virgil's is about as close as you're going to authentic barbecue on Broadway. Lively and loud, its walls lined with barbecue memorabilia, Virgil's is a great pre- and post-theater spot for regional American barbecue dishes like wet-cooked pork ribs, shredded Carolina pork shoulder, smoky and tangy roast lamb, all served with a variety of good side dishes, as well as great biscuits and corn bread. Dozens of beers, and a moderate wine list. Given its location, don't expect to find prices as low as you'd find at a real roadhouse down South.

BARS, SALOONS & TAVERNS

EAR INN

326 Spring St. (Greenwich St.), 10013
226-9060, *Lunch & Dinner daily*

The Ear Inn is reason to trek just about as far west as you
can without falling into the Hudson River. Look up at the neon
sign for a hint about where this tavern, a Landmark building
and open since 1817, got its name. Inside, grab a stool or a
table and order an eight-ounce prime sirloin burger for $6.50,
served on a seeded roll with a salad and home fries. Also on
the menu are salads and usually an Irish-accented special.
Catering to its regular crowd of writers and artists, the Ear Inn
stays open until 4 a.m. on weekends, and holds poetry readings
on Saturday afternoons.

ELEPHANT AND CASTLE

68 Greenwich Ave. (Sixth & Seventh Aves.), 10011
243-1400, *Breakfast, Lunch & Dinner daily, Brunch Sat.-Sun.*

There's one of these cheery Irish saloons in Dublin, and
one here in the Village. With its simple menu and efficient service, it is a perfect pit stop for shoppers in the daytime and,
since it's open until midnight, for night-owls as well. Among
the dozen omelets, we enjoy the lavish goat cheese version with
fresh and sun-dried tomatoes. The "Elephantburger" is a charcoal-grilled beauty topped with curried sour cream, bacon,
Cheddar cheese, tomato and scallions.

FANELLI'S

94 Prince St. (Mercer St.), 10013
226-9412, *Breakfast, Lunch & Dinner daily*

This downscale neighborhood bar in upscale SoHo always
attracts a crowd and is open until 2 in the morning. It's been
here since 1872, long before SoHo was transformed from a
warehouse-and-factory district to a trendy hub full of art gal-
leries and expensive shops. The hamburgers and french fries
are great. Be sure to take a look at the beautiful glass door.

MCSORLEY'S OLD ALE HOUSE

15 E. 7th St. (Second & Third Aves.), 10003
473-9148, *Lunch & Dinner daily*
No cards

This may be among the best places to eat a burger on a
rainy afternoon, or in the wee hours, when a musty old saloon,
especially one with this much history, seems the proper place
to be. Around since 1854, McSorley's has the faint odor of
more than a century's worth of stale beer. A working-class
neighborhood bar, it kept a men-only rule until 1970, when it

was targeted by feminists. It has since been discovered by the college crowd. Expect long lines just to get in the door some nights.

OLD TOWN BAR

45 E. 18th St. (Broadway & Park Ave.), 10003
529-6732, *Lunch & Dinner daily*

Open for business since 1892, the Old Town is loaded with character—tiled floors, a pressed tin ceiling, old lamps that once used gas. Unfortunately, everybody knows about the place, thanks in part to David Letterman using it on his show and in part to the yuppification of the neighborhood. After work, it can be hard just to get through the small doorway. Still, there are good burgers and a boisterous atmosphere to accompany the beer, which includes their own Old Town lager. Also available are salads and grilled sandwiches; try the chicken breast hero. Open until 1 a.m.

WHITE HORSE TAVERN

567 Hudson St. (11th St.), 10014
243-9260, *Lunch & Dinner daily*
No cards

This vintage New York bar that has satisfied the thirsts of such luminaries as Dylan Thomas, Jack Kerouac and Bob Dylan. Afternoons you still can find yourself in the company of writers, actors and musicians who live in the West Village neighborhood. But the nights—which extend to 4 a.m. on Fridays and Saturdays—belong to the young, making it the place to be if you want to feel like you're still in college. The standard bar food won't inspire a masterpiece, though the burgers and sandwiches are fine. But when it's quiet, the White Horse is a good place to sit and contemplate a lost love, and the outdoor tables are prime people-watching perches.

BREWPUBS

CHELSEA BREWING COMPANY

Westside Highway (18th St.), 10011
336-6440, *Lunch & Dinner daily, Brunch Sun.*

The largest microbrewery in Manhattan, this warehouse-like space on Pier 59 brews a changing array of beers, six at a time, and has its own line of bottled beer, labeled "Checker Cab Blonde Ale" and "Sunset Red." The fare runs from brick-oven-baked pizzas and pastas to grilled steaks and seafood. Since the 22-foot-high ceilings and seating for 350, upstairs and down, make for a lively—and noisy—beer hall atmosphere, if you want serenity, grab a sofa in the Cigar Room.

GREENWICH PIZZA & BREWING COMPANY

418 Sixth Ave. (9th St.), 10011
477-8744, *Lunch & Dinner daily, Brunch Sat.-Sun.*

This brick-walled, brass-trimmed beer-and-pizza joint keeps hopping 'til the wee hours. Over 75 beers are available, including imported microbrews and brews on tap from the Neptune brewery. This is a fun neighborhood hangout where friends share gourmet pizzas (fresh spinach buried in Mozzarella cheese; pink vodka sauce with peas and proscuitto), and beer by-the-yard. On weekends, there is a very reasonable prix-fixe brunch.

HEARTLAND BREWERY

35 Union Square West (16th & 17th Sts.), 10003
645-3400, *Lunch & Dinner daily*

Check out the huge glassed-in copper and steel vats where they brew their own beer at this Midwest-comes-to-Manhattan spot. The brews are evocative of the heartland—"Cornhusker Lager" ... "Harvest Wheat Beer" ... "Indiana Pale Ale" ... "Farmer Jon's Oatmeal Stout." The food, however, is all over the map: Maine crab-cakes, seafood jambalaya, a Kentucky whiskey burger and a pulled BBQ pork sandwich. When the Union Square Greenmarket is set up across the street on Saturdays, this exposed-brick-walled brewpub is packed. **Also at 1258 W. 51st St. (Sixth & Seventh Aves.) 582-8244).**

WESTSIDE BREWING COMPANY

340 Amsterdam Ave. (76th St.), 10024
721-2161, *Lunch & Dinner daily*

Owned by the folks who brought you the Chelsea Brewing Company, this small Upper West Side brewery always has red and blonde housemade beers on tap, along with such specials as amber, stout, porter and wheat. All the usual beer foods are served, from burgers and pasta to Mexican. Weekday lunch specials run $6.95.

BURGERS, DOGS & CHILI

ALL STATE CAFÉ

250 W. 72nd St. (Broadway & West End Ave.), 10023
874-1883, *Lunch & Dinner daily, Brunch Sat.-Sun.*
No cards

A hip jukebox and a roaring fire in winter are among the charms that make this below-ground brick-walled joint a perennial favorite of Upper West Siders until 3 in the a.m. Actors and literary types conduct serious conversations at the bar, then sit at the small wood-topped tables for a hearty and inexpensive meal, most likely the great burgers and fries. There also are daily specials for lunch and dinner such as roasted chicken, fresh fish and pastas, and a reasonably priced weekend brunch.

CORNER BISTRO

331 W. 4th St. (Jane St.), 10014
242-9502, Lunch & Dinner daily
No cards 👀

Open 'til 4 a.m. nightly, this West Village bar-and-burger joint has a reputation for serving Manhattan's best burgers (the secret is grilling them from both sides in a salamander). The vintage jukebox is well-stocked and the tables are scarred with graffiti. Nobody minds squeezing into the hard wooden booths for beer, Irish coffee and macho bowls of chili or bistro burgers made with high-quality beef and topped with cheese, bacon and onions—until 4 in the morning. Wear a bib.

GRAY'S PAPAYA

2090 Broadway (72nd St.), 10025
799-0243, Open 24 hours daily
No cards 👀

At these no-frills stand-up spots you get a 24-hour bargain and a chance to see all manner of New Yorkers, who come for what must be the cheapest and some of the best hot dogs for miles around, washed down with an assortment of tropical fruit drinks. Gray's Papayas are perfect for a speedy bite before the theater, or as a place to put down your packages after shopping. Don't miss the truly terrible puns on the signs, such as "Franks a lot for your business!" **Also at 402 Avenue of the Americas W. 8th St. (8th St.) 260-3532.**

JACKSON HOLE

517 Columbus Ave. (85th St.), 10028
362-5177, Breakfast, Lunch & Dinner daily
🔲 👀

Teenagers especially love these cowboy-themed eateries, where they can plop down and tuck into a seven-ounce burger prepared in any of 27 ways—topped with various cheeses, mushrooms, onions, bacon and so on. There's even a beefburger tartare for the adventurous diner. Sandwiches, salads and breakfast also are available. Take a window table to watch the passing scene; the interior decor is minimal. The Upper West Side spot is open until 4 a.m. on weekends. **Also at 1270 Madison Ave. (91st St.) 427-2820. Call for other locations.**

MANHATTAN CHILI COMPANY

1500 Broadway (W. 43rd St.), 10036
730-8666, Lunch & Dinner daily, Brunch Sat.-Sun.
VISA MasterCard DISC 🔲

A fun but touristy Times Square spot for a bowl of chili, fajitas, burgers and wings, along with dynamite margaritas and draft beer. Exotic chili renditions range from the "Texas Chain Gang" with coarse ground beef and smoked jalapeños to the "Pima City Green" with green peppers, potatoes and split peas.

MCDONALD'S

160 Broadway (Liberty St.), 10007
385-2063, *Breakfast, Lunch & Dinner daily*
No cards

This isn't your usual MickyD's. After all, there's a doorman in a tux to greet visitors, and music from a baby grand piano filling the double-deck dining room. Oh, and there isn't much of McDonald's signature Formica—each of the 250 tables here has a marble top. The usual McD menu has been expanded to appeal to the Wall Street types who stop in here. Fresh fruit and pastries are served in the morning; and espresso and herbal tea are available all day. But don't worry—you can still get a Big Mac and fries. Of course, given the decor, you're going to pay a bit more than at the other, less refined branches. **Numerous other locations.**

NATHAN'S FAMOUS

901 Avenue of the Americas (33rd St.), 10019
947-1259, *Open daily*
No cards

In 1916, long before golden arches began to dominate the fast-food business, Nathan Handwerker was stuffing ground beef into sausage casings at his tiny snack bar on Coney Island, and selling them quicker than you could say "wiener." His customers liked his "Coneys" so much that in a few years, Nathan's hot dogs had become as much a New York institution as the Brooklyn Dodgers. These days, the Dodgers are in California and Nathan's is a fast-food counter. At this and numerous other locations around the city, it shares space with the likes of Kentucky Fried Chicken. So much for history, but you can still get a hot dog and fries until midnight. For the real thing, go to the original in Coney Island, Brooklyn. **Numerous other locations.**

PAPAYA KING

179 E. 86th St. (Third Ave.), 10028
369-0648, *Open daily*
No cards

Since 1928, Papaya King has boasted that its frankfurter is tastier than filet mignon. Many regulars would agree, and the $1.29 price tag—including a topping of onions, sauerkraut or Papaya King's own tropical relish—doesn't hurt. A sign outside the shop claims that nearly 13 million franks have been sold since 1972. The fruit drinks also are a big attraction; the mango-strawberry "Tropical Breeze" has chunks of fruit in nearly every gulp. There's just a stand-up counter and not much room to maneuver, but who could argue with a hot-dog stand that has a photograph of Julia Child on the wall?

THE PRIME BURGER

5 E. 51st St. (Madison & Fifth Aves.), 10022
759-4729, *Breakfast, Lunch & Early Dinner Mon.-Sat.*
No cards

If you're on your own, this is a good spot for a good burger, because the burger "cubicles" where customers eat have fold-down wooden tabletops. The quality of the beef is so high, the cooks aren't afraid to serve it raw. Anyone for a burger tartare with eggs and onions?

SASSY'S SLIDERS

163 First Ave. (10th St.), 10003
228-2900, *Lunch & Dinner daily*
No cards 👀

Call them belly bombers—bite-size burgers on steamed white-bread buns that slide down into the tummy and make room for more, much more. Sassy's combos of four come in beef, chicken, turkey and veggie, along with garlic, sweet pota-to or Cajun fries. Top it off with a thick-as-cement milkshake for the ultimate guilty pleasure until 3 a.m. weekends.

SILVER SPURS

771 Broadway (9th St.), 10003
473-5517, *Breakfast, Lunch & Dinner daily*
A

There's a convoluted tale about a Miss Silver Spurs running a saloon in Texas that somehow led to the opening, in 1979, of this Greenwich Village cousin, a typical New York coffee shop done up in Western dress. The "colossal burger" is 10 ounces of beef before it hits the grill, and comes 22 ways. The "stage coach" is topped with mozzarella cheese, mushrooms, onions and peppers; the "buckin' bronco" is served with baked beans and bacon. To wash them down, there's sarsaparilla. Silver Spurs also serves breakfast, sandwiches and salads, and several kid-friendly children's meals. **Also at 490 La Guardia Place (Houston St.) 228-2333.**

SORRENTO COFFEE SHOP

4 W. 18th St. (Fifth & Sixth Aves.), 10004
627-0572, *Breakfast & Lunch Mon.-Sat.*
No cards

Okay, so they'll kill your cholesterol count, but these hand-made patties grilled in fat on a flat-top grill sure tempt burger lovers. Some Cuban dishes—rice and beans, pepper steak—too.

CAFÉS & COFFEEHOUSES

In addition to its scores of cafés and coffeehouses, New York has wholeheartedly adopted Seattle's love of coffee bars. These small, coffee-centric spots take their beans very seriously, and the result is an expensive but delicious cup of java. While not always homey, the city's coffee bars usually serve a smattering of pastries and sandwiches.

There is hardly a street corner without a **Starbucks**. Other major coffee-bar chains are **Dalton**, **Pasqua** and **Timothy's**. Among our other favorites are **Novocento**, 343 W. Broadway (Grand & Broome Sts.) 925-4706; **New World Coffee & Bagels** with several branches including 449 Sixth Ave. (10th & 11 Sts.) 633-1966; 1159 Third Ave. (67th & 68th Sts.) 472-1598; and 400 Madison Ave. (47th & 48th Sts.) 838-2854.

The mega-bookstores are cashing in on the coffee craze too. For example, the cafés in the huge **Barnes & Nobles** at 2289 Broadway (82nd & 83rd Sts.) 362-8835, and 675 Sixth Ave. (22nd St.) 727-1227, have tables and reputations as fertile singles spots. For more than just a latte and a light snack, there are cafés and coffeehouses galore:

ANGLERS & WRITERS

420 Hudson St. (St. Lukes Pl.), 10014
675-0810, *Breakfast, Lunch & Dinner daily*
No cards

With a nod to Hemingway, Anglers & Writers is full of fishing paraphernalia—mounted fish, fish prints, ship models, hurricane lamps. But it's as cozy as an English tearoom, with mismatched teapots and old wooden tables with fresh flowers. To go with coffee or tea, the homemade breads and scones are just right. There's also a menu of fish, pasta and chicken dishes, along with such daily specials as chicken pot pie and lamb stew.

BELL CAFFÈ

310 Spring St. (Greenwich & Hudson Sts.), 10013
334-2355, *Lunch & Dinner daily*

Located in the far western reaches of SoHo, Bell Caffè is convenient to the New York City Fire Museum, though not much else. It serves an eclectic mix of healthy food and has Newcastle Brown Ale on tap. Owned by a struggling actor, Bell Caffè features live music nightly and holds parties for artists the first Monday of the month (the paintings on the walls are for sale). A good place for a bite until 2 a.m. during the week, until 4 a.m. on Fridays and Saturdays.

LA BONNE SOUPE BISTRO

48 W. 55th St. (Fifth & Sixth Aves.) 10019
586-7650, *Lunch & Dinner daily*

La Bonne Soupe is the real thing—an inexpensive but quality bistro in midtown Manhattan, serving authentic and robust dishes like coq au vin, cassoulet, cheese fondue and hanger steak with frites. And as you might expect with such a name, particular attention is paid here to soups, like the fragrant and oozy tureen of onion soup blanketed in melted Gruyère. Like any restaurant dependent on theater-goers for weekday evening business, La Bonne Soupe's waitstaff will get you fed and out as quickly as possible if you inform them of your plans when you enter.

CAFÉ BORGIA

185 Bleecker St. (MacDougal St.), 10013
674-9589, *Breakfast, Lunch & Dinner daily*
No cards

Café Borgia attracts well-known locals like Al Pacino as well as regular New Yorkers and foreign tourists in search of an authentic Greenwich Village coffeehouse. On weekends, there's always a wait, but for steaming café au lait and cappuccino, French toast, Italian pastries and people-watching, there's no place better in the Village.

CAFÉ EUROPA

205 W. 57th St. (Seventh Ave.), 10019
977-4031, *Breakfast, Lunch & Dinner daily*

These glitzed-up Manhattan versions of Parisian brasseries (wood columns, ceiling fans and trompe l'oeil ceilings) are fine for a quick sandwich on fresh-baked breads (smoked salmon with scallions and cream cheese on black Russian bread; grilled chicken on Tuscan country bread), or a leisurely latte or espresso. Also available are thin-crusted pizzas, and low-fat, sugar-free muffins. **Also at 1177 Sixth Ave. (46th St.) 575-7272.**

CAFÉ LA FORTUNA

69 W. 71st St. (Central Park West & Columbus Ave.), 10023
724-5846, *Lunch & Dinner daily*
No cards

This cozy subterranean nook attracts a nightly crowd of locals and post-Lincoln-Center patrons who come for the best espresso on the Upper West Side until past midnight. There's a soothing pace here, enhanced by the decor of vintage opera records and yellowed photos of Tristans and Aidas peering sadly from the walls. A better-than-decent selection of pastries is on hand—anise cookies, chocolate cakes and rum-scented zuppa inglese. For sipping, you can choose from fragrant teas, fruit drinks and frothy hot chocolate. In summer, the garden terrace is open, and it's worth the half-hour wait in line to relax over iced cappuccino topped with a scoop of excellent homemade gelato.

CAFÉ REGGIO

119 MacDougal St. (W. 3rd & Bleecker Sts.), 10012
475-9557, *Breakfast, Lunch & Dinner daily*
No cards 👓

Open since 1927, and run by the Cavallacci family for over 40 years, this café has been going strong ever since. Plaster busts of Verdi and Wagner nestle in the niches of the smoke-darkened walls, and the faintly seedy air is vintage Fellini. Sip espresso, cappuccino or a devastating hot chocolate swirled with whipped cream while you eat pastry and study what passes for Bohemia these days in the tame Village streets. The foccaccia is homemade, and every day there's a homemade soup, perhaps cream of watercress or Tuscan vegetable. A good place to debate the meaning of life until 4 in the morning on Saturday night.

CAFFÈ DANTE

79-81 MacDougal St. (Bleecker St.), 10012
982-5275, *Breakfast, Lunch & Dinner daily*
No cards 💻👓

Neighborhood coffee-addicts make the Dante part of their daily routine for some of the most bracing, well-made espresso this side of the Trastevere. Cappuccino, hot chocolate, iced drinks and a good selection of teas and pastries also are available until well past midnight. In summer, sit outside at tiny tables for terrific people-watching. Even if you're not hungry, you'll want to try one of the lovely sandwiches, made with crisp rolls and top-quality imported Italian cold meats and cheeses.

CAFFÈ DELLA PACE

48 E. 7th St. (First & Second Aves.), 10003
529-8024, *Lunch & Dinner daily*
No cards

East Village regulars know exactly what they're getting at this small, unpretentious Italian café. Enjoy cappuccino, dessert and Italian sodas while sitting in a window a few steps above the street. A large plate of antipasti with hunks of mozzarella, thinly sliced prosciutto, roasted red peppers and tomatoes is served with Italian bread and is enough for a meal. The pasta specials change daily, and the tiramisu is deservedly popular. .

CAFFÈ TINA

184 Prince St. (Thompson & Sullivan Sts.), 10012
925-9387, *Lunch & Dinner daily*
No cards 💻

It helps if you speak Italian at this tiny but atmospheric SoHo coffeehouse. The pastries in the glass case look a bit tired, but we can vouch for the sandwiches and the strong espresso. A perfect place to sip a cappuccino while reading a book.

DEAN & DELUCA CAFÉ

9 Rockefeller Plaza (48th & 49th St.), 10020
664-1363, *Breakfast, Lunch & Dinner daily*

One of six cafés run by the owners of SoHo's ultra-chic gourmet food store, this bright, airy eatery features soups, sandwiches, salads, pastries and coffee, and does a brisk lunch business with Rockefeller Center execs. Dean & Deluca uses impeccable ingredients, and even the simplest sandwich can be elevated by dense, chewy breads and top-quality meats and cheeses. Most of the business here is take-out, but tables on two levels offer a pleasant spot to grab a quick bite or have a leisurely cup of coffee. You'll also find Dean & Deluca cafés in the trendy **Paramount Hotel** among other spots—and of course at their main store in SoHo. **Call for other locations.**

LAMARCA CHEESE SHOP & RESTAURANT

161 E. 22nd St. (Third Ave.), 10010
673-7920, *Lunch & Dinner Mon.-Fri.*
No cards

Originally a partner in Dean & DeLuca, the owner is a cheese connoisseur, and offers 75-100 varieties of cheese here—all aged on the premises. Custom-prepared trays are available, and they also sell delicious salads, soups, pastas and breads, as well as cappuccino, espresso and juice. Order to go, or take a seat at one of the café tables and indulge yourself.

THE LOTUS CLUB

35 Clinton St. (Stanton St.), 10002
253-1144, *Breakfast, Lunch & Dinner daily*

No, you're not in Berkeley, though it may feel that way at this Lower East Side bookshop/café. While you're browsing for books, $6 and less will get you warming soups, overstuffed sandwiches and big salads.

PARLOUR CAFÉ

ABC Carpet & Home, 888 Broadway (19th St.), 10003
677-2233, *Breakfast, Lunch & Tea Mon.-Fri., Dinner Tues.-Sat., Brunch Sat.-Sun.*

If Miss Havisham ran a restaurant, it would probably look a lot like the Parlour Café. Set inside ABC Carpet & Furniture, the decorator's dream store, the Parlour is a maze of funky mismatched tables and chairs and small, sparkling chandeliers illuminating the dim air. It all makes for a snug setting for brunch on the weekends—nothing fancy, just familiar stuff like blintzes, scrambled eggs and a bottomless stack of pancakes (eat as many as you want). Dinner is an equally cozy affair, with heartening dishes like French onion soup, crêpes and veal with polenta. During the week, the Parlour serves afternoon tea, so you can refresh yourself after feathering your nest with buys at the furniture store.

SAVORIES

30 Rockefeller Plaza (49th & 50th Sts.), 10020
332-7630, *Breakfast & Lunch Mon.-Fri.*

The beauty of Rockefeller Center and its statue of Prometheus are draw enough for Savories, the least expensive of several restaurants in an underground shopping area. In winter, diners gaze out through the glass walls onto a Currier & Ives-like vision of ice skaters on the surrounding rink. In summer, the rink turns into a colorful patio of umbrellas and tables. The scene is the real star—the sandwiches, salads, rotisserie chicken and pastas are fine, but don't expect any showstoppers. Call to hear the daily soups and specials on the answering machine.

VINEGAR FACTORY

431 E. 91st St. (First & York Aves.), 10128
628-9608, *Breakfast, Lunch & Dinner daily, Brunch Sat.-Sun.*

A roomy store by New York standards (in a former vinegar factory), Eli's Factory serves an unsurpassed selection of prepared salads, entrées and desserts—hearty Provençal tarts, roast chicken with tabouleh, sweet rugelach—as well as his best-selling breads, which are found at stores all over the city. A good selection of all packaged goods as well, and plenty of tables to enjoy a meal while you stock up for home.

COFFEE SHOPS & DINERS

AGGIE'S

146 W. Houston St. (MacDougal St.), 10012
673-8994, *Breakfast, Lunch & Dinner Mon.-Sat., Breakfast & Lunch Sun.*

This modern diner serves such trendy dishes as sandwiches with grilled vegetables and goat cheese—things you'd never find at a roadside diner in Arkansas. But they also serve hamburgers, which go well with its diner's old-fashioned, friendly ambience. Aggie herself is likely to be at the counter greeting customers, and if you come in a couple of times in a row, the waitresses will ask you if you'd like "the usual."

BARKING DOG LUNCHEONETTE

1678 Third Ave. (94th St.), 10128
831-1800, *Breakfast, Lunch & Dinner daily*
No cards

The Barking Dog Luncheonette may seem more cutesy than homey, with its doggy drinking fountain out front and case full of stuffed animals inside. But kids love it, and the food is the best bargain in the neighborhood. Popular dishes include the pan-fried Chesapeake Bay crabcakes and the crispy cornmeal-crusted fried calamari. The Cobb salad is commendable. The menu has a Southern accent, and everything is made in-house. The Barking Dog does breakfasts, burgers and sandwiches, too.

BENDIX DINER

219 Eighth Ave. (21st St.), 10011
366-0560, *Breakfast, Lunch & Dinner daily, Brunch Sat.-Sun.*

"Get Fat," proclaims the neon sign outside this funky Chelsea diner. And the menu notes, "Not responsible for personalities. In case of fire, please pay immediately." In addition to a sense of humor, the Bendix seems to have an identity crisis—the menu includes Swedish pancakes, Thai noodles, chili, stir-fried chicken teriyaki and a daily pasta special. The portions are huge and the homey dishes—meatloaf or pork chops with mashed potatoes—taste like Mom's. Sometimes there's even green Jell-O with whipped cream. Very hip, so expect a wait for a table, especially during weekend brunch.

BREAD & BUTTER

229 Elizabeth St. (Houston & Prince Sts.), 10012
925-7600, *Lunch daily*

Even if you're too busy shopping to break for lunch, you've still gotta have your Bread & Butter. This take-out shop serves sophisticated sandwiches, like grilled chicken with pesto and Parmesan, smoked turkey with artichokes, and grilled vegetables with goat cheese. Big spenders can splurge on a lobster club, and for the kid in you, how about peanut butter and jelly?

CAFÉ EDISON

228 W. 47th St. (Broadway & Eighth Ave.), 10036
354-0368, *Breakfast, Lunch & Dinner daily*
No cards

You can feel the sheer energy of Broadway in this boisterous theater district coffee shop, called by some "The Polish Tea

Room." Even if, like Broadway, it's a bit worn around the edges, it attracts such playwrights as August Wilson and Neil Simon. But you don't need to be a playwright to appreciate Café Edison's warp-speed waiters and terrific Eastern-European Jewish dishes, such as the fluffy, pillow-like cheese blintzes, borscht and gefilte fish. The $10.95 daily special includes a cup of delicious soup, a beverage and an entrée such as pot roast, broiled salmon or pork chops (this is not a kosher establishment). If you're staying at the adjoining Hotel Edison, you can charge your meal to your room. Watch for the hand-lettered sign: "We have kishka today!"

THE COFFEE MUG

233 Broadway (Park Pl. & Barclay St.), 10007
349-6040, *Breakfast & Lunch Mon.-Fri.*
No cards

The coffee shop food is just okay—grilled cheese sandwiches, burgers and onions rings—but the setting is mind-boggling: the ground floor of the Woolworth Building, with its soaring gold ceilings, mosaic-tiled floors and brass trim.

COFFEE SHOP

29 Union Square West (16th St.), 10003
243-7969, *Breakfast, Lunch & Dinner daily*

Coffee Shop with a capital "C" and "S"? Think coffee shop with attitude. This model hangout definitely has it. It's also filled with lots of '50s Formica and leatherette—and lots of smoke. Though the poseurs don't come here for the food, believe it or not, the food has a Brazilian bent: offering coconut-crisped shrimp, Bahian dumplings and seafood paella on some nights 'til 6 a.m.

THE COMFORT DINER

214 E. 45th St. (Second & Third Aves.), 10017
867-4555, *Breakfast, Lunch & Dinner daily*

From the outside, this little place looks like a tacky, run-down, old-fashioned metal-fronted diner. Step inside, however, and you realize it's a clean-and-neat, cool-and-hip retro version of an old-fashioned diner. The service is friendly and efficient, and you'll find not only meatloaf, macaroni-and-cheese and egg creams on the menu, but such updated comfort-food items as a Brie and sun-dried-tomato melted-cheese sandwich, Southwestern chicken pot pie and pineapple-banana smoothies. A great place for pancakes on a rainy Sunday morning. **Also at 146 E. 86th St. (Lexington) 426-8600.**

EJ'S LUNCHEONETTE

433 Amsterdam Ave. (80th & 81st Sts.), 10024
873-3444, *Breakfast, Lunch & Dinner daily, Brunch Sat.-Sun.*
No cards

These retro-1950s-style luncheonettes are big on breakfast: buttermilk flapjacks, Belgian waffles and challah french toast with or without a crunchy coating of almonds and corn flakes. There are also omelets, stewed fruit and such lunch and dinner items as black-bean-and-sirloin chili, Cobb salad and a chicken Reuben sandwich. **Also at 1271 Third Ave. (73rd St.) 472-0600, and 432 Sixth Ave. (9th & 10th Sts.) 473-5555.**

EMPIRE DINER

210 Tenth Ave. (22nd St.), 10011
243-2736, *Open 24 hours daily*

This art-deco railway car surges with megavolt energy at four in the a.m. on weekends, as club-hoppers stop by for breakfast. The menu offers glorified diner dishes—omelets, club sandwiches, chili, burgers, brownies, hot fudge sundaes. Much of the food wouldn't cut the mustard in a regular restaurant. But lots of leggy models love the place; some stockbroker types think it's wild. In warm weather, there are outdoor tables.

JONES DINER

371 Lafayette St. (Great Jones St.), 10012
673-3577, *Breakfast, Lunch & Early Dinner Mon.-Sat.*
No cards

Yep, it's the real thing: an old-fashioned long-and-narrow diner with red-topped stools at the counter and a handful of booths, where you can enjoy no-frills burgers and sandwiches at no-frills prices.

KIEV

117 Second Ave. (7th St.), 10003
674-4040, *Open 24 hours daily*
No cards

Got a craving for stuffed cabbage at 5 a.m.? Stop by this family-operated, East European coffee shop. Kiev attracts a large following of locals, who come for the blintzes, soft potato dumplings (pirogi), mushroom-barley soup and delicious slabs of french toast made with egg-rich challah bread. The generous portions and low prices make this place a popular student hangout.

LIFE CAFÉ

343 E. 10th St. (Ave. B), 10009
477-8791, *Lunch & Dinner daily*

You might recognize this Bohemian coffee house from the Broadway musical *Rent*. The Cal-Mex heavy-on-the-veggie menu offers everything from vegan burritos with soy cheese and tofu-sour cream to Southern-fried chicken with bourbon-mustard sauce. You can get a bowl of chili-dusted yam fries until 2 a.m. on weekends, then come back Sunday morning for a $1.99 hangover brunch of eggs, home fries, cornbread and coffee.

PICNIC

52 Irving Pl. (E. 17th St.), 10003
539-0240, *Breakfast, Lunch & Dinner daily*

Have you lost your picnic spirit? You can probably find it again at this corner café, which serves fresh, tasty salads and sandwiches. Take a seat at the communal table or order a picnic bag to go. If you like a simple sandwich that makes a meal, definitely try the meatloaf on a roll. But be sure to save room for dessert. The homemade "Ring Dings" deserve to be renamed "guaranteed death to your diet."

SILVER STAR RESTAURANT

1238 Second Ave. (65th St.), 10021
249-4250, *Open 24 hours daily*

This Greek-owned coffee shop is well-known in the neighborhood to bargain hunters who drop in for fresh seafood at moderate prices. Convenient to several movie theaters on the East Side, Silver Star is almost always full. The food ranges from such Greek specialties as pastitsio and moussaka to live lobsters and a fish of the day. In addition, there are burgers, sandwiches, omelets, grilled steaks and chops, salads and most other basics. Brunch is served on the weekends.

VESELKA

144 Second Ave. (9th St.), 10003
228-9682, *Open 24 hours daily*

True, this neighborhood is full of Eastern European diners, but Veselka's sprawling selection of pierogi and potato pancakes, blintzes and borscht has made it a local favorite. There's a small sidewalk café, and a funky cartoon film strip on the walls. Foreign newspapers are sold in front, service errs on the brusque side and lines for weekend brunch run out the door.

DELIS & BAGEL SHOPS

ABSOLUTE BAGELS

2700 Broadway (107th St.), 10025
932-2052, *Breakfast & Lunch daily*
No cards

A Thai bagel baker? Samak Thongkrieng, who learned his stuff at Ess-a-Bagel, turns out bagels that are huge and have an oh-so-soft texture more like that of a Chinese bun than an old-fashioned New York bagel. Still, Absolute's bagels get high marks for flavor, especially the egg, cinnamon-raisin and whole-wheat sesame. You can get bagel sandwiches and lox here, too.

BARNEY GREENGRASS

541 Amsterdam Ave. (86th & 87th Sts.), 10024
724-4707, *Breakfast & Lunch Tues.-Sun.*
VISA MasterCard during the week, No cards weekends

Since 1929, this noisy, dingy deli has hummed with hungry activity. Upper West Siders crowd in early to start the day on scrambled eggs with Nova and onions, or bagels with sturgeon, Nova or sable and cream cheese. If the line to get in is intimidating—on weekends, expect to wait—stop by the fish counter and pick up a few ounces of your favorite smoked fish, perhaps some pickled herring or one of the prepared fish salads, grab some bagels and a schmear, and build your own breakfast at home.

CARNEGIE DELICATESSEN

854 Seventh Ave. (54th & 55th Sts.), 10019
757-2245, *Breakfast, Lunch & Dinner daily*
No cards 🐶

A theater-district landmark, the Carnegie has cramped tables, big crowds, wisecracking waiters, and high prices, but it's the still one of the best places to get top-quality (and lean) corned beef and pastrami, enormous overstuffed sandwiches—and real New York deli ambience. Take home what you don't finish for another meal. We know many out-of-towners who make a beeline here the minute they set foot in Manhattan—even if it is 2 in the morning.

COLUMBIA HOT BAGELS

2836 Broadway (110th St.), 10025
222-3200, *Open 24 hours daily*
No cards 🐶

Columbia bakes the bagels for Zabar's and Murray's Sturgeon—need we say more? Columbia's bagels are bready but chewy, properly dense and great with lox. Especially delicious are the salt and rye bagels. They make bagel sandwiches too.

ESS-A-BAGEL

359 First Ave. (21st St.), 10010
260-2252, *Breakfast, Lunch & Dinner Mon.-Fri., Breakfast & Lunch Sat.-Sun.*
No cards

Many bagel aficionados argue that Ess-a makes the best bagels in New York. We're inclined to agree—except for when, once in awhile, we get one that isn't quite baked through. Cut and rolled by hand, their bagels are low in salt and preservative- and sugar-free. They're also huge. Flavors run the usual gamut, as do the many cream-cheese spreads. They also make bagel sandwiches galore, and, at the midtown shop, serve specialty coffee drinks. Ess-A-Bagel's bagels are kosher. **Also at 831 Third Avenue (51st St.) 260-2252.**

FINE & SCHAPIRO

138 W. 72nd St. (Broadway & Columbus Ave.), 10023
877-2874, *Lunch & Dinner daily*

When you see the big jars of peppers and olives in the window, the knishes and the roasted turkeys and chickens in the deli case, you'll know you've found this classic. Don't go for the decor; do go for the kosher hot dogs. For $17.95, the "Old World" sandwich-for-two sounds expensive, but it's a huge meal incorporating chopped liver, corned beef, pastrami, turkey and tongue topped with Russian dressing. If you want to throw high-cholesterol caution to the wind, this is the place.

KATZ'S DELI

205 E. Houston St. (Ludlow St.), 10002
254-2246, *Breakfast, Lunch & Dinner daily*

Opened in 1888, this Jewish-deli landmark in the historic immigrant neighborhood of the Lower East Side is a mammoth cafeteria-style place with great people-watching. You can get table service, but the most authentic way to go here is to take a ticket at the door, which employees at the counter punch with the prices as you order things to eat. Much of the food's not great. Stick with the grilled hot dogs and the hand-sliced corned beef that's as lean—and as good—as it gets.

MOM'S BAGELS & CATERING

15 W. 45th St. (Fifth & Sixth Aves.), 10036
764-1566, *Lunch Sun.-Fri.*

Mom's is a popular lunch spot for midtown office workers and can get incredibly crowded around noon. But the fresh-baked bagels—flying saucer-sized doughy delights that are wonderful spread with butter or soft cheese—are worth a stop. Also available: hard cheeses and a selection of meats. Mom's voicemail lists the daily specials and takes orders. Mom's is a kosher establishment, and is also a busy caterer.

SABLE'S SMOKED FISH

1489 Second Ave. (77th & 78th Sts.), 10021
249-6177, *Breakfast & Lunch daily*

At this Upper East Side spot, you'll find sensational smoked fish—from salmon, sable, whitefish and kippers to tuna and eel—along with fresh caviar, cold cuts and prepared to-go foods. (Kenny Sze, the owner, learned his craft at Zabar's.) There are a few tables for dining. Having a Sunday brunch party? Sable's will send over a lavish smoked-fish platter. They also make appealing cold-cut and cheese platters, jumbo sandwiches and chicken dishes.

SECOND AVENUE KOSHER DELI

156 Second Ave. (10th St.), 10003
677-0606, *Breakfast, Lunch & Dinner daily*

Got a craving for the most mouthwatering stuffed cabbage this side of Moscow? Juicy gefilte fish? Head to the East Village and New York's best kosher deli. The Lebewohl family has perfectly captured the frantic hustle and bustle of a turn-of-the-century eatery; the nostalgic atmosphere comes complete with cramped booths, pickles at every table and waitresses ordering you to finish every spoonful of the divine chicken-and-matzoh-ball soup. There are also kugel (noodle pudding), silky chopped liver and cholent (a casserole of beef, potatoes, beans and barley).

STAGE DELI

834 Seventh Ave. (54th St.), 10019
245-7850, *Breakfast, Lunch & Dinner daily*

The deli war between the Carnegie and the Stage is as partisan a fight as that between the Yankees and the Mets; these are serious issues in New York. Each accuses the other of atrocities such as steaming its corned beef with water from—gasp!—New Jersey. What's important is that the Stage and Carnegie have entirely different atmospheres. The Stage is more modern and less Brooklyn; it has window seats where you can watch people go by on Seventh Avenue and a full bar. Both delis are expensive. (At the Stage, the "Rosie O'Donnell" sandwich—corned beef, turkey, pastrami, roast beef and Swiss cheese, is $17.95.) The Stage's food is a matter of taste: its piles of lean, juicy corned beef between two pieces of doughy rye bread give the sandwich and New York delis a good name. The pastrami, however, while ample and tasty, loses to Carnegie by a nose.

ETHNIC FLAIR

AFGHAN

AFGHAN KEBAB HOUSE

764 Ninth Ave. (51st & 52nd Sts.), 10019
307-1612, *Lunch & Dinner Mon.-Sat.*
No cards

Afghan Kebab House is small and crowded, but it's worth the effort needed to grab one of the tiny tables for the food is tasty and inexpensive. Spit-roasted meats—chicken, lamb, beef and fish—cook slowly over open grills in a method apparently unchanged from ancient traditional modes. With a splash of one of the homemade hot sauces, the kebabs with rice are a perfect midtown bargain.

ARIANA AFGHAN KEBAB

878 Ninth Ave. (52nd & 53rd Sts.), 10019
262-2323, *Lunch & Dinner daily*
A

Hand-woven wall hangings and pictures of Afghanistan decorate every inch of this storefront restaurant that claims to cook dishes just like the owners' grandmothers did back in Kabul. Kadoo bolanee, pumpkin fritters with yogurt, and aushak, leek-filled dumplings in meat sauce, are satisfying examples of this hearty, exotic cuisine. One of our favorite meals here is a combo of savory sumac-dusted kebabs and aushe burida, a soothing noodle, yogurt and meat casserole. Bring your own wine or beer, and be prepared to wait for a table.

AMERICAN SOUTHWEST/ASIAN

BRIGHT FOOD SHOP

216 Eighth Ave. (21st St.), 10011
243-4433, *Brunch, Lunch & Dinner daily*
No cards

The 1930s sign still hangs outside this pink-and-gray-tiled luncheonette. But though the Bright Food Shop looks old-fashioned, its food is anything but. Chef/co-owner Dona Abramson invents dishes that blend Southwestern and Asian flavors, such as "moo shu Mex," a tortilla rolled around Chinese vegetables with a spicy peanut sauce, and black bean-and-chorizo wontons. Southwestern dishes include a hearty green chile posole, a New Mexican stew made with green chiles, and gingerbread made with dark Mexican beer, served with mango sauce and crema. The Caesar salad gets a tasty twist with cornbread croutons. A vegetarian can eat well here.

ARGENTINEAN

SOSA BORELLA

460 Greenwich St (Watts & Debrosses Sts.), 10013
432-5093, *Breakfast & Lunch Mon.-Fri., Dinner nightly, Brunch Sat.-Sun.*
A

A good place for fresh pastries and coffee in the morning, Sosa Borella, at lunch, serves sandwiches including bresaola, smoked turkey with Brie and roasted peppers, and prosciutto with mozzarella. It's not until dinner that the true Argentinean flavor of this quiet spot comes out. Then the menu features such specialties as garlic-zapped breaded-and-fried round steak with fried eggs on top, short ribs and grilled strip steaks.

BELGIAN

B. FRITES

1657 Broadway (51st & 52nd Sts.), 10019
767-0858, *Lunch & Dinner daily*
No cards

There's nothing quite like skinny, crisp and salty french fries, eaten out of a cardboard cone as they do in Belgium. B. Frites now sells them to New Yorkers, and they're the real thing: twice-fried in a genuine Belgian Rubbens frite-maker, and served with Vandemoortele mayonnaise, the mayonnaise used for frites in Belgium, or one of ten sauces flavored with everything from curry to peanuts. If the concept works here, look for B. Frites stands on every corner.

PETITE ABEILLE

466 Hudson St. (Barrow & Grove Sts.), 10014
741-6479, *Lunch & Dinner daily*

There are only about a half-dozen tables at this tiny spot, and they're usually full, but it's worth waiting for the sugary and buttery Belgian waffles, the sausages with stroemp, a sweet potato-and-vegetable purée, and the omelets served with crisp pommes frites and mayonnaise. **Also at 14th St. & Ninth Ave., 727-1505.**

POMMES FRITES

123 Second Ave. (7th & 8th Sts.), 10003
674-1234, *Lunch & dinner daily*
No cards

The name means french fries, but these twice-fried Belgian beauties aren't French. Take-out frites can now be found across the city, but Pommes Frites started the craze with paper cone carriers and dozens of special sauces. Try the roasted garlic mayo or sweet mango chutney. Or mix it up with especial sauce (ketchup, onions and frite sauce, a sweeter mayo). The first sample is free and raw onions come with everything; load up as late at 1 a.m. on weekends.

BRITISH

TELEPHONE BAR & GRILL

149 Second Ave. (9th & 10th Sts.), 10003
529-5000, *Lunch & Dinner daily*

Three (working) red English telephone booths stand out-side of this dark and cozy, Londonish-looking pub, where they serve fish and chips wrapped in the *New York Times*, Stilton cheese fritters and vegetarian shepherd's pie. Yes, there is Guinness on tap, but unlike in London, it's served cold here.

CAJUN

CHANTALE'S CAJUN KITCHEN

510 Ninth Ave. (38th & 39th Sts.), 10018
967-2623, *Lunch & Dinner Mon.-Sat.*

Serving mostly sandwiches and salads, Chantale's tiny nook also features authentic and inexpensive Cajun fare. Chantale's gumbo with shrimp, sausage, scallops, fish and chicken, is the best of five different gumbo varieties she offers regularly. The limited menu also includes a variety of salads, and a good selection of daily-changing specials. Though not particularly Cajun, the curried coconut vegetables, with or without chicken or shrimp, are terrific.

CARIBBEAN

CARIDAD   DOMINICAN

4311 Broadway (184th St.), 10033
928-4645, 928-9748, *Breakfast, Lunch & Dinner daily;*
open 24 hours Fri.-Sat.

This bright, spacious Dominican restaurant rocks with good will and merinque from the juke box all night long, and everything's good and cheap. From the kitchen come dishes like the mixed seafood, deep saucers brimming with lobster, crab, clams and mussels in pale-red broth. Like many Dominican places, the platters at Caridad arrive with working-class portions of beans, saffrony yellow rice and caramelized fried plantains. Bill Cosby is a good customer.

CASA ADELA   PUERTO RICAN

66 Avenue C (4th & 5th Sts.), 10009
473-1882, *Lunch & Dinner daily*
No cards

Avenue C is called Loisaida, where Puerto Rican cuisine still reigns with Adela Fargas as queen. Since 1973, she's been cooking up rotisserie chicken so tender, it falls apart on the fork. When Adela's visiting Puerto Rico, her kids are in the kitchen, dishing out pasteles (meat patties in plantain leaves) and pernil (shredded roast pork) with mugs of soupy beans to pour over fluffy rice. Between the blaring Spanish soap operas and whirring blender churning out frothy batidas (fruit milkshakes), don't expect intimate conversation.

NEGRIL ISLAND SPICE   JAMAICAN

362 W. 23rd St. (Eighth & Ninth Aves.), 10011
807-6411, *Lunch Tues.-Sun., Dinner nightly*

A

One of the best Caribbean spots in Manhattan, Negril Island Spice serves up tangy fish escoveitch, ginger-lime chicken and chewy bammie cake along with glasses of sweet sorrel. Though many dishes are not as spicy as some like, they're all well-cooked and nicely presented. A vegetarian menu includes steamed and seasoned callaloo and Ital stew. The colorful, lively setting is situated in an out of the way corner of Chelsea, but fans of roti will find their way.

CHINESE/DIM SUM

BIG WONG

67 Mott St. (Canal St.), 10013
964-0540, *Breakfast, Lunch & Dinner daily*
No cards

An unprepossessing Chinatown noodle and congee shop that's a favorite with locals, Big Wong prepares terrific wok-fried loofah-like crullers, and wonton soup chock-o-block with mai fun noodles and topped with room-temperature duck, chicken or pork. Whatever you order, don't leave without sampling the supernal spare ribs and duck, or a steaming bowl of rice congee topped with scallions, preserved pork or 1,000 year-old egg.

EVERGREEN SHANGHAI RESTAURANT

63 Mott St. (Canal & Bayard Sts.), 10013
571-3339, *Lunch & Dinner daily*
No cards

Don't be put off by the long menu. Forget the Cantonese, Szechuan and Hunan dishes and head straight for the Shanghai specialties: raw crabs marinated in ginger-and-garlic-haunted rice wine; thinly sliced aromatic beef; spicy cabbage, sweet-edged smoked fish; potent wine chicken; tofu in crab sauce; and sweet-and-peppery whole bass. Obviously, it's best to go with a group, so that you can share. Start off with juicy soup dumplings.

GOLDEN UNICORN

18 E. Broadway (Catherine St.), 10002
941-0911, *Breakfast, Lunch & Dinner daily*

Take the elevator up from the street level—past hostesses in black tie speaking rapidly into walkie-talkies—and emerge in one of two bustling, brightly lit Hong Kong-style dining rooms. A combination lunch buffet and dim sum parlor in the round, Golden Unicorn attracts Chinatown's best-dressed, but its prices are low. The dim sum is the best reason to eat here: waitresses in pink wheel by carts laden with taro-coated fried seafood, savory warm pork buns, shrimp cakes with nuts and meat and five different types of wontons. In fact, this is arguably the best dim sum in Chinatown.

JOE'S SHANGHAI

9 Pell St. (Mott & Bowery Sts.), 10013
233-8888, *Lunch & Dinner daily*
No cards

If you can't round up dining partners, come to Joe's alone, for you'll make friends quickly at one of the big communal tables, where everyone oohs and aahs over the xiao lung bao—Shanghai steamed buns that somehow manage to enclose hot soup in pastry. Order them with shrimp or pork, then suck out some of the savory broth before dipping the dumpling into black vinegar and ginger sauce and gobbling it whole. Other Shanghai delights to try here: cabbage-draped meatballs; razor clams with black beans; turnip cakes; and crispy whole yellow fish. **Also in Queens (82-74 Broadway, Elmhurst, 718-639-6888).**

KAM CHUEH

40 Bowery (Canal & Bayard Sts.), 10013
791-6868, 791-6866, *Lunch & Dinner daily*
No cards

With its fish tanks and spare interior, Kam Chueh looks pretty much like all of the other no-frills restaurants in Chinatown. But you can taste the difference in such house specials as squid in salted pepper, which is deep-fried to crisp perfection with no trace of oiliness. Even standard fare like sweet-and-sour chicken is done so well that it seems exciting. As Kam Chueh is open until 5 a.m., it's a great place to satisfy your post-karaoke bar cravings.

MA MA BUDDHA

578 Hudson St. (W. 11th St.), 10014
929-7800, *Lunch & Dinner daily*

A couple of notches up from your typical neighborhood Chinese restaurant, Ma Ma Buddha prides itself (or is it herself) on the perfectly cooked stir-fried veggies—with which you can have with any assortment of meats or fish. Though we've found the steamed dumplings a bit doughy, we love the delicately fried soft-shell crabs in season and the barbecued dishes. And how many other Chinese places have outdoor seating?

MANDARIN COURT

61 Mott St. (Canal & Bayard Sts.), 10002
608-3838, *Breakfast, Lunch & Dinner daily*

Do visions of pork buns and shrimp dumplings dance in your head? They will after a visit to Mandarin Court, where dim sum is served from 7:30 a.m. to 3:30 p.m. daily. Located on one of most touristy blocks in Chinatown, this sparingly decorated restaurant is popular with diners who can't tell a spring roll from an egg roll, as well as with demanding dim-sum snobs. There are also good lunch specials, and a dinner menu boasting such tasty surprises as crab meat with corn soup, and baked scallops in mayonnaise sauce.

MEE NOODLE SHOP

922 Second Ave. (49th St.), 10022
888-0027, *Lunch & Dinner daily*
🅐 ♥

Okay, so it's not much to look at. Mee Noodle Shop is an outpost of fresh, simple and delicious Chinese noodle cookery in midtown Manhattan. A busy lunch spot, Mee Noodle has an extensive menu offering seven varieties—rice stick, lo mein, mei fun—with endless combinations of additional ingredients. There are some less authentic choices, like egg and spinach noodles, but stick to the Asian variety. Try roast pork lo mein, or perhaps dan dan noodles under a dense meat sauce, but with portions large and prices low, you can afford to take a chance on the new here.

NEW YORK NOODLETOWN

28 1/2 Bowery (Bayard St.), 10013
349-0923, *Lunch & Dinner daily*
No cards

Be prepared to share a table in this noisy Hong-Kong-style noodle restaurant, but the noodles are worth the hassle. On the long non-noodle menu are such tasty dishes as salt-baked soft-shell crabs in season, stir-fried pea shoots, and shrimp with black-pepper sauce.

OLLIE'S NOODLE SHOP & GRILLE

2315 Broadway (84th St.), 10024
362-3111, *Lunch & Dinner daily*

Their scallion pancakes alone—made with just the right oiliness, light dough and flavor—put Ollie's ahead of the pack of your typical street-corner Manhattan Chinese restaurant. The steamed vegetable dumplings are made with delicate wrappers, and the huge, reasonably priced bowls of noodle soup are as comforting as Mom's chicken noodle. You can watch the cooks at work in the open kitchen as you wait. **Also at 200B W. 44th St. (Seventh Ave.) 921-5988, and 1991 Broadway (W. 68th St.) 595-8181.**

69 MOTT STREET

69 Mott St. (Canal St.), 10013
233-5877, *Breakfast, Lunch & Dinner daily*
No cards

Aromatic five-spice-scented roast duck, moist, succulent smoked spare ribs and roast pork with wonderfully crackling skin are the main reasons for coming to this modest Chinatown neighborhood restaurant. Served at room temperature with a bowl of scallion-topped congee (boiled rice), they are among the most consistently good quick snacks you can get in Chinatown. Other dishes are good and cheap as well.

CUBAN-CHINESE

LA CHINITA LINDA

166 Eighth Ave. (18th St.), 10011
633-1791, *Lunch & Dinner daily*

We're lucky to have a number of Cuban-Chinese restaurants in New York, run by Chinese families who fled Cuba in the fifties. Among the best is this popular West Side eatery, where the zesty roast meats and poultry Cuban-style are the best bets. The noodles on the Chinese side of the menu are good as well, and everything's great with a Tsingtao beer.

LA NUEVA VICTORIA

2536 Broadway (95th & 96th Sts.), 10025
865-1810, *Breakfast, Lunch & Dinner daily*

Another popular—and very good—Cuban-Chinese restaurant on the Upper West Side, La Nueva Victoria serves such multi-cultural mixes as chicharron de pollo, wonton soup and a plate of fried plantains. Black beans, saffron rice and boiled congee with shrimp or pork are reliable and satisfying staples, but if you're really hungry, order them with Chinese-style roast pork or Dominican-style steak, perhaps with a Chinese beer and a silken flan for dessert.

GREEK

UNCLE NICK'S

747 Ninth Ave. (50th & 51st Sts.), 10019
245-7992, *Lunch & Dinner daily*
A

This old-fashioned taverna is a fun and friendly place to enjoy big portions of well-prepared Greek classics, from gyros and spinach pie to grilled fish, at excellent prices. Gather a party together and share a combo of appetizers, including tarama, melitzanosalata and tsadziki, scooped up with pita bread and washed down with retsina or beer. Good for pre- or post-theater dining.

INDIAN

CURRY IN A HURRY

119 Lexington Ave. (28th St.), 10016
683-0900, *Lunch & Dinner daily*

If you get an Indian taxi driver, ask him for the name of a good, cheap Indian restaurant. Chances are he'll mention this Gramercy Park hole-in-the-wall. They take credit cards only if your bill is over $10.

MITALI EAST

334 E. 6th St. (First & Second Aves.), 10003
533-2508, *Lunch & Dinner daily*

On a block filled with Indian restaurants, Mitali East is perhaps the most popular. There long have been rumors that all the restaurants share a single kitchen, but Mitali's food is better than many of its neighbors. Chana bhajee, spicy sautéed chickpeas, make a good first course. Mitali's chicken tandoori is moist and mild. Be sure to try some of the breads, including the aloo paratha, stuffed with spiced potatoes. Mitali is comfortable, with a colorful red-and-yellow decor.

MITALI WEST

296 Bleecker St. (Seventh Ave. South), 10014
989-1367, *Lunch & Dinner daily*

See review of Mitali East above.

PASSAGE TO INDIA

308 E. 6th St. (First & Second Aves.), 10003
529-5770, *Lunch & Dinner daily*

Another of the 6th Street Indian restaurants, this eatery features pretty wood paneling and a soothing ambience, and you can see the tandoor (clay oven) from the dining room. The tandoori dishes—beef, chicken, lamb or shrimp—are well prepared, but the vindaloo, made with chicken, lamb or shrimp, is incendiary, so beware. There are a few Indonesian dishes as well.

ITALIAN

CAFFÈ BUON GUSTO

236 E. 77th St. (Second & Third Aves.), 10021
535-6884, *Lunch & Dinner daily*
No cards ☎

These Italian cafés serve delicious—and very reasonably priced—Italian favorites such as homemade ravioli and penne alla vodka. The Buon Gustos are not such well-kept secrets, and without a reservation, there's usually a wait. **Also at 71 W. 71st St. (Columbus Ave.) 875-1512, 1009 Second Ave. (53rd St.) 755-1476, and 151 Montague St., Brooklyn Heights, 718-624-3838.**

CARMINE'S

2450 Broadway (90th & 91st Sts.), 10024
362-2200, *Lunch & Dinner daily*

You could almost call these two Carmine's "theme" restaurants—the theme being an old-fashioned crowded and noisy family-style Southern Italian restaurant, where everyone at the table shares huge platters of inexpensive and garlic-punched pasta and chicken in various red sauces. Get a big party together and prepare to wait for seating. **Also at 200 W. 44th St. (Broadway & Eighth Ave.) 221-3800.**

COLA'S

148 Eighth Ave. (17th & 18th Sts.), 10011
633-8020, *Dinner nightly*

A reliable pasta restaurant in Chelsea, Cola's has a small menu with gentle prices. Favorites include whole wheat penne with shiitake mushrooms, sage, rosemary and tomatoes, and risotto with shrimp and broccoli.

CUCINA STAGIONALE

275 Bleecker St. (Sixth & Seventh Aves.), 10014
924-2707, *Lunch & Dinner daily*
No cards

This popular Village pasta house looks like a cozy dining room, featuring old-fashioned flowered wallpaper hung with family photographs. Pastas are under $10 and include vegetable lasagne, penne with eggplant, onions, tomatoes and ricotta cheese, and shells with sautéed calamari, anchovies and capers. There's also a range of fish and meat dishes. Bring your own wine.

LA FOCACCERIA

128 First Ave (7th & 8th Sts.) 10009
254-4946, *Lunch & Dinner Mon.-Sat.*
No cards

It's plain and tiny, but La Focacceria has been serving homey Italian meals—thick bean-and-pasta soup, chicken livers Madeira, spaghetti in red clam sauce—for decades, along with thick slabs of fresh-baked foccacia.

MANGANAROS GOURMET FOODS

488 Ninth Ave. (37th & 38th Sts.), 10018
563-5331, 800-4SALAMI, *Lunch daily, closed Sun. in summer*
A

Untold numbers of Manganaros fans have trod the old wooden floors of the old-fashioned, ancient-looking Italian grocery store for its famous sandwiches, among other goods. In front, there's a good selection of imported oils, vinegars, cheeses and dried pastas available, and you can eat a meal here at one of the dozen little tables.

MANGANARO'S HERO BOY RESTAURANT

492 Ninth Ave. (38th St.), 10018
947-7325, *Lunch & Dinner Mon.-Sat.*

You call them heroes; others call them subs or grinders. Under any name, these torpedo-sized monsters, overstuffed with hearty Italian cold cuts, are some of New York's best sandwiches. The environment is somewhat run-down and the roster of hot Italian dishes that fill out the menu is pretty lackluster, but the aroma of imported cheeses, fresh bread and olives is intoxicating. Sandwiches range from individual heroes to order-in-advance specialties such as the six-foot champion for up to 40 hungry people.

MAPPAMONDO (UNO)

11 Abingdon Square (Bleecker & 12th Sts.), 10014
675-3100, *Dinner nightly*

MAPPAMONDO (DUE)

581 Hudson St. (Bank & 11th Sts.), 10014
675-7474, *Dinner nightly, Brunch Sat.-Sun.*
No cards

Maps and globes decorate these tiny, cramped West Village Italians, where the crowd is young and the noise-level is high. (Due is slightly bigger than Mappamondo Uno down the street.) At Uno, you can get farfalle al salmon.

MELAMPO IMPORTED FOODS

105 Sullivan St. (Prince & Spring Sts.), 10014
334-9530, *Open Mon.-Sat.*
No cards

Although it is primarily a well-stocked Italian grocery store, Melampo is most well-known for the sandwiches: Slices of mortadella, prosciutto, coppa and fresh mozzarella cheese join sun-dried tomatoes, vinegary roast peppers and a splash of good extra virgin olive oil on top of focaccia or other Italian breads for a most satisfying Little Italy lunch. Breads, cheese, sliced meats and Italian soft drinks and sweets are also available, along with San Pellegrino water.

OROLOGIO

162 Ave. A (10th & 11th Sts.), 10009
228-6900, *Dinner nightly*
No cards

Clocks, clocks and more clocks decorate this cramped but charming spot. The food is good and very reasonably priced: thin-crusted pizzas and homemade pastas for under $9, and such entrées as marinated grilled tuna for $13.50.

SALUMERIA BIELLESE

378 Eighth Ave. (29th St.), 10001
736-7376, *Lunch & Dinner Mon.-Sat.*

Many of the sausages served in the best restaurants and shops in New York and around the country come from this deli and restaurant. Traditional Genoa salami, prosciutto and other spicy Italian pork sausages are the most popular, but you can get boudin blanc, boudin noir, cotechino and French-style chipolatas. The stock varies, depending on what's being made that day, but it's all good. The deli is open for breakfast, too.

JAPANESE

MENCHANKO-TEI

39 W. 55th St. (Fifth & Sixth Aves.), 10019
247-1585, *Lunch & Dinner daily*

On a cold day, you can't beat the restorative powers of a steaming bowl of Japanese noodles, which Menchanko-Tei serves up with efficiency and grace. It's an especially good choice for lone diners in midtown, who can sit at the convivial, black-lacquer counter in front. For under $10, you can get the Menchanko luncheon combination, which includes a huge metal cauldron filled with tasty things: a rich broth, home-style noodles, shrimp, fish balls, rice cakes, chicken and cabbage. **Also at 131 E. 45th St. (Lexington & Third Aves.) 986-6805.**

OISHI NOODLE

1117 Sixth Ave. (43rd St.), 10036
764-3075, *Lunch & Dinner Mon.-Sat.*
No cards

This neat and clean hole-in-the-wall not far from Times Square, serves noodles with mixed vegetables, pork and roast beef toppings, all suspended in one of four house soups: soybean, soy sauce, butter and salt, and curry. The noodles are the perfect texture—neither crunchy nor slithery, but somewhere in between. Oishi also serves delicious dumplings; one fine dish is the stir-fried udon noodles with pork dumplings and salad.

SOBAYA

229 E. 9th St. (Second & Third Aves.), 10012
533-6966, *Lunch & Dinner daily*

If you think Japanese food begins and ends with sushi, you might want to check out Sobaya to see what you've been missing. Soba and udon are served at this sleekly appointed, tranquil little noodle haven on East 9th Street, which in recent years has become somewhat of a Little Tokyo community. Best of all, slurping your noodles is not only allowed, but according to Japanese custom, encouraged.

KOREAN

DOK SUNI'S

119 First Ave. (Seventh St. & St. Mark's Pl.), 10003
477-9506, *Dinner nightly*
No cards

This hip East Villager doesn't have a Korean decor, but the food's the real thing: pork spareribs seasoned with garlic and chili paste, and kim chee in lots of things, even pancakes.

EMPIRE KOREA

6 E. 32nd St. (Madison & Fifth Aves.), 10016
725-1333, *Open 24 hours daily*

Empire Korea has the look and feel of a once-grand casino. During the week, the restaurant offers 15 different kinds of daily-changing lunch-box specials. For under $10, you can choose from traditional Korean dishes like bibimbap and bul kogi or Japanese specialties like sashimi or shrimp teriyaki, all served with rice, salad, tempura and, of course, kim chee.

HAN BAT

53 W. 35th St. (Fifth & Sixth Aves.), 11232
629-5588, *Open 24 hours daily*

Perhaps the only place for a kim-chee fix in the middle of the night, this garment district Korean is most crowded at lunchtime, when mostly Korean business execs come for the country dishes of South Korea, served family-style. Share a pajun, a scallion pancake the size of a small pizza, topped with squid and shrimp, or a bindae duk, a pancake of ground mung beans, pork and bean sprouts. Pots of sul long tank, a milky beef soup, simmer for 12 hours in the open kitchen. The best antidote for the spiciness of such dishes as nakji bokum, stir-fried baby octopus with peppers, vegetables and noodles, is a glass of O.B. Korean beer.

KANG SUH RESTAURANT

1250 Broadway (W. 32nd St.), 10001
564-6845, *Open 24 hours daily*

The most carnivorous appetites can be satisfied at Kang Suh—even in the middle of the night. Choose from 16 different kinds of marinated Korean barbecues, including bul kogi and kal-bi, and cook them at your own tabletop wood-charcoal grill.

WON JO KOREAN-JAPANESE RESTAURANT

23 W. 32nd St. (Fifth Ave. & Broadway), 10001
695-5815, *Open 24 hours daily*

Before Korean became the hot cuisine craze of the moment, Won Jo was where those in the know could go for a dependably delicious meal, any time of the day or night. They still do, and unlike some of the hipper, new places downtown, you don't have to order (and get charged for) the kim chee. Try some of the Seoul-satisfying soups, seafood casseroles, noodle dishes and, of course, barbecues.

KOSHER

ESS-A-BAGEL

359 First Ave. (21st St.), 10010
980-1010, *Breakfast, Lunch & Dinner daily*
No cards

831 Third Ave. (51st St.), 10022
260-2252, *Breakfast, Lunch & Dinner daily*

See review under "Delis & Bagel Shops"

FINE & SCHAPIRO

138 W. 72nd St. (Broadway & Columbus Ave.), 10023
877-2874, *Breakfast, Lunch & Dinner daily*

See review under "Delis & Bagel Shops"

MOM'S BAGELS & TABLES

15 W. 45th St. (Fifth & Sixth Aves.), 10036
764-1566, *Open Sun.-Fri.*

A

See review under "Delis & Bagel Shops"

SECOND AVENUE KOSHER DELI

156 Second Ave. (10th St.), 10003
677-0606, *Breakfast, Lunch & Dinner daily*

See review under "Delis & Bagel Shops"

SIEGEL'S KOSHER DELI & RESTAURANT

1646 Second Ave. (85th & 86th Sts.), 10028
288-2094, *Breakfast, Lunch & Dinner daily*

This all-kosher deli and gourmet-platter store on the Upper
East Side features a wide selection of fresh-baked breads, overstuffed sandwiches, whole roast turkeys, hors d'oeuvres and
pastries.

MALAYSIAN

MALAYSIA RESTAURANT

46-48 Bowery (Canal & Bayard Sts.), 10013
964-0284, 964-2257, *Lunch & Dinner daily*

Malaysia, the restaurant, isn't exactly easy to find, tucked
away as it is in a shopping arcade—but what a find it is. Only
now are Americans starting to discover the melange of
Chinese, Thai and even Indian flavors that make up Malaysian
cuisine, and this is a pleasant place to make your introduction.
Such dishes as chicken with asparagus in spicy sauce will leave
you wondering how you went so long without it. An absolute
must-have is the roti canai, a flaky flatbread served with a spicy
curried dipping sauce.

MEXICAN & LATIN AMERICAN

BENNY'S BURRITOS

113 Greenwich Ave. (Jane St.), 10014
727-3560, *Lunch & Dinner daily*
No cards

Think of Benny's Burritos as hip meets black beans, and
you'll have the right idea. It's rightfully crowded at all hours.

Enjoy a Mission Burrito, a $6 bargain filled with beans, rice, Monterey Jack cheese, guacamole and sour cream (although the kitchen could offer more guacamole). Benny's Bay Burrito is the identical creation with beef or chicken for $6.75. **Also at 93 Ave. A (6th St.) 254-2054.**

CAFÉ CON LECHE

424 Amsterdam Ave. (80th & 81st Sts.), 10024
595-7000, *Breakfast, Lunch & Dinner daily*

A charming little place, Café Con Leche is an upscale Latin American café with downscale prices. Decorated in shades of yellow with colorful masks on the brick wall, it feels warm and welcoming. Try the delicious Cuban sandwich ($4.95), made with roast pork, ham, cheese and pickles, and heated in a press. We also like the empanadas and the rice with Spanish sausage. Among the authentic dishes are mashed green plantains with crispy pork rinds, chicken and rice, pork chops with garlic, and flan. The menu is varied, the coffee strong.

EL POLLO

1746 First Ave. (90th & 91st Sts.), 10128
996-7810, *Lunch & Dinner daily*

It won't be difficult for fans of Southern-fried to appreciate South American-roasted at El Pollo. Apparently, Peru is home not only to some high quality ruins (Macchu Picchu), but also to some finger-licking good chicken. Be sure to try some of the side dishes, too, like rice and beans, fried plantains and spicy curly fries.

EL SOMBRERO

138 Ludlow St. (Stanton St.), 10002
254-4188, *Lunch & Dinner daily*
No cards

New York City never has been known for great Mexican food, especially if you want it cheap and fast. But down on the Lower East Side, El Sombrero (colloquially known as The Hat) has been serving up Tijuana-style rice and refried beans for years. The place isn't pretty—just Formica tables, cheap plates and a jukebox that has to compete with Spanish television—but the guacamole is fresh, the arroz is yellow and the frosty margaritas really hit the spot.

EMPANADA OVEN

826 Seventh Ave. (53rd & 54th Sts.), 10019
977-3072, *Lunch & Dinner Mon.-Fri.*

This tiny storefront specializes in a variety of the savory Latin American pastries known generically as empanadas. The golden, flaky pastry pockets (around $2.95 each) come stuffed with a variety of fillings—spicy chicken, peppery sausage,

shredded beef, manchego cheese, mixed vegetables with potatoes—and for $10 you can leave with a bagful. Though this is
primarily a take-out spot, there is counter service for a lucky
few.

LOS DOS RANCHEROS

507 Ninth Ave. (38th St.), 10018
868-7780, *Lunch & Dinner daily*
No cards

Good, authentic and inexpensive soft taco stands in New
York are rare, so Los Dos is a welcome, if funky, addition.
Stuffed with carnitas (fried pork), barbecued goat, or pork
skin in green sauce, the folded soft tacos at $2 each are a steal.
Platters of chicken in pipian sauce, or enchiladas con mole
poblano arrive heaped high, along with tortillas, rice and
beans, and cost only $7. Dishes like posole and stewed-chicken
tostadas are served on weekends only. Los Dos Rancheros also
sells a wide selection of Mexican beers and sodas.

MARY ANN'S

116 Eighth Ave. (16th St.), 10011
633-0877, *Lunch & Dinner daily, Brunch Sat.-Sun.*
No cards

The original Mary Ann's is among the first authentic
Mexican restaurants in New York, and despite substantial com-
petition now, it still draws a crowd. A big basket of homemade
tortilla chips and tangy salsa arrive when you're seated. Then
comes the real eating. Mary Ann's tacos are not made with the
tasteless prefabricated shells served at so many places. Try the
Azteca, a combination platter of a tender white-meat chicken
enchilada in a green sauce, a cheese chile relleno or a soft taco
stuffed with guacamole. **Also at 500 E. 5th St. (Second Ave.)
475-5939. Two newer locations—1503 Second Ave. (78th St.)
2499-6165, and 2454 Broadway (91st St.) 877-0132—take credit
cards and have bars.**

MEXICANA MARNA

525 Hudson St. (W. 10th & Charles Sts.), 10014
924-4119, *Lunch Mon.-Sat., Dinner nightly*
No cards

A tiny new spot for homemade Mexican food in the Village:
tacos and flautas made with rich corn tortillas, chips and fresh
salsas. Beware: if you eat at one of the few colorful tables, you
may be watched by the line of people awaiting take out.

PANCHITO'S

103-105 MacDougal St. (Minetta Ln. & Bleecker St.), 10012
473-5239, *Lunch & Dinner daily*

A raucous Village hangout for over 30 years, this dark,
kitschy cantina serves pitchers of sangria and such exotic

frozen drinks as "French Sex on the Beach" keep flowing 'til 4 a.m. Oh yes, and there's food too—huge and cheap portions of all the Mexican usuals, from quesadillas and tacos and enchiladas to huevos rancheros.

TACO TACO

1726 Second Ave. (89th & 90th Sts.), 10128
289-8226, *Lunch & Dinner daily*
No cards

A storefront restaurant where the tables are draped with serapes and Latin music plays in the background, Taco Taco offers good, inexpensive Mexican food. The waiters may not speak much English, but they're helpful and friendly. The soft tacos are heavenly; the marinated pork is just spicy enough. The burritos hold delicious beans, rice, and your choice of several fillings. We are partial to the spinach-and-chicken rendition. Quesadillas are a revelation to those accustomed to the tired versions available elsewhere.

MIDDLE EASTERN

SALAM

104 W. 13th St. (Sixth & Seventh Aves.), 10001
741-0277, *Dinner nightly*

Dim lighting, warm colors and mirrored walls make Salam a romantic setting for Syrian and Moroccan specialties. The soft booths invite the diner to sit and peruse the inexpensive menu and wine list by candlelight. Tasty appetizers like chunky baba gannouj, spicy kibbeh and tangy meat pies can be a meal in themselves, or leave room for savory main courses like chicken baked in filo or shrimp with nuts and raisins.

TURKISH GRILL

193 Bleecker St. (MacDougal St. & Sixth Ave.), 10012
674-8833, *Lunch & Dinner daily*

A mostly take-out spin-off of the fit-for-a-pasha Turkish Kitchen on Third Avenue, this Village spot serves a variety of exotic Turkish appetizers (stuffed grape leaves, hummus and taramasalata) and charcoal-grilled kebabs (lamb, chicken, swordfish and veggies), served with crusty sesame-seeded Turkish pide flatbread—until two a.m. weekdays and until 4 a.m. on weekends.

MOROCCAN

ANDALOUSIA

28 Cornelia St. (Sixth & Seventh Aves.), 10014
929-3693, *Dinner Wed.-Mon.*

Okay, so the floor is sort of on a slant at this cramped little West Village restaurant, but it's a homey spot for reasonably priced Moroccan b'stilla (made here with chicken, not the traditional pigeon) and aromatic tajines, Moroccan stews served in earthenware pots with couscous. Bring your own wine or beer.

SALAM

104 W. 13th St. (Sixth & Seventh Aves.), 10001
741-0277, *Lunch & Dinner daily*

See Review under "Middle Eastern" above.

PAN-ASIAN

CHAO CHOW

111 Mott St. (Canal & Hester Sts.), 10013
226-2590, *Breakfast, Lunch & Dinner daily*
No cards

The menu is scribbled on the wall in at least three Asian languages. Their "special soup noodles" come in a variety of flavors; they're sometimes spicy, usually soul warming and quite delicious. You'll find such Indonesian-influenced items as Cambodian rice-stick soup.

REPUBLIC

37 Union Square West (16th & 17th Sts.), 10003
627-7172, *Lunch & Dinner daily*

"Noodle shop" and "chic" aren't words you expect to use together. Then again, Republic is not what you expect of a noodle shop. Think Zen-meets-disco and you get an idea of what the place looks and feels like. But what keeps this place packed are the noodles in spicy duck broth, chicken udon, salmon sashimi salad and other Asian-inspired pickings, all for under $10 a bowl/plate. **Also at 2290 Broadway (82nd & 83rd Sts.), 579-5959.**

POLISH

KK POLISH-AMERICAN

194 First Ave. (11th & 12th Sts), 10009
777-4430, *Breakfast, Lunch & Dinner daily*
No cards

Go all out at this cheerful Polish eatery and order the works—a platter of stuffed cabbage, pirogi, kielbasa sausage and kraut. In fair weather, the courtyard is a rare treat.

SOUL FOOD/SOUTHERN

COPELAND'S

547 W. 145th St. (Broadway & Amsterdam Ave.), 10027
234-2357, *Dinner Tues.-Sun., Brunch Sun.*

There's live jazz at this Harlem soul-food institution, where regulars go through the cafeteria line for everything from ribs, fried catfish and yams to fresh banana pudding. The all-you-can-eat buffet on Tuesday through Thursday nights is a bargain $13.95, the popular gospel brunch (with a gospel choir) on Sundays is $16.95.

MAMA'S FOOD SHOP

200 E. 3rd St. (Aves. A & B), 10009
777-4425, *Lunch & Dinner Mon.-Sat.*
No Cards

Just like you'd find at any soul food buffet down South, Mama serves up crispy fried chicken, grilled salmon or steaming meatloaf with a choice of traditional sides, like fluffy mashed potatoes, mac-and-cheese or cole slaw. And just so you don't forget you're in the East Village, there's also couscous of the day. In a hurry? Head across the street to **StepMama** for take-out sandwiches.

OLD DEVIL MOON

511 E. 12th St. (Aves. A & B), 10009
475-4357, *Brunch Sat.-Sun., Dinner nightly*

The staff describes it as "Southern gothic," mixing low country cooking with the East Village kitsch of colored lights, paper lanterns and a disco ball in the dining room. Weekend brunch is famous for oversized biscuits and gravy, salty country ham, gluey cheese grits, fried catfish and cornmeal hotcakes in a variety of fruit flavors, like pear and mango. If you prefer a spicy breakfast, huevos Oaxaca will light your fire.

SOUL FIXINS'

371 W. 34th St. (Eighth & Ninth Aves.), 10001
736-1345, *Lunch & Dinner Mon.-Sat.*
No cards

The fresh down-home fare at this tiny place near Penn Station includes chicken—baked, fried, barbecued or smothered—ribs, fish and meatloaf, along with such sides as collard greens and black-eyed peas. Every order comes with thick squares of buttery, fresh-baked cornbread.

WELLS RESTAURANT

2247-49 Adam Clayton Powell Blvd. (132nd & 133rd Sts.), 10027
234-0700, *Lunch & Dinner daily*

Swing dancing, and fried chicken served Southern-style with waffles and syrup, are the house specials at Wells in Harlem. You might feel like you're at a dressed-up Howard Johnson's, but the food is so fine and the folks here so friendly that you wouldn't want any little piece of this place to change, right down to how they cook the collard greens. Wells is open until 4 a.m. on Fridays and Saturdays. A live big band orchestra swings the house on Monday nights.

SPANISH

CAFÉ ESPAÑOL

172 Bleecker St. (MacDougal & Sullivan Sts.), 10012
505-0657, *Lunch & Dinner daily*

You can almost imagine Hemingway eating at this darkly lit Spanish restaurant, where the sangria flows and you can get a lobster for $13.95, a three-course meal of garlic-infused mariscada or paella for $16.95, a selection of tapas and even a few Mexican dishes.

THAI

JAI-YA THAI RESTAURANT

396 Third Ave. (28th St.), 10016
889-1330, *Lunch daily, Dinner Mon.-Sat.*

A long-time Thai staple in Elmhurst, Queens, Jai-ya opened this Manhattan branch some years ago and has been drawing not only old regulars from across the river, but Thai-loving Manhattanites as well. They do a dynamite crispy whole fish with chili sauce, sensational coconut milk soup with spicy chicken and good phad Thai noodles.

TIBETAN

TIBET SHAMBALA

488 Amsterdam Ave. (83rd & 84th Sts.), 10024
721-1270, *Lunch & Dinner daily*

Shambala looks like a mythical heaven on earth. We don't think the food at this handsome storefront restaurant is other-worldly, but it's pretty good. Among the soups, there is a note-worthy tomato-based broth with spinach, tofu, beef dumplings and scallions. Also intriguing is the salad of potatoes, chickpeas and greens. The lamb curry is popular, as are several beef dish-es. A lovely dessert is made of sweetened rice with raisins and homemade yogurt. Service is friendly and enthusiastic.

TSAMPA

212 E. Ninth St. (Second & Third Aves.), 10003
614-3226, *Lunch Mon.-Sat., Dinner nightly*

Among the few Tibetan restaurants in New York, Tsampa stands out as much for its soothing atmosphere as for the inno-vative, healthy cuisine that borrows from neighboring India, China, Nepal, Bhutan and Japan. Most ingredients are organic, and with choices like tender chicken curry in tangy yogurt-and-onion sauce and grilled whole trout with crispy, gingered skin, you'll hardly notice that red meat is missing from the menu. Warm up with a pot of Tibetan tea—either nutty barley or tra-ditional bocha—made with butter and salt.

VIETNAMESE

MONSOON

435 Amsterdam Ave.(81st St.), 10024
580-8686, *Lunch & Dinner daily*

A bamboo ceiling and straw peasant hats on the walls lend a Vietnamese ambience to this Upper Westside eatery. If you enjoy the bold spicing of Thai food, you may be disappointed by the subtlety of Vietnamese cuisine, but you'll appreciate its delicacy. We recommend the summer rolls with a peanut dip-ping sauce, sugar cane wrapped in grilled shrimp paste and steamed shrimp dumpling "lady fingers" to start. Among the entrées are sweet and smoky lemon-grass-marinated pork chops and many delicious versions of stir-fried or steamed noo-dles. Rice lovers will marvel at the sticky black rice.

NHA TRANG

87 Baxter St. (Canal & Bayard Sts.), 10013
233-5948, *Lunch & Dinner daily*
No cards

Named for a village in Vietnam, Nha Trang is one of the best (and friendliest) of Chinatown's Vietnamese restaurants, and it makes up for its lack of decor with fresh light food. The lengthy menu occasionally misses something in translation, as in "beef balls with egg noodles soup" (we're sure they mean beef dumplings). The shrimp rolls—a rice paper wrapping around shrimp, rice vermicelli, mint and basil—make a perfect first course, and any of the varieties of pho, rice noodle soups with coriander and crushed peanuts on top, are a meal. End with iced coffee, made with sweetened condensed milk.

VIETNAM

11 Doyers St. (Bowery St.), 10013
693-0725, Lunch & Dinner daily

Hidden in an alley off of Chinatown's most crooked street, you'll find a set of stairs leading down to one of New York's oldest Vietnamese restaurants. Atmosphere is not at a premium here, but with light, healthy and exotic food like this who cares: Crunchy spring rolls tempt the palate for a huge steaming bowl of shrimp-sour soup or perhaps a plate of salt-and-pepper shrimp. Diners can cut and roll their own shrimp and sugarcane in pancakes with mint leaves.

ICE CREAM & MORE

BASKIN-ROBBINS

215 W. 125th St. (Seventh & Eighth Aves.), 10027
864-9039, Open daily
No cards

Before there were Häagen-Dazs and Ben & Jerry's, there was Baskin-Robbins. One of the oldest ice cream chains in the country, 31 Flavors is still going strong, serving quality ice cream in a multitude of—sometimes ingenious—flavors. They also have several low-and non-fat and sugar-free ice creams and yogurts, including soft-serve "Truly Free" (which isn't half-bad for yogurt with no fat and no sugar added.) **Call for other locations.**

BEN & JERRY'S

41 Third Ave. (9th & 10th Sts.), 10003
995-0109, Open daily
No cards

If you're into ice cream with lots of chunky ingredients and unique flavors, this is the place. Ben & Jerry's, in fact, has become one of the two premium ice cream superpowers based on its ability to develop the likes of Heath Bar Crunch, New York Super Fudge Chunk and Cherry Garcia. The stores go beyond just offering ice cream. They also sell some pretty fine brownies and cookies not to mention a range of coffees. Most of them also offer seats, giving guests a chance to relax and enjoy their ice cream treats rather than just eating them on the run. **Call for other locations.**

CHINATOWN ICE CREAM FACTORY

65 Bayard St. (Mott & Elizabeth Sts.), 10002
608-4170, *Open daily*
No cards

Dessert is not a high point at most of Chinatown's restaurants, so pay your dinner tab and meander over to the Chinatown Ice Cream Factory. Among its 42 flavors, you'll find the familiar vanillas and chocolates, but for an unusual experience, try lychee, almond cookie, green tea or red bean. The pink color and sweetness of the red bean make it popular with youngsters. Also good are tangerine sherbet and ginger ice cream. They also sell candy.

CONES

272 Bleecker St. (Seventh Ave.), 10014
414-1795, *Open daily*
No cards

This is where foodies from the James Beard Institute stop for ice cream after lunch. Raoul, the Argentinean owner, makes 32 flavors of Italian-style ice creams and sorbets from a secret family recipe. The flavors are intense, the texture rich, yet the gelati have 30% fewer calories than most premium creams, and the sorbets are fat-free. In addition to some wonderful variations on chocolate (chocolate-mocha-chocolate chip), you'll find such exotic flavors as dulce de leche (caramel), and zabayone tasting of port wine, marsala and Cognac.

CUSTARD BEACH

2 World Financial Center (The Winter Garden), 10281
786-4707, *Open Mon.-Sat.*
No cards

Frozen custard was invented 80 years ago on Coney Island, but with the advent of factory-made ice cream, it was rendered obsolete—until now. Allan Silberman has re-introduced it at the first New York outlet of a quickly expanding chain. It's creamier than ice cream (though somewhat less fattening), and comes in such intense flavors as peach cobbler, crème brûlée as well as chocolate and vanilla.

HÄAGEN-DAZS

77 Bayard St. (Mott St.), 10002
571-1970, *Open daily*
No cards

Häagen-Dazs is one of several companies with ice cream stands scattered all over Manhattan (19 at press time.) Astoundingly rich, its ice cream is very high in butterfat and calories, but you'll feel your splurge was worth it. We've tasted no better vanilla, and with chocolate-covered almonds added, it becomes the enchanting Swiss almond vanilla. If you can keep your vow to count calories once you walk in the door, order the soft-frozen, sugar-free yogurt; there's none better. **Call for other locations.**

MINTER'S ICE CREAM KITCHEN

250 Vesey St. (West Side Hwy.), 10281
945-4455, *Open daily*
A

After shopping or dining in TriBeCa, if you crave a luscious and creamy cone, come to Minter's. They offer super-rich homemade ice cream in 16 flavors, including Kahlúa-and-cream and triple chocolate. There's a range of goodies on hand for mixing into your cone—brownies, crumbled Heath Bars and fresh strawberries. Minter's also serves frozen yogurt.

PEPPERMINT PARK

1225 First Ave. (66th St.), 10021
288-5054, *Breakfast, Lunch & Diner daily*

Decked out in crisp peppermint green, PP makes home-made ice cream and chocolates, along with sandwiches and sal-ads. Although it's not the best we've tasted, the ice cream comes in 45 flavors, from vanilla and chocolate to black rasp-berry, chocolate peanut butter and strawberry cheesecake. As its name suggests, Peppermint Park is popular with kids.

SANT AMBROEUS

1000 Madison Ave. (77th & 78th Sts.), 10021
570-2211, *Lunch & Dinner daily*
A

Everything at this New York branch of a famed Milanese pastry shop is expensive, but if you stick to the gelato case at the entrance, you'll walk out satisfied with what you bought with your well-spent dollars—superb gelato in such magnifi-cent flavors as hazelnut and cappuccino. They also serve lunch and dinner, as well as specialty coffee drinks.

SERENDIPITY 3

225 E. 60th St. (Second & Third Aves.), 10022
838-3531, *Lunch & Dinner daily*
A

Part expensive toy boutique, part ice cream parlor, part casual restaurant, this charming hodgepodge has been a teenager's favorite dessert hangout after the movies for over two decades. The young waiters are scrubbed fresh, all bright eyes and smiles, and the white-on-white decor with its marble tables and wire chairs add to the sensation that you've just entered a Victorian sugar-plum fantasy. As for the menu, there are better-than-average burgers, omelets and salads, but most regulars come for the colossal sundaes and banana splits. There are some great iced drinks, such as the absurdly named "frozen hot chocolate."

PIZZA

ARTURO'S

106 W. Houston St. (Thompson St.), 10012
475-9828, *Dinner nightly*

Though not New York's best, Arturo's pizzas have a chewy crust is delicious. And, after all, Arturo's is a family-owned neighborhood institution that's been on this SoHo corner for over 40 years. The most expensive pizza is $17, for a large pie with sausage, mushrooms, peppers and onions. Although there's a full menu, you'll do best by sticking to the pizza and perhaps a salad. There's live music nightly, mostly jazz.

FAMOUS BEN'S PIZZA OF SOHO

177 Spring St. (Thompson St.), 10012
966-4494, *Lunch & Dinner daily*
No cards

Ben's is famous not only for its terrific Sicilian-style pizza (in big squares with lots of sweet tomato sauce and cheese), but also for its ham-and-cheese knots, overstuffed calzones, eggplant parmigiana rolls, and even fried dough for dessert.

JOE'S PIZZA

233 Bleecker St. (Carmine St.), 10014
366-1182, *Lunch & Dinner daily*
No cards

There's nothing glamorous about this tiny storefront, but for over 25 years, Pino "Joe" Pozzuoli has been turning out 'za on a crust that keeps its crispiness even under the weight of its creamy mozzarella-and tangy-sweet tomato sauce topping. Pepperoni, peppers and sausages are among the extras. If you're a believer that authentic street pizza has got to be served by the slice, come to Joe's for New York's best.

JOHN'S

278 Bleecker St. (Sixth & Seventh Aves.), 10014
243-1680, *Lunch & Dinner daily*
No cards

After nearly 70 years in the same Village spot, New York's best-loved pizzeria just keeps getting better. Maybe it's the coal-fired oven that deliciously chars the thin crust, the mound of fragrant fresh garlic that tops off every piece, or the first-rate ingredients like crumbly sweet Italian sausage, green peppers and fresh mushrooms. Most likely, it's the combination of all of those things that makes for a truly excellent rendering of pizza at its basic best. **Also at 408 E. 64th Street (York & First Aves.), 935-2895.**

PATSY'S PIZZA

2287 First Ave. (117th & 118th Sts.), 10029
534-9783, *Lunch & Dinner daily*
No cards

There are a few pizzerias that share the name, but East Harlem's Patsy's is New York's most authentic old-style pizzeria, and claims to be the first to use a coal-fired pizza oven when it opened in the thirties. With a thin crust that manages to be both crispy and chewy, tangy, homemade tomato sauce and a variety of traditional toppings, Patsy's produces a pizza among the city's best. Play some Sinatra tunes on the jukebox while enjoying your large sausage-and-mushroom pie, and undergo the full Italian East Harlem nostalgia trip.

RAY'S OF GREENWICH VILLAGE

465 Ave. of the Americas (11th St.), 10011
243-2253, *Lunch & Dinner daily*
A

Despite many pretenders to the throne, this is the one, the only, the original Ray's Pizza, and it consistently rates as one of the best pizzerias in the city. Try a hefty cheese-smothered slice, or indulge in one of Ray's 18-inch whoppers. Prices are modest by New York standards.

SERAFINA FABULOUS PIZZA

1022 Madison Ave. (79th St.), 10021
734-2676, *Lunch & Dinner daily*

A neighborhood favorite for thin-crusted pizzas baked in a wood-burning oven, plus fresh pastas. The upstairs terrace is a fine spot for al fresco dining in warm weather.

TOTONNO'S

1544 Second Ave. (80th St.), 10021
327-2800, *Lunch & Dinner daily*

A spin-off of Brooklyn's famous hole-in-the-wall pizzeria, where the pizzas have been emerging piping hot from coal-fired ovens for nearly 75 years, Totonno's on the Upper East Side is certainly tonier, with a full bar and outdoor dining.

TWO BOOTS

37 Ave. A (2nd & 3rd Sts.), 10009
505-2276, *Lunch & Dinner daily, Brunch Sat.-Sun.*

Two Boots was founded on a clever geographic and culinary notion to combine the foods of the world's boots: Italy and Louisiana. The dining room is loud and funky, decorated with strings of chiles, cowboy boots and red-checked tablecloths. The pizza is inspired: great crispy crusts and such toppings as Cajun andouille sausage, barbecued shrimp, crawfish or jalapeño peppers, as well as the more customary garlic, olive or eggplant. The menu also includes other Cajun and Italian dishes, and there's a kids' menu. Early in the evening, the restaurant can be filled with families. Later, it's a young, hip crowd that's drawn to the Lower East Side clubs. **Also at 75 Greenwich Ave. (Seventh Ave.) 633-9096, 74 Bleecker St. (Broadway & Lafayette) 777-1033, 42 Ave. (3rd & 4th Sts.) 254-1919, and 514 Second Ave., Park Slope, Brooklyn, 718-499-3253.**

SOUP

SOUP KITCHEN INTERNATIONAL

259-A W. 55th St. (Eighth Ave. & Broadway), 10019
757-7730, *Lunch & Dinner Mon.-Fri.*
No cards

We've seen several imitators since *Seinfeld* portrayed owner Al Yeganeh as the despotic "Soup Man of West 55th Street." It's true that Yeganeh posts stern rules at this take-out spot, and if you don't obey them you're likely to get no bread or fruit, sides which are sometimes added gratis: "Know what you want when you reach the counter, speak quickly and ask no questions, have your money ready and move to the left after ordering!" So why do customers queue up outside every day, even in the freezing cold winter and sweltering summer? They love Yeganeh's repertory of more than 200 bean, nut, fish, vegetable and meat soups, which change daily and always include 10 or so thick, hot soups, including seafood bisque, and a selection of four or five cold soups. Regulars don't mind paying $6 for a 12-ounce cup, $13 for a 32-ounce container; they swear Yeganeh's soup isn't soup at all, that it's "art".

TEA ROOMS & PÂTISSERIES

DANAL

90 E. 10th St. (Third & Fourth Aves.), 10003
982-6930, *Lunch Mon.-Fri., Dinner nightly, High Tea Fri.-Sat.,
Brunch Sat.-Sun., $*

With the smells of good cooking, the jazz singer on the stereo and the old French farmhouse tables and chairs, Danal seems to be very far away from the Big City. There are comfy couches by the fireplace (it's an artificial blaze, unfortunately) and lots of objets scattered around—photos in frames, candlesticks, pitchers. Choose from more than 20 teas offered with scones, tea sandwiches and desserts. Danal is also a restaurant (see review in "Greenwich Village—And Also...").

TAKASHIMAYA TEABOX CAFÉ

693 Fifth Ave. (54th & 55th Sts.), 10022
350-0180, *Lunch & Tea Mon.-Sat.*

This serene, East-meets-West café can be found in the basement of Takashimaya, the transplanted Tokyo department store on Fifth Avenue. It's not what we'd call a bargain-basement café, but you can get a wonderful smoked-salmon-on-pressed-rice sandwich, or a daily-changing bento box-lunch for $15. The Teabox Café offers over 35 kinds of tea, but watch your wallet. Some go for around $10 a pot.

TEA & SYMPATHY

108 Greenwich Ave. (Jane St.), 10011
807-8329, *Lunch, Tea & Dinner daily*
No cards

A good spot for a spot of tea on a rainy day if you don't mind cramped quarters. They not only serve afternoon tea, but also such English basics as Welsh rarebit, shepherd's pie, bangers and mash and tweed-kettle pie. In addition to the Stilton-and-walnut salad, there is a salad with chicken, egg, bacon and tomatoes they've dubbed "Absolutely Fabulous." Next door is a shop selling everything English, from tea to videotapes.

THEME RESTAURANTS

Credit Hard Rock Café founder Peter Morton with coming up with the idea first: build a restaurant around a theme and make it as much a place for entertainment as for food, and people will not only flock there, but they'll leave with at least one piece of "merch" (merchandise) with your name on it. Theme restaurants are cropping up as fast as people (often celebrities) can think of a new hook—many of them near West 57th Street, which is quickly becoming "Theme Restaurant Row," or Times Square. Styled around everything from Harleys to horror flicks, they're colorful and they're fun, but keep in mind that all of the theme restaurants consider themselves "entertainment complexes"—which means that the food often takes a back seat to...well...the theme. Theme restaurants attract tourists by the busload and are great for kids, but generally don't take reservations. They planned it that way: while you're waiting...and waiting...for a table, they hope you'll stock up on their "merch."

BROOKLYN DINER

212 W. 57th St. (Broadway & Seventh Ave.), 10019
977-1957, *Breakfast, Lunch & Dinner daily, Brunch Sat.-Sun.*
A

Nostalgic for the good old days when the Dodgers still played in Brooklyn and you could get a real egg cream without worrying about cholesterol? This shiny metal-trimmed restaurant looks like a Brooklyn snack shop right out of the '50s, complete with a soda fountain and Brooklyn Dodgers memorabilia. You can get a malt, an authentic 15-bite Brooklyn hot dog, and macaroni and cheese that's pretty darn good.

HARD ROCK CAFÉ

221 W. 57th St. (Seventh Ave. & Broadway), 10019
489-6565, *Lunch & Dinner daily*

A

This 57th Street branch of the worldwide chain is a spectacle and there is almost always a line. But the bouncers don't turn anyone away, so if you can wait it out, you'll be rewarded inside with rock music blasted at a formidable decibel level, a guitar-shaped bar, good burgers and great lime-grilled chicken, and the famous, enormous collection of rock-and-roll memorabilia from every musician from Chubby Checker to Bruce Springsteen.

HARLEY DAVIDSON CAFÉ

1370 Sixth Ave. (56th St.), 10019
245-6000, *Lunch & Dinner daily, Brunch Sat.-Sun.*

A

A giant American flag graces the ceiling of this noisy, two-level, all-American roadhouse where pseudo bikers and their babes can ogle the shiny Harleys on display and "hog" on burgers, roadhouse chicken wings, meatloaf, chocolate-peanut-butter pie and other down-home dishes Elvis would dig.

JEKYLL & HYDE

91 Seventh Ave. South (Barrow & Grove Sts.), 10014
989-7701, 800-992-HYDE, *Lunch & Dinner daily, Brunch Sat.-Sun.*

If you like eating in the dark with skeletons dangling over your head, you'll enjoy this cross between a London pub and Disneyland's "Haunted House." Jekyll & Hyde features over 250 beers, eight-ounce "monster" burgers, grilled chicken sandwiches, pizzas, and an $9.95 weekend brunch that comes with all the Bloody Marys, Mimosas or Screwdrivers you can drink. At intervals, the Sphinx on the wall "comes to life" to croon (off-key) requests and tell bad jokes. If you need to go to the john, good luck—the bathrooms are hidden behind a bookcase. There's an upstairs "Laboratory Bar & Lounge" for more partying, and lots of Jekyll &Hyde merchandise for sale, from $17.95 T-shirts to a $300 leather bomber jacket.

THE JEKYLL & HYDE CLUB

1409 Sixth Ave. (57th & 58th Sts.), 10019
541-9517, *Lunch & Dinner daily*

A bigger and glitzier version of the Greenwich Village J&H (see entry above), this mega-haunted house decorated with

everything creepy and crawly, is strictly for tourists and the kid-
dies. As for the food—some say the reason they have all the
special effects and the costumed actors roaming around trying
to scare you, is to keep your mind off what's on your plate.

MARS 2112

1633 Broadway (51st St.), 10019
582-2112, *Lunch & Dinner daily*

A

What will they think of next? This Times Square newcomer
is an over-the-top version of the red planet, where the surroundings are out of this world even if the food isn't. The
menu zig zags all over the universe, and serves everything from
Mariner pizza and smoked-duck quesadillas to sushi. If the kids
can't sit still, send them into the interactive game room.

MOTOWN CAFÉ

104 W. 57th St. (Sixth & Seventh Aves.), 10019
581-8030, *Lunch & Dinner daily*

Decorated with the gold records and memorabilia of
Motown recording artists, this purple-neon-trimmed, two-level
home of soul music serves such all-American "comfort" and
soul food dishes as macaroni and cheese, collard greens, meat
loaf and barbecued ribs. Live entertainers perform—you
guessed it—Motown songs.

PLANET HOLLYWOOD

140 W. 57th St. (Sixth & Seventh Aves.), 10019
333-7827, *Lunch & Dinner daily*

A

A chain restaurant franchise owned, in part, by Arnold
Schwarzenegger, Sylvester Stallone and Bruce Willis, this raucous, touristy treat for movie buffs sets itself apart from its pre-
decessor, the Hard Rock Café (one block away), by offering up
a grand collection of movie memorabilia. The restaurant also
offers a surprisingly decent bill of fare, sizzling fajitas being
among the best.

THE SLAUGHTERED LAMB PUB

182 W. 4th St. (Sixth & Seventh Aves.), 10014
627-LAMB , *Lunch & Dinner daily, Brunch Sat.-Sun.*

This dark, gothically decorated pub takes its name from the
movie *American Werewolf in London*. You'll find a scary but fun
decor (heavy on the werewolves), over 75 beers, a menu of
steaks, sandwiches and pastas, and downstairs, a "haunted"
dungeon where you can shoot pool and play darts surrounded
by the "remains of imprisoned pub patrons from the past"
until 4 in the morning.

VEGGIE/ORGANIC

ANGELICA KITCHEN

300 E. 12th St. (First & Second Aves.), 10003
228-2909, *Lunch & Dinner daily*
No cards ♥

The menu changes daily at Angelica Kitchen, where fresh and wholesome vegetarian food is served in a peaceful East Village setting. Everything is organic, and the seasonal menu is carefully prepared. This does not mean boring. A rice, millet, kasha and sweet potato croquet is flavored with pecans, garlic, fennel and caraway and gets an onion-dill glaze. A stew is made of shiitake mushrooms, carrots, turnips, parsnips, squash and burdock and served over udon noodles. For dessert, try a lemon-almond torte or a pear upside-down cake. Angelica Kitchen should satisfy whether you're a serious macrobiotic or you just want to eat well.

BLANCHE'S ORGANIC CAFÉ

22 E. 44th St. (Madison Ave.), 10017
599-3445, *Breakfast, Lunch & Dinner Mon.-Sat.*

Fresh, delicious and reasonable meals are the reason people line up for lunch and take-out at these organic—mostly vegetarian—restaurants. A rotating menu can include squash bisque, bulghur wheat salad with dried fruits, walnuts and rosemary, barbecued tofu teriyaki, herb-roasted vegetables or burritos. A few non-veg dishes, mostly made with chicken and turkey. **Also at 972 Lexington Ave. (71st St.) 717-1923, 247 Columbus Ave. (73rd St.) 579-3179, and 14 14th St. (Seventh Ave. South) 337-9798.**

CANDLE CAFÉ

1307 Third Ave. (74th & 75th Sts.), 10021
472-0970, *Lunch & Dinner daily, Brunch Sun.*

Candle Café may be the only restaurant in Manhattan where no animal or animal products appear on the menu. Light appetizers like hummus, flavorful salads made from tangy sea vegetables, and entrées based on imaginative uses of tofu, tempeh and seitan make Candle Café a good place for healthful and tasty foods.

KATE'S JOINT

58 Avenue B (4th & 5th Sts.), 10003
777-7059, *Lunch & Dinner daily*

This veggie haven specializes in surprisingly tasty meat substitutions, like "fake steak," "unchicken" and "mock shrimp."

True, the meatless Jamaican patty filled with spicy ground tempeh won't fool a meat-eater, and the Southern-fried tofu cutlets don't taste like chicken. But that won't keep you from eating them. Don't overlook more traditional vegetarian fare, either, like garlicky hummus, lemony steamed Swiss chard and super-sugary vegan brownies. The diner doubles as a juice, beer and wine bar that stays open until 1 a.m.

NAVIA'S DINER

133 Ludlow St. (Rivington St.), 10003
353-8136, Open 24 hours daily

Top fashion model Navia Nguyen gave up photo shoots to create a diner that serves cheap-and-tasty meat-free comfort food. But if you think this is just another Fashion Café filled with leggy lookers and bland fare, check out her crusty mac-and-cheese, tangy veggie-burger Reuben and everyone's childhood favorite, tater tots. At night, the diner becomes a vegetarian party zone, with deejay music until 4:30 a.m., and coming soon, a full juice bar and soda fountain.

SOUEN

210 Sixth Ave. (Prince St.), 10014
807-7421, Breakfast, Lunch & Dinner daily, Brunch Sat.-Sun.

For almost three decades, these earnest, casual restaurants have been serving organic and macrobiotic foods according to the policy: no meat, no sugar, no dairy products and no preservatives. The result is not the awful meal you might expect. In fact, you'll eat quite well and feel virtuous too. The fish is fresh and well prepared, often with an Asian accent. **Also at 28 E. 13th St. (Fifth Ave. & University Pl.) 627-7150.**

WHOLE WHEAT 'N' WILD BERRYS

57 W. 10th St. (Fifth & Sixth Aves.), 10011
677-3410, Lunch Mon.-Sat., Dinner nightly

Whole Wheat 'n' Wild Berrys aims to be the kind of restaurant to which a vegetarian college student could happily bring his meat-eating dad. We're not sure it succeeds completely, but this charming health food spot has been here for over 20 years. Everything but the bread is homemade and much of the produce is organic. Try the spinach pie, nutburgers, fish and pasta.

Manhattan Gourmet Markets & More

INTRODUCTION	220
GOURMET MARKETS	220
ETHNIC MARKETS	223
BAKERIES	225
CAVIAR	226
CHEESE & PASTA	226
CHOCOLATES	227
DELIS & SMOKED FISH	228
GREEN MARKETS	229
HEALTH/ORGANIC FOODS	229

MANHATTAN TO GO

Manhattan is a gourmet's paradise, and there is no end to the number of shops selling everything from upscale staples such as imported olive oils and vinegar to exotica like frozen coconut milk and watermelon seeds. Short of putting together another book devoted to gourmet food markets, we've compiled our favorite places in Manhattan where you can shop for delicacies to eat at home. Most restaurants prepare food to-go as well.

You'll find just about everything imaginable that's edible in the "Gourmet Markets" listed first. But we've listed our favorite specialty stores below as well:

GOURMET MARKETS

All phone numbers are (212) unless otherwise indicated

BALDUCCI'S

424 Ave. of the Americas (9th & 10th Sts.), 10011
673-2600, *Open daily*

A

Balducci's has come a long way from the mom-and-pop stand it once was. A foodie institution, the family-owned emporium is a gathering place in Greenwich Village, a neighborhood feast for the senses. As you walk into this European-style market, you can see the quality is top-notch. Balducci's is pleasantly crowded during weekday working hours, but can become overwhelming after 5:30 when the pace quickens. The array of merchandise is impressive: English biscuits, fine Dijon mustards, the best Greek olive oils, mineral waters from around the world and German cookies are only some of the finds. In addition to an immense selection of cheeses, are the likes of home-made cannelloni and shrimp primavera, and a produce section stocking mangos, asparagus and strawberries even in the dead of winter. Place your mail orders by phone.

CAMPAGNA HOME

29 E. 21st St. (Park Ave. & Broadway), 10010
420-1600, *Open daily*

A

Across the street from **Campagna**, Mark Strausman's warm and colorful Tuscan restaurant, is Strausman's upscale recreation of an old-fashioned green grocers (with an emphasis on the upscale). You can buy take-out meals prepared in the restaurant, plus imported gourmet products and Campagna-label pasta sauces, olive oils and pastas. What sets this apart from other gourmet markets is that in addition to food products, it sells home furnishings, and Italian ceramic vases and pottery pieces like those used in Campagna.

CHELSEA MARKET

75 Ninth Ave (15th & 16th Sts.), 10011
243-6005, *Open daily*
Cards vary according to shop

An old factory was converted into one of New York's most intriguing food emporiums, with not only food and wine shops and places to eat, but food-preparation facilities as well. **Amy's Breads**, for example, are baked here, as are **Fat Wich** brownies. Other purveyors include **Ruthy's Cheesecake**, **The Manhattan Fruit Exchange**, **Hale & Hearty Soups**, **Ronnybrook Farm Dairy**, **The Lobster Place** for fresh seafood and **Buon Italia** for good buys in Italian-imported products.

DEAN & DELUCA

560 Broadway (Prince & Spring Sts.), 10012
431-1691, *Open daily*

A

The mother of all New York gourmet-food stores since 1977, D&D is worth a visit even if you have no intention of buying a thing. You'll be amazed by the in-depth selection in almost every gourmet-food category imaginable. Breads, for example, come from a dozen different bakeries around the city. The cheese counter stocks over 200 cheeses from such countries as France, Spain, Belgium, Denmark, England and Canada. Dean & DeLuca also carries nearly three dozen varieties of coffee beans, handmade chocolates, and the best in meats, fish, fowl, pastas, produce and take-out food. The tiny coffee bar up front is prime for people-watching. Don't miss the housewares section—you'll want to buy everything in sight, from oversized café-au-lait cups to wrought-iron candle holders to hot-off-the press cookbooks.

FAIRWAY MARKET

2127 Broadway (74th & 75th Sts.), 10023
595-1888, *Open daily*

Even if you don't live in the neighborhood, the abundance of fresh produce makes the trip here worthwhile. Fairway does an incredible business and prices are reasonable. You'll enjoy admiring the pyramids of exotic kiwis, cherimoyas and cactus pears, as well as all sorts of cheeses. How to choose between the chèvres (beautifully displayed, on vine leaves with charcoal), and the American "Camembert"? Throughout the market are homemade signs indicating the how-tos of vegetable care and offering mouth-watering, foolproof recipes. There are also breads, grains, jams and vinegar, as well as extensive deli-take-out-and fresh-fish sections.

GOURMET GARAGE

453 Broome St. (Mercer St.), 10012
941-5850, *Open daily*

The Gourmet Garage sells fruits, vegetables, poultry and seafood wholesale to local restaurants and caterers, and allows the public buy the same high-quality produce at almost the same prices. If you buy in volume (e.g., 100 pints of strawberries), you'll get a good deal. You can buy prepared foods to go as well.

VINEGAR FACTORY

451 E. 91st St. (York Ave.), 10128
628-9608, *Open daily*

Eli Zabar transformed a warehouse where vinegar was once made into a gourmet's heaven. A roomy store by New York standards, Eli's Factory serves an unsurpassed selection of prepared salads, entrées and desserts, as well as his best-selling breads, and a good selection of packaged goods. You can have weekend brunch on the balcony. New a few blocks away, with the same phone number and similar offerings: **Eli's Manhattan, 1411 Third Ave. (80th St.).**

ZABAR'S

2245 Broadway (80th St.), 10024
787-2000, *Open daily*

Pick a number when you enter this always-crowded Upper West Side foodie haven (different numbers are necessary for the cheese and prepared-meat departments), then enjoy the show while you're waiting: The lox men, for example, handle their knives with the skill of surgeons. Zabar's carries everything you've ever heard of, and much that you haven't, at reeasonable prices. The aisles are loaded with coffees, teas, spices, preserves, mustards, chocolates and breads. Climb to the second floor for an extensive selection of up-to-the-minute cookware and kitchen appliances, all at rock-bottom prices. The store has the ambience of a subway car at rush hour, but to regulars, it's home.

ETHNIC MARKETS

AGATA & VALENTINA   ITALIAN

1505 First Ave. (79th St.), 10021
452-0690, *Open daily*

Agata & Valentina has won fans among choosy East Siders for its flair with Sicilian-style prepared foods such as rustic baked penne with cauliflower, olives, anchovies, garlic and bread crumbs. There are many other dishes, along with a great selection of Italian and Sicilian breads and pastries, fresh mozzarella and fresh pastas. These riches of southern Italy combine with friendly, helpful service to make this a favorite stop on Manhattan's extremely food-competitive Upper East Side.

EAST VILLAGE MEAT MARKET   EASTERN EUROPEAN/JEWISH

139 Second Ave. (St. Mark's Pl. & 9th St.), 10003
228-5590, *Open daily*
No cards

Who has the best Ukrainian, Polish and Lithuanian-style cured pork products on the Lower East Side is a continuing argument, but the East Village Meat Market has a strong core of devotees who favor their twice-smoked pork chops, thin and chewy kabanosy and powerful kielbasa that drips with garlic-infused fat. Little English is spoken here as the shopping ladies clamor for service. Both Polish and Ukrainian foods are stocked here. They carry fluffy cheese babkas, dense Lithuanian bread, broad selections of pickles, soups, mustards and jams, and cookies and pastries.

FOODS OF INDIA   INDIAN

121 Lexington Ave. (28th & 29th Sts.), 10016
683-4419, *Open daily*

A

Indian restaurant chefs favor this spot for its own brand of basmati rice, imported from India. There are also lots of hard-to-find ingredients like fenugreek seed, whole coriander and dried mints. Many different types of lentils, beans, nuts and fruit as well, along with a large selection of packaged chutneys, oils, marinades, pickles and breads.

ITALIAN FOOD CENTER   ITALIAN

186 Grand St. (Mulberry St.), 10012
925-2954, *Open daily*

Beneath a ceiling hung with salamis, prosciutto, sopresset-ta, spicy pepperoni and cured sweet sausages, grandmotherly ladies shop for olives, pasta, pecorino romano, bread, roasted sweet red peppers in oil, marinated artichoke hearts, and an excellent selection of oils, vinegar and Italian staples. The Center's countermen also make sandwiches, which are popular among downtowners at lunchtime. Take-out entrées and sauces are also sold, along with Italian sodas, San Pellegrino water and nectars.

KAM MAN FOODS   CHINESE
200 Canal St. (Mott St.), 10013
571-0330, *Open daily*

Kam Man is the antithesis of the dingy Chinatown market, and on weekends, it is packed with upscale suburban Chinese in the city to do their weekly shopping. In addition to the smoked ducks hanging in the window, you'll find towers of dried mushrooms, peppers and salted cuttlefish, barrels full of pickles and all kinds of Asian noodles, as well as shelves stocked with dozens of varieties of soy sauce, fish sauce and such fiery condiments as sriracha, the Southeast Asian version of Tabasco sauce. There are many varieties of tea, of course, and an especially good selection of seafood, herbs, roots and curatives.

KATAGIRI   JAPANESE
224 E. 59th St. (Second & Third Aves), 10022
755-3566, *Open daily*

In a store jammed full like a Tokyo subway train, you'll find all foods Japanese: soy sauces, condiments, dried and fresh noodles, frozen ingredients and entrées; umeboshi plums, mirin, nori and other sushi ingredients; snacks, junk food, beers, sakes, soft drinks—if you can find it in a market in Osaka, Katagiri probably stocks it. Imported and local fresh fish and a butcher counter help provide New York's growing Japanese population, as well as fans of Japanese food, with just about every culinary need.

LIKITSAKOS   GREEK
1174 Lexington (80th & 81st Sts.), 10028
535-4300, *Open daily*

You'll find everything here you'll need to throw a Zorba party—except the plates to break. In addition to stocking imported Greek olives and stuffed grape leaves, this store makes its own taramosalata and hummus daily, along with a changing variety of entrées that might include not just the usual eggplant moussaka, but artichoke moussaka as well. And of course, there's always fresh pita bread.

MYERS OF KESWICK   ENGLISH
634 Hudson St. (Horatio & Jane Sts.), 10014
691-4194, *Open daily*

Where does an Englishman in New York go for some pork pie? Myers stocks this British staple, along with Cornish pasties, herby, home-made Cumberland pork sausages and chipolata sausages known in the U.K. as "bangers." Everything from the mundane—boxes of porridge oats and enough HP condiments to keep even Keith Richards satisfied—to sensational holiday mincemeat pies can be found here, with the help of the veddy British staff.

BAKERIES

AMY'S BREAD

The Chelsea Market, 75 Ninth Ave. (16th & 16th Sts.)
462-4338, *Open daily*
No cards

Amy's crusty breads are sold all over town, but this is where to get them hot out the oven: semolina with golden raisins and fennel or with black sesame seeds; country sourdough; black-olive loaf; organic whole-wheat with oats, pecans and golden raisins. **Also at 672 Ninth Ave. (46th & 47th Sts.), 977-2670.**

BALTHAZAR BAKERY

80 Spring St. (Crosby St.), 10012
965-1785, *Open daily*

Even if you can't get a reservation at the oh-so-chic Balthazar Restaurant, you can always buy their crusty baquettes, rosemary-scented ciabatta, buttery croissants and glistening fresh-fruit tarts at this adjoining bakery. Sandwiches and soups are served all day long for take-out, but there are no tables for lingering.

BOULEY BAKERY

120 W. Broadway (Duane St.)
964-2525, *Open daily*

The aroma of fresh bread will lure you inside this chic TriBeCa bakery and restaurant, where chef David Bouley turns out such signature breads as pistachio-hazelnut, walnut-saffron and apple-raisin, and big, crusty wheat-rye-and sourdough French country bread. The pastries range from a Valhrona chocolate tart, and fresh berry tarts to perhaps the best brownies in town.

ECCE PANIS

1126 Third Ave.(65th St.), 10021
535 2099, *Open daily*

Name it, Ecce Panis makes it: dense rye breads, airy brioche, oniony focaccia, olive fougasse, tart lemon sponge cake, even a stunning bittersweet-chocolate-sourdough bread. The Italian biscotti with pistachios, almonds or even macadamia nuts are sensational. In fact, you'd be hard pressed to find a baked good that's not done superbly here. **Also at 1260 Madison Ave. (90th St.) 348-0040, & 434 Sixth Ave. (10th St.) 460-5616).**

PAYARD PATISSERIE   FRENCH

1032 Lexington Ave. (73rd & 74th Sts.), 10021
717-5252, *Open Mon.-Sat.*

A

Francois Payard, a third-generation pastry chef who won a huge following at Restaurant Daniel, opened this jewel of a bakery with his former boss Daniel Boulud. Now his authentic French breads and delicate pastries are served in restaurants all over town, as well as in his adjoining bistro. Arrive early to get the best selection.

CAVIAR

CAVIARTERIA

502 Park Ave. (59th St.), 10022
759-7410, *Open daily*

A

If caviar is your downfall, Caviarteria is a good place to succumb, either in the handsome new dining room or when you get your precious roe home. They now have a **Caviar Bar** in SoHo. The store also stocks a selection of smoked salmon and pâtés. **Also in the SoHo Grand Hotel at 310 W. Broadway (Canal St.), 925-5515. To order by phone, call 1-800-4-CAVIAR.**

PETROSSIAN

182 W. 58th St. (Seventh Ave.), 10019
245-2214

You can dine in the art-deco dining room decorated with etched Erté mirrors and Lalique appointments, or order their sublime caviar and smoked fish to go. This is the place for buttery foie gras too.

CHEESE & PASTA

MURRAY'S CHEESE SHOP

257 Bleecker St. (Sixth & Seventh Aves.), 10014
243-3289, *Open daily*

This cheery shop is crammed with rare, boutique and specialty cheeses as well as traditional favorites at bargain-hunter's prices. At any one time, you might find more than a dozen international varieties of blue cheese, obscure English and American farmhouse cheeses, and international delicacies from Spain, Ireland and Italy. Lots of breads, crackers and appetizers as well, and a friendly, helpful staff.

RAFFETTO'S

144 W. Houston St. (Sullivan & MacDougal Sts.), 10012
777-1261, Open Tues.-Sat.
No cards

Dried pasta cut into a multitude of wheels, curls and tubes; bags of cornmeal-dusted ribbons of fresh fettuccine flavored with cheese or garlic; and a good selection of home-made ravioli pillows make Rafetto's an absolute most for food tourists. Other Italian basics are available here, too. After trying to count the different types of pasta stored in the wooden bins and refrigerator, though, you will probably forget about everything else.

THE RAVIOLI STORE

75 Sullivan St. (Spring & Broome Sts.), 10012
925-1737, Open daily
No cards

The Ravioli Store has been on the cutting edge of New York's pasta boom. You can find such fresh pastas as wild mushroom and white-truffle ravioli made with saffron-flavored pasta, or sage-honey-perfumed pumpkin ravioli in a no-cholesterol egg-white pasta. Also available: agnolotti, tortellini, gnocchi, fresh pastas and organic varieties made with buckwheat, oat bran and kamut.

CHOCOLATES

LA MAISON DU CHOCOLAT

25 E. 73rd St. (Madison & Fifth Aves.), 10021
744-7117, Open daily
A

At this tiny jewel of a store on a quiet residential street, the chocolates are all handmade in Paris and flown in weekly. There are about 30 types of fillings, but our favorite is the bittersweet ganache. Boxes come in many sizes and prices.

NEUCHATEL CHOCOLATES

Plaza Hotel, Fifth Ave. at Central Park South (59th St.), 10019
751-7742, Open daily
A

Enthusiasts swoon over these handmade Swiss chocolates—handmade in New York, not Switzerland—in spite of the steep prices. You'll find over 70 varieties of chocolates, along with silken truffles, the shops' specialty. **Also at 60 Wall St. (Pearl St.), 480-3766.**

RICHART DESIGN ET CHOCOLAT

7 E. 55th St. (Fifth & Madison Aves.), 10022
371-9369, Open Mon.-Sat.

A branch of a Parisian confectioner, Richart has the ambience of a fine jewelry store, and its tiny chocolates look like jewels. The delicate design atop each piece designates what's inside: ganache with cream and ultra-bitter cocoa, praline of Italian hazelnuts and Arabica coffee, mousse of pineapple—you get the idea. The gift boxes are gorgeous but, need we say, expensive. Still, you can't find more impressive-looking chocolates. They're almost too beautiful to eat.

TEUSCHER CHOCOLATES OF SWITZERLAND

620 Fifth Ave. (49th & 50th Sts.), 10017
246-4416, *Open daily*

We love Teuscher's seasonal window displays showing off their whimsical gift boxes. What's inside: truffles, truffles and more truffles made of renowned Swiss chocolate and flown in fresh from Zurich every week. The specialty of the house is the "Champagne"—a luscious blend of fresh cream, butter and chocolate with a Champagne-cream center and a dusting of confectioner's sugar. You'll also find nougat, almond, walnut, kirsch, orange, cocoa and solid milk-, dark- and white-chocolate truffles. **Also at 25 E. 61St St. (Madison Ave.), 751-8482.**

DELI & SMOKED FISH

GUSS PICKLES   EASTERN EUROPEAN/JEWISH

35 Essex St. (Hester St.), 10002
254-4477, *Open Sun.-Fri.*

At this colorful slice of lower East Side New York, they sell pickles and more pickles: huge and tiny, sour, half-sour and spicy pickles soaking in buckets of brine lined up all the way out onto the sidewalk. You can also pick up pickled tomatoes, cauliflower and hot peppers, along with sauerkraut, sweetkraut and grated horseradish.

RUSS AND DAUGHTERS

179 E. Houston St. (Orchard & Allen Sts.), 10002
475-4880, *Open daily*

On weekends, New Yorkers flock to this modest shop for excellent smoked fish: Scotch, Atlantic or Icelandic salmon, along with sable, tuna and whitefish. You'll also find a wide variety of "go-withs," from pickled herring, sour pickles, bagels and bialys, to dried fruits and nuts. This neat, bright and appetizing shop is one of New York's longtime favorites.

SARGE'S

548 Third Ave. (36th & 37th Sts.), 10016
679-0442, *Open 24 hours daily*

It doesn't look like much, but Sarge's turns out bounteous deli and smoked-fish platters, and can cater everything from caviar and Nova Scotia salmon canapés to hot dogs or whole turkeys. Sarge's will also provide serving pieces, condiments and the staff for a party. And they deliver 24 hours a day.

YONAH SCHIMMEL

137 Houston St. (First & Second Aves.), 10002
477-2858, *Open daily*
No cards

The Cadillac of knishes—a thin flaky crust enveloping hot, irresistible filling. Each is handmade, and come stuffed with potato, buckwheat, spinach and a half-dozen other flavors. Yonah Schimmel started out selling knishes among the push-carts on the Lower East Side, and has since been named in national magazines. If there's a "King of Knishes," it's Schimmel.

GREENMARKETS

You'll find a warm community spirit at New York's open-air greenmarkets. Farmers from upstate truck in their home-grown fresh vegetables and fruits, home-made jams, jellies, maple syrup, apple cider and baked goods, which are sold along with milk, fresh eggs, homemade cheese, fresh seafood, poultry and flowers. The largest greenmarket is held Mondays, Wednesdays, Fridays and Saturdays at **Union Square** year-round. It's a terrific place to shop for not only fresh produce, but such delicacies as venison sausages. In the late afternoon, you'll hear vendors shouting out their "buck-a-bag" specials. The popularity of the Union Square Greenmarket has led to the opening of greenmarkets—some seasonal—in many neighborhoods. Call 477-3220 to request a map of New York's green-markets.

HEALTH/ORGANIC FOODS

COMMODITIES

117 Hudson St. (N. Moore St.), 10013
334-8330, *Open daily*

These large stores share an excellent reputation that's well-deserved. Both are so well-stocked with health foods and relat-ed products that they are really health-food supermarkets. The organic produce is a particular attraction because of its quality and reasonable prices. **Also at 165 First Ave. (10th & 11th Sts,) 260-2600.**

THE BRONX

MAP	232
DINING	233
AND ALSO...	234
QUICK BITES	235

BAKERY CAFÉS	235
DOMINICAN	235
ITALIAN	236
PIZZA	236
SEAFOOD	236

THE
BRONX

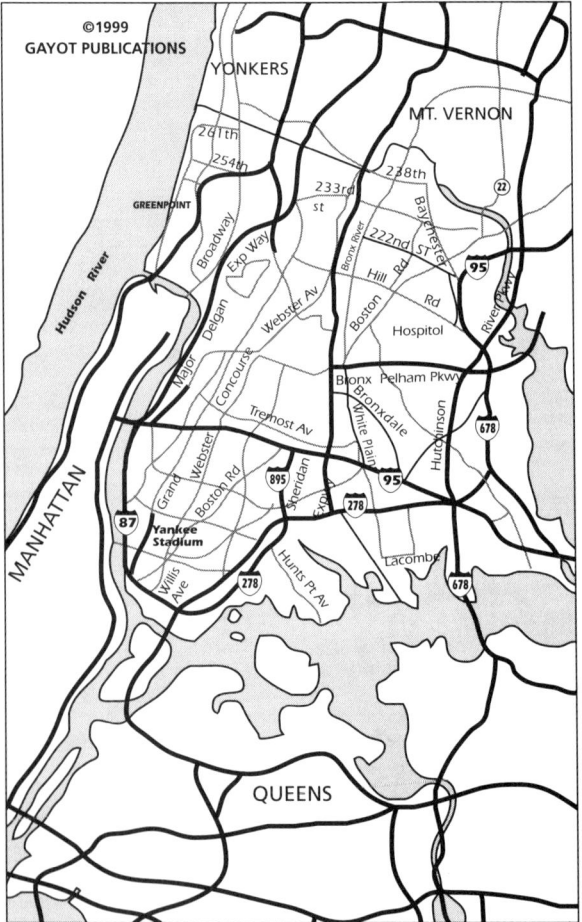

©1999
GAYOT PUBLICATIONS

YONKERS

MT. VERNON

261th

254th

233rd St

238th

GREENPOINT

Broadway

Exp Way

Bronx River

Baycherster ST

22

222nd ST

Hudson River

Major Delgan

Webster Av

Hill Rd

Boston

Rd

95

River Pkwy

Concourse

Hospitol

Bronx Pelham Pkwy

Tremost Av

Bronxdale

White Plain

Hutchinson

678

Grand

Webster

Boston Rd

895

Sheridan

95

87

MANHATTAN

Yankee
Stadium

278

Exp

278

Lacombe

Willis Ave

278

Hunts Pt Av

678

QUEENS

DINING

CAFÉ SEVILLA SPANISH 11/20

1209 White Plains Rd. (Westchester & Gleason Aves.),
Parkchester 10472
718-792-3367, *Lunch & Dinner daily, $$*
A

Café Sevilla is one of the Bronx's restaurant secrets. A congenial, homey spot located not too far from the Bronx Botanical Gardens and Zoo, Café Sevilla serves such solid Spanish fare as arroz con pollo, codfish stew, mixed seafood stew and other familiar dishes.

DOMINICK'S ITALIAN 10/20

2335 Arthur Ave. (187th & Crescent Sts.), Belmont 10458
718-733-2807, *Lunch & Dinner Wed.-Mon., $$*
No cards

Dominick's in the Bronx is one of those places that never seems to change. No reservations are taken, so the wait can be long, and the servers keep the menu and the wine list in their heads. The decor is limited to a simple wood-paneled room with rows of tables. Yet Dominick's continues to draw from the neighborhood and beyond. It is best to start with an antipasto or perhaps the fish zuppa, not soup but a platter of seafood served in a red sauce with pasta. The braised pork chops or roast pork are usually fine and come with cabbage cooked in pan juices. Surprisingly, the pastas are often uneven. The better ones include the homemade fettuccine with fresh mushrooms and the linguine with seafood. There are no desserts, but make sure to try some of the bread from a local bakery.

MARIO'S ITALIAN 12/20

2342 Arthur Ave. (184th & 187th Sts.), Belmont 10458
718-584-1188, *Lunch & Dinner Tues.-Sun., $$*
A ☎ 🚗

Here in this colorful family-style restaurant, Neapolitan cooking has ruled the busy Italian neighborhood street for more than 75 years. Try the bracingly fresh seafood salad of shrimp, squid and octopus; the plump gnocchi in a biting marinara sauce are excellent. If the place looks familiar, that's because some scenes from The Godfather were shot here.

TITO PUENTE'S CARIBBEAN 11/20

64 City Island Ave. (Rochelle St.), City Island 10464
718-885-3200, *Lunch & Dinner daily, $$*
A ☎ 🦉

A theme restaurant of sorts owned in part by Latin-jazz great Tito Puente. Sit on congo-drum barstools while nursing a "Frozen Mango Mambo." The fare includes lots of lobster dishes, baked clams, salads, plus Caribbean specialties from Cuban sandwiches and black beans to Puerto Rican-style seafood paella.

AND ALSO...

ANN & TONY'S   ITALIAN

2407 Arthur Ave. (187th & Belmont Sts.), 10458
718-933-1469, *Lunch & Dinner Tues.-Sun.,* **$$**

A neighborhood Italian in a neighborhood that's famous for its Italian food, Ann & Tony's has been feeding customers for 75 years. Okay, so the decor features mirrored walls, patterned tablecloths and year-round Christmas lights. The old-fashioned dishes like mixed antipasti and pollo Ann & Tony's are pretty good—and generous in portion.

COSENZA'S FISH MARKET   SEAFOOD

2354 Arthur Ave. (186th St.), Belmont 10458
718-364-8510, *Lunch & Dinner Mon.-Sat.,* **$**
No cards

Cosenza's primarily sells fresh and dried Mediterranean fish, as well as crabs, lobsters, striped bass and other local fish, all at great prices. But if you're not looking to buy some seafood to take home, stop here for achingly fresh clams, oysters, cockles and sea urchins, as well as cooked mussels and snails, served al fresco at the stand-up street-side clam bar.

IL BOSCHETTO   ITALIAN

1660 E. Gun Hill Rd. (Tiemann Ave.), 10469
718-379-9335, *Lunch & Dinner daily,* **$$**

A tried and true Bronx institution for over 30 years, Il Boschetto serves up generous portions of such fresh pastas as linguine di mare and green fettuccine. Depend on friendly service and a warm atmosphere.

JIMMY'S BRONX CAFÉ   CARIBBEAN/SEAFOOD

281 W. Fordham Rd. (Major Deegan Pkwy.), Fordham Heights 10468
718-329-2000, *Lunch & Dinner daily,* **$$**

Always crowded and noisy, this lively spot serves up huge portions of Caribbean and fresh seafood dishes. On their enclosed terrace, The Patio nightclub features live entertainment on the weekends until 4 a.m.

THE LOBSTER BOX   SEAFOOD

34 City Island Ave. (Belden St.), City Island 10464
718-885-1952, *Lunch & Dinner daily*, $$$

🅰 ☎ 📷

This City Island landmark offers fresh lobster any way you like it—broiled, steamed, stuffed, fra diavolo or marinara. The portions are generous and the water views are terrific. Also such pasta specials as shrimp and chicken primavera, shrimp fra diavolo, and lobster ravioli with sun-dried tomatoes and basil in a light cream sauce.

QUICK BITES

BAKERY CAFÉS

EGIDIO'S BAKERY

622 E. 187th St. (Hughes Ave.), Belmont 10458
718-295-6077, *Open daily*
No cards

Have a cappuccino and sit at one of the small tables before leaving with your bounty of napoleons, mixed Italian mini-cookies and cakes, biscotti, cannoli and other goodies that are arguably the best in this Italian bakery-laden neighborhood.

TRADITIONAL IRISH BAKERY/THE SNUG IRISH RESTAURANT

4268 Katonah Ave. (235th St.) Woodlawn 10470
718-994-0846, *Open daily*
No cards

The authentic Irish baked goods here may be the best in all of New York. Fluffy soda bread, currant-encrusted scones, and hard-to-find specialties like light Irish fruitcake, are terrific. The adjoining restaurant serves everything from Irish sardines and Irish sausage to roast ham with stuffing.

DOMINICAN

SCHOOL BUS

Webster Ave. (166th & 167th Sts.), South Bronx
No phone, *Open daily 7 a.m.-6 p.m.*
No cards

The South Bronx has more than a few refitted school busses serving Dominican comidas criollas, and this is one of the best. For under $5, you can get steak in Creole sauce or stewed chicken with rice and beans or mashed plantains.

ITALIAN

CAFÉ AL MERCATO

2344 Arthur Ave. (Crescent Ave. & 186th St.), The Bronx 10458
718-364-7681, Breakfast, Lunch & Dinner Mon.-Sat.
No cards

Old-fashioned Italian favorites, including pizzas, pastas, hero sandwiches and such entrées as chicken pizziola with rigatoni and a side of garlicky broccoli rabe, served in a friendly, family-run market.

PIZZA

CATANIA'S PIZZA CAFÉ

2305 Arthur Ave. (184th St. & Crescent Ave.), 10458
718-584-3583, Breakfast, Lunch & Early Dinner Mon.-Sat.
No Cards

The pizza is fine here, but the real reason to visit this hole-in-the-wall is for the dynamite calzones bursting with everything from cheese and more cheese, sausage, to a veal meatball and peppers.

SEAFOOD

JOHNNY'S REEF

2 City Island Ave., City Island, The Bronx 10464
718-885-2086, Lunch & Dinner daily, Closed Dec. 1-March 1)
No cards

The reason for the trip to this ramshackle restaurant at the end of the island: terrific old-fashioned, deep-fried, batter-dipped seafood. Shrimp, clams, oysters, porgies and whiting are served up along the cafeteria line still steaming from the boiling oil, and are served piled high on paper plates. Try steamed shrimp and clams with cole slaw and french fries, grab a cup of beer and enjoy the view of the tethered sailboats, Long Island and Manhattan. You won't believe you're in the gritty Bronx, but technically City Island's waterfront and beaches are part of the borough.

BROOKLYN

MAP	238
DINING	239
AND ALSO...	246
QUICK BITES	247

BARS, SALOONS & BREWPUBS	247
CAFÉS & COFFEE SHOPS	248
DELIS	248
ETHNIC FLAIR	249
AFRICAN	249
CAMBODIAN	249
CARIBBEAN & LATIN AMERICAN	249
INDONESIAN	251
ITALIAN	251
MALAYSIAN	252
MIDDLE EASTERN	252
POLISH	253
SOUL FOOD	254
THAI	254
HEALTHY	255
ICE CREAM & MORE	255
PIZZA	255

BROOKLYN

©1999
GAYOT PUBLICATIONS

DINING

ACADIA PARISH CAJUN CAFÉ   CAJUN   10/20
148 Atlantic Ave. (Clinton & Henry Sts.), Cobble Hill 11201
718-624-5154, *Lunch & Dinner Wed.-Mon., $*

A

This small family-run spot is plain and simple, and serves plentiful portions of down-home Cajun food. Resist filling up on the piping-hot corn muffins, and save room for the shrimp-and-crawfish Creole, the Louisiana-style crabcakes and the chicken and andouille jambalaya. There are fresh pies for dessert, but they don't have a liquor license.

ABBRACCIAMENTO ON THE PIER   ITALIAN   11/20
2200 Rockaway Pkwy., Canarsie Pier 11236
718-251-5517, *Lunch & Dinner daily, $$*

The view of Jamaica Bay and the wildlife preserve across the water are the major attractions here. Boaters pull up for cocktails and dinner on the pier, or sit inside near the piano bar, facing the sea-view windows. Dinner is a mix of Italian grill and Italian-American seafood, most of it good (but not as good as the view). Best bets are the tangy clams possilipo, orecchiette with garlicky broccoli rabe and sausage, the veal chop with vinegary peppers and the shrimp fra diavolo.

BRAWTA CARIBBEAN CAFÉ   CARIBBEAN   11/20
347 Atlantic Ave. (Hoyt St.), Boerum Hill 11217
718-855-5515, *Lunch & Dinner daily, $$*
No cards

At this bright, colorful space on busy Atlantic Avenue, everything is fresh and tasty. Most compelling are the rich curried coconut shrimp, and the hard-to-find ackee-and-codfish stew, the Jamaican national dish flecked with fiery scotch bonnet peppers. The steamed red snapper and curried goat with potatoes and carrots are also good, and don't miss two of the house drinks: pine-ade, a mix of ginger and pineapple; and the reputed virility aide called sea moss, which is boiled seaweed with vanilla, nutmeg and condensed milk.

CHEZ NIC   INTERNATIONAL   10/20
0303 Third Ave, (83rd & 84th Sts.), 11209
718-491-6618, *Dinner nightly, Brunch Sun, $$*

Chez Nic may look the part of a French bistro with its copper ceilings, lace curtains and pretty backyard garden, but the menu features much more than Gaelic fare. We're talking Italian fettuccine, Caribbean spice-rubbed chicken, Asian sesame-crusted salmon and even Southwestern ancho chili-flavored pork. That may sound like a hodgepodge, but the dishes work well together even when shared. Start with a steaming bowl of Prince Edward Island mussels in a fragrant wine-and-pesto broth or lobster cake with a tangy red-pepper remoulade. Skip the fashionable-but-bland sesame-crusted salmon in favor of sautéed skate. For dessert, share a towering duo of double-chocolate napoleons, one filled with whipped cream, the other with praline cream.

CUCINA   ITALIAN   14/20   ♟
256 Fifth Ave., (Carroll St. & Garfield Pl.), Park Slope 11215
718-230-0711, *Dinner Tues.-Sun.*, **$$**

Manhattan-style raves go to this elegant Northern Italian in a pair of newly renovated dining rooms. The menu changes often, but the antipasti and pasta are reliably authentic, the meats hearty and aromatic. Try the spinach and three-cheese ravioli, the farfalle with shrimp, or the roast snapper and clams. Or just sit at the bar and watch the Park Slope crowd, pleased with themselves for saving on a subway trip into Manhattan to eat.

GAGE & TOLLNER   SOUTHERN   13/20   ♟
372 Fulton St. (Smith St.), 11201
718-875-5181, *Lunch & Dinner daily*, **$$$**

Restored to its original splendor in 1996, this 1879 landmark has been here longer than the Brooklyn Bridge. In fact, it's the oldest continuously operating restaurant in New York City. New are a mahogany-and-marble-topped bar and sumptuous private dining suites. The menu still offers such classics as pan-roasted oysters, sherry-laced lobster bisque and lobster Newburg, but you can also get such up-to-date dishes as filet mignon with shiitake mushrooms and grilled tuna. For dessert, you can't beat the peach cobbler. The mostly American wine list has some fairly priced selections.

GARDEN CAFÉ   FUSION   10/20
620 Vanderbilt Ave. (Prospect Pl.), Prospect Heights 11217
718-857-8863, *Dinner Tues.-Sat.*, **$$**

"International ingredients mixed with contemporary American and European basics" is wordy but it best describes the Garden Café's approach. Inside this small corner café with a ramshackle charm, the mostly neighborhood crowd samples dishes ranging from green lip mussels steamed in wine with fennel and shallots, to seared salmon with vegetable vinaigrette and delicate roasted sea bass topped with leeks, sage and golden raisins. In addition to seafood, they do the occasional pasta and pork loin.

GARGIULO'S ITALIAN 10/20

2911 W. 15th St. (Surf & Mermaid Aves.), Coney Island 11235
718-266-4891, *Lunch & Dinner Wed.-Mon.*, $$$

A

There was a time when Gargiulo's attracted Manhattanites with its classic Neapolitan seafood recipes, shiny marble dining room and Coney Island setting. Since the turn of the century, the Gargiulo's enormous menu has offered fritto misto, baked scungilli, lobster Fra Diavolo, housemade lasagna, manicotti, chicken cacciatore and other red-sauce dishes to daytrippers and locals alike. Once, a gigantic octopus sculpture adorned the exterior of the place; rumor has it that in the middle of a Sunday rush, the chef cooked it.

HENRY'S END NEW AMERICAN 12/20

44 Henry St. (Cranberry St.), Brooklyn Heights 11201
718-834-1776, Dinner nightly, $$

A 🖀 ♥

This crowded, convivial neighborhood bistro offers European beers and ale, and has a formidable wine list. The braised duckling with honey and ginger or wild mushrooms and lingonberries, is top-notch. You can also get chicken, fish, veal and steak done just about any way you want it, plus game—venison, elk, alligator, even kangaroo—in season.

KALIO FUSION/NEW AMERICAN 10/20

245 Court St. (Butler & Kane Sts.), Carroll Gardens 11201
718-625-1295, *Dinner Tues.-Sun.*, $$

A

Fusion/New American comes to Brooklyn in a nice if narrow room on Court Street. Seafood gets fine treatment here, with cod baked in a potato crust and tuna tartare leading the way. Frequently changing specials can be odd, but they are generally worth the trouble, and when something's wrong, the friendly attitude of the neighborhood servers quickly reminds you why places like Kalio thrive in Brooklyn.

LA BOUILLABAISSE FRENCH 12/20

145 Atlantic Ave. (Clinton & Henry Sts.), Brooklyn Heights 11201
718-522-8275, Lunch Mon.-Fri., Dinner nightly, $
No cards

There's no written menu, dishes change daily, and you'll have to wait for a table on weekends at this popular Brooklyn/French bistro, where the bouillabaisse and Provençal-style seafood are terrific. Patrons are expected to bring their own wine—which helps keep the tab down.

LEMONGRASS GRILL THAI 10/20

61A Seventh Ave., (Lincoln Ave. & Berkeley Pl.), Park Slope 11215
718-399-7100, *Lunch & Dinner daily*, $

VISA MasterCard 💳

Though this modern Thai spot is trendy and usually jam-packed, we prefer the food at nearby Thai Taste (see entry below). Best bets are the seared salmon pla jean, the lemon-grass pork chops, and kwaytio ki mow, broad rice noodles sautéed with chili, basil, tomatoes, onions and yes, lemon grass. If you prefer your Thai food mild, be sure to tell them, or head to the newer Lemongrass Grill on Manhattan's Upper West Side.

LUNDY BROS.   SEAFOOD   11/20
1901 Emmons Ave. (Ocean Ave.), Sheepshead Bay 11214
718-743-0022, *Lunch & Dinner daily, Brunch Sun.*, $$
A ☎

A restored Brooklyn landmark, this enormous bay-side din-ing hall seats hundreds of people, and feeds them well on lob-ster, steamers and chowder served with old-fashioned biscuits and side dishes. There's wood-fired pizza too.

MARCO POLO   ITALIAN   12/20
345 Court St. (Union St.), Carroll Gardens 11231
718-852-5015, *Lunch & Dinner daily*, $$$
A ☎

A glorious hot and cold buffet of such shimmering antipasti as roast peppers, vegetables tossed in vinaigrette and chilled shellfish, are served graciously by an experienced wait-staff at this long-time Carroll Gardens favorite. The veal dishes are uniformly good, as are the many varieties of seafood. Old-fashioned murals cover the walls depicting the restaurant's namesake and his journeys in Asia, from where he brought Italy its first noodles. The minestrone is excellent, as are the cuttlefish in ink sauce, the black pasta and the snapper in Pernod sauce.

MAX & MORITZ   NEW AMERICAN   10/20
426A Seventh Ave. (14th St.), Park Slope 11215
718-499-5557, *Dinner nightly, Lunch & Brunch Sat.-Sun.*, $$
A 🍽

Grilled pork chops, shrimp ravioli in tomato reduction, baked Brie with fruit compote, beef tenderloin in crushed pep-per, roast chicken—Max & Moritz has a menu like many bistros that fiercely compete in Manhattan, but Park Slopers have few to choose from and so flock to the exposed brick, candle-lit spot. The narrow dining room and roomy back gar-den are hits with the Upper West Siders who've come to the Slope to raise kids, and weekend brunch can be jammed with tots playing with Mommy's poached eggs, zucchini pancakes and grilled tomatoes.

MIKE & TONY'S   AMERICAN   10/20
239 Fifth Ave. (Carroll St.), Park Slope 11215
718-857-2800, *Lunch Sun., Dinner nightly*, $$$
A ☎

As owner of Cucina (see review above) and retail stores across the street, Michael Ayoub has planted his flag firmly in this part of the Slope. Here, he's established a small dining room with a dark-wood, low-lit saloon up front where his dinners can sip old Scotch and light up cigars. The menu leans toward Guy Food—steaks and crabcakes—along with such other stylishly prepared dishes, as grilled sea bass with tomato-cream sauce and savory chicken pot pie. Since in addition you'll find good wine list, a well-stocked bar and lots of local camaraderie, expect a wait.

MONTE'S VENETIAN ROOM   ITALIAN   11/20

451 Carroll St. (Clinton St.), Carroll Gardens 11231
718-624-8984, *Lunch & Dinner daily*, $$

Once a hangout for famous Italian saloon singers, this old-fashioned spot boasts a giant mahogany bar, '30s murals of Venice's canals, and a stupendous Venetian crystal chandelier. The food is more Southern Italian then Venetian, but Monte's chefs know their way around seafood—shrimp alla Monte especially.

NEW CITY CAFÉ   NEW AMERICAN   11/20

246 DeKalb Ave. (Vanderbilt Ave.), Fort Greene 11205
718-622-5607, *Dinner Fri.-Sat.*, $$

A

Open only two nights, New City offers a limited menu of carefully prepared and innovative fare in a warm, cozy setting, with a fireplace crackling away if the weather suits. (The other five nights, the 35-seat dining room is available for private parties) Velvety black bean soup, inventive puréed vegetable spring rolls, grilled duck breast with corn pudding and fried cornmeal-crusted catfish are among the offerings on the frequently changing menu.

NEW PROSPECT CAFÉ   AMERICAN   12/20

393 Flatbush Ave. (Eighth Ave.), Prospect Heights 11217
718-638-2148, *Lunch Tues.-Sun., Dinner nightly*, $

The cozy New Prospect gets high marks for its commitment to quality preparation and creativity with vegetarian food, as well as its relaxed, efficient setting. Try the corn-and-shrimp chowder, the Cajun meatloaf with garlic mashed potatoes or the occasional (and unexpectedly good) jerk tempeh. If you like their baked goods, desserts and salads, try the New Prospect at Home, its bakery around the corner on Seventh Avenue.

ODESSA   RUSSIAN   11/20

1113 Brighton Beach Ave. (13th St.), Brighton Beach 11235
718-332-3223, *Lunch & Dinner Tues.-Sun.*, $$

Grab some friends for a night out at the Odessa, a party that starts out with cold duckling, pickled vegetables and chicken Kiev, and ends with raucous music, inspired dancing and vodka, vodka, vodka. The gigantic second-floor hall can hold 300, and sometimes does on Friday and Saturday nights when the bands play and the local Russian émigrés dress up for a family night out.

OZNOT'S DISH   MEDITERRANEAN   12/20
79 Berry St. (9th St.), Williamsburg 11211
718-599-6596, *Lunch & Dinner daily*, $$
No cards

As Williamsburg continues to remake itself as the new SoHo, an artists' neighborhood full of funky galleries and hip boutiques, Oznot's Dish fits right in. With its cracked-tile mosaic walls and eclectic outdoor garden, the restaurant is as much art scene as dining venue. The cuisine (heavy on modern-style Moroccan) is imaginative and fresh, with lots of choices including Tunisian brik, delicate snack purses of tangy goat cheese wrapped in thin phyllo dough and a mezze plate featuring somewhat skimpy samples of feta, hummus, baba ghanouj and stuffed grape leaves. Try instead such intriguing soups as a hot beet and pomegranate blend that works surprisingly well. Other unique dishes include grilled salmon with a ginger-tomato sauce, a rib-eye steak with coriander jus and plum chutney, and, for dessert, the red plum-and-pistachio tart. Ask help in selecting from the 40 varieties of tea, 250 international wines (many selections under $25) and 50 imported or local microbrewed beers.

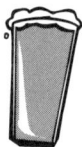

PETER LUGER   STEAKHOUSE   13/20
178 Broadway (Driggs Ave.), Williamsburg 11211
718-387-7400, *Lunch & Dinner daily*, $$$
No cards

Established in 1887, this old New York steakhouse predates the Williamsburg Bridge, in whose shadow it stands. Brooklynites and Wall Streeters flock here for the huge top quality steaks, large orders of french fries or hash browns, spinach and cheesecake. The two-story restaurant (try to reserve a table in the downstairs dining room) sports well-worn oak tabletops, wood-handled knives and forks and waiters who have worked here for years. Don't ask for a menu; you'll be branded as a tourist. The porterhouse steaks, basted with butter and always cooked rare, are tender and juicy. Order one steak for two people, and a steak-for-two for three. There are also two-inch-thick loin lamb chops and thick slabs of prime rib, both of which are as good as the steaks. A limited but reasonably priced wine list offers mostly red wines from California, with some French and Italian offerings.

PETE'S DOWNTOWN   ITALIAN   10/20

1 Old Fulton St.(Water St.), Downtown Brooklyn 11201
718-858-3510, *Lunch & Dinner Tues.-Sun., $$*

Within sight of the Brooklyn Bridge and the lower
Manhattan skyline, Pete's Downtown keeps the old waterfront
area alive with its golden-age Brooklyn atmosphere of tin ceil-
ings and southern Italian favorites, like mozzarella in carrozza,
a world-class pasta e fagioli, and other regional dishes like
gnocchi, baked ravioli and penne alla vodka. This isn't the
trendy northern Italian or Tuscan-style spot, but typically old-
fashioned Italian American Brooklyn at its best, with many con-
temporary updates. Enjoy the comfort and the view.

QUEEN   ITALIAN   12/20

84 Court St., (Livingston & Schermerhorn Sts.), Brooklyn Heights 11201
718-596-5955, *Lunch & Dinner daily, $$*

Once, Queen was a humble downtown pizzeria, but after
brothers Pasquale and Vincent Vitielo took over down the
block from their father's original location, the cooking headed
uptown. Brooklyn politico and courthouse regulars fill Queen's
apricot-hued dining room at lunch, while families often return
to the old neighborhood for special occasions and favorite
items like house-made mozzarella, fried fennel with blood
oranges, saccettini stuffed with spinach and gorgonzola, fava
beans with butter and oil, and monkfish tossed with raisins,
onions and pignolis—all in generous portions.

THE RIVER CAFÉ   NEW AMERICAN   15/20

1 Water St. (under pediment of the Brooklyn Bridge), 11201
718-522-5200, *Lunch Mon.-Fri., Dinner nightly, Brunch Sat.-Sun., $$$$*

You can't beat this elegant barge-restaurant's drop-dead
view of the Manhattan skyline and the Brooklyn Bridge. It's
one of our favorite spots for a celebration, and we applaud the
excellent wine list and the inviting piano bar. Chef Rick
Laakkonen has steadily improved the innovative New
American cuisine. The house-smoked dishes, such as the fruit-
wood-smoked salmon with johnnycakes, are wonderful, and
you can always count on the steaks. Intriguing entrées include
charred filet of pork with spinach purée, pan-roasted partridge
with lentils and vinegar sauce, and braised stuffed veal flank
with piquillo peppers and shiitake mushrooms. For dessert, go
for the gimmicky but delicious chocolate Brooklyn Bridge,
made with Valrhona chocolate, no less.

TOMMASO'S   ITALIAN   13/20

1464 86th St. (14th & 15th Aves.), Bensonhurst/Dyker Heights 11228
718-236-9883, *Lunch Mon.-Sat., Dinner Tues.-Sun., $$*

If you like robust Italian food and an occasional aria during
dinner, you'll love Tommaso's, for owner Thomas Verdillo is a
gracious host and an able singer. At holiday time, it's the place
to go for a classic Neapolitan Christmas Eve dinner, especially
in the back room with its frescoed walls and soft light. You can
get your fix of wonderful antipasti: creamy mozzarella and
roasted peppers with olive oil and garlic, mozzarella in carroz-
za, pasta with red clam sauce, sausages and broccoli rabe.
During truffle season, Tommasso brandishes the truffle shaver
over delicate pasta and risotti. Tommasso knows his wines and
stocks some intriguing labels at good value.

TWO TOM'S   ITALIAN   11/20

255 Third Ave. (President & Union Sts.), Park Slope 11215
718-875-8689, *Lunch & Dinner Tues.-Sun., $$*
No cards

Talk about atmosphere! On most nights, you're surrounded by laughing families devouring enormous veal chops or
choice steaks, plates of bitter rapini and platters of pasta.
There's no menu; just listen as your waiter hurriedly rambles
through the evening's choices. Nothing seems to have changed
in this storefront restaurant in the run-down Casket District for
fifty years, and that's the way we like it

AND ALSO...

RASPUTIN   RUSSIAN

2670 Coney Island Ave. (Ave X), Coney Island 11235
718-332-8333, *Dinner nightly, $$$$*

Go late, go hungry, and go with enough cash for a taxi
home, as you may find yourself downing too much vodka to
drive. A favorite with Russian émigrés, this is a kitschy cabaret
more than a restaurant, and customers really let their hair
down. The waiters are as no-nonsense as they come.

QUICK BITES

BARS, SALOONS & BREWPUBS

THE GATE

321 Fifth Ave. (3rd St.), Park Slope 11205
718-768-4329, *Lunch & Dinner daily*
No cards

With a dozen taps or more churning out an eclectic, comprehensive selection of regional, seasonal and international brews, a rockin' blues/reggae/pop music jukebox, a big selection of single-malt Scotches and small batch bourbons, outdoor seating and a decidedly laissez-faire attitude, The Gate is Park Slope's best bar. Most everyone comes for the beer, which can include hard-to-find Americans and temporarily available international ales and such, but especially satisfying is the Gate's food policy: They don't cook, but they do keep a sheaf of local delivery menus handy in case you want to eat while enjoying your Brooklyn Chocolate Stout. And you won't have to leave your seat, which can be hard to come by in the thick of the evening, especially during live music nights

MUGS ALE HOUSE

125 Bedford Ave., Greenpoint 11211
718-384-8494, Lunch & Dinner daily
No cards

Greenpoint's best beer bar, Mugg's runs 30 taps of imported and regional beers and has even installed two old-style beer engines for pouring handcrafted ales. A long bar and backroom with ancient booths can hold lots of beer fans, and an outdoor garden fills in the warm months, especially with adventurous Manhattanites who've caught the nearby 'L' train, only one stop away from the last East Side station. Casual pub grub—sandwiches, burgers, fries—is served in the evening until midnight, and the friendly neighborhood crowd is a pleasure.

PARK SLOPE BREWING COMPANY

356 Sixth Ave. (5th St.), Park Slope 11215
718-788-1756, *Lunch Fri.-Sat., Dinner nightly, Brunch Sat.-Sun.*

This neighborhood tavern in Park Slope is a local favorite and one of the most attractive brew pubs around, with old-fashioned ceiling fans run by an antique-pulley system. The fare—mostly comfort food, like macaroni and cheese—is only passable, but favorite brews made here include Park Slope's Pale Ale and Big Shippy's Barley Wine. **Also in Park Slope (62 Henry St., 718-522-4801).**

CAFÉS & COFFEE SHOPS

BAM CAFÉ

30 Lafayette St. (Ashland St.), Downtown Brooklyn 11217
718-636-4100, *Lunch & Dinner daily*

[VISA]

Lodged on the top floor of the imposing Brooklyn Academy of Music (BAM), BAM Café has the coolest location and interior in Brooklyn, with lit arches spanning the spacious dining area, overstuffed chairs arrayed across the back of the room and a hip-looking (if slow) wait staff. Great for pre-theater sandwiches (chicken cobb on ciabatta roll), or post-movie snacks (pumpkin and corn cake with salsa fresca), slightly overpriced, but hey, BAM Cafe is about the space, the scene and the continuing rebirth of downtown Brooklyn.

TOM'S RESTAURANT

782 Washington Ave. (Sterling Pl.), Prospect Heights 11238
718-636-9738, *Breakfast & Lunch daily*
No cards

For 60 years, Tom's has been serving breakfast all day long to young and old. Everyone basks in the friendly and festive atmosphere, and fills up on all the usual breakfast favorites, from bacon and eggs to apple pancakes to golden challah french toast.

DELIS

JUNIOR'S

386 Flatbush Ave. Extension (DeKalb Ave.), 11201
718-852-5257, *Breakfast, Lunch & Dinner daily*

[A]

There's always a knot of cars double-parked outside the busy and gaudy Junior's, with its blinking lights and hustling wait staff. Lots of typical deli fare at this Brooklyn institution, like sandwiches and such, but they all take a back seat to Junior's main attraction—cheesecake. Just off the Manhattan Bridge, Junior's sells a traditional creamy New York-style cheesecake in many flavors. It's a blast from the dessert past, and one of New York's best.

MRS. STAHL'S KNISHES

1001 Brighton Beach Ave. (Coney Island Ave.), Brighton Beach 11235
718-648-0210, *Open daily*
No cards

It might be a long way to go for fresh and flaky knishes, but this tiny, dingy eatery under the elevated train in Brighton Beach is always worth a stop. Choose from over 20 kinds of freshly baked knishes stuffed with everything from kasha, potato and broccoli, to sweet potato—and you won't want to eat for another day. And don't pass us the transcendently rich cherry-cheese knish. Call and charge mail orders.

ETHNIC FLAIR

AFRICAN

JOLOFF

930 Fulton St. (St. James Pl. & Washington Ave.), Fort Greene 11238
718-636-4011, *Lunch & Dinner daily*
No cards

Joloff is the name for Senegal's national dish—rice cooked in tomato sauce—and Senegalese food in all its richness is celebrated here. Savory stews served with a variety of scented and flavored rice dishes are the best bet. Try the golden stew of onion and chicken, or the national dish of red rice with carrots, eggplants, yams, and fish in a fiery tomato-thickened sauce. Joloff is a good place for vegetarian fare as well.

KEUR N'DEYE

737 Fulton St. (S. Elliot & S. Portland Sts.), Fort Greene 11217
718-875-4937, *Lunch & Dinner Tues.-Sun.*
No cards

Keur N'Deye appeals with its warm dining room where carved wooden instruments and hand-woven tapestries from Dakar decorate the walls, and Senegalese music plays in the background. Whet your appetite with one of the unusual juices like sorrel or guava, before moving on to a succulent feast of Senegalese home cooking. Try the yassa guinaar, chicken smothered in sautéed onions with a tangy lemon sauce, mafe dieun, bluefish in peanut sauce, or yassa yap, tender lamb and beef in a lemon-onion sauce, all served on mounds of couscous.

CAMBODIAN

CAMBODIAN CUISINE

87 S. Elliott Pl. (Lafayette St.), Fort Greene 11205
718-858-3262, *Lunch & Dinner daily*

Few Cambodians make their way to New York, and this may be the only outpost in Brooklyn for the fragrant and enticing southeast Asian cuisine. Fresh fish fried and served in a creamy sauce flavored with lemon grass and basil, spicy ground beef salad appetizer and marinated chicken slowly steamed in a galanga-scented coconut milk head the menu, but all here is worth a try, especially at these prices.

CARIBBEAN & LATIN AMERICAN

BOURDA GREEN BAKERY & RESTAURANT   WEST INDIAN

1861 Nostrand Ave. (Ave. D), Flatbush 11226
718-693-0052, *Lunch & Dinner daily*
No cards

John Bell prides himself on his fish patties, cod cakes wrapped in flaky yellow pastry pockets. He also makes all kinds of West Indian breads and sweets, like casava pone and pineapple tarts. Try some black pudding, made with beef blood, rice and a seasoning called married-man's pork, or the hangover-curing pepperpot.

CASTILLOS   DOMINICAN

302 Flatbush Ave. (Seventh Ave.), Prospect Heights 11217
718-638-2907, *Breakfast, Lunch & Dinner daily*

A

A friendly neighborhood Dominican restaurant that vibrates with the sounds of meringue and salsa. Lots to choose from here in the way of hearty and inexpensive country-style food throughout the day. Try some sancocho (beef and root vegetable stew) and mofongo (boiled mashed plantains with garlic and oil served with fried cheese and salami for breakfast). To wash them down, there's nothing like the refreshing morir sonando milkshake, which tastes like an orange creamsicle.

LA TAQUERÍA   MEXICAN

72 Seventh Ave. (Berkeley Pl.), Park Slope 11217
718-398-4300, *Lunch & Dinner daily*

La Taquería offers authentic East Los Angeles-style tacos, with many shades of heat in their salsas, burritos, rotisserie chicken, enchiladas and tamales. They also offer "San Francisco gourmet wraps," filled with Caesar salad or grilled chicken with spicy peanut sauce.

MEZCAL'S   MEXICAN

223 Fifth Ave. (President St.) 11220
718-783-3276, *Lunch & Dinner daily*

The Mezcal's chain brings the complex cuisine of Mexico's Puebla region to Park Slope, Bay Ridge and Brooklyn Heights. Overlook the bland standards and opt for shrimp Mocambo, bathed in white wine and smoky mesquite chips, or adobo Alitxqueño, thick slices of pork smothered in chipotle peppers and cinnamon. For dessert, don't pass up bola de fuego, deep-fried ice cream balls. **Also at 7508 Third Ave. (76th & Bay Ridge Parkway), 718-748-7007, and 151 Atlantic Ave. (Clinton & Henry Sts.), 718-643-6000.**

SYBIL'S   GUYANESE

2210 Church Ave. (Flatbush Ave.), Flatbush 11226
718-469-3220, *Lunch & Dinner daily*

Sybil Bernard-Kerrutt may be the uncrowned queen of Guyanese food in New York. Shoppers leave her bakery/carry-out with armloads of lemony tennis rolls, sweet pineapple tarts and dense cassava pone. Expatriate Guyanese seek out three of her best dishes: pepperpot (a zesty oxtail stew enriched with inexpensive cuts of beef, pork, and chicken, and the distinctive aroma and flavor of cassarep,) East Indian-style chicken roti, and Guyanese chow mein.

INDONESIAN

JAVA INDONESIAN RIJSTTAFEL

455 Seventh Ave. (16th St.), 11215
718-832-4583, *Lunch Wed.-Sun., Dinner nightly*

A

Java's exotic, reasonably priced fare and homey atmosphere make it a popular spot after a quiet afternoon strolling—or more likely, Rollerblading—through Prospect Park. Two can easily share the rijsttafel (literally "rice table" or smörgasbord) featuring 16 samples of Indonesian dishes that blend Indian and Thai with a touch of the bizarre, including gado-gado, similar to pad-Thai noodles in a peanut dressing; soto madura, a lemony chicken soup full of noodles, potatoes and a hard-boiled egg; and ikan bumbu Bali, crispy cod fish balls with a tart-and-fruity dipping sauce.

ITALIAN

NORTHSIDE CAFÉ

119 Kent Ave. (N. Seventh St.), Greenpoint 11211
718-388-9000, *Lunch Sun.-Fri, Dinner nightly*

A 📷 🍽

It only seems like you're at the end of the world, as Manhattan looms just across the river and beyond the waterside landscape. Northside is as much a bar as a restaurant, but the kitchen does great things with Italian-influenced chicken with peppers, sausage and onions, pastas and fried seafood. Otherwise, the large selection of beers, the spacious window-lined tile-and-wood bar room, cozy booths and courtyard garden make Northside a neat hangout.

RANDAZZO'S CLAM BAR

2017 Emmons Ave. (21st St.), 11235
718-615-0010, *Lunch & Dinner daily*
No cards 📷 🍽 👓

After 75 years in Sheepshead Bay, Randazzo's is king of clams—and lobster, shrimp and calamari, too. Order up a mess of steamers and battered calamari rings to eat out on the deck, or pack a soft shell crab sandwich for a trip on the fishing boats across the pier. Come back for more until 1:30 a.m. on weekends. Just don't expect complex flavors and sophisticated atmosphere: This Italian red-sauce-style cooking just wouldn't be complete without Formica tabletops, Naugahyde barstools and waitresses who say "Here you go, hon" as they pass out plastic beer cups.

THE RED ROSE

315 Smith St. (President & Union Sts.), Carroll Gardens 11231
718-625-0963, *Dinner Wed.-Mon.*

This friendly, small neighborhood restaurant offers a wide selection of Italian favorites, from zucchini marinara and fettuccine Alfredo to chicken picante with croquettes.

MALAYSIAN

NYONYA

5323 54th St. (Eighth Ave.), 11220
718-972-2943, *Lunch & Dinner daily*
No Cards

Situated in the up-and-coming Chinatown of Brooklyn's Sunset Park neighborhood, Nyonya serves the subtly spicy cuisine of Malaysia with real flair. We recommend the squid with Chinese watercress in a red curry sauce and cold Hainanese chicken, but if you have difficulty choosing from the menu, the staff is eager to help. With its warm, stylish bamboo and brick interior, Nyonya is also a step up from the ascetic coffee-shop look of many Asian restaurants. **Also in Manhattan at 194 Grand St. (Mott & Mulberry Sts.), 212-334-3669.**

MIDDLE EASTERN

FOUNTAIN CAFÉ

183 Atlantic Ave. (Court & Clinton Sts.), Cobble Hill 11201
718-624-6764, *Lunch & Dinner daily*

Middle Easterners have done business for a hundred years along Atlantic Avenue. Today, the modest and brightly lit Fountain Café serves the best falafel sandwiches and platters on the street. Pita pockets emerge packed with falafel balls, moist, hot and drenched in tahini. Have an appetizer platter of smoky baba ghanouj and tangy hummus with warm pita bread and olives first, and you'll leave inexpensively satisfied.

MOUSTACHE—BROOKLYN

405 Atlantic Ave. (Bond & Nevins Sts.), Cobble Hill 11217
718-852-5555, *Lunch & Dinner daily*
No cards

Not to be confused with what was once its sister restaurant in Manhattan, Moustache-Brooklyn serves the same savory and cheap Middle Eastern food in an extremely casual setting—no frills—although dining in the back garden during the summer is charming. The usual array of Mediterranean appetizers—baba ghanouj, tabbouleh, hummus, cracked olives—are good here, but the main attractions are the fresh-baked puffy pita sandwiches stuffed with sliced lamb or falafel and salad topped with tahini, and the Brooklyn-invented pitza, a large round of the freshly house-made bread topped with highly spiced meats and vegetables with small slices of whole-milk cheese.

OLIVE VINE

131 Sixth Ave. (Sterling Pl.) Park Slope 11217
718-636-4333, *Lunch & Dinner daily*
No Cards

Falafel, kefta kebabs, house-made baba ghanouj, hummus and fool madamas top the menu list, but the most popular dish is the thin, pita-crust pitza, a uniquely Brooklyn treat: a pizza-sized hand-made pita (without pocket) topped with everything from sun-dried tomatoes and roasted chicken to ground lamb, and sprinkled with the zatar, the savory green Middle Eastern spice mixture that zings the palate. Though casual in the extreme and nothing to look at, olive vine has picnic tables out front which allow you to watch Park Slope stroll by on quiet, tree-lined Sixth Ave.

WALID DEMIS MOUSTACHE PITZA

405 Atlantic Ave. (Bond & Nevins Sts.), Cobble Hill 11217
718-852-5555, *Lunch & Dinner daily*
No cards

Their homemade pita bread is sensational. Therefore, the made-to-order Jordanian "pitzas" are too: large, freshly baked pitas the size pizzas topped with savory ground lamb, lamb sausage, lemony chicken or just leeks and scallions. Excellent baba ghanouj and hummus, as well as zingy zatar bread, pita coated in olive oil and dusted with ground sesame seeds, thyme and sumac. A rear garden is enclosed for outdoor dining year round.

POLISH

POLSKA

136 Greenpoint Ave. (Manhattan Ave.), Greenpoint 11222
718-389-8368, *Breakfast, Lunch & Dinner daily*
No cards

Many immigrant Poles and their descendants still thrive in this neighborhood, and this plain counter-and-booth eatery is one of their favorites. Any soup in the winter is good here, and the old-world veal shank is remarkable. If your waitress struggles with English, just point on the menu to goulash, placki (potato pancakes) with sour cream, a dark Polish beer and perhaps some strawberry blintzes.

SOUL FOOD

CAROLINA COUNTRY KITCHEN

1993 Atlantic Ave. (Saratoga Ave.), Brownville 11216
718-346-4400, *Breakfast, Lunch & Dinner daily*
No cards

African-American cookery like this can be found all across the South, but few places serve it up this good in New York. Fried chicken, kale and collard greens, grits, beef ribs, pig's feet, barbecue, chitlins and a myriad of sides and super-sweet desserts are all worth trying. Have an iced tea, step up to the steam tables and let the ladies behind the counter make your day. Hearty, cheap and satisfying—that's the style here.

THE MCCAFÉ

327 Stuyvesant Ave. (Macon St.), Bedford-Stuyvesant 11233
718-574-3728, *Breakfast, Lunch and Dinner Tues.-Sun.*

Not to be confused with Mickey D's, this landmark has been serving home-style Southern cooking in a modest, clean and friendly setting since the 1940s. A big after-church crowd fills the tables on Sundays for platters of smothered pork chops, salmon cakes and grits. There are few old-style Bedford-Stuyvesant dining establishments as friendly, or as inexpensive.

THAI

PLAN EAT THAI

184 Bedford Ave. (N. 7th St.), 11211
718-599-5758, *Lunch & Dinner daily*
No cards

Quite possibly the city's best cheap Thai food, Plan Eat Thai is just a single subway stop from Manhattan in Williamsburg, the new artists' enclave that's become Brooklyn's answer to the East Village. The loud, crowded diner serves standard favorites: peanutty phad Thai, spicy basil beef, crunchy papaya salad, whole fish in sweet-and-sour tamarind sauce. It's all hot and fast, but be prepared to cool your heels in line for a while, for Plan Eat Thai doesn't take reservations and it's always packed. As for the name, it was originally Planet Thai, but Planet Hollywood threatened to sue, so...

THAI TASTE

125 Seventh Ave.(President St.) Second Floor, Park Slope 11215
718-622-9376,*Lunch &Dinner daily*

A

When your friends try to take you to Lemongrass Grill down the block, show them you know better and walk up the block and upstairs to Thai Taste, where there is no waiting, the service is friendly and the food is superior. Try Thai asparagus in green curry sauce with seafood, boneless duck roasted with honey and ginger, or Chinese-style eggplant. Sticky rice is extra and worth it, and all the usual dishes (fried fish with basil, pad thai, and pork with string beeans) are reliably well-prepared, if unspectacular. For the experimental, specials like frog legs in garlic, basil and chilis might do. And don't miss the Thai iced coffee.

HEALTHY

CAMILLE'S CLOVER HILL

272 Court St. (Kane & DeGraw Sts.), Carroll Gardens 11201
718-875-0895, *Lunch Sat.-Sun., Dinner Tues.-Sun., $*

With a frequently changing menu and an emphasis on vegetarian and healthy cuisine at reasonable prices, Camille's Clover Hill is perfectly suited to yuppie-boomed Carroll Gardens, where strollers are beginning to push the old-timers playing cards off the sidewalks. Camille's kitchen has an winning way with such meat-substitutes as tofu, seitan and tempeh, so don't let them put you off. There are also good poultry and pasta dishes and even (gasp!) red meat sightings on occasion, and an all-around light hand with very fresh ingredients.

ICE CREAM & MORE

PETER'S ICE CREAM PARLOR & COFFEE HOUSE

185 Atlantic Ave. (Clinton & Court Sts.), Cobble Hill 11201
718-852-3835, *Open daily*
No cards

In the midst of many Middle Eastern bakeries and restaurants, you'll find this old-fashioned ice-cream parlor, where cozy church-pew booths and ice-cream chairs clash. The ice cream is rich and thick, in varying flavors. The coffee is good as well.

PIZZA

GRIMALDI'S

19 Old Fulton St. (Water & Front Sts.), Brooklyn Heights 11201
718-858-4300, *Lunch & Dinner Wed.-Mon.*
No cards

Think Patsy's. They only recently changed their name to Grimaldi's because they didn't want to be confused with the Manhattan chain of Patsy's pizza parlors. Some fans insist Brooklyn's best-known coal-fired pizzeria is the best in New York. Chewy and lightly charred, Grimaldi's crust has loyal devotees who willingly wait as long as it takes, which can be awhile on a busy weekend. Homemade sauce, fresh mozzarella, tangy sausage, hand-cut mushrooms and fresh basil decorate the best offerings. Parking can be difficult, but the views of the Old Fulton Street neighborhood under the Brooklyn Bridge is worth a walk.

LENTO'S

7003 Third Ave. (Ovington), Bay Ridge 11209
718-745-9197, *Lunch & Dinner daily*

For thin-crusted pizza, this is the place. Seafood salad, nightly pasta specials and robust Neapolitan dishes are also good, but don't miss their roasted red pepper, hot sausage and eggplant pizza combination. **Also in Park Slope (833 Union Street, 718-399-8782).**

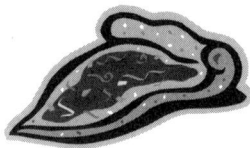

TOTONNO'S

1524 Neptune Ave. (W. 15th & 16th Sts.), Coney Island 11224
718-372-8606, *Lunch & Dinner Wed.-Sun.*
No cards

For almost 75 years, pizza has been everything here, and Totonno's coal-fired ovens send out lip-searing, bubbling pies. But if you want to try them, you must be persistent. Open only from noon to 8:30 p.m. Wednesdays through Sundays—and only until the freshly made pizza dough lasts, this is the classic hole-in-the-wall pizzeria, with only a small sign in the window. It's worth the trip and the wait.

TWO BOOTS

514 2nd St. (Seventh & Eighth Aves.), Park Slope 11215
718-499-3253, *Lunch in summer only, Dinner nightly, Brunch Sat.-Sun.*
A

This Two Boots, one of several in the city, welcomes kids with crayons, pizzas garnished with vegetable faces—and raw pizza dough to play with. The "boots" are Italy and Louisiana, the progenitors of the house cooking style. Some creative pizza combinations here—like spicy shrimp, smoked mozzarella and roasted peppers—and pastas along with spicy Cajun food. There is a small but fun bar scene with occasional music.

QUEENS

MAP	**258**
DINING	**259**
AND ALSO...	**263**
QUICK BITES	**264**

ETHNIC FLAIR	264
AFGHAN	264
CARIBBEAN	264
CHINESE/DIM SUM	264
GREEK	265
INDIAN	265
LATIN AMERICAN	266
ICE CREAM & MORE	267
PIZZA	267

QUEENS

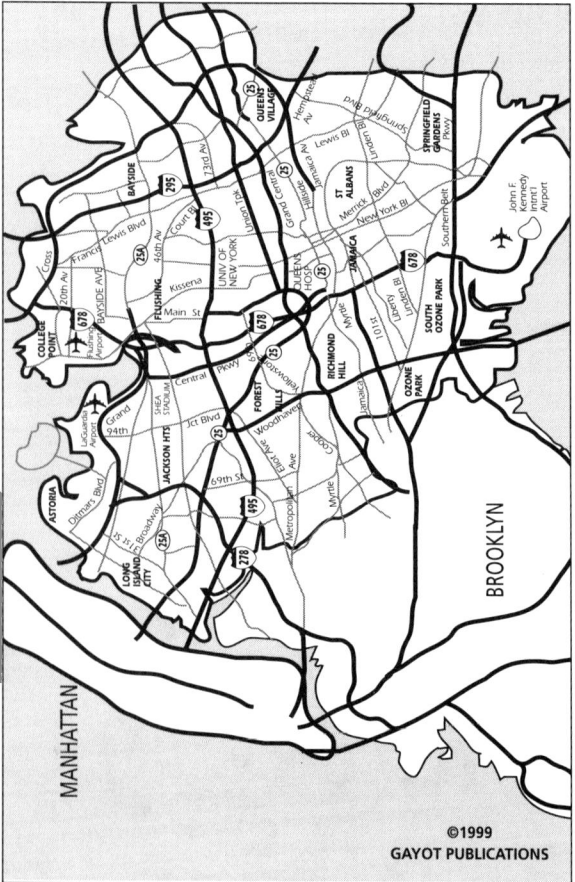

Map of Queens showing MANHATTAN, BROOKLYN, and neighborhoods including COLLEGE POINT, BAYSIDE, QUEENS VILLAGE, SPRINGFIELD GARDENS, ST ALBANS, FLUSHING, JAMAICA, SOUTH OZONE PARK, RICHMOND HILL, OZONE PARK, FOREST HILLS, JACKSON HTS, ASTORIA, LONG ISLAND CITY, John F. Kennedy Int'n'l Airport, and LaGuardia Airport.

©1999
GAYOT PUBLICATIONS

DINING

CABANA
CARIBBEAN   11/20

107-10 70th Rd. (Austin St.), Forest Hills 11375
718-263-3600, Lunch & Dinner daily, $$

While Cabana is definitely a colorful party scene, the food here is often authentic and creative. Some of chef/owner Glenn Flechter's recipes come from his Puerto Rican mother-in-law. Spicy Jamaican jerk chicken, Bahamian conch fritters and golden brown codfish cakes called baccalaitos are great starters. Not Caribbean, but very good, is the steak churrasco, lathered with garlic, oil and parsley. You won't find salmon with tangerine glaze in Kingston or Santo Domingo, but it's still good here.

GIANNI'S RISTORANTE
ITALIAN   11/20

75-61 31st Ave. (76th & 77th Sts.), Jackson Heights 11372
718-899-2555, Lunch & Dinner Mon.-Sat., $

A

What was formerly Ralph's Italian restaurant has a more Italian name now. The food is nothing fancy, just lovingly prepared Italian specialties served the old-fashioned, checked-tablecloth spaghetti-house way. Good bets include hearty spaghetti carbonara and other slightly out of favor but soulfully satisfying Italian classics such as osso buco.

GOLDEN MONKEY
CHINESE   12/20

133-47 Roosevelt Ave. (Prince St.), Flushing 11354
718-762-2664, Lunch & Dinner daily, $
No cards

If you enjoy spicy Szechuan-style cooking, you'll be happy with the battered and fried sweet-and-sour yellowfish, mouth-numbingly hot beef covered with ground black pepper, and eggplant with garlic-meat sauce speckled with fiery dried chiles. Try the crunchy vegetable rolls with a sesame dipping sauce. Fans of properly cooked eel will also find happiness at the Golden Monkey.

GOODY'S
CHINESE   13/20

94-03 63rd Dr. (Queens Blvd.), Rego Park 11374
718-896-7163, Lunch & Dinner daily, $
No cards

At Goody's, and don't miss the Shanghai soupy buns, pastry skins filled with a savory broth with crab, pork and chicken. Try cold appetizers like salty duck, pickled cabbage and tofu with bamboo and mushroom. Experiment with marvelous flaky pastries filled with shrimp, pork and shredded turnip. Also sample the fried dumplings, the Shanghai noodles with seafood and the fried slivers of seaweed-battered yellowfish. Bring your own beer. **Also in Manhattan's Chinatown (1 E. Broadway, 212-577-2922).**

JADE PALACE   CHINESE   12/20

136-14 38th Ave. (Main St.), Flushing 11354
718-353-3366, *Lunch & Dinner daily*, $$
No cards

Hong Kong cookery as well as Cantonese are the trademarks of this restaurant in Chinese Flushing. Smart and very busy, the Palace bustles on the weekends with Chinese families. Fiery black-pepper pork or beef and snappy squid with green chile baked in salt are always good, and from the large tank in the dining room, you can select your fish to be steamed Canton-style, or crab to be cooked in black bean sauce. Also, try blanched fresh shrimp with chili sauce.

JAI-YA THAI   THAI   12/20

81-11 Broadway (81st St.), Elmhurst 11373
718-651-1330, *Lunch & Dinner daily*, $$

Thai aficionados are more than willing to make the trip to Elmhurst for Jai-Ya Thai's renderings of classic soups like chicken with coconut milk. There are also tangy minced fishcakes called tod mun, barbecued beef sauté, fiery deep-fried crispy fish with chili or basil, various seafood curries and, of course, phad Thai noodles. Peanuts, coconut milk, cilantro, finger chilies, kaffir lime leaf and lemon grass all are put to wonderful use here, and some claim it's the best Thai in the city.

KUM GANG SAN   KOREAN   11/20

138-28 Northern Blvd. (Bowne & Union Sts.), Flushing 11354
718-461-0909, *Open 24 hours daily*, $

Kum Gang San recreates a little Korean village in the old village of Flushing, yet offers a menu in English. On a busy weekend evening at this huge restaurant with its own parking lot, waterfall and 24-hour service, Korean families enjoy the night out by grilling their bul goki and other meats at the table. Dig into the fiery kim chee, or the naeng myon—cold rice noodles in broth with beef, egg cake and hot oil—and ask your waiter to make a selection for you from the various sides and appetizers; they're all good.

LA CABAÑA ARGENTINA   ARGENTINEAN   11/20

95-51 Roosevelt Ave. (Warren & Johnson Blvds.), Jackson Heights 11372
718-429-4388, *Lunch & Dinner daily*, $$

La Cabaña's classic Argentinian parillada (mixed grill) is a smoking-hot platter heaped with strip steak, sausages, ribs, kidneys, sweetbreads and other char-grilled cuts of beef. Simple cooking of quality meats are the by-words here. The best addition might be the chef's churrasco—a garlic, basil, parsley and oil sauce that's spread on the meats. Or simply try a sizzling oversized steak.

LONDON LENNIE'S   SEAFOOD   12/20

63-88 Woodhaven Blvd. (Penelope & Fleet Ct.), Rego Park 11374
Lunch Mon.-Fri., Dinner nightly, $$

The specialty in these spacious wooden-walled dining rooms is bracingly fresh seafood, cooked with care. Briny raw clams and oysters, sweet sautéed bay scallops, golden-brown Maryland-style crabcakes with herb mayonnaise, fried calamari with spicy marinara sauce, fresh striped bass filets—anything in season can be found on the cozy tables at Lennie's. Wait for a table at the bar crowded with locals, or take a peek at the fresh fish arranged at the take-out counter.

MANDUCATIS   ITALIAN   13/20

13-27 Jackson Ave. (47th Ave.), Long Island City 11104
718-729-4602, *Lunch Mon.-Fri., Dinner nightly, $$$*

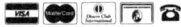

In Latin, the name means "You guys, eat!" You won't need any further encouragement after trying Ida Cerbone's sauce made from family-grown tomatoes. In fact, with extra-virgin unfiltered olive oil and wine from the family vineyard in Italy, and many of the pickled vegetables put up by Ida each summer, this is as close to a real family osteria as you can get in Queens. It's also hearty Lazian cooking, so don't look for truffles. Enjoy such specialties as braised or stuffed rabbit, homemade pasta, grilled lamb and veal and smartly garlicky broccoli rabe.

MI COLOMBIA   LATIN AMERICAN/SEAFOOD   12/20

76-18 Roosevelt Ave., Jackson Heights 11372
No phone, *Lunch & Dinner daily, $$*
No cards

As you can tell from its elaborate window display, Mi Colombia specializes in seafood. From a gargantuan mixed seafood grill for two to octopus, red snapper and grouper, Mi Colombia's cooks have a light hand at the grill and fryer. Make sure to include room for side orders of arepas, black sausage, sweet plantains and a whipped papaya or guanabana batido.

O LAVRADOR   PORTUGUESE   11/20

138-40 101st Ave. (Liberty Ave.), Richmond Hill 11418
718-526-1526, *Lunch & Dinner Mon.-Sat., $$*

One of the few Portuguese restaurants in New York, the modest O Lavrador if worth a trip for such Portuguese treats as an appetizer of clams, chorizo and ham, tender veal sautéed in wine and lemon, arroz de mariscos with clams, scallops, shrimp, squid and yellow rice, and marinated pork in a rich brown sauce with clams and rice.

PENANG CUISINE MALAYSIA   MALAYSIAN   11/20

38-04 Prince St. (Roosevelt Ave.), Flushing 11354
718-321-2078, *Lunch & Dinner daily,* $
No cards

This friendly family-run restaurant in pan-Asian Flushing serves good food, and has spawned offshoots in Manhattan, Boston and Philadelphia. Malaysian food combines many Asian influences, which means such dishes as beef marinated in tamarind and slowly simmered in a coconut-milk broth, or fried turnip rolls with spicy sauce. The SoHo branch is trendier but more expensive.

TIERRAS COLOMBIANAS   COLOMBIAN   11/20

82-18 Roosevelt Ave. (82nd & 83rd Sts.), Jackson Heights, 11372
718-426-8868, *Lunch & Dinner daily,* $
No Cards

Just say sí to some of the squarest meal deals you can find anywhere in New York. The platos tipicos or "typical plates" turn out to be small platters of beef, pork, chicken or fish served with generous portions of rice and beans, salad, fried plantains, potatoes or cassava—enough to feed a small family with plenty of South American flair to spare. The friendly service and filling fare at this bustling Colombian diner clearly has people coming back for more. **Also at 33-01 Broadway, Astoria, 718-956-3012.**

WATER'S EDGE   NEW AMERICAN   13/20

44th Dr. at the East River, Long Island City 11101
718-482-0033, *Lunch Mon.-Fri., Dinner Mon.-Sat.,* $$$$

Sitting on a barge on the East River, Water's Edge offers a drop-dead view of the Manhattan skyline. The straightforward menu is seafood-intensive, with such appetizers as seared tuna sashimi and herb-marinated shrimp, and entrées of roast Chilean sea bass, seared diver sea scallops and grilled Alaskan king salmon. They also do a fine grilled veal chop, hearty braised beef shortribs and such game dishes as loin of venison. The desserts are appropriately festive for this good-for-special-celebrations restaurant, and the free ferry ride to Long Island City is a kick. Try to book a reservation during the sunset.

ZENON   GREEK   15/20

34-10 31st Ave. (34th & 35th Sts.), Astoria 11106
718-956-0133, *Lunch & Dinner daily,* $
No cards

Zenon transports culinary flavors from the heart of Greece to the heart of Astoria. The oversized faux-ancient water jugs on the tables transport you to another time and place. Superb meze like creamy melitzanasalata, piquant tsadziki, crusty spinach pie and savory saganaki, served flaming at your table, can begin a meal that leads to such classic dishes as moussaka, octopus and savory grilled meats. On Wednesday nights, traditional music complements the patter of Greek conversation.

AND ALSO...

DAVID'S TAIWANESE GOURMET   CHINESE

84-02 Broadway (82nd. St.), Elmhurst 11373
718-429-4818, *Lunch & Dinner daily*, $
No cards

David's is known for its authentic Taiwanese cuisine: oyster pancakes, fermented bean curd, marinated seaweed and clams with basil.

ELIAS CORNER   GREEK/SEAFOOD

24-01 31st St. (24th Ave.), Astoria 11102
718-932-1510, *Dinner nightly*, $$
No cards

Tucked away under the subway, this friendly Greek spot doesn't have menus. Choose your fresh seafood (even octopus and porgies) from what's on display in a glass butcher case, and they'll grill it for you.

KARYATIS   GREEK

35-03 Broadway (35th & 36th Sts.), Astoria 11106
718-204-0666, *Lunch & Dinner daily*, $$
A

This warm and lively Greek restaurant serves such authentic dishes as charcoal-grilled octopus, lamb stew, chicken with sausages, and baklava. You can make a meal of the traditional Greek appetizers, and dips scooped up with wedges of pita bread. There's live music on Tuesday through Saturday nights.

PIER 25A   SEAFOOD

215-16 Northern Blvd. (215th & 216th Sts.), Bayside 11361
718-423-6395, *Lunch & Dinner daily*, $
A

A cross between a diner and a nautically themed restaurant, this family-style fish house serves generous portions of fresh seafood. They also offer steaks, and veal and chicken dishes.

WATERFRONT CRAB HOUSE   SEAFOOD

2-03 Borden Ave. (2nd St.), Long Island City 11101
718-729-4862, *Lunch & Dinner daily*, $$
A 🕿

For a quick getaway from Manhattan, hop the 34th Street ferry to Queens, and walk across the parking lot to this old standby. In the antique-filled dining room, you'll find all the usuals, done usually quite well: from Manhattan and New England clam chowder and garlicky crabs to lobster tail and steak.

QUICK BITES

ETHNIC FLAIR

AFGHAN

SPEENGAR SHISH KEBAB HOUSE

40-09 69th St. (Roosevelt Ave.), Woodside 11377
718-426-8850, *Lunch & Dinner daily*

In this modest, tiny storefront restaurant, you can watch kebabs cook on the traditional Afghani-style spit. Marinated meats—leg of lamb, lamb rib chops, ground beef balls, chicken breast, king fish—are skewered and cooked slowly over the open fire, and served with brown rice and salad. Choose from the many combination dishes of brown rice with lamb curry, spinach or vegetables. The most expensive dish is under $9.

CARIBBEAN

EL SITIO   CUBAN

68-28 Roosevelt Ave. (69th St.), Woodside 11377
718-424-2369, *Lunch & Dinner daily*

You can get all the usual Cuban dishes here—roast pork, rice and beans with bananas, yucca with garlic, shredded beef. But what makes El Sitio worth a trip is their Cuban sandwich, a perfect assemblage of prosciutto-thin ham, pork and mild Swiss cheese, steamed with pickles and mojito garlic sauce between two crispy slices of bread. Since it's priced at only $3.80, who needs MickyD's?

SANDY'S ROTI SHOP   TRINIDADIAN

121-10 Liberty Ave., (120th & 121st Sts.), Richmond Hill 11419
718-659-8000, *Breakfast, Lunch & Dinner daily*
No cards

Back from the Islands and need a taste of goat roti, curried conch or fried kingfish? Sandy's has that, and lots of Trinidadian versions of East Indian dishes as well, like rice and dhal with coconut chutney. Or try some fried allo served with "buss-up-shot" (Caribbean for Indian paratha bread). Chase it all with a glass of whipped sea moss or a tangy sorrel drink.

CHINESE/DIM SUM

JOE'S SHANGHAI

136-21 37th Ave. (Main St.), Flushing 11354
718-539-3838, *Lunch & Dinner daily*
No cards

If you've got a hankering for sweet and fragrant Shanghai-style cooking, and you don't mind eating in a Chinese restaurant where little English is spoken, Joe's is the place to go in Flushing. Steamed buns—crabmeat with pork especially—are also filled with shimmering broth and are the special treat here. Eel and other elusive seafood also get the royal treatment at Joe's.

K.B. GARDEN RESTAURANT

136-28 39th Ave., (Main St.), Flushing 11354
718-961-9088, *Breakfast, Lunch & Dinner daily*

A

From 9 a.m. until 3 p.m. daily, this a big, bustling Hong-Kong-style dim sum parlor, which means you choose from the carts being wheeled furiously through the room, and call a captain over when you're finished, to tally up the bill. Don't stop with the steamed dumplings and buns; the braised chicken feet and sesame balls are good too. This is also a wonderful place for Cantonese-style seafood. See the live shrimp and fish swimming in the tank? Soon you'll be eating them, steamed or deep-fried, with ginger and scallions or black-bean sauce.

GREEK

UNCLE GEORGE'S

33-19 Broadway (34th St.), Astoria 11103
718-626-0593, *Open 24 hours daily*
No cards

This no-nonsense, family-atmosphere establishment in the heart of Greek Astoria serves standard Greek specialties—creamy taramasalata, garlicky skordalia, stewed rabbit, sautéed octopus, roast chicken. The lamb burgers are especially juicy, oniony and flavorful. That is, if you can resist the chicken, whole lamb and suckling pig (in season) turning on the open rotisserie.

INDIAN

DELHI PALACE

37-33 74th St. (Roosevelt & 37th Aves.), Jackson Heights 11372
718-507-0666, *Lunch & Dinner Mon.-Sat.*

Good Southern Indian food is the specialty of this no-frills restaurant near Jackson's Diner (see review following). That translates into such specialties as deep-fried lentil "doughnuts" (iddly), wafer-thin crêpes (dosai) wrapped around a number of fillings, and rice pancakes topped with tomatoes, peas, mixed vegetables or a hot peppers or onions (uthappam). All come with creamy lentils and cilantro-mint-accented yogurt sauce.

JACKSON DINER

37-47 74th St. (37th Ave.), Jackson Heights 11372
718-672-1232, *Lunch & Dinner daily*
No cards

It looks like an American diner and the name is American, but the food is all Indian, including vegetarian Indian dishes from different regions of the sub-continent. Crisp pakora, tasty samosas and tender lamb rogan josh are all served in the culture-shock decor featuring pink Formica and red-and-white checked tablecloths. Don't miss the kulcha, a puffy onion- and ginger-scented bread.

SHAMIANA RESTAURANT

42-47 Main St. (42nd Ave.), Flushing 11355
718-445-2262, *Lunch & Dinner daily*
No cards

This is one of the few Indian vegetarian restaurants serving food from the Gujarat, in the northwest corner of the country. The buffet offers good bhel puri, crispy samosas, a wide selection of Gujarati-style vegetable dishes, crêpe-like dosas and thicker, pancake-like uttapams. Try the sweet ras mali, a custardy milk dessert.

LATIN AMERICAN

EL POTRERO

46-12 Greenpoint Ave. (46th & 47th Sts.), Sunnyside 11372
718-472-4123, *Lunch & Dinner daily*

El Potrero serves a range of excellent Latin American food, including hearty posole stewed with delectable bits of pernil (roast pork). Soups are savory and satisfying, filled with vegetables like yucca and pumpkin, and entrées like fluffy poblano rellenos come piled high with guacamole, beans and rice.

IZALCO   SALVADORIAN

64-05 Roosevelt Ave., Woodside 11377
718-533-8373, *Lunch & Dinner Thurs.-Tues.*

Perhaps the best Salvadorian spot in New York, Izalco has a bright home under the elevated train. Once inside the neat, cozy restaurant, try the tangy chopped beef appetizer called salpicon, pastelitos filled with beef or chicken, creamy cheese-filled pupusas, and dense, tasty tamales.

LA PICADA AZUAYA   ECUADORAN

84-19 37th Ave. (84th & 85th Sts.), Jackson Heights, 11372
718-424-9797, *Lunch & Dinner daily*

It's about time the rest of the world woke up and smelled the llapingachos. If you're curious about Ecuadoran cuisine or are already a convert to it, plan a visit to this pleasant, unassuming restaurant in Jackson Heights, one of the city's most multicultural communities. Traditional dishes, including soups, ceviches and llapingachos (potato omelets) are sure to please your palate; and don't forget to try the batidos or shakes, made from papaya, pineapple and other exotic fruit juices.

ICE CREAM & MORE

BENFAREMO, THE LEMON ICE KING OF CORONA

2-02 108th St. (52nd Ave.), Corona 11373
718-699-5133, Open daily
No cards

No one ever regrets traveling for an audience with Peter Benfaremo, the Lemon Ice King of Corona, as he and his store are known. He's been making authentic Italian ices here in Corona since the '40s. Beside lemon, Ben offers a variety of fruit ices that taste like fruit, not artificially flavored sugar ice. This is the way Italian ices should taste, and that's why Benfaremo's the king.

PIZZA

RIZZO'S

30-13 Steinway St. (30th Ave.), Long Island City 11105
718-721-9862, *Lunch & Dinner daily*
No cards

Rizzo's thin-crusted pan pizza is a delight—spicy and still served in traditional Sicilian rectangles. Remember that the next time you get the too-thick, too-doughy and too-mushy pizza that passes for Sicilian-style.

Staten Island

MAP   270

DINING   271

AND ALSO...   272

STATEN ISLAND

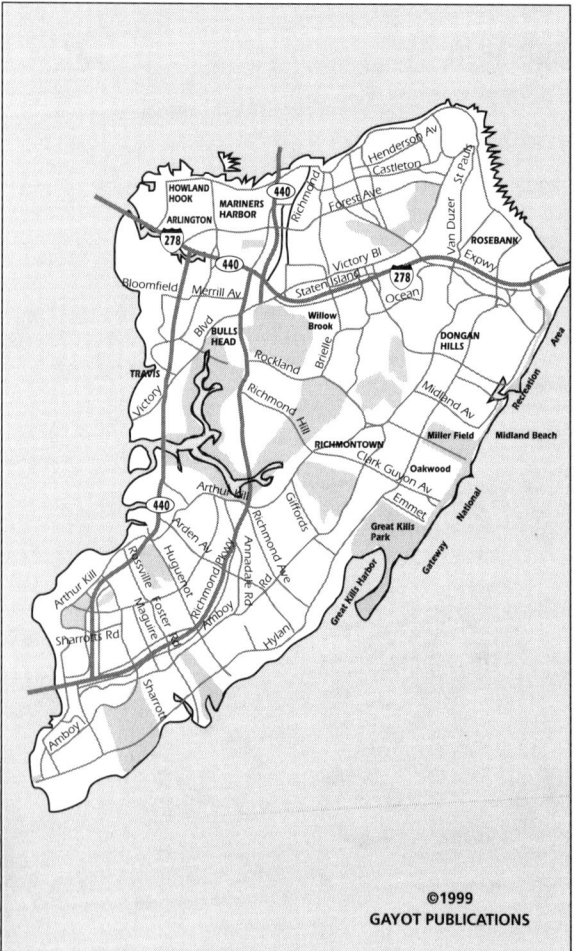

©1999
GAYOT PUBLICATIONS

DINING

ADOBE BLUES   SOUTHWESTERN   10/20
63 Lafayette Ave. (Filmore St.), New Brighton, 10310
718-720-2583, *Lunch & Dinner daily, $$*

Staten Island's free ferry has become a popular tourist destination for on-the-water views of Manhattan and the Statue of Liberty. Go at sunset and you've got a great excuse to stay for dinner, when a five minute bus ride will drop you at the flickering neon sign for this Southwestern saloon with live music and plenty of cowboy kitsch. Sidle up to the bar and select from among 45 tequilas and 200 bottles of beer on the wall; microbrews like Cave Creek Chili Beer, with a hot jalapeño bobbing inside, will fire you up faster than the weak house sangria. Don't fill up on the fresh salsa and store-bought chips when you can order spicy ground chicken mini-tacos, then skip the mundane quesadillas in favor of beer-soaked "Drunken Mexican" shrimp or a sizzling platter of grilled ostrich fajitas. Then loosen your belt for low-brow cowboy desserts like "Butch Cassidy Chocolate-Peanut Butter Pie." Bands play three times a week, and on weekends, the kitchen serves until 1 a.m.

AESOP'S TABLES   NEW AMERICAN   11/20
1233 Bay St., Rosebank 10305
718-720-2005, *Lunch & Dinner Tues.-Sat., $$*

This New American oasis in Staten Island is cozy, countrified and eclectic. Choose among the fresh seafood dishes prepared Mediterranean-style, like grilled red snapper dressed with fresh pesto sauce, large baked clams strongly seasoned with bread crumbs, garlic and shallots, and fluffy cod cakes served with spicy and vinegary greens. Also good are jerk chicken, and pork chops in a red chile crust. Summer and autumn are the best times to dine here, as the local Long Island and New Jersey farm bounty allows the kitchen greater fresh combinations, and diners not wishing to eat in the charmingly simple wood-floor dining room can dine outside in the pretty patio garden and take the salt air under the stars.

TRATTORIA ROMANA   ITALIAN   11/20
1476 Hylan Blvd., South Beach 10305
718-980-3113, *Lunch & Dinner daily, $$*

In a city dominated by Neapolitan and Northern Italian restaurants, Trattoria Romana's owners offer a rarity: authentic Roman-style cooking. At this modest restaurant, both the hot and cold mixed antipasti are good, as are the ever-changing versions of minestrone, a variety of creamy al dente risottos with vegetables and mushrooms, or seafood in red sauce. The pastas are good, especially the homemade spinach-and-cheese ravioli in walnut sauce. Choose from an ample selection of veal, fish and chicken dishes; in season, we recommend the baby lamb with wine and fresh herbs. Don't miss the 20 or so brick-oven pizza possibilities.

AND ALSO...

GOODFELLAS BRICK OVEN PIZZA   PIZZA
1718 Hylan Blvd., South Beach 10305
718-987-2422, *Lunch & Dinner daily, $*

Goodfellas' pizza alla vodka, made with an oddly pink tomato-vodka cream sauce, won Pizza and Pasta magazine's "Best Pizza" recipe in 1993, but on this pizza-crazy island that was no surprise. The wood-burning oven at Goodfella's yields a nicely crisp and slightly charred crust. The plain tomato-sauced pie is also good, with fresh mozzarella, basil and other toppings good enough to challenge Brooklyn and Manhattan's best. The pasta is good, too, but most regulars, including Mayor Giuliani, come for the pizza.

LUM CHIN   CHINESE
4326 Amboy Rd. (Armstrong & Richmond Aves.), 10312
718-984-8044, *Lunch & Dinner daily, $*

1640 Forest Ave. (Willowbrook Rd.) 10314
718-442-1707, *Lunch & Dinner daily, $*

Chinese on Staten Island; dine in either of these two modern settings, or take-out the usually good food.

OLD BERMUDA INN   CONTINENTAL
2512 Arthur Kill Rd. (Bloomingdale Rd. & Roseville Ave.), 10309
718-948-7600, *Dinner Wed.-Sun., Brunch Sun., $$*

A restaurant known more for its charm than its Continental food, though the $16.50 Sunday buffet brunch is usually a sell-out.

Glossaries & Restaurant Indexes

MENU SAVVY   274

COFFEE SAVVY   283

WINE SAVVY   287

FOOD & WINE EVENTS   297

FOOD & WINE PAIRINGS   300

WATER SAVVY   304

RESTAURANT INDEXES   312

   Restaurants By Cuisine   312
   Restaurants By Notable Features   323
   Restaurants By Area   328

MENU SAVVY

A GUIDE TO INTERNATIONAL FOOD TERMS

FRENCH

Agneau: lamb

Aïoli: garlicky mayonnaise

Américaine: sauce of white wine, Cognac, tomatoes and butter

Andouille: smoked tripe sausage, usually served cold

Anglaise: boiled meats or vegetables

Béarnaise: sauce made of shallots, tarragon, vinegar and egg yolks, thickened with butter

Béchamel: sauce made of flour, butter and milk

Beurre blanc: sauce of wine and vinegar boiled down with minced shallots, then thickened with butter

Beurre noisette: lightly browned butter

Bisque: rich, velvety soup, usually made with crustaceans, flavored with white wine and Cognac

Blinis: small, thick crêpes made with eggs, milk and yeast

Boeuf bourguignon: beef stew with red wine, onions and lardons (Lardoon; larding fat cut into long strips and threaded through lean cuts of meat by a special larding needle in order to moisten the meat as it cooks).

Bombe glacée: molded ice cream dessert

Bordelaise: fairly thin brown sauce of shallots, red wine and tarragon

Borscht: thick Eastern European soup of beets and boiled beef, often garnished with a dollop of sour cream

Boudin noir: blood sausage

Bouillabaisse: various fish cooked in a soup of olive oil, tomatoes, garlic and saffron

Bourride: sort of bouillabaisse, usually made with large white fish, thickened with aïoli; served over slices of bread

Brie: cow's milk cheese with a soft, creamy inside and a thick crust, made in the shape of a disk and sliced like a pie

Brioche: a soft loaf or roll, often sweetened and used for pastries

Brochette: on a skewer

Canapé: small piece of bread topped with savory food

Canard: duck

Carbonnade: pieces of lean beef, first sautéed then stewed with onions and beer

Carré d'agneau: rack of lamb

Cèpes: prized wild mushroom, same family as the Italian porcini

Chanterelles: prized wild mushroom, trumpet-shaped

Charcutière: sauce of onions, white wine, beef stock and gherkins

Charlotte: dessert of flavored creams and/or fruit molded in a cylindrical dish lined with ladyfingers (if served cold) or strips of buttered bread (if served hot)

Chèvre: goat cheese

Choucroute: sauerkraut; often served with sausages, smoked bacon, pork loin and potatoes

Clafoutis: a dessert of fruit (usu. cherries) baked in an eggy batter

Confit: pork, goose, duck, turkey or other meat and sealed in its own fat

Coquilles St-Jacques: sea scallops

Coulis: thick sauce or purée, often of vegetables or fruit

Court-bouillon: stock in which fish, meat and poultry are cooked

Crème chantilly: sweetened whipped cream

Crêpe Suzette: crêpe stuffed with sweetened mixture of butter, Curaçao, tangerine juice and peel

Croque-monsieur: grilled ham and cheese sandwich

Croûte (en): in pastry crust

Crudités: raw vegetables

Daube: beef braised in red wine

Ecrevisses: crayfish

Entrecôte: "between the ribs"; steak cut from between the ribs

Epinards: spinach

Escalope: slice of meat or fish, flattened slightly and sautéed

Escargots (la bourguignonne): snails (with herbed garlic butter)

Financière: Madeira sauce enhanced with truffle juice

Florentine: with spinach

Foie gras: liver of a specially fattened goose or duck

Fondue: a bubbling pot of liquid into which which pieces of food are dipped—most commonly cheese and bread; can also be chocolate and fruit or various savory sauces and cubes of beef. Also, vegetables cooked at length in butter and thus reduced to pulp

Forestière: garnish of sautéed mushrooms and lardons (Lardon; larding fat cut into long strips and threaded through lean cuts of meat as it cooks)

Galantine: boned poultry or meat, stuffed and pressed into a symmetrical form, cooked in broth and coated with aspic

Galettes and crêpes (Brittany): galettes are thin pancakes made of buckwheat flour and are usually savory. Crêpes are made of wheat flour and are usually sweet

Gâteau: cake

Gelée (en): in aspic (gelatin usually flavored with meat, poultry or fish stock)

Génoise: sponge cake

Granité: lightly sweetened fruit ice

Gratin dauphinois: sliced potatoes baked in milk, sometimes with cream and/or grated Gruyère

Grenouille: frog (frogs' legs: cuisses de grenouilles)

Hollandaise: egg-based sauce thickened with butter and flavored with lemon

Jambon: ham

Julienne: vegetable soup made from a clear consommé, or any shredded food

Langoustine: saltwater crayfish

Lapin: rabbit

Limon: lime (also, citron vert)

Lotte: monkfish or anglerfish; sometimes called "poor man's lobster"

Madrilène (la): garnished with raw, peeled tomatoes

Magret (Maigret): breast of fattened duck, cooked with the skin on; usually grilled

Médaillon: food, usually meat, fish or foie gras, cut into small, round pieces

Moules marinière: mussels cooked in the shell with white wine, shallots and parsley

Noisettes: hazelnuts; also, small, round pieces of meat (especially lamb or veal)

Nougat: sweet made with roasted almonds, egg whites, honey and sugar

Oeufs: eggs

Pain: bread

Parfait: sweet or savory mousse; also a layered ice cream dessert

Parisienne: garnish of fried potato balls

Paupiettes: thin slices of meat stuffed with forcemeat and shaped into rolls

Pissaladière: tart with onions, black olives and anchovy filets

Pommes: apples

Pommes de terre: potatoes

Poulet: chicken

Profiteroles: small puffs of choux paste often filled with whipped cream of crème patissiere and piled high in a dish with chocolate sauce poured over

Provençale (' la): with garlic or tomato and garlic

Quiche: tart of eggs, cream and various fillings (such as ham, spinach or bacon)

Ratatouille: stew of eggplant, tomatoes, bell peppers, zucchini, onion and garlic, all sautéed in oil

Rémoulade: mayonnaise with capers, onions, parsley, gherkins and herbs

Rouille: sort of mayonnaise with pepper, garlic bread soaked in bouillon, olive oil and possibly saffron

Sabayon: fluffy, whipped egg yolks, sweetened and flavored with wine or liqueur; served warm

Saint-Pierre: John Dory, a white-fleshed fish

Salade niçoise: salad of tomatoes, hard-boiled egg, anchovy filets, tuna, sweet peppers, celery and olives (also can include green beans, potatoes, basil, onions and/or broad beans)

Sole meunière: sole dipped in flour and sautéed in butter with parsley and lemon

Sorbet: sherbet

Spätzle: round noodles, often made from eggs

Steak au poivre: pepper steak; steak covered in crushed peppercorns, browned in a frying pan, flambéed with Cognac; also sauce deglazed with cream

Tapenade: a paste of olives, capers and anchovies, crushed in a mortar with lemon juice and pepper

Tartare: cold sauce for meat or fish; mayonnaise with hard-boiled egg yolks, onions and chopped olives

Tarte: tart, round cake or flan; can be sweet or savory

Tarte tatin: upside-down apple tart

Truffe: truffle; highly esteemed subterranean fungus, esp. from Périgord

ITALIAN

Acciughe: anchovies

Aceto: vinegar

Aglio: garlic

Agnello: lamb

Agnolotti: crescent-shaped, meat-filled pasta

Amaretti: crunchy almond macaroons

Anguilla: eel

Aragosta: spiny lobster

Arrosto: roasted meat

Baccalo: dried salt cod

Bagna cauda: hot, savory dip for raw vegetables

Bierra: beer

Biscotti: cookies

Bistecca (alla fiorentina): charcoal-grilled T-bone steak (seasoned with pepper and olive oil)

Bolognese: pasta sauce with tomatoes and meat

Bresaola: air-dried spiced beef; usually thinly sliced, served with olive oil and lemon juice

Bruschetta: toasted garlic bread topped with tomatoes

Bucatini: hollow spaghetti

Calamari (calamaretti): (baby) squid

Calzone: stuffed pizza-dough turnover

Cannellini: white beans

Carbonara: pasta sauce with ham, eggs, cream and grated cheese

Carciofi (alla giudia): (flat-tened and deep-fried baby) artichokes

Carpaccio: paper thin, raw beef (or other meats)

Cassata: ice-cream bombe

Cipolla: onion

Conchiglie: shell-shaped pasta

Coniglio: rabbit

Costoletta (alla milanese): (breaded) veal chop

Cozze: mussels

Crespelle: crêpes

Crostata: tart

Fagioli: beans

Fagiolini: string beans

Farfalle: bow-tie pasta

Fegato alla veneziana: calf's liver sautéed with onions

Focaccia: crusty flat bread

Formaggio: cheese

Frittata: Italian omelet

Fritto misto: mixed fry of meats or fish

Frutti di mare: seafood (esp. shellfish)

Funghi (trifolati): mush-rooms (sautéed with garlic and parsley)

Fusilli: spiral-shaped pasta

Gamberi: shrimp

Gamberoni: prawns

Gelato: ice cream

Gnocchi: dumplings made of cheese (di ricotta), potatoes (di patate), cheese and spinach (verdi) or semolina (alla romana)

Grana: hard grating cheese

Granita: sweetened, fla-vored grated ice

Griglia: grilled

Insalata: salad

Involtini: stuffed meat or fish rolls

Maccheroni: macaroni pasta

Manzo: beef

Mela: apple

Melanzana: eggplant

Minestra: soup; pasta course

Minestrone: vegetable soup

Mortadella: large, mild Bolognese pork sausage

Mozzarella di bufala: fresh cheese made from water-buffalo milk

Noce: walnut

Orecchiette: ear-shaped pasta

Osso buco: braised veal shanks
Ostriche: oysters
Pane: bread
Panettone: brioche-like sweet bread
Panna: heavy cream
Pancetta: Italian bacon
Pappardelle: wide, flat pasta noodles
Pasticceria: pastry; pastry shop
Patate: potatoes
Pecorino: hard sheep's-milk cheese
Penne: hollow, ribbed pasta
Peperoncini: tiny, hot peppers
Pepperoni: green, red or yellow sweet peppers
Pesca: peach
Pesce: fish
Pesce spada: swordfish
Pesto: cold pasta sauce of crushed basil, garlic, pine nuts, parmesan cheese and olive oil
Piccata: thinly-sliced meat with a lemon or Marsala sauce
Pignoli: pine nuts
Polenta: cornmeal porridge
Pollo: chicken
Polipo: octopus
Pomodoro: tomato
Porcini: prized wild mushrooms, known also as boletus
Prosciutto: air-dried ham
Ragu: meat sauce
Ricotta: fresh sheep's-milk cheese
Rigatoni: large, hollow ribbed pasta
Risotto: braised rice with various savory items
Rucola: arugula
Salsa (verde): sauce (of parsley, capers, anchovies and lemon juice or vinegar
Saltimbocca: veal scallop with prosciutto and sage
Semifreddo: frozen dessert, usually ice cream, with or without cake
Spiedino: brochette; grilled on a skewer
Spumone: light, foamy ice cream
Tartufi: truffles
Tiramisu: creamy dessert of rum-spiked cake and triple-crème Mascarpone cheese
Tonno: tuna
Tortellini: ring-shaped dumplings stuffed with meat or cheese
Uovo (sodo): egg (hard-boiled)
Verdura: greens, vegetables
Vitello (Tonatto): veal (in a tuna and anchovy sauce)
Vongole: clams
Zabaglione: warm whipped egg yolks flavored with Marsala
Zucchero: sugar
Zucchine: zucchini
Zuppa: soup
Zuppa inglese: cake steeped in a rum-flavored custard sauce

SPANISH & LATIN AMERICAN

Because there are so many regional dialects in Spain and Latin America, the term for one food product might easily have four or five variations. We've chosen those ingredients and dishes most often found in Southern California restaurants.

Aceite: oil
Ajo: garlic
All-i-oli: aïoli; garlicky mayonnaise
Arroz: rice
Bacalao: dried, salted codfish
Burrito: soft, wheat-flour tortilla rolled and stuffed with meats, refried beans, cheese and vegetables
Caldo: broth
Camarones: shrimp
Carne: meat
Cerveza: beer

Ceviche: raw fish marinated in citrus juice

Chalupa: a small, thick corn tortilla folded into a boat shape, fried and filled with a mixture of shredded meat, cheese and/or vegetables

Chilequile: flat tortilla layered with beans, meat, cheese and tomato sauce

Chile relleno: large, mild chile pepper, stuffed with cheese and fried in an egg batter

Chorizo: spicy pork sausage flavored with garlic and spices

Empanada: pie or tart filled variously with meat, seafood or vegetables

Enchilada: a tortilla, fried and stuffed variously with meat, cheese and/or chiles

Entremeses: appetizers

Flan: a baked custard with a caramel coating (also crema caramela)

Frito (frita): fried

Gambas: shrimp

Garbanzo: chick pea

Gazpacho: Andalusian; a cold soup of fresh tomatoes, peppers, onions, cucumbers, olive oil, vinegar and garlic (also celery, breadcrumbs)

Guacamole: an avocado dip or filling, with mashed tomatoes, onions, chiles and citrus juice

Higado: liver

Huachinango: red snapper

Huevos: eggs

Huevos rancheros: tortillas topped with eggs and a hot, spicy salsa

Jalapeño: very common hot chile pepper, medium size

Jamón: ham

Licuado: fruit milkshake

Lima: lime

Limón: lemon

Mariscos: shellfish

Masa: cornmeal dough; essential for making tortillas

Menudo: a stew featuring tripe

Mole: sauce; most often a thick, dark sauce made with mild chiles and chocolate

Nachos: a snack dish of tortilla chips topped with melted cheese and chiles

Nopales: leaves of the prickly pear cactus; simmered and used in various dishes

Paella: a dish of saffron-flavored rice studded with meat (chicken, ham, sausages, pork), shellfish and vegetables

Papas: potatoes (also, patatas)

Papas fritas: literally "fried potatoes "; french fries

Parrillada: grilled

Pescado: fish

Pez espada: swordfish

Pimiento: red chile pepper; can be sweet or hot

Plátano: plantain; a starchy, mild-tasting variety of banana popular in Latin American; usu. cooked and served as a side dish

Pollo: chicken

Poblano: large, mild, dark green chile pepper; used for chile rellenos

Puerco: pig

Quesadilla: a soft, folded tortilla filled with cheese (and/or other savory stuffings) and toasted or fried

Queso: cheese

Salchicha: sausage

Salsa: sauce; also, an uncooked condiment employing fresh tomatoes, onions and chiles

Sangría: Spanish drink made with red wine, soda water, chopped fresh fruits and sugar, often with a touch of brandy; served on ice

Sopa: soup

Taco: a folded, fried tortilla filled with ground beef (or other meats or fish), refried beans, shredded lettuce, tomatoes, onion, cheese and salsa

Tamale: Corn dough made with lard, filled with a savory stuffing, wrapped up in a piece of corn husk, and steamed

Tapa: appetizer, Spanish in origin; usu. enjoyed with an apéritif such as dry sherry

Tortilla: a flat, unleavened bread made with cornmeal flour (masa) or wheat flour

Tostada: a fried tortilla topped with a saladlike mix of ground beef or chicken, beans, lettuce, tomato, guacamole

ASIAN

Chinese

Bao bun: dim sum item; small, steamed buns, white in color, stuffed with a variety of minced fillings (often chicken, shrimp, pork or lotus beans)

Bird's-nest soup: soup that has been thickened and flavored with the gelatinous product derived from soaking and cooking the nests of cliff-dwelling birds

Bok choy: Chinese white cabbage

Chop suey: strictly a Chinese American dish; meat or shrimp and vegetables (mushrooms, water chestnuts, bamboo shoots, bean sprouts) stir-fried together and served over rice

Chow mein: strictly a Chinese American dish; meat or shrimp and vegetables (mushrooms, water chestnuts, bamboo shoots, bean sprouts) stir-fried and served over crispy egg noodles

Dim sum: figuratively, "heart's delight"; a traditional meal featuring a variety of small dumplings, buns, rolls, balls, pastries and finger food, served with tea in the late morning or afternoon

Egg roll: thin wrapper stuffed with pork, cabbage or other vegetables, rolled up, and deep-fried or steamed

Fried rice: cooked, dried rice quickly fried in a wok with hot oil, various meats or vegetables and often an egg

Hoisin: a sweet, rich, dark brown sauce made from fermented soy beans; used as a base for other sauces

Lo mein: steamed wheat-flour noodles stir-fried with bean sprouts and scallions and either shrimp, pork, beef or vegetables

Lychee: small, round, fleshy fruit; used fresh, canned, preserved and dried

Mu shu: a delicate dish of stir-fried shredded pork and eggs rolled up in thin pancakes

Oyster sauce: a thick, dark sauce of oysters, soy and brine

Peking duck: an elaborate dish featuring duck that has been specially prepared, coated with honey and cooked until the skin is crisp and golden; served in pieces with thin pancakes or steamed buns, and hoisin

Pot sticker: dim sum item; dumpling stuffed with meat, seafood or vegetables, fried and then steamed

Shark's fin soup: soup thickened and flavored with the cartilage of shark's fins, which provides a protein-rich gelatin

Shu mai: dim sum item; delicate dumpling usu. filled minced pork and vegetables

Spring roll: a lighter version of the egg roll, with fillings such as shrimp or black mushrooms

Szechuan: cuisine in the style of the Szechuan province, often using the peppercorn-like black Chinese pepper to make hot, spicy dishes

Thousand-year-old eggs: chicken, duck or goose eggs preserved for 100 days in ashes, lime and salt (also, 100-year-old eggs)

Wonton: paper-thin, glutinous dough wrapper; also refers to the dumpling made with this wrapper, stuffed with minced meat, seafood or vegetables

Wonton soup: a clear broth in which wontons are cooked and served

Japanese

Amaebi: sweet shrimp

Awabi: abalone

Azuki: dried bean; azuki flour is often used for confections

Ebi: shrimp

Edamame: soy beans, served boiled and salted as an appetizer

Enoki (Enokitake): delicate mushrooms with long stems and small caps

Hamachi: yellowtail

Hibachi: small, open charcoal grill

Ikura: salmon roe

Kaiseki: Multicourse menu of luxury dishes reflecting the seasons with the use of seasonal foods and artistic dinnerware and presentation

Kappa: cucumber

Kobe beef: cattle raised in exclusive conditions (frequent massages and a diet featuring large quantities of beer), which results in an extraordinarily tender, very expensive beef

Konbu: dried kelp; used in soup stock, for sushi and as a condiment

Maguro: tuna

Maki: rolled

Mako: shark

Mirugai: giant clam

Miso (soup): soybean paste from which a savory broth is made, usu. served with cubes of tofu or strips of seaweed

Ono: wahoo fish; a relative of the mackerel often compared in taste to albacore

Ramen: soup noodles

Saba: mackerel

Sake: salmon

Saké: traditional rice wine served hot or cold

Sashimi: thinly sliced raw fish on rice, usually served with soy sauce and wasabi

Shabu shabu: similar to sukiyaki; beef and vegetables cooked tableside in a broth

Shiitake: Prized cultivated

mushroom, dark brown with a large cap

Shoya: soy sauce

Soba: buckwheat noodles

Sukiyaki: braised beef and vegetable dish with broth added after cooking

Sushi: Rounds of vinegared rice wrapped in dried seaweed with a center of raw rish or vegetables, served with wasabi and soy

Tako: octopus

Tamago: egg

Tamari: dark sauce similar in composition and taste to soy; often used for dipping

Tempura: deep-fried, batter-dipped fish or vegetables

Teriyaki: A marinade of soy and sweet saké, used on meats, fish and poultry

Tofu: bean curd, processed into a liquid and then molded into large cubes

Toro: fatty belly cut of tuna

Udon: wheat noodles

Uni: sea-urchin roe

Wasabi: a hot, spicy condiment made from the roots of Japanese horse-radish, chartreuse in color

Yakitori: a dish of pieces of chicken and vegetables, marinated in a spicy sauce, skewered and grilled

Thai

Kaeng (or Gaeng): large and diverse category of dishes; loosely translates as "curry"

Kaeng massaman: a variety of coconut-milk curry

Kaeng phed: a red, coconut-cream curry

Kaeng som: a hot-sour curry

Khao: rice

Khao suai: white rice

Khao phad: fried rice

King: ginger

Kung: prawns

Lab (or Larb): dish of minced meat with chilies and lime juice

Mu: pork

Nam: sauce

Nam pla: fish sauce

Nam phrik: a hot chili sauce

Nuea: beef

Ped: duck

Phad: fried

Phad king: fried with ginger

Phad phed: fried hot and spicy

Phad Thai: pan-fried rice noodles with chicken, shrimp, eggs, peanuts and bean sprouts

Phrik: chili pepper

Si racha (or Sri racha): spicy chili condiment

Tom kha kai: chicken coconut-cream soup flavored with lemongrass and chilies

Tom yam kung: hot-sour shrimp soup flavored with lemon grass, lime and chilies

Yam: flavored primarily with lime juice and chilies, resulting in a hot-sour taste; usually "salads" but can also be noodle dishes or soup

Yam pla: raw fish spiked with lime juice, chili, lemongrass, mint and fish sauce

COFFEE SAVVY

THE ORIGINS OF THE COFFEE CRAZE

Nearly every culture in the world has a passion for coffee, and there are various stories about how it all started. One of our favorites has to do with a goat herder in ancient Abyssinia (Ethiopia) who one morning discovered his goats gleefully cavorting around a shiny, dark-leafed shrub with red berries. After nibbling a few of the red berries himself, the goat herder joined his goats in their spirited romp. Another story attributes the discovery to an Arabian dervish who, when exiled by enemies to the wildnerness, survived by making a broth from water and the berries he plucked from coffee trees.

Regardless of which story is true, botanical evidence indicates that coffea arabica actually originated on the high plateaus of what is now Ethiopia in Africa. Traders undoubtedly brought it across the Red Sea to what is now Yemen, where it was cultivated from the sixth century on. Though at first coffee was used as a medicine—and by dervishes readying for a spin—it soon became a popular social beverage, resulting in coffeehouses where men exchanged ideas and gossip while sipping cups of hot brew in cities from Cairo to Mecca.

Though the Arabs jealously guarded their discovery, a few sneaky coffee fanatics managed to smuggle seeds from Arabia into India and Java, where it was cultivated with great success. By the seventeenth century, the coffee culture had spread to Europe. Coffeehouses attracted politicians, seafarers, merchants, authors and scholars, who often used the premises for discussions, reading, musical performances and even duels. At a time when Europeans wealthy enough to afford exotic luxuries were enjoying their two, three or four cups a day, the greatest French lover of luxury, King Louis XIV, supposedly built the first greenhouse to house a coffee tree given him by the mayor of Amsterdam. It's said that from the Sun King's royal coffee tree, sprang billions of arabica trees, including those growing today in Central and South America.

THE COFFEEHOUSE FOR THE NINETIES

Cut, as they say in Hollywood, to Seattle, in the rainy Pacific Northwest. Here, the current coffee craze was born just over a decade ago with a—then tiny—coffee company named **Starbucks** (after the first mate in the classic novel, *Moby Dick*). Starbucks re-invented the coffeehouse for modern times, creating attractive, relaxed and congenial meeting places where men and women exchange ideas and gossip—or read, work or simply think—while enjoying a cup of coffee. And we're not just talking about *a cup of coffee*. The choices of specialty coffee drinks made with "specialty" coffee beans—those of the highest quality—are endless, which is why we've put together this brief primer on the vocabulary of specialty coffees:

THE WORLD OF COFFEE

Like wine grapes, specialty coffee beans get much of their distinctive flavor from the growing conditions and preparation methods of the regions in which they're produced. We can classify coffee flavor and aroma according to geographic origin:

CENTRAL & SOUTH AMERICAN COFFEES

The most popular origins in the U.S. market, these are usually light-to-medium bodied, with clean lively flavors. Their balance and consistency make them the foundation of good coffee blending as well. Among these are beans from Colombia, Costa Rica, Guatemala and Mexico. Kona, though geographically a product of the Pacific islands, falls within this Latin American range of taste and aroma.

EAST AFRICAN COFFEES

These unique beans—from Kenya, Ethiopia, Tanzania and Zimbabwe—often combine the sparkling acidity of the best Central Americans with unique floral or winy notes, and typically are medium-to-full bodied.

INDONESIAN COFFEES

Usually full-bodied and smooth, low in acidity, and often possessing earthy and exotic taste elements, coffee beans from Java, Sumatra, Papua New Guinea and Sulawesi are an important "anchor" component of choice blends.

DARK ROASTS

Coffees from varying geographic origins are dark-roasted to provide a specific range of flavors, from the caramel spice of Espresso, to the smoky tang of Italian Roast, to the pungent French Roast.

BLENDS

Typically, a blend might play off Central American acidity with Indonesian smoothness, or spice up a delicate origin with the tang of a dark roast. At its best, blending coffee is high art, offering a balance or diversity which few straight coffees can match.

DECAFFEINATED

Some coffee-drinkers find the effects of too much caffeine unpleasant; others are looking for a hot cup to enjoy before bedtime. For that reason, coffee beans from many geographic origins are put through a decaffeinating process.

GLOSSARY OF COFFEE TASTING TERMS

THE BASICS:

Flavor: the total impression of aroma, acidity and body.

Acidity: the sharp, lively quality characteristic of many high-grown coffees. Acid is not the same as bitter or sour. Acidity is the brisk, snappy, spicy quality which makes coffee refreshing and palate-cleansing.

Body: the tactile impression of the weight of the brewed beverage in the mouth. It may range from watery and thin, through light, medium and full, to buttery or even syrupy in the case of some Indonesian varieties.

OTHER USEFUL TERMS:

Aroma: the fragrance of brewed coffee. Terms used to describe aroma include: caramelly (candy or syrup-like), carbony (for dark roasts), chocolaty, fruity, floral, herbal, malty (cereal-like), rich (over-used), rounded, spicy.

Bitter: a basic taste perceived primarily at the back of the tongue. Dark roasts are intentionally bitter, but bitterness is more commonly caused by over extraction (too little coffee at too fine a grind).

Bland: the pale, insipid flavor often found in low-grown coffees. Under-extracted coffee (made with too little coffee or too coarse a grind) is also bland.

Briny: a salty sensation caused by application of excessive heat after brewing. (The familiar smell of "truck stop" coffee.)

Earthy: the spicy, "of the earth" taste of Indonesian coffees.

Exotic: coffee with unusual aromatic and flavor notes, such as floral, berry, and sweet spice-like qualities. Coffees from East Africa and Indonesia often have such characteristics.

Mellow: the term for well-balanced coffee of low-to-medium acidity.

Mild: a coffee with harmonious, delicate flavor. Fine, high-grown Latin American coffee is often described as mild.

Soft: low-acid coffees such as Indonesians, that may also be called mellow or sweet.

Sour: a primary taste perceived mainly on the posterior sides of the tongue, characteristic of light-roasted coffees.

Spicy: an aroma or flavor reminiscent of a particular spice. Some Indonesian arabicas, especially aged coffees, evoke an association with sweet spices like cardomom. Others, such as Guatemala Antiqua, are almost peppery.

Strong: technically the relative proportion of coffee solubles to water in a given brew.

Sweet: a general term for smooth, palatable coffee, free from defects and harsh flavors

Tangy: a darting sourness, almost fruit-like in nature, related to wininess. A fine high-grown Costa Rican coffee is frequently tangy.

Wild: a coffee with extreme flavor characteristics; it can be a defect or a positive attribute, and denotes odd, racy nuances of flavor and aroma. Arabian Mocha Sanani nearly always exhibits such flavors.

Winy: a desirable flavor reminiscent of fine red wine; the contrast between fruit-like acidity and smooth body creates flavor interest. Kenyan coffees are examples of winy coffee flavor.

GLOSSARY OF SPECIALTY COFFEE DRINKS

made by a **Barista**, an expert at preparing espresso drinks

Espresso: A small but intense shot of coffee produced by forcing hot water under pressure through tightly packed coffee, one cup at a time.

Espresso Con Panna: A shot of espresso with a dollop of whipped cream.

Espresso Macchiato: Espresso lightly "marked" with foamed milk.

Caffè Americano: A shot of espresso diluted with hot, purified water, to produce a full-flavored but still mild cup of coffee.

Caffè Latte: A shot of espresso plus steamed milk, topped off with foamed milk.

Caffè Mocha: A squirt of chocolate syrup on the bottom of the cup, then espresso topped by steamed milk, a crown of whipped cream and a sprinkle of cocoa powder.

Cappuccino: Espresso topped with steamed milk and a generous cap of foamed milk.

Frappuccino: A cold and creamy low-fat blend of fresh-brewed Starbucks Italian roast coffee, milk and ice. Variations: with a shot of espresso (**Espresso Frappuccino**), with dark chocolate syrup (**Mocha Frappuccino**), or with a protein and vitamin supplement (**Power Frappuccino**).

*The Glossary of Coffee Tasting Terms and Specialty Coffee Drinks was provided courtesy of **Starbucks Coffee Company***.

WINE SAVVY

WINE OF THE NORTHEAST REGION: BEYOND TRADITION

The Northeast, with its long and not infrequently severe winters, has never been an easy place to grow grapes, except for such native species as Concord, Catawba, Niagara (vitis labrusca), and a dozen other types best suited to fruit juice, jams, and jellies. Yet throughout the eighties, this long-established commercial wine-producing region, comprising New York, Connecticut, Maine, Massachusetts, New Hampshire, New Jersey, Pennsylvania, Rhode Island, and Vermont, has evolved dramatically.

Led in part by the establishment of premium wineries on the eastern end of Long Island, New York, in particular, made considerable strides to overcome its traditional image as the home of "jelly-jar" wines. And who would have predicted that in rival New Jersey there would one day be 17 wineries, all within 50 miles of Manhattan's Times Square or that Philadelphia would come to have an equal number of wineries located less than an hour away from its City Hall? Make no mistake about it: With its excellent Merlots, Cabernets, Rieslings, and Chardonnays, one of America's oldest wine regions is today making its mark worldwide as among the very finest regions, and one just beginning to realize its full potential.

The Promise of the Empire State

New York State boasts America's oldest wine industry, established in the early 1800s in the Finger Lakes region of western New York and in the Hudson Valley, an hour or so north of New York City. The vineyards were planted mostly with labrusca species until the 1950s and 1960s, when cold-resistant French hybrids made significant inroads. Viticulture scientists had always maintained that the climate made it impossible to grow vinifera grapes, not only here, but virtually anywhere east of the Rockies. By the late seventies and early eighties, however, increasing numbers of venturesome growers shifted to cool region varieties such as Riesling and Chardonnay. Today, vinifera varieties are at least surviving in the Northeast, struggling in some areas and doing quite well in other areas.

More importantly, winemaking skills have improved significantly in this region, as is evident not only in the attractive Chardonnay, Riesling, Merlot, Cabernet Sauvignon and the occasional Pinot Noir or Gamay produced here, but in French hybrid varieties as well. Some of the whites from this region, such as Vidal Blanc, Cayuga, Seyval Blanc, and Ravat, can be similar in style to Muscadet or Sauvignon Blanc. Well-made and reasonably priced, they've more than found a niche in the local marketplace. Dessert wines from the Northeast, including some traditional ice wines, have improved greatly, and some are now consistently excellent. And the long-established sparkling wine industry here has made great advances with vinifera-based wines, effectively exploiting the region's relatively high-acid, lean Chardonnay juice to produce clean, crisp bubblies.

New York has the largest vineyard acreage in the region— over 100,000 acres total (only a third of it in vinifera grapes)— and produces by far the largest volume of wine, 30 million gallons annually. In the U.S., it ranks second only to California in total production.

New York's Neighbors: Good and Getting Better

In each of the other northeastern states, including Pennsylvania which contains a few relatively large estates and many smaller ones, vineyard acreage is limited to well under a thousand acres. Pennsylvania has achieved a reputation for its Chardonnay. New Jersey wineries have produced creditable Gewürztraminer and Riesling, and a few stylish hybrids such as Vidal Blanc. In the New England states, where winter's cold is most severe, winegrowing is a daunting challenge. Still, Connecticut has nine wineries producing a mix of vinifera wines (mostly Chardonnay and Riesling) and French hybrids, Rhode Island has five, Massachusetts about the same. Northernmost Maine, Vermont, and New Hampshire produce primarily fruit wines, though table wines made from local grapes are in evidence as well. Maine blueberry and Vermont apple wines (dry versions as well as semi-dry and sweet) are well worth a try. Rhode Island, which enjoys a climate moderated by the Atlantic Ocean, produces vinifera varieties such as Chardonnay, Gewürztraminer, and Pinot Noir. Sakonnet, founded in 1974, is the state's most successful winery. Years of struggle here have paid off in stylish wines that are among the best in the Northeast.

Connecticut's small wineries feel safest with French hybrids, bred to handle cold and sudden freezes. A couple of wineries, notably Crosswoods, near Stonington, also grow vinifera varieties such as Chardonnay, Merlot, Riesling, and Gamay; the generation of wineries that came of age in the eighties, such as Chamard Vineyards (founded in 1983), are planted over completely to vinifera. Chardonnay has been the most successful so far in this area. These and other wineries meet consumer tastes and market demand by buying additional grapes (most often Chardonnay) from Long Island and Finger Lakes vineyards.

New Jersey rediscovered its winegrowing potential in the 1980s. The Garden State's best wines now come from small operations such as Alba, but growers and vintners across the state have lately organized to work for greater quality and increased recognition.

Efforts at grapegrowing in Pennsylvania go back to 1683, when William Penn, founder of Philadelphia, tried to grow vines imported from France and Spain; the attempt failed. Penn's gardener, James Alexander, subsequently domesticated America's first wild grapes for cultivation. Prior to Prohibition, Pennsylvania was a leading producer of bulk wine. Today, the state has more than 50 wineries, but only a handful produce wines worth recommending. Acreage planted in vinifera varieties, particularly Chardonnay, Riesling, and Cabernet Sauvignon, is on the increase in the eastern part of the state and also on its far western edge, on the shores of Lake Erie.

GUIDE TO NEW YORK REGIONS

New York has five officially-designated wine regions. The three largest are around the eastern end of Lake Erie, on the Niagara Peninsula, and in the Finger Lakes area. Chardonnay and Riesling attract the most attention here; some white hybrids (Seyval, Vidal) also do well. The biggest acreage is still planted in Concord, Catawba and other native grapes that are now used more for juice and jam than for wine, though significant quantities of wine continue to be made from these varieties to meet existing demand.

The Hudson River region, with vineyards and wineries situated east and west of the Hudson River some 50 to 75 miles north of New York City, is smallest in production and acreage. The river here offers some protection from frost and cold. Millbrook Vineyard, east of the Hudson near Millbrook, has proved that vinifera varieties can succeed in this region when planted in an appropriate spot. West Park Vineyards is devoted exclusively to Chardonnay; Seyval Blanc, however, is the most widely-planted white grape in the Hudson River region at the moment. But that is fast changing.

New York's youngest wine region, on the eastern reaches of Long Island, has done the most to combat New York's comparatively low profile with consumers outside of the region. This area was planted almost exclusively to vinifera from its beginnings in the early seventies. Most vineyards here are on the North Fork; a few are in the Hamptons to the south. Taking their cue from Bordeaux, where the maritime climate and soils are similar, Long Island growers have concentrated on Merlot, Cabernet Sauvignon, Cabernet Franc, and Sauvignon Blanc, though Chardonnay has proven more consistently successful in yielding good white wines. Reds from this region can be lean and rather hard, but they are well structured and some improve with age. As Long Island's vines have matured, the quality and concentration of fruit in the wines made here has increased markedly. Barrel-fermented Chardonnay, Sauvignon

Blanc, and Riesling are often flavorful and polished. This region is only now beginning to hit its stride with these varieties, and promises to one day become the source of some of the finest wines made in North America—and beyond.

WINE TOURING NEW YORK

Visiting the wineries of New York State can provide a pleasant day or two's break from the big city excitement of Manhattan. Some of the wineries below have tasting rooms and are open to the public on a regular basis; others can be visited only by appointment. (All are in New York State.) You'll do well to phone ahead before setting out on your wine touring adventure. For comprehensive information on the wineries of New York and the Northeastern Region, see Gault Millau/AAA's The Best Wineries of North America (order form in back of this book).

Adair Vineyards   *(Hudson River Valley)*
75 Allhusen Rd., New Platz 12561
(914) 255-1377

Bedell Cellars   *(Long Island)*
Route 25, Main Rd., Cutchogue 11935
(516) 734-7537

Benmarl Wine Company, Ltd.   *(Hudson River Valley)*
156 Highland Ave., P.O. Box 549, Marlboro 12542
(914) 236-4265

Bidwell Vineyards   *(Long Island)*
Route 48, Cutchogue 11935
(516) 734-5200

Brotherhood Winery   *(Hudson River Valley)*
35 North St., Washingtonville 10992
(914) 496-9101

Dr. Frank's Vinifera Wine Cellars   *(Finger Lakes)*

9749 Middle Rd., Hammondsport 14840
(607) 868-4884

Glenora Wine Cellars, Inc.   *(Finger Lakes)*
5435 Route 14, Dundee 12837
(607) 243-5511

Gristina Vineyards   *(Long Island)*
Main Road, P.O. Box 1009, Cutchogue 11935
(516) 734-7089

Hargrave Vineyard   *(Long Island)*
Box 927, Route 48, Cutchogue 11935
(516) 734-5111

Hermann J. Wiemer Vineyard   *(Finger Lakes)*
Route 14, Box 38, Dundee 14837
(607) 243-7971

Heron Hill Vineyards, Inc.   *(Finger Lakes)*
9249 County Rte. 76, Hammondsport 14840
(607) 868-4201

Lamoreaux Landing Wine Cellars   *(Finger Lakes)*
9224 Route 414, Lodi 14860
(607) 582-6011

Millbrook Vineyards   *(Hudson River Valley)*
Wing Rd., R.R.#1, Box 1670, Millbrook 11525
(914) 677-8383

Palmer Vineyards   *(Long Island)*
P.O. Box 2125, Aquebogue 11931
(516) 722-9463

Pindar Vineyards   *(Long Island)*
P.O. Box 332, Peconic 11958
(516) 734-6200

Wagner Vineyards   *(Finger Lakes)*
9322 Route 414, Lodi 14860
(607) 582-6450

Woodbury Vineyards   *(Lake Erie)*
3230 South Roberts Rd., Fredonia 14063
(716) 679-9463

GLOSSARY OF WINE-TASTING TERMS

Acidity: a principal component of wine that shows up as a sharpness or tartness, giving it snap.

Aroma: the smell the wine acquires from the grapes themselves and fermentation process.

Astringency: the mouth-puckering quality found in many young red wines.

Austere: a wine unusually high in acidity; lacking roundness or wholeness.

Balanced: no individual component of the wine stands out; all the elements contribute to a harmonious whole.

Berry: taste characteristic found in many red wines, it resembles the taste of fruit like blackberry, blueberry and cherry.

Body: the weight of the wine in the mouth; usually manifested by a richness, fullness or viscosity.

Bouquet: the smell that develops from the process of aging wine in the bottle.

Buttery: a component that gives white wines a rich, roundness that resembles the taste of butter

Chewy: a rich red wine with big body and dense flavor.

Clarity: the appearance of a young wine should be clear, not cloudy.

Complex: a wine that displays many levels of flavor.

Dry: a wine with no apparent residual sugar. Novice wine drinkers may describe this as "sour."

Earthy: positive characteristics of loamy topsoil, mushrooms or truffles sometimes found in red wines. In French, "goût de terroir."

Fat: a wine with good fullness and length, although it may lack finesse.

Floral: flowery aromas and tastes, usually associated with white wines.

Fruity: the taste of the fruit of the grapes themselves; it often manifests itself as other fruit flavors, such as apples, strawberries or black currants.

Grassy: an herbaceous flavor, like new-mown grass, common to Sauvignon Blanc; negative if extreme.

Hard: a wine that does not have generous flavors; applied to red wines that have excessive tannins.

Herbaceous: general term descriptive of various herbal flavors in wine, recognized by aroma and taste.

Hot: a wine in which the high level of alcohol is out of balance with the other elements.

Intense: powerful, dense, and rich in flavor

Jammy: in red wines, intense fruitiness combined with berry-like flavors.

Nose: all the elements detected by the sense of smell, including both the aroma and bouquet.

Oaky: flavors of the oak in which the wine is fermented and/or aged.

Smoky: a roasted aroma or taste characteristic attributable to aging in oak barrels.

Spicy: descriptive of spicelike flavor elements found in wine such as pepper, cardamom, clove and cinnamon.

Supple: a wine that tastes soft and smooth; easy to drink.

Tannic: a mouth puckering astringency found in young red wines.

GLOSSARY OF GRAPES

Red Wine Varietals:
CABERNET SAUVIGNON

The king of red wines in California, Cabernet's reputation was established by wineries in the Napa Valley, although it has proved distinctive in other regions as well. While sometimes a bit harsh in its youth, it has the ability to mature into a most complex and full-bodied wine, much like the great wines of Bordeaux. Its flavors are comfortable with simple grilled meats as well as more complex dishes like venison in mushroom sauce. Great and consistent producers of Cabernet can be found in the Napa and Sonoma Valley, as well as Australia, Chile, Argentina and, of course, the châteaux of Bordeaux which produce the true benchmark of this varietal.

MERLOT

This variety was once relegated to blending into other lots of red wine. But in the last twenty years it has taken on an identity of its own. Merlot has herbal and fruity flavors similar to Cabernet, but it has a smooth and supple character in the mouth without the bite of tannins. It complements the same type of foods that Cabernet does, albeit less distinctively. Top producers hail from Bordeaux (where the wine is mostly blended, but sometimes bottled seperately, depending on the region) Chile, Argentina, Napa, Sonoma and Washington State.

PINOT NOIR

Pinot Noir has the potential to be the most seductive, beguiling red wine in existence. Unfortunately past examples from California left a lot to be desired. In the past ten years, however, Pinot Noir has shown the greatest increase in quality of any varietal. The perseverance of younger winemakers and traditional winemaking methodology is resulting in Pinots that can stand side by side with the wines of Burgundy. Lighter than Cabernet, Pinots have a richness and intensity of fruit that is unparalleled. The best of them drink like velvet and accompany a wide variety of foods. Top French Burgundys are bottled under a variety of different names and labels, depending on region, vineyard and producer. In America, considerable success with this Burgundian varietal has been from Napa, Sonoma (Carneros), Santa Barbara and Oregon.

SYRAH

The great grape of the Rhône Valley has become more widely planted in California in the last ten years. Highly aromatic wines with meaty, smoky, spicy flavors are the trademark of the Syrah grape. When made in a lighter style, it's a good quaffing wine to pair with simple bistro type food. When made in a richer style, it's a good accompaniment to lamb and all manner of wild game. Syrah is the grape found in French Côte Rotie, St. Joseph and Cornas and plays a major role in the spicy Châteauneuf-du-Papes of the southern Rhône too. In California, the Syrah grape is being cultivated in such diverse regions as Santa Barbara, Sonoma, Monterey, the Amador Foothills and Yolo County.

ZINFANDEL

Real Zinfandel is red, a fact many wine drinkers are rediscovering now that the trend for "white" zinfandel has stabilized. Peppery, briary, brawny and chewy are only a few of the adjectives used to describe this mouth-filling wine. It has a real zest for matching up with tomato-based pasta dishes and other highly herbalized preparations. There is no European counterpart for this variety; it is one that the first Italian winemakers propagated and cultivated when they came to California. It's origins are obviously European, but today it's a grape variety that is unique to California. Vintners in Napa, Sonoma and Amador seem to do the best job with it.

White Wine Varietals:

CHARDONNAY

In the '80s it became de rigeur to ask for "a glass of Chardonnay" in a restaurant and passé to simply request "a glass of white wine." This is the most popular wine in California for a reason: it's cold, fruity and easy to drink. It's pleasant with just about any dish involving cheese, eggs, fish or fowl. Winemakers have divided into two camps over the style of Chardonnay; one school of thought emphasizes the high-toned, steely, fruit-like qualities of the wine through little or no use of oak, while the other school emphasizes barrel and malolactic fermentation in addition to the fruit characteristic, giving the wine a rounder, buttery taste. Benchmarks for Chardonnay are white Burgundies (rich and extracted) and Chablis (steely andcrisp). In California, there are fine Chardonnays from just about every region, including Napa, Sonoma, Mendocino, Monterey and Santa Barbara.

GEWÜRZTRAMINER

This so called "aromatic" varietal is making a minor comeback in California. "Gewürz" translates as "spice" and it's immediately detectable when poured into a glass. The flavors echo the fragrant and flowery nose echoes, while providing an additional punch from a piquant, spicy component. Made with some residual sweetness, the wine seems to be a good counterpoint for spicy Chinese and Thai dishes. The Alsatian region of France has about four centuries of experience in producing these wines in the traditional style. In California, the cooler growing regions, like Sonoma, Mendocino and Santa Barbara, do well with this grape.

RIESLING

Another "aromatic" that is finding a home in California again; it can be a particularly refreshing alternative to the Chardonnay/Sauvignon Blanc white wine tandem. Unlike its cousin, Gewürztraminer, this varietal has little spice and instead relies on its delicate aromas and subtle flavors for its special niche. Usually lighter in style and sometimes with residual sweetness, it's better paired with lighter fare. The Riesling is a mainstay of German winemaking and also ripens to full maturity in Alsace. The top California producers have generally been those who have also had success with Gewürztraminer.

SAUVIGNON BLANC

This variety is often considered the poor man's Chardonnay; it can be vinified similarly but costs only half as much. But Sauvignon Blanc has a number of identities ranging from a clean, slight grassy white wine to a herbaceous, full-bodied wine backed up with oak aging. It does its best service at the table when paired with strong, forceful, herbal flavors like goat cheese and raddichio salad. Unheralded but excellent examples come from Sancerre and Pouilly-Fume in the Loire Valley. In California, just about every region produces a Sauvignon Blanc, although the North Coast counties seem to have a real knack for it.

SPARKLING WINES

Domaine Chandon (owned by Moët & Chandon) set up shop in Napa Valley less than twenty years ago and, after its initial success, almost every French Champagne house has come to California to establish its foothold. The main reason for their interest in the New World is that Champagne is a geographically limited area which is almost fully planted to the grape, and California was almost virgin territory for sparkling wine. While the legacy of Champagne seems to be tiny pinpoint bubbles that reveal delicate and subtle flavors, their California counterparts are more often bold, upfront and fruity with their flavors. The prevailing wisdom is that the delicate nuances of the wine (in particular, Champagne) get lost when paired up with hearty, complex or highly seasoned dishes. It's certainly the perfect aperitif wine. All the California sparklers are of high quality so it seems to be a matter of house style as to what is preferred. Names to remember are Domaine Carneros, Domaine Chandon, Gloria Ferrer, Mumm-Napa, Piper-Sonoma, Mirassou, Roederer Estates, Scharffenberger, Schramsberg, Iron Horse, Handley, Cordonui, J, and Maison Deutz.

VINTAGE WINE CHART

VINTAGE CHART: The World's Wines

	FRANCE												GER.	ITALY		CALIFORNIA			
	Red Bordeaux	White Bordeaux	Sauterne	Red Burgundy	White Burgundy	Beaujolais	Côtes du Rhône	Provence	Alsace	Loire: Anjou, Muscadet	Pouilly, Sancere	Champagne	Rhine, Moselle, Nahe	Piedmonte	Chianti	Cabernet Sauvignon	Chardonnay	Pinot Noir	Zinfandel
1995	5	4	3	3	4	4	5	4	5	4	4	—	4	4	3	5	5	4	Ex
1994	4	3	2	2	4	3	3	4	5	3	3	—	4	2	3	Ex	5	5	Ex
1993	4	3	3	3	3	4	3	4	4	4	4	—	5	4	2	5	5	4	5
1992	3	3	3	3	5	2	3	3	3	3	3	—	5	3	2	5	5	4	5
1991	3	3	2	4	4	Ex	4	3	3	1	3	1	4	2	2	4	5	4	5
1990	5	4	5	Ex	4	4	5	5	5	5	5	Ex	5	5	5	5	5	4	5
1989	5	4	Ex	5	5	Ex	5	5	Ex	5	5	5	5	5	2	4	3	4	4
1988	4	4	Ex	5	5	4	4	4	5	4	4	5	5	5	3	5	5	4	4
1987	3	4	1	4	3	2	1	2	3	3	2	3	4	4	2	4	3	4	5
1986	5	5	5	3	3	3	3	3	4	4	4	3	4	3	4	5	5	4	4
1985	5	5	2	Ex	5	5	5	3	5	5	5	5	4	5	5	Ex	4	4	5
1983	5	5	Ex	3	5	—	5	4	Ex	4	4	5	5	2	3	3	4	4	3
1982	Ex	4	3	2	4	—	4	—	2	5	5	5	3	5	4	4	3	4	3
1981	4	5	4	—	—	—	3	—	3	5	5	5	4	3	3	4	4	4	4
1979	4	4	3	3	5	—	4	—	—	—	—	5	4	4	2	4	4	3	4
1978	4	5	—	Ex	5	—	Ex	—	—	—	—	4	2	5	4	5	4	4	4

EX: EXCEPTIONAL
5: VERY GREAT
4: GREAT
3: GOOD

2: MEDIUM
1: PASSABLE
—: SMALL YEAR

* This is only meant to be a general guide. Start by learning which regions and years are better than others; once you develop a good knowledge, buy according to your preferences.

The European wines are categorized by the region in which the grapes were grown. This is their "appellation," displayed on the label along with the phrase *Appéllation controlée or Denominazione di origine contrallata* to guarantee the wine's authenticity. The California wines are categorized by grape name, as they are throughout the United States.

NEW YORK
FOOD & WINE EVENTS
& SEASONAL FOOD TIPS

(Dates vary with the year)

JANUARY

- Oysters are fresh now—eat them with Champagne to ring in the New Year. Also, this is the month for wild mushrooms, tangerines, oranges, red apples, Camembert and blue cheeses.
- **International Beer & Food Festival**—International beer and food tasting sponsored by the American Institute of Wine & Food (447-0456).
- **Wine & Spirits Education Courses**—On-going courses begin for individuals in the wine trade and consumers who wish to gain substantial knowledge of wine. Classes held in the Chelsea Wine Vault in the Chelsea Market, given by the International Wine Center (627-7170).
- **Chinese New Year (late January to mid-February)**—Annual celebration in Chinatown, with food and fanfare. Expect special dishes at many Chinese restaurants.
- **Ice Carving Exhibition**—Fantasies in ice carved by creative chefs in City Hall Park, sponsored by Paris Gourmet Patisfrance and Chartreuse Liqueur (201-939-5656, ext. 202).
- **Annual Cookbook Sale**—To benefit the James Beard Foundation, at the James Beard House (800-36-BEARD)

FEBRUARY

- Artichokes are best this time of year.
- **American Institute of Wine & Food Gala**—Diner, dance and an auction, at Windows on the World (447-0456).
- **American Wine Appreciation Week**—The last week of February has been proclaimed "American Wine Appreciation Week" by a resolution of the U.S. Congress. The intention of this commemoration is to recognize the contributions of wine-grape fruit growers and vintners to the U.S. economy and to the nation's cultural, religious and family traditions. Look for corresponding celebrations, wine tastings and other activities to be sponsored by wineries and wine retailers across the country.
- **Kids Sports Cook-Fest**—Tastings from top NYC chefs, celebrity and athlete guests, and a basketball game, to benefit charity, Madison Square Garden (243-9090 ext 219).

MARCH

- Spring lamb comes fresh to markets this month. So does asparagus.

APRIL

- This is the month for strawberries, red onions, haricots verts, mangoes and goat cheese.
- **International Wine Fair**—Extensive international wine tasting paired with creations by New York chefs, sponsored by Morell & Co. (688-9370).

MAY

- **James Beard's Birthday Dinner**—A Gala dinner celebrating the late great culinary legend, held at the James Beard House (800-36-BEARD).
- **The James Beard Awards**—"Rising Stars of the 21st Century". The Oscars of the food world, this televised awards ceremony honoring chefs, cookbook authors, restaurateurs and journalists, is coupled with a food-and-wine tasting, at the New York Marriott Marquis. (627-2090, 800-36-BEARD)
- **Eighth Annual Windows on Long Island**—Wine tasting and dinner, to benefit "Partnership for the Homeless", Windows on the World (645-3444 ext 102).
- **The James Beard Foundation Annual Festival at the World Financial Center**—In 1999, Portuguese cuisine is the focus, with food and wine seminars, cooking classes, demonstrations, book signings and tastings (633-9145).
- **Ninth Avenue International Food Festival**—Street fair running from 37th to 57th Streets on Ninth Avenue, celebrating the Big Apple's vast and rich variety of culinary offerings, with local restaurants preparing their specialties from more than 30 different countries (581-7217).

JUNE

- Peaches ripen this month. So do nectarines, cherries, boysenberries and melons.
- **Taste of Times Square**—Food tastings of specialties from Times Square-area restaurants (788-7418).
- **Restaurant Day**, June 18—Restaurants all over New York City sell sampels of their signature dishes in front of their establishments with a portion of the proceeds going to Citymeals-On-Wheels and Share Our Strength (620-7027).
- **Restaurant Week,** June 21-26—The premiere restaurants of New York City offer a $19.99 prix-fixe lunch menu—some extend through Labor Day (620-7027).
- **Feast of St. Anthony**—A 13-day street festival runs for two blocks on Sullivan from Houston to Spring Street, with rides, entertainment and food, to benefit the St. Anthony Church (777-2755).

JULY

- Corn is at its peak. So are tomatoes, basil, avocados and garlic.
- **Meet the Tastemakers/James Beard Foundation Cookbook Expo,** July 11-14—A part of the NASFT Fancy Food Show where authors sign copies of their cookbooks and the public can meet some of the great chefs participating in the show (620-7027).

Chefs & Champagne, the Hamptons—A Champagne-and-food tasting with dishes prepared by chefs from Hamptons-area restaurants, at Sag Pond Vineyards (800-36-BEARD).

AUGUST

- Bordeaux wines arrive in the U.S. This is the last good month for corn and summer fruits.

SEPTEMBER

- Wine-grape harvesting begins this month, which means tastings and celebrations in New York's wine-growing areas.
- **Dine-Around Downtown,** September 14—The great restaurants of downtown New York come together at the World Trade Center to sell samples of their signature menu items (620-7027).
- **San Gennaro Festival**—Food, wine, music and games run the length of Mulberry Street for Little Italy's annual Italian celebration (226-9546).
- **Autumn Gourmet Gala to benefit Share Our Strength**—Grammercy Tavern (477-0777).
- **Columbus Avenue Festival**—An Upper West Side street fair with food and fun (541-8880).
- **Fine & Rare Wine Auction**—Sponsored by Philips International Auctioneers & Park Avenue Liquor Shop (800-825-2781).

OCTOBER

- Truffles and chanterelles are unearthed this month. Also pears and Dungeness crab are good.

NOVEMBER

- Beaujolais Nouveau is released, with celebrations everywhere.
- **James Beard Annual Holiday Auction & Dinner**—Auction of international and domestic trips to hotels, spas and cooking schools combined with dinners and events in the destination cities, followed by a theme dinner that changes annually (620-7027).

DECEMBER

- It's black truffle month!
- **Fine & Rare Wine Auction**—Philips International Auctioneers & Park Avenue Liquor Shop (800-825-2781).
- A New York Christmas—Celebrity chefs' food and wine tasting, wine auction, and entertainment to benefit the Volunteers of America (873-2600).
- **Grand Gourmet Luncheon**—A food and wine tasting of Italy with the French Culinary Institute, to benefit Partnership for the Homeless (645-3444 ext.102).
- **Culinary Pas de Deux**—Champagne reception, tastings and silent auction to benefit the American Ballet Theater (477-3030 ext. 3239).

FOOD & WINE PAIRINGS

Consider the myriad foods available at our grocers and food preparations that can be enjoyed in our restaurants. Then consider the number of varietal wines available and all their styles. It quickly becomes clear that the enterprise of pairing food and wine can be as complicated as you wish to make it. If you'd like some rules of thumb to help you sort out the possibilities, here are two that have stood the test of time. Rule One: Drink red wine with meat, and white wine with fish and poultry. Rule Two: Forget about Rule One and marry any food with any wine you wish; when it comes to personal preferences, there are no rights and wrongs.

There are, of course, some classic food and wine matches that satisfy again and again. And there are exciting new standards being discovered daily as the range of foods and wines available continues to expand. Based on our experience, the following matches of widely available dishes and cuisines with the wines of North America are worthy of special consideration. One caveat: Sauces can change everything, so ask the cook or a waiter for a flavor forecast.

APPETIZERS & FIRST COURSES

ANTIPASTO

Pinot Gris, (Dry) Chenin Blanc, Sauvignon Blanc, Pinot Blanc, Gamay Beaujolais, Barbera

ASPARAGUS

Sauvignon (Fumé) Blanc, (Dry) Riesling, Vidal Blanc

CARPACCIO (BEEF)

Barbera, Cabernet Rosé, Rhône Blends

CARPACCIO (TUNA)

Sauvignon (Fumé) Blanc, Vin Gris

CAVIAR

Brut Sparkling Wine

CLAMS (RAW OR CASINO)

Sauvignon (Fumé) Blanc, Brut Sparkling Wine, (Dry) Chenin Blanc, Pinot Blanc, Seyval Blanc

COLD MEATS

Vin Gris, Riesling, Gamay Beaujolais, Barbera, Seyval Blanc, (Dry) Vignoles, Chambourcin Rosé

CRUDITÉS

Pinot Blanc, Chenin Blanc, Chardonnay, Gamay Beaujolais

FOIE GRAS

Brut Sparkling Wine; Late-Harvest Riesling, Sauvignon Blanc, or Gewürztraminer, Muscat, Pinot Noir

NIÇOISE SALAD
Sauvignon (Fumé) Blanc

NUTS AND/OR OLIVES
Brut Sparkling Wine

OYSTERS (RAW)
Sauvignon (Fumé) Blanc, Brut Sparkling Wine, Pinot Gris, Chardonnay, (Dry) Riesling, Pinot Blanc, Chenin Blanc

PASTA SALAD
Sémillon, Sauvignon (Fumé) Blanc, (Dry) Chenin Blanc, (Dry) Riesling

PASTA WITH CREAM SAUCE
Chardonnay, Pinot Blanc

PASTA WITH SHELLFISH
Sauvignon (Fumé) Blanc, Chardonnay

PASTA WITH TOMATO SAUCE
Barbera, Sangiovese, Zinfandel, Rhône Blends

PASTA WITH VEGETABLES
Pinot Blanc, Dry Riesling, Sauvignon Blanc, Viognier, Gamay Beaujolais, Barbera

PATÉS
Gewürztraminer, Seyval Blanc, Gamay Beaujolais, Riesling, Brut Sparkling Wine, Cabernet Franc, Vin Gris

PROSCIUTTO AND MELON
Pinot Blanc, Riesling, Late Harvest Riesling or Gewürztraminer, Muscat

QUICHE
Riesling, Chenin Blanc, Chardonnay, Viognier, Gamay Beaujolais

SCALLOPS
Sauvignon (Fumé) Blanc, Chardonnay, Brut Sparkling Wine, Pinot Noir, Sémillon

SMOKED FISH (TROUT, HERRING)
Riesling, Gewürztraminer, Pinot Blanc, Brut Sparkling Wine

SOUPS
Usually none, or (Solera) Sherry

FISH & SHELLFISH

CRAB
Sauvignon (Fumé) Blanc, Brut Sparkling Wine, Chardonnay

LOBSTER
Brut Sparkling Wine, Chardonnay

MUSSELS
Chenin Blanc, Pinot Blanc, Pinot Gris, Sauvignon (Fumé) Blanc

RED SNAPPER
Chardonnay, Sauvignon (Fumé) Blanc

SALMON
Pinot Noir, Sauvignon Blanc, Pinot Gris, Sémillon, Vin Gris

SALMON TARTARE
Brut Sparkling Wine, Pinot Gris

SASHIMI, SUSHI
Brut Sparkling Wine, Semi-Dry Riesling

SCALLOPS, OYSTERS, CLAMS
See appetizers

SHRIMP
Pinot Blanc, Chenin

Blanc, Sauvignon (Fumé)
Blanc, Chardonnay,
Colombard, Vidal Blanc

STRIPED BASS
Chardonnay, Pinot
Blanc, Viognier, (Dry)
Vignoles

SWORDFISH
Sauvignon (Fumé)
Blanc, Brut Sparkling Wine,
Vin Gris, Pinot Noir

TUNA
Sauvignon (Fumé)
Blanc, Pinor Noir, Merlot,
Vin Gris, Chardonnay

OTHER WHITE FISH
Chardonnay, Viognier,
Dry Riesling, Semillon

MEAT & POULTRY

CHICKEN
Chardonnay, Vin Gris,
Riesling, Merlot, Gamay
Beaujolais, Chenin Blanc,
Pinot Noir, (Lighter)
Cabernet Sauvignon

CHICKEN SALAD
Riesling, Chenin Blanc,
Gewürztraminer, Pinot Blanc

CHICKEN (SMOKED)
Vin Gris, Pinot Noir,
Zinfandel

DUCK
Pinot Noir, Merlot, Rosé
Sparkling Wine, Cabernet
Sauvignon, Zinfandel

FRANKFURTER
Riesling, (Chilled)
Gamay Beaujolais

HAM
Vin Gris, Gamay
Beaujolais, Merlot

HAMBURGER
Cabernet Sauvignon,
Gamay, Syrah, Chancellor,
Barbera, Zinfandel, Rhône
Blends

LAMB (GRILLED, BROILED)
Meritage, Cabernet
Sauvignon, Merlot, Pinot
Noir, Marechal Foch,
Chancellor, Zinfandel

PHEASANT
Pinot Noir, Syrah

QUAIL
Pinot Noir

RABBIT
Riesling, Pinot Noir,
Barbera, Merlot, Zinfandel

SAUSAGE
Riesling, Brut or Rosé
Sparkling Wine, Barbera,
Gamay Beaujolais, Norton or
Cynthiana, Syrah, Zinfandel

STEAK (GRILLED, BROILED)
Cabernet Sauvignon,
Merlot, Rhône Blends,
Zinfandel, Meritage, Norton
or Cynthiana, Brut Sparkling
Wine

TURKEY
Zinfandel, Merlot,
Chardonnay, Gamay
Beaujolais

VEAL
Chardonnay, Barbera,
Merlot, Cynthiana

VENISON
Syrah, Rhône Blends,
Petite Sirah, Zinfandel,
Pinot Noir, Norton,
Chancellor, Cabernet
Sauvignon

OTHER MAIN COURSES

COUSCOUS
Cabernet Franc, Merlot, Petite Sirah, Rosé Sparkling Wine, Syrah, Vin Gris

CURRY, FISH OR CHICKEN
Riesling, (Chilled) Gamay Beaujolais, Sauvignon (Fumé) Blanc, Zinfandel

MOUSSAKA
Merlot, Sangiovese, Barbera, Zinfandel

PIZZA
Barbera, Zinfandel, Sangiovese, Brut or Rosé Sparkling Wine, Cabernet Rosé

SPICY CHINESE
Dry (and off-dry) Riesling, Pinot Gris, Pinot Blanc, Brut or Rosé Sparkling Wine, Merlot

SPICY MEXICAN
Dry (and off-dry) Riesling, Vin Gris, Chenin Blanc, (Chilled) Gamay Beaujolais

THAI
Chenin Blanc, Pinot Blanc, Riesling, Gewürztraminer, Brut or Rosé Sparkling Wine

CHEESES

GOAT
soft: Brut or Rosé Sparkling Wine, Sauvignon (Fumé) Blanc, Cabernet Sauvignon, Merlot, Pinot Noir

hard: Pinot Noir, Merlot, Syrah, Cabernet Sauvignon

COW & SHEEP
medium: Pinot Noir, Petite Sirah

hard: Cabernet Sauvignon, Petite Sirah, Zinfandel, Port Blue, Late-Harvest Riesling, Chenin Blanc, Gewürtraminer, Muscat, Zinfandel

DESSERTS

APPLE PIE, TART & BAKED
Late-Harvest Riesling, Various Ice Wines, Muscat, Demi-sec Sparkling Wines, Blueberry Wine

BERRIES
Brut Sparkling Wines, Demi-sec Sparkling Wines, Late-Harvest Riesling, Muscat, Zinfandel

CHOCOLATE
Late-Harvest Riesling, Raspberry Wine, Black Muscat, Cabernet Sauvignon

CAKES
Demi-sec Sparkling Wines, Late-Harvest Riesling, Muscat, Various Ice Wines

CREAMS, CUSTARDS, PUDDINGS
Demi-sec Sparkling Wines, Late-Harvest Riesling, Muscat, Various Ice Wines

FRESH FRUIT
Late-Harvest Chenin Blanc, Riesling, Gewürztraminer, Muscat

ICE CREAMS, SORBETS
Usually none, perhaps fruit wine or fruit liqueurs

NUTS
Port, Brut Sparkling Wine, Angelica

TIRAMISU
Angelica

WATER SAVVY

Knowing Your Bottled Water

The bottled-water boom over the past decade and a half has transcended the elements of fashion, and has made bottled water a staple in American homes and restaurants. In 1995, according to Beverage Marketing Corp., bottled-water sales increased 8 percent, making it the fastest-growing segment of the beverage industry. Today, yearly sales of bottled water total about $3.4 billion. What spurred this need among consumers to buy what you can get out of the tap for free?

Baby boomers are maturing, and their tastes, as well as concerns over their waistlines, are guiding them toward more natural, less caloric beverages than the Cokes, Buds and margaritas they enthusiastically consumed in their younger party days. America's passion for fitness, combined with, in some cases, a near-prohibitionist attitude toward alcohol, has also driven consumers to seek PC beverage alternatives. Furthermore, the deteriorating taste and quality of tap water—and the fear of the contaminants it may contain—have made bottled water not just a choice for some people, but a necessity.

Trouble at the Tap

The basic belief that American tap water is safe to drink may no longer hold water. Virtually every day, the media reports incidents of contamination and pollution of our municipal water sources. Water quality varies from city to city, street to street and tap to tap. New York City is said to have better-tasting tap water than Los Angeles. Yet both are subject to such chemical treatments as chlorination, which kills bacteria but can produce trihalomethanes (THMs) when it interacts with organic matter in water. THMs have been found to be carcinogenic. From toxic dumps leaking into the aquifers to agricultural pesticides seeping into our reservoirs, our taps are under constant threat. Even the very delivery system that brings tap water from the reservoir to the glass has been found to contain contaminants: lead, copper, radon and a potpourri of other elements that can cause everything from severe headaches to cancer.

When we turn our taste buds to bottled water, we have a long list of "don't wants," but only a hazy idea of what things we do want in our water. Understanding all the bottled water options is the first step.

Not All Water is Created Equal

Within the bottled-water business there are two distinct divisions. The biggest, by volume, is the 5-gallon or jug-water business. Deer Park and Great Bear are among the leaders in this field. Bottlers also are capitalizing on consumers' fondness for their office water coolers, selling two-and-a-half as well as one-gallon containers in supermarkets. This type of bottled water is sold as an alternative to tap water. Premium—or "gourmet"—bottled waters, such as San Pellegrino, Poland Spring and Perrier, are sold as alternatives to soft drinks and alcohol. Packaging ranges from six-ounce to two-liter bottles, from custom glass and PET plastic to aluminum cans. These waters are sometimes carbonated and may have added essences, juices or flavorings.

To make an informed choice about which of the various types of bottled waters is for you, scrutinize the labels. European bottled mineral waters come from springs, which are simply underground water sources that flow naturally to the surface. Waters labeled "spring water" must come from a spring source. Federal labeling standards in the United States, which came into force in May, 1996, now require that bottlers disclose on the label where the water originated.

Purified water is a different story—it's usually produced by distillation, de-ionization or reverse osmosis. This water can originate from either the tap or from ground water. Often labeled "purified" or "drinking water," this processed water often has minerals added to it to give it taste. If the water is produced by vaporization and condensation, it may be labeled "distilled water".

Eight Glasses a Day Keeps the Doctor Away

In Europe, bottlers tout the reputed healthful properties of good water. Almost every European bottled water is "bottled at the source," which means that it comes from a spring where people have gone for hundreds of years to "take the waters" in curative spa treatments. Spas like Vittel and Contrexeville have medical programs designed to address specific ailments. Most spa treatments involve consuming more than eighty ounces of water a day, which is said to remove toxins from the body and to be effective in the treatment of obesity. In Europe, these bottled waters—with their mineral contents listed on the label—are sold not only in supermarkets but also in pharmacies. Doctors even prescribe certain mineral waters for specific ailments.

In the U.S., however, bottled water is marketed with an emphasis on taste, its contribution to fitness regimens, and in some cases, its trendiness. The U.S. Food and Drug Administration does not recognize any therapeutic values of bottled water because the existing medical research does not conform to FDA guidelines. However, the therapeutic value of certain bottled waters is becoming a subject of discussion in American scientific and medical circles.

The Taste of H20

We have approximately 100,000 taste buds, each one connected to our brain by a nerve. Each taste bud senses four basic stimulations from various parts of the tongue; saltiness and sweetness are experienced from taste buds on the tip of the tongue; sourness is perceived on the outer edge of the tongue, and bitterness is perceived on the rear surface of the tongue. Aiding the total tasting experience are two nerves in the upper passage of the nose. The aromatics of a substance pass through the nose when we exhale. Experiment: pinch your nostrils closed and notice how much less vivid your sense of taste is. When evaluating water, it is important to draw the water into the mouth and cover all your taste-sensitive areas with it.

Tap-water taste varies depending on where you live and how your municipal water supply treats or processes the water. The slightly acidic taste of chlorine is one of the most commonly perceived tastes in municipal tap water. Chlorine and other chemicals can affect the taste of beverages, ice cubes, soups and even vegetables. Water impurities can also affect the taste of foods and beverages. Certainly, tea and coffee's natural aromatic constituents will diminish when made with poor-tasting tap water. In fact, Julia Child once said that her Santa Barbara tap water turns her "Chinese tea into mud."

When Carl Rosenberg became the chief baker at the Century Plaza Hotel in Los Angeles, he was asked to duplicate the famous dinner rolls baked at the Olympic Hotel in Seattle. Rosenberg tried out the recipe in Los Angeles, but the rolls' distinctive flavor and texture were both missing. He rechecked the ingredients, and all were correct and of the highest quality. "Could it be the water?" he wondered. After ordering several gallons of Seattle tap water, Rosenberg tried the recipe again. This time the rolls were perfect. Since it was not practical to ship Seattle water each time he baked the rolls, Rosenberg used distilled water, which produced better dough fermentation than L.A. tap water.

But though distilled water may be better to cook with than tap water, it does not score well in water tastings. At a recent

"Homage to H20" held by The American Institute of Food and Wine, ten non-carbonated bottled waters were judged in a blind tasting. The distilled bottled water scored the lowest number of points, and judges used words like "dull" and "flat" to describe its taste. People tend to prefer drinking spring water because it tastes better than distilled water. Use distilled water to fill your car battery and steam-iron.

The taste of spring water reflects the different geologic strata underground, where the water absorbs minerals and trace elements—some over a year or two, and others over centuries. These minerals are described in the water's mineral analysis (printed on the label) and are perceived in its taste. Highly mineralized water can sometimes taste metallic; highly bicarbonated water can taste salty. Water with a high content of hydrogen sulfide tastes like rotten eggs, and water with a high concentration of iron can taste like a rusty nail. People tend to prefer their non-carbonated water with a range of 30 to 100 parts-per-million of total dissolved solids—that being the measure of these minerals and trace elements. For carbonated waters, higher levels of minerals are acceptable.

The taste of water can be affected not only by what's in the water, but what the water is in: Lower-grade plastic bottles can impart a plastic taste to the water. If the bottles are stored in the sunlight, the plastic taste can become even stronger.

Bubbly Water

The taste of carbonated water is effected by its level of carbonation—the more carbon-dioxide gas present, the more acidic the water's taste. This sensation, sometimes described by tasters as "bracing," "sharp" and "spritzy," can be positive or negative, depending upon which minerals are in the water. Certain minerals bind the carbonation into the water. Seltzers tend to lose their carbonation quickly because of the lack of minerals. In bottled-water tastings, the more highly mineralized carbonated waters have scored best.

Become bottled-water savvy with this brief primer about popular brands available in New York restaurants.

The Major Brands

Calistoga

Nestled at the north end of Napa Valley, Calistoga is a spa-resort town where a geyser second in size only to Yellowstone's Old Faithful shoots up from the ground, and people have been coming to "take the waters"—in pools and in mud-baths—since before the turn of the century. Of the town's three commercially bottled waters, Calistoga comes from water which emerges from the ground at 212 degrees Fahrenheit and is then cooled to 39 degrees F for bottling. The hydrogen-sulfide aroma is removed from the water at the bottling plant by filtering it through sand. The finished water is then ozonated and carbonated. Calistoga also bottles a non-carbonated water sourced from a Napa County spring.

Crystal Geyser

Also bottled in the town of Calistoga, Crystal Geyser water comes from an aquifer 240 feet below the bottling plant. The water surfaces at a temperature of 140 degrees F, and through a method of heat exchanges, is cooled, filtered to remove sediment, ozonated, carbonated and bottled. The company also produces the non-carbonated Natural Alpine Spring water near the town of Olancha, California. Its source is high in the Sierra Mountains, where glacial waters have seeped over eons through cracks in the granite rocks. Crystal Geyser also produces Natural Alpine spring water, which comes from a source near the base of Mt. Whitney.

Dannon Natural Spring Water

You know the name "Dannon" from the company's line of milk products. Now you'll find it on bottles of non-carbonated water. The source this newcomer to the bottled-water biz is a spring in the Laurentian region of Quebec, Canada. Test-marketed in Florida and Colorado, initial results showed that Dannon's brand name and moderate pricing produced positive sales, as consumers associate the name with taste, trust and natural products.

Deer Park

Deer Park's source is a spring 3,000 feet above sea level surrounded by hundreds of acres of woodlands in the Allegheny Mountains, near Deer Park, Maryland. When it was first bottled in 1880, the non-sparkling water was called Boiling Spring because of the action of the water as it bubbled through white sand. The Deer Park Hotel and Spa, which opened in 1873, became a watering ground for distinguished guests, including U.S. Presidents Garfield, Cleveland, Harrison and Taft.

Evian

This famous non-sparkling European water comes from Source Cachat in France, where the water emerges from a tunnel in the mountain at 52.88 degrees F. The source is fed from the melted snow and rain that filters through glacial sand from the Vinzier Plateau over a period of 15 years. The glacial sand is surrounded by clay which protects the water from pollution. The water is bottled at a nearby bottling plant, which is highly automated and exceptionally hygienic.

Great Bear

Great Bear Spring has been known since the Onondaga Indian tribe lived near the source in Central New York State, where it is protected by remote woodlands and sheltering rock formations. The spring water filters through layers of gray and white sand and fine sandstone gravel, emerges from the earth at a temperature of about 52 degrees F, and is bottled as a still spring water.

Ice Mountain

Early Indians were the first to discover Ice Mountain Spring, located in the remote woodlands of Mt. Zircon, near Rumford, in central Maine. They noticed it seemed to rise and fall with the cycles of the moon and called it Moon Tide Spring. The water was first bottled by the Abbott family In 1859, and is now bottled as both still and sparkling.

Mountain Valley

This water springs from a source in a 500-acre forest in the hills between Glazypeau and Cedar Mountains, in Arkansas. Adjacent is a timberland preserve, all of which protects the Mountain Valley aquifer. It was first bottled in 1871 and has been continuously bottled since then, both as carbonated and non-carbonated water. Mountain Valley's source emerges at 65 degrees F; the bottling plant draws approximately 50 gallons per minute from the spring. The source's aquifer is estimated to be at 1,600 feet below earth's surface, where the water filters through levels of shale, Blakely sandstone and limestone.

Perrier

Dating back more than 100 million years to the Cretaceous Period, when limestone deposits began to form faults and fissures that captured water deep within the earth below what is now Vergèze, France. Hannibal's Carthaginian army is said to have paused by the spring, Les Bouillens, in 218 B.C. Remains in the area suggest that the Romans also refreshed themselves in the waters of Perrier, which have a bit of natural carbonation. When it is bottled, extra fizz is created by adding filtered CO_2 gas captured at a nearby natural source.

Poland Spring

The history of Poland Spring, Maine, dates back to 1793, when the area around the spring was first settled and the Ricker family opened a small inn. Soon afterward Joseph Ricker lay dying, and to ease his fever someone fetched water from the spring. The story is that Ricker drank it and lived another fifty-two years to tell the tale! Iin 1845, Hiram Ricker began to bottle the water and, in 1893, Poland Spring was awarded the Medal of Excellence at the World's Columbian Exposition in Chicago. Today, Poland Spring comes both still and sparkling.

Quibell

The source for Quibell's sparkling product is a spring on heavily wooded Sweet Springs Mountain, West Virginia, at the pinnacle of the Great Eastern Divide. Geologists from Virginia Tech have indicated that the water flows naturally at about two million gallons per day. The water filters through limestone rock strata and emerges from the spring at 42 degrees F.

San Pellegrino

The spring of San Pellegrino is sequestered in the mountains north of Milan, Italy, and was first made famous by quenching the thirst of Leonardo da Vinci. Today the Fonte Termale, an opulent marbled drinking hall is a monument to the glamour of "taking the waters." San Pellegrino's sources are three deep springs which emerge from the ground at 69.8 degrees F. The waters come from an aquifer 1,300 feet below the surface, where limestone and volcanic rocks impart unique minerals and trace elements. Among its several bottled waters, San Pellegrino also bottles and imports to the U.S. Acqua Minerale Naturale Panna, a still water that comes from a spring in the hills of Tuscany near Florence.

Saratoga

In the southern foothills of New York's Adirondack Mountains is the famous town of Saratoga Springs, where, in the Gay '90s, celebrities like Lillian Russell and Diamond Jim Brady drank Saratoga's carbonated water from monogrammed cups. Saratoga's original source was a hand-drilled well that went through 30 feet of sand and 150 feet of rock. Natural carbonation occurs in the water, although the water is re-injected with additional carbonation during the bottling process.

Solé

The Fonte Solé Spring is located in the foothills of the Lombardy region of the Italian Alps, and has been revered for its health-giving waters since Roman times. In the Middle Ages, the source was controlled by a monastery when both plague and pestilence threatened the population. A belief grew up that those who drank from the spring would be . Today, the water is recognized as being low in sodium. The University of Pavia has declared it as being microbiologically pure. Solé is packaged in green glass bottles, both non-carbonated and lightly carbonated. The latter, be warned, is not the best mixer to use for spritzers because of the fragility of its bubbles.

Spa

First discovered by the ancient Romans, the source for Spa's non-sparkling mineral water is located in Belgium's

Ardennes Valley. Spa was the first town to develop an international bottled water industry (in 1583, the water was exported to none less than King Henri II of France). In the process, the town inadvertently exported its name; since then, "spa" has been synonymous with most natural springs and health resorts. On the edge of the High Venn near Spa is the spring called Reine (the Queen's Spring). Rain and melted snow falls on a moss area of La Fagne, a plateau 575 meters above sea level. It percolates down through layers of clay, slate, flint, sand and quartz where it finally surfaces at 440 meters above sea level.

Tynant

Springing from a source in Wales' Cambrian Mountains, this carbon-filtered sparkling water first made a name for itself in London's high-end hotels in 1989. Today, the lightly carbonated beverage is more widely distributed, and imported to the United States as well. Tynant is recognizable by its striking blue glass bottles, the hue that apothecary bottles were colored during the Victorian era.

Vittel

This still mineral water comes from three springs in the small town of Vittel, protected within a 5,000 hectare forest in the Vosges Mountains in Northeastern France. Vittel Grande Source comes from an immense underground aquifer where rock strata and sandstone charge the water with calcium, magnesium and sulphates. The spring surfaces at 11.1 degrees C. and its waters are renowned for its stimulating effects on the kidneys, gall bladder and liver.

By Arthur von Wiesenberger, the author of a number of books about water, the most recent, The Taste of Water (Best Cellar Books). He is also a consultant to the bottled-water industry.

RESTAURANT INDEXES

RESTAURANTS BY CUISINE

We find it harder and harder to classify restaurants by cuisine these days, because more and more restaurants are serving dishes that reflect a variety of ethnic influences. Many of the restaurants that were once classified as "Californian" (lots of fresh ingredients and grilling) are now incorporating elements of American regional cooking and calling themselves "New American," though with all the Asian, Latin American, European and Middle Eastern influences in their cooking as well, we could probably label them "Pacific Rim/New American," "Pan-Asian/New American," or "Mediterranean/New American." We have also found that many old-fashioned American restaurants have updated to "New American"—and that even some French restaurants (especially in hotels) have switched to "New American." If you're an adventurous eater, take note of the esoteric categories below—Eclectic, Pacific Rim, International and Nuevo Latino, for example. To best understand what you'll be served at the restaurants included in our book, however, we suggest you ignore the cuisine "labels" and read the text of the reviews.

AFGHAN

Afghan Kebab House
Ariana Afghan Kebab
Pamir
Speengar Shish Kebab
House

AFRICAN

Joloff
Keur N'Deye

AMERICAN

American Festival Café
Cigar Room at Trumpets
City Hall
Elaine's
Garage
Home
Independent
Mike & Tony's

New Prospect Café
The Post House
Sam's
SoHo Kitchen & Bar
"21" Club
Vince & Eddie's
Ye Waverly Inn

AMERICAN/HEALTHY

The Grange Hall

AMERICAN/SEAFOOD

Manhattan Ocean Club

ARGENTINEAN

La Cabaña Argentina
Sosa Borella

ASIAN/CUBAN

Asia de Cuba

BAKERY/CAFÉS

Bleecker Street Pastry &
    Café
Cupcake Café
E.A.T.
Eatzi's Market & Bakery
Edgar's
Egidio's Bakery
Friend of a Farmer
La Bonne Soupe
La Boulangère
Panya
Rocco Pastry Shop
Sarabeth's
Traditional Irish Bakery
TriBakery
Veniero's

BARBECUE

Brothers Bar-B-Que
Dallas B-B-Q
Duke's
Virgil's Real Barbecue

BARS, SALOONS & BREWPUBS

Chelsea Brewing Company
Ear Inn
Elephant & Castle
Fanelli's
The Gate
Greenwich Pizza & Brewing
    Company
Heartland Brewery
McSorley's Old Ale House
Mugs Ale House
Old Town Bar
Park Slope Brewing
    Company
Westside Brewing Company
White Horse Tavern

BELGIAN

B. Frites
Petite Abeille
Pommes Frites
Waterloo

BELGIAN/FRENCH

Café de Bruxelles

BELGIAN/MIDDLE EASTERN

Mesopotamia

BRAZILIAN

Cabana Carioca
Churrascaria Plataforma
Delícia

BRITISH

Telephone Bar & Grill

BURGERS, DOGS & CHILI

All State Café
Corner Bistro
Gray's Papaya
Jackson Hole
Manhattan Chili Company
McDonald's
Nathan's Famous
Papaya King
The Prime Burger
Sassy's Sliders
Silver Spurs
Sorrento Coffee Shop

BURMESE

Mandalay Kitchen
Mingala West

CAJUN

Acadia Parish Cajun Café
Chantale's Cajun Kitchen
Delta Grill

CAJUN/TEX-MEX

L-Ray

CAFÉS & COFFEEHOUSES

Angler's & Writers
Bam Café
Bell Caffè
Café Borgia
Café Europa
Café La Fortuna
Café Reggio
Caffè Dante
Caffè Della Pace
Caffè Tina
Dean & Deluca Café
Lamarca Cheese Shop &
    Restaurant
The Lotus Club
Parlour Café
Savories
Vinegar Factory

CAMBODIAN
Cambodian Cuisine

CARIBBEAN
Bourda Green
Brawta Caribbean Café
Cabana
Tito Puente's

CARIBBEAN FUSION
Bambou Restaurant & Bar

CARIBBEAN/SEAFOOD
Jimmy's Bronx Café

CAVIAR/FRENCH
Caviar Russe
Petrossian

CAVIAR & GOURMET BAR FOOD
Caviarteria Champagne
Caviar Bar

CHAMPAGNE & GOURMET BAR FOOD
Flute

CHINESE/AMERICAN
Wong Kee

CHINESE/DUM SUM
Big Wong
Canton
Chin Chin
David's Taiwanese Gourmet
Evergreen Shanghai
    Restaurant
Golden Monkey
Golden Unicorn
Goody's
Jade Palace
Joe's Shanghai
Kam Chueh
K.B. Garden Restaurant
Lum Chin
Ma Ma Buddha
Mandarin Court
Mee Noodle Shop
Mr. K's

New York Noodletown
Ollie's Noodle Shop & Grille
Oriental Pearl
Pig Heaven
Shun Lee Palace
69 Mott Street
Tai Hong Lau
20 Mott Street

COFFEE SHOPS & DINERS
Aggie's
Barking Dog Luncheonette
Bendix Diner
Bread & Butter
Café Edison
The Coffee Mug
Coffee Shop
The Comfort Diner
EJ's Luncheonette
Empire Diner
Jones Diner
Kiev
Life Café
Picnic
Silver Star Restaurant
Veselka
Tom's Restaurant

COLOMBIAN
Tierras Colombianas

CONTEMPORARY
Astor Restaurant & Lounge

CONTEMPORARY AMERICAN
Restaurant EQ

CONTINENTAL
Old Bermuda Inn
The Pembroke Room
Sardi's

CONTINENTAL/GLOBAL
Windows on the World

CUBAN
El Sitio

CUBAN-CHINESE
La Chinita Linda
La Nueva Victoria

DELIS & BAGEL SHOPS

Absolute Bagels
Barney Greengrass
Carnegie Delicatessen
Columbia Hot Bagels
Ess-A-Bagel
Fine & Schapiro
Junior's
Katz's Deli
Mom's Bagels & Catering
Mrs. Stahl's Knishes
Sable's Smoked Fish
Second Avenue Kosher Deli
Stage Deli

DOMINICAN

Caridad
Castillos
School Bus

EASTERN EUROPEAN/JEWISH

Sammy's Roumanian
Steakhouse

ECLECTIC

Island
Restaurant 222

ECLECTIC/FRENCH

Blue Ribbon

ECUADORIAN

La Picada Azuaya

EGYPTIAN

Casa la Femme

ETHIOPIAN

Blue Nile
Ghenet

FRENCH

Alison on Dominick
Au Troquet
Balthazar Restaurant
Bouley Bakery Restaurant
Bouterin
The Box Tree
Café Adriana
Café Boulud

Café Centro
Café Loup
Capsouto Frères
Chateaubriand
Chelsea Bistro & Bar
Chez Jacqueline
Chez Ma Tante
Cité
Demarchelier
Destinée
Félix
Ferrier
Flea Market
Florent
The 14 Wall Street
Restaurant
Gasgogne
Jean-Claude
Jean Georges
Jo Jo
Jules
L'Absinthe
L'Acajou
La Boîte en Bois
La Bouillabaisse
La Caravelle
La Colombe d'Or
La Côte Basque
La Fourchette
La Goulue
La Grenouille
La Métaire
La Mirabelle
La Réserve
La Ripaille
Le Bernardin
Le Cirque 2000
Le Périgord
Le Refuge
Le Régence
Le Solex
Le Tableau
Le Veau d'Or
Le Zoo Restaurant
Les Célébrités
Les Halles
Lespinasse
Lutèce
Metisse
Montrachet
Park Bistro
Payard Patisserie & Bistro
Peacock Alley
Pitchoune

Quatorze Bis
Raoul's
Raphaél
René Pujol
Restaurant Daniel
Sud
Steak Frites
Trois Jean

FRENCH/AMERICAN

Café Nicole

FRENCH BISTRO

Balthazar Restaurant
Café Luxembourg
L'Orange Bleue
Provence
Steak au Poivre

FRENCH/CONTINENTAL

Cafés des Artistes
The Carlyle Restaurant

FRENCH/ ECLECTIC

Sonia Rose

FRENCH/FUSION

Bayard's
La Bohème

FRENCH-INDIAN FUSION

Salient

FRENCH/ITALIAN

Frontière

FRENCH/KOSHER

Le Marais

FRENCH/MEDITERRANEAN

Picholine
Scarabée

FRENCH/MEXICAN

Coup

FRENCH/MOROCCAN

Bar Six
Chez Es Saada

FRENCH/NEW AMERICAN

Café Pierre
Chanterelle
Etats-Unis
Mercer Kitchen
Tatous

FRENCH/SEAFOOD

Le Bernardin
Le Pescadou

FUSION

Garden Café

FUSION/NEW AMERICAN

Kalio

GOURMET BAR FOOD

The Bubble Lounge
The Library
Spy

GREEK

Eros
Karyatis
Molyvos
Periyali
Uncle George's
Uncle Nick's
Zenon

GREEK/SEAFOOD

Elias Corner
Estiatorio Milos

GUYANESE

Sybil's

HEALTHY

Camille's Clover Hill

HEALTHY/AMERICAN
KPNY (Ken's Place New York)

HEALTHY/ORGANIC
Heartbeat

ICE CREAM & MORE
Baskin-Robbins
Ben & Jerry's
Benfaremo, The Lemon Ice King of Corona
Chinatown Ice Cream Factory
Cones
Custard Beach
Häagen-Daz
Minter's Ice Cream Kitchen
Peppermint Park
Peter's Ice Cream Parlor & Coffee House
Sant Ambroeus
Serendipity 3

INDIAN
Akbar
Bay Leaf Brasserie
Curry in a Hurry
Dawat
Delhi Palace
Jackson Diner
Jewel of India
Mitali East
Mitali West
Passage to India
Raga
Shaan
Shamiana restaurant

INDIAN/FUSION
Surya

INDIAN/VEGETARIAN
Mavalli Palace

INDONESIAN
Java Indonesian Rijsttafel

INTERNATIONAL
Boom Restaurant
Chez Nic
Match Downtown

ITALIAN
Abbracciamento on the Pier
Ann & Tony's
Arqua
Babbo
Baci
Bar Cichetti
Bar Pitti
Barbetta
Barocco
Barolo
Basta Pasta
Becco
Bellini
Bice
Bottino
Briscola
Café al Mercato
Caffè Buon Gusto
Caffè Rosso
Campagna
Cellini
Carmine's
Cent'Anni
Chelsea Trattoria
Cipriani Wall Street
Coco Pazzo
Cola's
Contrapunto
Cucina
Cucina Stagionale
Da Silvano Restaurant
Da Umberto
Delícia
Diva
Dominick's
Downtown
Eli's
Ennio & Michael's Restaurant
Erminia
Felidia Ristorante
F.illi Ponte Ristorante
Fino
Follonico
Fresco by Scotto
Frico Bar Restaurant
Gabriel's

Gargiulo's
Gemilli
Gianni's Ristorante
Harry Cipriani
I Coppi
I Tre Merli
I Trulli
Il Bagatto
Il Boschetto
Il Buco
Il Cantinori
Il Mulino
Il Nido
Il Valletto
La Focacceria
La Pizza Fresca
La Vineria
Le Madri
Limoncello
Luca
Lusardi's
Manducatis
Manganaro's Hero Boy
    Restaurant
Mappamondo Uno
Mappamondo Duo
Marco Polo
Mario's
Mad 28
Mangia
Melampo Imported Foods
Mazzei
Mezzaluna
Mezzogiorno
Monte's Venetian Room
Monzù
Moreno Ristorante
Naples 45
Nino's
Northside
Novitá
Orologio
Orso
Osteria del Circo
Paggio
Palio
Paola's Restaurant
Paper Moon
Parioli Romanissimo
Patsy's
Pelegrinos
Petaluma
Pete's Downtown
Piadina

Pò
Portico
Primavera
Primola
Queen
Randazzo's Clam Bar
Rao's
The Red Rose
Remi
Restivo Ristorante
Rosemarie's
Salumeria Biellese
San Domenico
San Giusto
Sant Ambroeus
Serafina Fabulous Grill
Siena
Sistina
Sorrento
S.P.Q.R.
Taormina
Tommaso's
Torre di Pisa
Trattoria Romana
Trattoria Venti Trè
Two Toms
Uzie & Marco's
Vincent's Restaurant

ITALIAN/CONTEMPORARY

The Park

ITALIAN/MEDITERRANEAN

Fantino

ITALIAN/STEAKHOUSE

Frank's Restaurant

JAMAICAN

Negril Island Spice

JAPANESE & SUSHI

Blue Ribbon Sushi
Chikubu
Hasaki
Hatsuhana
Honmura An
Hyotan-Nippon

Inagiku
Kuruma Zushi
Menchanko-Tei
Mie
Nippon
Oishi Noodle
Sakagura
Seryna
Sobaya
Sushi Bar
Sushisay

JAPANESE/FUSION

Bond Street

KOREAN

Bop
Dok Suni's
Empire Korea
Han Bat Kang Suh
Restaurant
Kum Gang San
Woo Chon

KOREAN/JAPANESE

Kum Gang San
Won Jo

KOREAN/VEGETARIAN

Hangawi

KOSHER

Ess-a-Bagel
Fine & Schapiro
Mom's Bagels & Tables
Second Avenue Kosher Deli
Siegel's Kosher Deli &
    Restaurant

LATIN AMERICAN

Bolivar
Boca Chica
Empanada Oven

LATIN AMERICAN/SEAFOOD

El Potrero
Mi Colombia

LEBANESE

Al Bustan

MALAYSIAN

Malaysia Restaurant
Nyonya
Penang Cuisine Malaysia
Penang SoHo
Penang West

MEDITERRANEAN

Café Crocodile
Café M
Cal's
Istana
Matthew's
Oznot's Dish

MEXICAN

Benny's Burritos
Café Con Leche
El Sombrero
El Teddy's
La Taquería
Los Dos Rancheros
Mary Ann's
Maya
Mexicana Marna
Mezcal's
Mi Cocina
Panchito's
Rocking Horse Café
Mexicano
Rosa Mexicano
Taco Taco
Zarela

MEXICAN/SOUTHWESTERN

Radio Mexico Café

MIDDLE EASTERN

Cedars of Lebanon
Fountain Café
Layla
Moustache—Brooklyn
Olive Vine
Walid Demis Moustache
    Pitza

MOROCCAN

Andalousia
Salam

NEW AMERICAN

Across the Street
Adrienne
Aesop's Tables
An American Place
Aureole
B Bar
The Barclay Bar & Grill
Bridge Café
Bryant Park Grill
Butterfield 81
Cafeteria
Cena
Cibo
City Wine & Cigar Company
Clementine
Cub Room
Duane Park Café
Eighteenth & Eighth
Eleven Madison Park
Fifty Seven Fifty Seven
Flowers
"44"
Gertrude's
Gotham Bar & Grill
Grammercy Tavern
Halcyon
Henry's End
Hudson River Club
Indigo
Jerry's
Judson Grill
Kokochin
Lemon
Lenox Room
Liam
The Lobster Club
Lucky Strike
March Restaurant
Mark's Restaurant
Match Uptown
Max & Moritz
Merchant's NY
Merlot Bar & Grill
Michael's
Monkey Bar
Mono
Moomba
New City Café

One if by Land, Two if
   by Sea
Park Avalon
Park Avenue Café
Park View at the Boathouse
Patroon
Quilty's
Restaurant 147
Rialto
The River Café
Savoy
The Screening Room
Syrah
Taliesin
Tavern on the Green
Terrace
TriBeCa Grill
Treehouse
27 Standard/The Jazz
   Standard
Union Pacific
Union Square Café
Verbena
Veritas
The Vinegar Factory
Water's Edge
Zoë

NEW AMERICAN/CONTINENTAL

Four Seasons

NEW AMERICAN/INDIAN

Tabla

NEW AMERICAN/ITALIAN

Fred's

NEW AMERICAN/SEAFOOD

Wilkinson's Restaurant

NUEVO LATINO/CUBAN

Patria

ORGANIC

Josie's

PAN-ASIAN

Chao Chow
China Grill
Lucky Chang
Rain
Republic

PERUVIAN

El Pollo

PIZZA

Arturo's
Catania's Pizza Café
Famous Ben's Pizza of SoHo
Goodfellas Brick-Oven Pizza
Grimaldi's
Joe's Pizza
John's
Lento's
Patsy's Pizza
Ray's of Greenwich Village
Rizzo's
Serafina Fabulous Pizza
Totonno's
Two Boots

POLISH

KK Polish-American
Polska

PORTUGUESE

O Lavrador

PUERTO RICAN

Casa Adela

RUSSIAN

Firebird
Odessa
Rasputin
Russian Samovar

RUSSIAN/GOURMET BAR FOOD

Pravda

SALVADOREAN

Izalco

SCANDINAVIAN

Aquavit
Christer's

SEAFOOD

American Park
Atlantic Grill
Blue Water Grill
City Crab & Seafood
   Company
Cosenza's Fish Market
Johnny's Reef
The Lobster Box
London Lennie's
Lundy Bros.
Oceana
Pearl Oyster Bar
Pier 25A
Shaffer City Oyster Bar
   & Grill
Waterfront Crab House

SEAFOOD/FUSION

Tropica

SEAFOOD/NEW AMERICAN

Aquagrill
Oyster Bar & Restaurant
Redeye Grill
The Seagrill

SOUL FOOD/CARIBBEAN

Mekka

SOUL FOOD/SOUTHERN

Carolina Country Kitchen
Copeland's
Emily's
Jezebel
MaMa's Food Shop
The McCafé
Old Devil Moon
Soul Fixins'
StepMama
Sylvia's Restaurant
Wells Restaurant

SOUP

Soup Kitchen International

SOUTHERN/AMERICAN

B. Smith's
Gage & Tollner

SOUTHERN/CARIBBEAN
Lola

SOUTHWESTERN
Adobe Blues
Citrus Bar & Grill
Mesa Grill
Miracle Grill
Tapika

SOUTHWESTERN/ASIAN
Bright Food Shop

SPANISH
Bolo
Café Español
Café Sevilla
El Faro
El Rincon de España

SPANISH/ITALIAN
Acquario

STEAKHOUSE/AMERICAN
Ben Benson's
Bobby Van's Steakhouse
Gallagher's
Keen's
Maloney & Porcelli
Michael Jordan's The Steak
    House NYC
Morton's of Chicago
Old Homestead Restaurant
The Palm
Peter Luger
Ruth's Chris Steakhouse
Smith & Wollensky
Sparks Steakhouse
Tupelo Grill

TEA ROOMS & PATISSERIES
Danal
Takashimaya Teabox Café
Tea & Sympathy

THAI
Kin Khao
Jai-Ya Thai
Lemongrass Grill
Plan Eat Thai
Thai Taste
Thailand Restaurant

THAI/BREWPUB
Typhoon Brewery

THAI/FRENCH
Vong

THEME RESTAURANTS
Brooklyn Diner
Hard Rock Café
Harley Davidson Café
Jekyll & Hyde
The Jekyll & Hyde Club
Mars 2112
Motown Café
Planet Hollywood
The Slaughtered Lamb Pub

TIBETAN
Tibet Shambala
Tsampa

TRINIDADIAN
Sandy's Roti Shop

TURKISH
Turkish Grill
Turkish Kitchen

VEGETARIAN
Zen Palate

VEGETARIAN/ORGANIC
Angelica Kitchen
Blanche's Organic Café
Candle Café
Kate's Joint
Navia's Diner
Souen
Whole Wheat 'n Wild Berrys

VIETNAMESE/FRENCH
Can

VIETNAMESE
Cuisine de Saigon
Cyclo
Indochine
Le Colonial
Monsoon
Nha Tran
Vietnam

RESTAURANTS BY NOTABLE FEATURES

We've included only the BEST in each category:

BREAKFAST	323
BRUNCH	323
BUSINESS DINING	324
GOOD FOR KIDS & TEENS	324
HOTEL DINING ROOOMS	325
PLACE TO MEET FOR A DRINK	325
LATE-NIGHT DINING	325
LIGHT & HEALTHY FARE	326
LIVE MUSIC/ENTERTAINMENT	326
OPEN 24 HOURS	326
OUTDOOR DINING	326
ROMANTIC	326
VIEW	327
GREAT WINE LIST	327

BREAKFAST

Adrienne
Barney Greengrass
Bendix Diner
Cupcake Café
Café Europa
The Comfort Diner
EJ's Luncheonette
Ess-A-Bagel
Fifty Seven Fifty Seven
Friend of a Farmer
The Grange Hall
Jerry's
Junior's
Le Solex
Mercer Kitchen
Payard Patisserie

Sarabeth's
Tom's Restaurant
TriBakery
The Vinegar Factory

BRUNCH

Bridge Café
Café des Artistes
Café M
Chelsea Brewing Company
Copeland's
Emily's
Greenwich Pizza & Brewing
    Company
Home
Le Zoo
Matthew's

Monzù
Old Devil Moon
Park View at the Boathouse
Parlour Café
The Pembroke Room
The Redeye Grill
The River Café
Tavern on the Green
The Vinegar Factory

The Post House
Remi
Restaurant Daniel
Ruth's Chris Steakhouse
Smith & Wollensky
Taliesin
Tupelo Grill
"21" Club
Union Pacific
Union Square Café

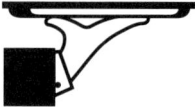

BUSINESS DINING

Aquavit
Bayard's
Bice
Cena
Chikubu
Cigar Room at Trumpets
Cipriani Wall Street
Cité
City Hall
Coco Pazzo
Cub Room
Eleven Madison Park
Four Seasons
The 14 Wall Street
    Restaurant
Gemelli
Grammercy Tavern
Hatsuhana
Hudson River Club
Jean Georges
Judson Grill
Keen's
Le Bernardin
Le Cirque 2000
Maloney & Porcelli
Mark's Restaurant
Michael's
Montrachet
Morton's of Chicago
Nippon
Oyster Bar & Restaurant
The Palm
Palio
Peter Luger
Patroon

GOOD FOR KIDS & TEENS

Barking Dog Lunchonette
Brooklyn Diner
City Crab & Seafood
    Company
The Comfort Diner
Duke's
Greenwich Pizza & Brewing
    Company
Grimaldi's
Hard Rock Café
Jackson Hole
The Jeckyll & Hyde Club
John's
Manhattan Chili Company
Mars 2112
Max & Moritz
Motown Café
The Nice Restaurant
Peppermint Park
Pig Heaven
Planet Hollywood
Serafina Fabulous Pizza
Serendipity 3
Silver Spurs
Tavern on the Green
Tommaso's
Two Boots
The Vinegar Factory
Virgil's

HOTEL DINING ROOMS

Adrienne (The Peninsula)
Café Nicole (Novotel NY)
Café Pierre (The Pierre)
The Carlyle Restaurant
    (The Carlyle)
Fantino (The Westin)
Fifty Seven Fifty Seven (The
    Four Seasons)
Inagiku (The Waldorf-
    Astoria)
Istana (The NY Palace)
Halcyon (Rihga Royal)
Jean Georges (Trump
    International)
Kokachin (The Omni
    Berkshire)
Les Célébrités (The Essex
    House)
Lespinasse (The St. Regis)
Mercer Kitchen (The
    Mercer)
The Park (The Lombardy)
Post House (The Lowell)
Peacock Alley (The Waldorf-
    Astoria)
Taliesin (The Millenium
    Hilton)

PLACE TO MEET FOR A DRINK

Aquavit
B Bar
Bar Cichetti
The Bubble Lounge
Caviar Russe
Caviarteria Champagne &
    Caviar Bar
City Hall
Clementine
Elephant & Castle
Fanelli's
Flute
"44"
Four Seasons
The Gate
Grammercy Tavern
Harry Cipriani
Le Colonial
The Library
Mercer Kitchen
Monkey Bar
Moomba
Old Town Bar
Palio
The Park
Park Slope Brewing
    Company
Pravda
Spy
Terrace
TriBeCa Grill
Union Square Café
Waterloo
White Horse Tavern

LATE-NIGHT DINING

Adobe Blues
Astor Restaurant & Lounge
B Bar
Balthazar
Bluc Ribbon
Blue Ribbon Sushi
Cafeteria
Carnegie Deli
Clementine
El Teddy's
Flute
Lucky Strike
Merchant's NY
Odéon
Match Downtown
Match Uptown

Restaurant 147
Stage Deli
Sushi Bar

LIGHT & HEALTHY FARE

Akbar
Angelica Kitchen
Atlantic Grill
Camille's Clover Hill
Candle Café
Hangawi
Kate's Joint
KPNY (Ken's Place New
   York)
Mavalli Palace
The SeaGrill
Sushisay
Whole Wheat 'n' Wild Berrys
Zen Palate

LIVE MUSIC/ENTERTAINMENT

Adobe Blues
Blue Water Grill
Copeland's
Emily's
Firebird/Café Firebird
Jezebel
Lucky Cheng
Merlot Bar & Grill/Iridium
Jazz Club
Odessa
Sam's
Sylvia's Restaurant
27 Standard/The Jazz
Standard
Tatou
Well's Restaurant

OPEN 24 HOURS

Empire Diner
Empire Korea
Florent (on weekends)
Han Bat
Kang Suh Restaurant
Kiev
Silver Star Restaurant
Veselka
Won Jo Korean-Japanese
Restaurant

OUTDOOR DINING

Abbracciamento on the Pier
American Festival Café
Bouterin
Frico Bar Restaurant
Home
Jean Georges
Miracle Grill
Park View at the Boathouse
Provence
Randazzo's Clam Bar
Raphaél
The SeaGrill
Tavern on the Green
Terrace
Verbena
Water's Edge
Ye Waverly Inn

ROMANTIC

Au Troquet
Aureole
Bambou Restaurant & Bar

Barbetta
Bond Street
Bouterin
The Box Tree
Bryant Park Grill
Café des Artistes
Casa La Femme
Caviar Russe
Cellini
Chelsea Bistro & Bar
Destinée
Erminia
Eros
Felidia
Firebird
Follonico
Four Seasons
Gasgogne
Il Bagatto
Jean Georges
Jewel of India
La Caravelle
La Fourchette
La Grenouille
La Ripaille
Le Cirque 2000
Le Colonial
Le Refuge
Le Regénce
Lespinasse
Lutèce
March Restaurant
Mark's Restaurant
Maya
Mr. K's
One if by Land, Two if
    by Sea
Pamir
Parioli Romanissimo
The Park
Park View at the Boathouse
Restaurant Daniel
The River Café
Salam
Savoy
Shaan
Tatou
Terrace
Treehouse
Verbena
Water's Edge

VIEW

American Park
Bryant Park Grill
Chelsea Brewing Company
Hudson River Club
Pete's Downtown
The River Café
Taliesin
Restaurant 222
Water's Edge
Windows on the World

GREAT WINE LIST

An American Place
Aureole
Barolo
Chanterelle
City Wine & Cigar Company
Eleven Madison Park
Felidia
Fresco by Scotto
Grammercy Tavern
Hudson River Club
Jean Georges
Keen's
La Caravelle
Le Bernardin
Le Cirque 2000
Lespinasse
Lutèce
March Restaurant
Mark's Restaurant
Merlot Bar & Grill
Michael's
Montrachct
Patroon
Picholine
Post House
Restaurant Daniel
Smith & Wollensky
Taliesin
TriBeCa Grill
Union Square Café
Veritas
Windows on the World
Zoë

RESTAURANTS BY AREA

BELOW HOUSTON

Acquario
Aggie's
Alison on Dominick
American Park
Anglers & Writers
Aquagrill
Arqua
Arturo's
B Bar
Balthazar Restaurant
Bar Cichetti
Barocco
Barolo
Bayard's
Bell Caffè
Big Wong
Blue Ribbon
Blue Ribbon Sushi
Bond Street
Boom Restaurant
Bouley Bakery Restaurant
Bread & Butter
Brothers Bar-B-Que
Bridge Café
The Bubble Lounge
Caffè Tina
Can
Canton
Capsouto Frères
Casa La Femme
Caviarteria Champagne &
    Caviar Bar
Chanterelle
Chao Chow
Chinatown Ice Cream
    Factory

Cipriani Wall Street
City Hall
City Wine & Cigar Company
Cub Room
Custard Beach
Diva
Downtown
Duane Park Café
Ear Inn
El Sombrero
El Teddy's
Evergreen Shanghai
Restaurant
Famous Ben's Pizza of SoHo
Fanelli's
Félix
F.illi Ponte Ristorante
The 14 Wall Street
Restaurant
Frontière
Gemelli
Ghenet
Golden Unicorn
Haägen-Dazs
Honmura An
Hudson River Club
Independent
I Tre Merli
Jean-Claude
Jerry's
Joe's Shanghai
Jones Diner
Kam Chueh
Kin Khao
Layla
Le Pescadou
Liam

L'Orange Bleue
The Lotus Club
Lucky Strike
Ma Ma Buddha
Malaysia Restaurant
Mandalay Kitchen
Mandarin Court
Match Downtown
McDonald's
Mee Noodle Shop
Melampo Imported Foods
Mercer Kitchen
Mezzogiorno
Minter's Ice Cream Kitchen
Montrachet
Monzü
Morton's of Chicago
Navia's Diner
New York Noodletown
Next Door Nobu
Nha Trang
The Nice Restaurant
Nobu
The Odéon
Ollie's Noodle Shop & Grille
Omen
Oriental Pearl
Paggio
Pearl Oyster Bar
Peligrinos
Penang SoHo
Pravda
Provence
Quilty's
Radio Mexico Café
Raoul's
Rialto
Rosemarie's
Salient
Sammy's Roumanian
    Steakhouse
Savoy
The Screening Room
69 Mott Street
SoHo Kitchen & Bar
Sorrento
Souen
S.P.Q.R.
Spy
Tai Hong Lau
Taliesin
Taormina
Telephone Bar & Grill

Thailand Restaurant
Trattoria Venti Trè
TriBakery
TriBeCa Grill
20 Mott Street Restaurant
Vietnam
Vincent's Restaurant
Windows on the World
Wong Kee
Zoë

**GREENWICH VILLAGE
& ENVIRONS**

Andalousia
Angelica Kitchen
Astor Restaurant & Lounge
Au Troquet
Babbo
Bar Pitti
Bar Six
Ben & Jerry's
Benny's Burritos
Bleecker Street Pastry &
    Café
Boca Chica
Bop
Briscola
Café Borgia
Café de Bruxelles
Café Español
Café Loup
Café Reggio
Caffè Dante
Caffè Della Pace
Caffè Rosso
Casa Adela
Cent'Anni
Chez es Saada
Chez Jacqueline
Chez Ma Tante
Clementine
Cones
Corner Bistro
Coup
Cucina Stagionale
Cuisine de Saigon
Cyclo
Da Silvano Restaurant
Danal
Delicia
Dok Suni's
El Faro

El Rincon de España
Elephant & Castle
Ennio & Michael's
    Restaurant
Flea Market
Florent
Garage
Gotham Bar & Grill
The Grange Hall
Greenwich Pizza & Brewing
    Company
Hasaki
Heartland Brewery
Home
I Coppi
Il Bagatto
Il Buco
Il Cantinori
Il Mulino
Indigo
Indochine
Jekyll & Hyde
Joe's Pizza
John's
Jules
Kate's Joint
Kiev
KPNY (Ken's Place New
    York)
La Bohème
La Focacceria
La Métaire
La Ripaille
Le Tableau
Le Zoo Restaurant
Life Café
L-Ray
Lucky Cheng
Mama's Food Shop
Mappamondo Uno
Mappamondo Due
McSorley's Old Ale House
Mekka
Mesopotamia
Mexicana Marna
Mi Cocina
Mie
Miracle Grill
Mitali East
Mitali West
Mono
Moomba
Old Devil Moon

One if By Land, Two if
    By Sea
Oroglogio
Panchito's
Panya
Passage to India
Petite Abeille
Piadina
Pò
Pommes Frites
Raga
Ray's of Greenwich Village
Restaurant EQ
Rocco Pastry Shop
Salam
Sassy's Sliders
Second Avenue Kosher Deli
Silver Spurs
The Slaughtered Lamb Pub
Sobaya
Sosa Borella
Sud
Surya
Tea & Sympathy
Treehouse
Tsampa
Turkish Grill
Two Boots
Veniero's
Veselka
Waterloo
White Horse Tavern
Whole Wheat 'n' Wild Berrys
Ye Waverly Inn

14TH STREET TO 42ND STREET

An American Place
Asia de Cuba
Bambou Restaurant & Bar
Basta Pasta
Bendix Diner
Blue Water Grill
Bolo
Bottino
Bright Food Shop
Bryant Park Grill
Cafeteria
Cal's
Campagna
Cedars of Lebanon

Cena
Chantale's Cajun Kitchen
Chelsea Bistro & Bar
Chelsea Brewing Company
Chelsea Trattoria
Cibo
City Crab & Seafood
    Company
The Coffee Mug
Coffee Shop
Cola's
Cupcake Café
Curry in a Hurry
Da Umberto
Duke's
Eatzi's Market & Bakery
Eighteenth & Eighth
Eleven Madison Park
Empire Diner
Empire Korea
Ess-a-Bagel
Fino
Flowers
Follonico
Frank's Restaurant
Friend of a Farmer
Gasgogne
Gramercy Tavern
Han Bat
Hangawi
I Trulli
Jai-Ya Thai Restaurant
Kang Suh Restaurant
Katz's Deli
Keen's
KK Polish American
Kum Gang San
L'Acajou
La Boulangère
La Chinita Linda
La Colombe D'Or
La Pizza Fresca
Lamarca Cheese Shop &
    Restaurant
Le Madri
Le Solex
Les Halles
Lemon
Lola
Mad 28
Manganaro's Hero Boy
    Restaurant
Mary Ann's

Mavalli Palace
Mesa Grill
Moreno Ristorante
Nathan's Famous
Negril Island Spice
Novitá
Old Homestead Restaurant
Old Town Bar
Park Avalon
Park Bistro
Parlour Café
Patria
Periyali
Picnic
Pitchoune
Republic
Restaurant 147
Restivo Ristorante
Rocking Horse Café
Salumeria Biellese
Shaffer City Oyster Bar
    & Grill
Siena
Sonia Rose
Sorrento Coffee Shop
Soul Fixins'
Steak Frites
Tabla
The Tonic
Trois Canards
Tupelo Grill
Turkish Kitchen
27 Standard/The Jazz
    Standard
Union Pacific
Union Square Café
Verbena
Veritas
Won Jo Korean-Japanese
    Restaurant
Woo Chon

MIDTOWN EAST

Akbar
Al Bustan
The Barclay Bar & Grill
Bellini
Bice
Blanche's Organic Café
Bobby Van's Steakhouse
Bouterin
The Box Tree

Café Adriana
Café Centro
Caviar Russe
Cellini
Chikubu
Chin Chin
Cigar Room at Trumpets
The Comfort Diner
Dawat
Eros
Felidia Ristorante
Fifty Seven Fifty Seven
Four Seasons
Fresco by Scotto
Hatsuhana
Heartbeat
Il Nido
Inagiku
Istana
Kokachin
Kuruma Zushi
La Grenouille
Le Cirque 2000
Le Colonial
Le Périgord
Lespinasse
Lutèce
Maloney & Porcelli
March Restaurant
Michael Jordan's The Steak
    House NYC
Monkey Bar
Morton's of Chicago
Mr. K's
Naples 45
Nippon
Oceana
Oyster Bar & Restaurant
The Palm
Pamir
The Park
Patroon
Peacock Alley
The Prime Burger
Rosa Mexicano
Ruth's Chris Steakhouse
Sakagura
San Giusto
Scarabée
Seryna
Shun Lee Palace
Smith & Wollensky
Sparks Steakhouse

Sushi Bar
Sushisay
Takashimaya Teabox Café
Tatou
Tropica
Typhoon Brewery
Vong
Zarela

MIDTOWN WEST

Adrienne
Afghan Kebab House
American Festival Café
Aquavit
Ariana Afghan Kebab
B. Frites
B. Smith's
Barbetta
Bay Leaf Brasserie
Becco
Ben Benson's Steak House
Brooklyn Diner
Café Edison
Café Europa
Carnegie Delicatessen
Cabana Carioca
Café Nicole
Chateaubriand
China Grill
Christer's
Churrascaria Plataforma
Cité
Dean & Deluca Café
Delta Grill
Empanada Oven
Estiatorio Milos
Fantino
Firebird
Flute
Frico Bar Restaurant
"44"
Gallagher's
Halcyon
Hard Rock Café
Harley Davidson Café
The Jekyll & Hyde Club
Jewel of India
Jezebel
Judson Grill
La Bonne Soupe Bistro
La Caravelle
La Côte Basque

La Réserve
La Vineria
Le Bernardin
Le Marias
Les Célébrités
Limoncello
Los Dos Rancheros
Mangia
Manhattan Chili Company
Manhattan Ocean Club
Mars 2112
Menchanko-Tei
Michael's
Molyvos
Motown Café
Oshi Noodle
Orso
Osteria del Circo
Palio
Patsy's
Petrossian
Planet Hollywood
The Rainbow Room
Raphaël
The Redeye Grill
Remi
René Pujol
Russian Samovar
Sam's
San Domenico
Sardi's
Savories
The Seagrill
Shaan
Soup Kitchen International
Stage Deli
Tapika
Torre Di Pisa
21 Club
Uncle Nick's
Virgil's Real Barbecue
Wells Restaurant
Zen Palate

UPPER EAST SIDE

Across the Street
Atlantic Grill
Aureole
Barking Dog Luncheonette
Bolivar
Busby's
Butterfield 81

Café Boulud
Café Crocodile
Café M
Café Pierre
Caffè Buon Gusto
Candle Café
The Carlyle Restaurant
Coco Pazzo
Contrapunto
Demarchelier
Destinée
E.A.T.
El Pollo
Elaine's
Eli's
Emily's
Erminia
Etats-Unis
Ferrier
Fred's
Gertrude's
Harry Cipriani
Hyotan-Nippon
Il Valetto
Island
Jo Jo
L'Absinthe
La Fourchette
La Goulue
Le Refuge
Le Régence
Le Veau d'Or
Lenox Room
The Library
The Lobster Club
Luca
Lusardi's
Mark's Restaurant
Match Uptown
Matthew's
Maya
Mazzei
Mezzaluna
Nino's
Pamir
Paola's Restaurant
Papaya King
Parioli Romanissimo
Park Avenue Café
Park View at the Boathouse
Patsy's Pizza
Payard Patisserie & Bistro
The Pembroke Room

Peppermint Park
Petaluma
Pig Heaven
Portico
The Post House
Primavera
Primola
Quatorze Bix
Rao's
Restaurant Daniel
Sable's Smoked Fish
Sant Ambroeus
Serafina Fabulous Grill
Serafina Fabulous Pizza
Serendipity 3
Siegel's Kosher Deli &
    Restaurant
Silver Star Restaurant
Sistina
Steak au Poivre
Sylvia's Restaurant
Syrah
Taco Taco
Totonno's
Trois Jean
Uzie & Marco's
The Vinegar Factory
Wilkinson's Restaurant

UPPER WEST SIDE

Absolute Bagels
All State Café
Baci
Barney Greengrass
Baskin-Robbins
Blue Nile
Café Con Leche
Café des Artistes
Café La Fortuna
Café Luxembourg
Caridad
Carmine's
Columbia Hot Bagels
Copeland's
Citrus Bar & Grill
Dallas B-B-Q
Edgar's
EJ's Luncheonette
Fine & Schapiro
Gabriel's
Gray's Papaya
Jackson Hole

Jean Georges
Josie's
La Boîte en Bois
La Mirabelle
La Nueva Victoria
Merchant's NY
Merlot Bar & Grill
Metisse
Mingala West
Monsoon
Penang West
Picholine
Rain
Restaurant 222
Sarabeth's
Tavern on the Green
Terrace
Tibet Shambala
Vince & Eddie's
Westside Brewing Companay

THE BRONX

Ann & Tony's
Café al Mercato
Café Sevilla
Catania's Pizza Café
Cosenza's Fish Market
Dominick's
Edgio's Bakery
Il Boschetto
Jimmy's Bronx Café
Johnny's Reef
The Lobster Box
Mario's
School Bux
Tito Pente's
Traditional Irish
    Bakery/The Snug
    Restaurant

BROOKLYN

Acadia Parish Cajun Café
Abbracciamento on the Pier
Bam Café
Bourda Green Bakery &
    Restaurant
Brawta Caribbean Café
Cambodian Cuisine
Camillel's Clover Hill
Carolina Country Kitchen
Castillos

Chez Nic
Cucina
Fountain Café
Gage & Tollner
Garden Café
Gargiulo's
The Gate
Grimaldi's
Henry's End
Java Indonesian Rijsttafel
Joloff
Junior's
Kalio
Keur N'Deye
La Bouillabaisse
La Taquería
Lemongrass Grill
Lento's
Lundy Bros.
Marco Polo
Max & Moritz
The McCafé
Mezcal's
Mike & Tony's
Monte's Venetian Room
Moustache–Brooklyn
Mrs. Stahl's Knishes
Mugs Ale House
New City Café
New Prospect Café
Northside Café
Nyonya
Odessa
Olive Vine
Oznot's Dish
Park Slope Brewing
    Company
Peter Luger
Peter's Ice Cream Parlor &
    Coffee Shop
Pete's Downtown
Plan Eat Thai
Polska
Queen
Randazzo's Clam Bar
Rasputin
The Red Rose
The River Café
Sybil's
Tom's Restaurant
Totonno's
Thai Taste
Tommaso's

Two Boots
Two Tom's
Walid Demis Moustache
Pitza

QUEENS

Benfaremo, The Lemon Ice
    King of Corona
Cabana
David's Taiwanese Gourmet
Delhi Palace
El Portrero
El Sitio
Elias Corner
Gianni's Ristorante
Golden Monkey
Goody's
Izalco
Jackson Diner
Jade Palace
Jai-Ya Thai
Joe's Shanghai
Karyatis
K.B. Garden Restaurant
Kum Gang San
La Cabaña Argentina
La Picada Azuaya
London Lennie's
Manducatis
Mi Colombia
O Lavrador
Penang Cuisine Malaysia
Pier 25A
Rizzo's
Sandy's Roti Shop
Shamiana Restaurant
Speengar Shish Kebab
    House
Tierras Colombianas
Uncle George's
Waterfront Crab House
Water's Edge
Zenon

STATEN ISLAND

Adobe Blues
Aesop's Tables
Goodfellas Brick Oven Pizza
Lum Chin
Old Bermuda Inn
Trattoria Romana

INDEX

A

A New York Christmas . 299
Abbracciamento
   on the Pier. 239
Absolute Bagels. 183
Acadia Parish Cajun
   Café 239
Acquario. 44
Across the Street. 152
Adobe Blues 271
Adrienne. 128
ADVICE & COMMENTS . 10
Aesop's Tables 271
AFGHAN CUISINE 186, 264
Afghan Kebab House . . 186
AFRICAN CUISINE 249
Agata & Valentina. 223
Aggie's 179
Akbar 89
Al Bustan. 89
Alison on Dominick 19
All State Café 171
American Festival Café . 128
American Institute of
   Wine & Food Gala . 297
American Park. 19
American Southwest/
   Asian 187
American Wine Appreciation
   Week. 297
Amy's Bread 221, 225
An American Place 67
Andalousia 204
Angelica Kitchen. 217
Anglers & Writers 175
Ann & Tony's. 234
Annual Cookbook Sale . 297
Aquagrill. 19
Aquavit. 111
ARGENTINEAN CUISINE 187

Ariana Afghan Kebab . . 187
Arqua 20
Arturo's 211
Asia de Cuba. 67
Astor Restaurant
   & Lounge 47
Atlantic Grill. 131
Au Troquet. 47
Aureole. 131
Autumn Gourmet Gala . 299

B

B Bar 44
B. Frites 188
B. Smith's. 111
Babbo. 47
Baci 155
BAKERIES 225
BAKERY CAFÉS . . . 164, 235
Balducci's 220
Balthazar Bakery 20
Balthazar Restaurant 20
BAM Café. 248
Bambou Restaurant
   & Bar 68
Bar Cichetti 20
Bar Pitti 48
Bar Six 48
BARBECUE 167
Barbetta 111
The Barclay Bar & Grill. 109
Barking Dog
   Luncheonette 180
Barnes & Nobles. 175
Barney Greengrass 184
Barocco 21
Barolo. 21

BARS, SALOONS
    & BREWPUBS 247
BARS, SALOONS
    & TAVERNS 169
Baskin-Robbins. 208
Basta Pasta 68
Bay Leaf Brasserie 128
Bayard's 44
Becco 112
Beer Bar 90
BELGIAN CUISINE 188
Bell Caffè 175
Bellini. 89
BELOW HOUSTON 18
Ben & Jerry's 208
Ben Benson's
    Steak House 112
Bendix Diner 180
Benfaremo, The Lemon Ice
    King of Corona 267
Benny's Burritos 200
Bice 90
THE BIG NOSH 164
Big Wong 190
Blanche's Organic Café . 217
Bleecker Street Pastry
    & Café 164
BLENDS 284
Blue Nile 155
Blue Ribbon 21
Blue Ribbon Sushi . . . 21-22
Blue Water Grill 68
Bobby Van's Steakhouse 109
Boca Chica 48
Bolivar 131
Bolo 68
Bond Street 22
Boom Restaurant 22
Bop 49
Bottino 69
Bouley Bakery 225
Bouley Bakery
    Restaurant 22
Bourda Green Bakery &
    Restaurant 249
Bouterin 90
The Box Tree 109
BP Café 69
Brawta Caribbean Café . 239
Bread & Butter 180
BREWPUBS 170
Bridge Café. 23
Bright Food Shop 187
Briscola. 49
BRITISH CUISINE 188
THE BRONX 231
BROOKLYN 237

Brooklyn Diner 214
Brothers Bar-B-Que . . . 167
Bryant Park Grill 69
The Bubble Lounge 45
BURGERS, DOGS & CHILI. . 171
Busby's 132
Butterfield 81 132

C

Cabana 259
Cabana Carioca 112
CABERNET SAUVIGNON 292
Café Adriana 109
Café al Mercato 236
Café Borgia 176
Café Boulud 132
Café Centro 90
Café Con Leche 201
Café Crocodile 133
Café de Bruxelles 49
Café des Artistes 155
Café Edison 180
Café Español. 206
Café Europa 176
Café Firebird. 115
Café La Fortuna 176
Café Loup. 50
Café Luxembourg 156
Café M 152
Café Nicole. 112
Café Pierre 133
Café Reggio 177
Café Sevilla 233
CAFÉS & COFFEE SHOPS . . 248
CAFÉS & COFFEEHOUSES . 175
Cafeteria 69
Caffè Buon Gusto 195
Caffè Dante 177
Caffè del Corso. 129
Caffè della Pace. 177
Caffè Rosso. 50
Caffè Tina 177
CAJUN CUISINE 189
Cal's 70
CAMBODIAN CUISINE . 249
Camille's Clover Hill. . . 255
Campagna 70, 221
Campagna Home 221
Can 23
Candle Café 217
Canton 23
Capsouto Frères 24
CARIBBEAN 189, 264
CARIBBEAN &
    LATIN AMERICAN . . 249

Caridad. 189
The Carlyle Restaurant . 134
Carmine's. 195
Carnegie Delicatessen . . 184
Carolina Country
    Kitchen 254
Casa Adela 189
Casa La Femme 24
Castillos 250
Catania's Pizza Café . . . 236
CAVIAR. 226
Caviar Bar. 226
Caviar Russe 110
Caviarteria 226
Caviarteria Champagne
    Caviar Bar 45
Cedars of Lebanon 70
Celebrities in the
    Kitchen 11
Cellini. 91
Cena. 71
Cent'Anni. 50
CENTRAL & SOUTH
    AMERICAN COFFEES284
Chai Salon 89
Chantale's Cajun
    Kitchen 189
Chanterelle. 24
Chao Chow 204
CHARDONNAY 294
Chateaubriand 113
CHEESE & PASTA 226
Chefs & Champagne, the
    Hamptons 299
Chelsea Bistro & Bar. . . . 71
Chelsea Brewing
    Company. 170
Chelsea Market. 221
Chelsea Trattoria. 71
Chestnut Room 160
Chez es Saada 50
Chez Jacqueline 51
Chez Ma Tante 51
Chez Nic 239
Chikubu. 91
Chin Chin. 91
China Grill 113
Chinatown Ice Cream
    Factory 209
Chinese New Year. 297
CHINESE/
    DIM SUM 190, 264
CHOCOLATES. 227
Christer's 113
Churrascaria Plataforma 114
Cibo. 72
Cigar Room at Trumpets 92

Cipriani Wall Street 25
Cité 114
Cité Grill 114
Citrus Bar & Grill 156
City Crab & Seafood
    Company. 72
City Hall 25
City Wine & Cigar
    Company. 25
Clementine. 51
Coco Pazzo 134
The Coffee Mug 181
COFFEE SAVVY 283
COFFEE SHOP 181
COFFEE SHOPS & DINERS . 179
THE COFFEEHOUSE FOR
    THE NINETIES 283
Cola's 195
Columbia Hot Bagels . . 184
Columbus Avenue
    Festival 299
The Comfort Diner. . . . 181
Commodities 229
Cones. 209
Contrapunto. 134
Copeland's 205
Corner Bistro 172
Cosenza's Fish Market . 234
Coup 52
Crystal Room 160
Cub Room 26
CUBAN-CHINESE CUISINE. 193
Cucina 240
Cucina Stagionale 195
Cuisine de Saigon 52
Culinary Pas de Deux . . 299
Cupcake Café 164
Curry in a Hurry. 194
Custard Beach. 209
Cyclo 52

D

Da Silvano Restaurant . . . 53
Da Umberto. 72
Dallas B-B-Q 168
Dalton 175
Danal 64, 213
DARK ROASTS 284
David's Taiwanese
    Gourmet 263
Dawat. 92
Dean & DeLuca 221
Dean & Deluca Café. . . 178
DECAFFEINATED COFFEE . 285
Delhi Palace 265

DELI & SMOKED FISH . 228
Delícia 53
Delis. 248
DELIS & BAGEL SHOPS 183
Delta Grill. 114
Demarchelier 134
Destineé 135
Dine-Around
    Downtown 299
Diva 26
Dok Suni's 198
Dominican Cuisine 235
Dominick's 233
Downtown 26
Drovers Tap Room 56
Duane Park Café. 26
Duke's 168

E

E.A.T. 165
Ear Inn 169
EAST AFRICAN COFFEES 284
East Village
    Meat Market 223
EATING THE BIG APPLE. . 5
EatZi's Market
    & Bakery. 165
Ecce Panis. 225
Edgar's 165
Egidio's Bakery. 235
Eighteenth & Eighth . . . 73
Eighth Annual Windows
    on Long Island 298
EJ's Luncheonette 182
El Faro 53
El Pollo 201
El Potrero. 266
El Rincon de España. . . . 53
El Sitio 264
El Sombrero 201
El Teddy's. 45
Elaine's. 152
Elephant & Castle. 169
Eleven Madison Park . . . 73
Eli's 135
Elias Corner 263
Emily's 135
Empanada Oven 201
Empire Diner 182
Empire Korea 198
Ennio & Michael's
    Restaurant. 54
Erminia. 136
Eros 92
Ess-A-Bagel 184, 199

Estiatorio Milos 115
Etats-Unis. 136
ETHNIC FLAIR. 186, 249, 264
ETHNIC MARKETS 223
Evergreen Shanghai
    Restaurant. 190

F

F.illi Ponte Ristorante . . . 27
Fairway Market. 221
Famous Ben's Pizza
    of SoHo 211
Fanelli's 169
Fantino. 115
Fat Wich. 221
Feast of St. Anthony . . . 298
Felidia Ristorante 93
Félix 27
Ferrier. 136
Fifty Seven Fifty Seven . . 93
FINE & RARE WINE
    AUCTION 299
Fine & Schapiro . . 185, 200
Fino 73
Firebird. 115
Flea Market. 54
Florent 54
Flowers. 74
Flute. 129
Follonico 74
FOOD & WINE EVENTS 297
FOOD & WINE PAIRINGS. . 300
Foods of India 223
"44". 116
Fountain Café. 252
Four Seasons. 93
The 14 Wall Street
    Restaurant. 27
14th Street to
    42nd Street 67
Frank's Restaurant 74
Fred's 152
Fresco by Scotto 94
Frico Bar Restaurant . . . 129
Friend of a Farmer 166
Frontière. 28
FUSION OR CONFUSION? 10

G

Gabriel's 156
Gage & Tollner. 240
Gallagher's 116

Garage 65
Garden Café 240
Gargiulo's 241
Gasgogne 74
The Gate 247
Gemelli 28
Gemelli Mare 28
Gertrude's 137
Gewürztraminer 294
Ghenet 28
Gianni's Ristorante 259
GLOSSARIES & RESTAURANT
    INDEXES 273
Glossary of Coffee
    Tasting Terms 285
GLOSSARY OF GRAPES . 292
GLOSSARY OF SPECIALTY
    COFFEE DRINKS . . . 286
GLOSSARY OF WINE
    TASTING TERMS . . . 291
Golden Monkey 259
Golden Unicorn 190
Goodfellas Brick
    Oven Pizza 272
Goody's 259
Gotham Bar & Grill 55
Gourmet Garage 222
GOURMET MARKETS
    & MORE 219-220
Gramercy Tavern 75
Grand Gourmet
    Luncheon 299
The Grange Hall 55
Gray's Papaya 172
GREEK CUISINE . . 193, 265
GREENMARKETS 229
Greenwich Pizza &
    Brewing Company . . 171
GREENWICH VILLAGE &
    ENVIRONS 47
Grimaldi's 255
GUIDE TO NEW YORK
    REGIONS 289
Guss Pickles 228

Hatsuhana 94
Health/Organic Foods . 229
Healthy Cuisine 255
Heartbeat 94
Heartland Brewery 171
Henry's End 241
Home 56
Honmura An 29
HOW MUCH IS ENOUGH? . . 12
Hudson River Club 29
Hyotan-Nippon 137

I

I Coppi 56
I Tre Merli 30
I Trulli 75
Ice Carving Exhibition . 297
ICE CREAM
    & MORE . 208, 255, 267
Il Bagatto 56
Il Boschetto 234
Il Buco 56
Il Cantinori 57
Il Mulino 57
Il Nido 95
Il Valletto 137
Inagiku 95
Independent 29
Indian Cuisine . . . 194, 265
Indigo 65
Indochine 57
INDONESIAN CUISINE . 251
INDONESIAN COFFEES . 284
International Beer &
    Food Festival 297
International Wine Fair . 298
Iridium Jazz Club 161
Island 153
Istana 95
Italian
    Cuisine . . 195, 236, 251
Italian Food Center 223
Izalco 266

H

Häagen-Dazs 209
Halcyon 116
Hale & Hearty Soups . . 221
Han Bat 199
Hangawi 87
Hard Rock Café 215
Harley Davidson Café . . 215
Harry Cipriani 137
Hasaki 55

J

Jackson Diner 266
Jackson Hole 172
Jade Palace 260
Jai-Ya Thai 206, 260
James Beard Annual
    Holiday Auction &
    Dinner 299

The James Beard
Awards 298
The James Beard
Foundation Annual
Festival 298
James Beard Foundation
Cookbook Expo . . . 298
James Beard's Birthday
Dinner. 298
Japanese Cuisine 197
Java Indonesian
Rijsttafel 251
Jean Georges. 157
Jean-Claude 30
Jekyll & Hyde. 215
The Jekyll & Hyde
Club 215
Jerry's. 30
Jewel of India 117
Jezebel 117
Jimmy's Bronx Café . . . 234
Jo Jo. 138
Joe's Pizza 211
Joe's Shanghai . . . 191, 264
John's. 211
Johnny's Reef 236
Joloff 249
Jones Diner. 182
Josie's. 161
JUdson Grill 117
Jules 58
Junior's. 248
JUST HOW DRESSY IS
DRESSY? 11

K

K.B. Garden Restaurant 265
Kalio. 241
Kam Chueh 191
Kam Man Foods 224
Kang Suh Restaurant. . . 199
Karyatis. 263
Katagiri. 224
Kate's Joint. 217
Katz's Deli 185
Keen's. 76
Keur N'Deye 249
Kids Sports Cook-Fest . 297
Kiev 182
Kin Khao 30
KK Polish-American . . . 205
Kokachin 96
KOREAN CUISINE 198
KOSHER. 199
KPNY (Ken's Place New

York) 58
Kum Gang San 76, 260
Kuruma Zushi. 96

L

L'Absinthe 138
L'Acajou. 76
L'Orange Bleue 32
L-Ray 59
La Bohème 65
La Boîte en Bois 158
La Bonne Soupe Bistro . 176
La Bouillabaisse 241
La Boulangère 166
La Cabaña Argentina. . . 260
La Caravelle 118
La Chinita Linda. 193
La Colombe d'Or 76
La Côte Basque. 118
La Focacceria 196
La Fourchette 138
La Goulue. 139
La Grenouille 96
La Maison du Chocolat. 227
La Métairie 58
La Mirabelle 158
La Nueva Victoria 193
La Picada Azuaya 267
La Pizza Fresca 77
La Réserve 118
La Ripaille. 58
La Taquería. 250
La Vineria. 129
Lamarca Cheese Shop &
Restaurant 178
LATIN AMERICAN CUISINE 266
Layla. 31
Le Bernardin. 119
Le Cirque 2000 97
Le Colonial. 97
Le Madri. 77
Le Marais 119
Le Périgord. 98
Le Pescadou 31
Le Refuge 139
Le Régence 140
Le Solex 77
Le Tableau 59
Le Veau d'Or 140
Le Zoo Restaurant 59
Lemon 78
Lemongrass Grill. 241
Lenox Room. 140
Lento's. 256
Les Célébrités 120

Les Halles 78
Lespinasse 98
Liam 31
The Library 153
Life Café 182
Likitsakos 224
Limoncello 120
The Lobster Box 235
The Lobster Club 141
The Lobster Place 221
Lola 78
London Lennie's 261
Los Dos Rancheros 202
The Lotus Club 178
Luca 153
Lucky Cheng 60
Lucky Strike 32
Lum Chin 272
Lundy Bros. 242
Lusardi's 141
Lutèce 98

M

Ma Ma Buddha 191
Mad 28 79
Malaysia Restaurant . . . 200
MALAYSIAN 200, 252
Maloney & Porcelli 99
Mama's Food Shop 205
Mandalay Kitchen 32
Mandarin Court 191
Manducatis 261
Manganaro's Hero Boy
    Restaurant 196
Manganaros Gourmet
    Foods 196
Mangia 120
Manhattan Chili
    Company 172
The Manhattan Fruit
    Exchange 221
Manhattan Ocean Club . 121
MANHATTAN TO GO . . 220
MANHATTANDINING . . . 17
MANHATTANQUICK BITES . 163
Mappamondo (Due) . . . 196
Mappamondo (Uno) . . . 196
March Restaurant 99
Marco Polo 242
Mario's 233
Mark's Restaurant 141
Mars 2112 216
Mary Ann's 202
Match Downtown 32
Match Uptown 142

Matthew's 142
Mavalli Palace 79
Max & Moritz 242
Maya 142
Mazzei 143
The McCafé 254
McDonald's 173
McSorley's
    Old Ale House 169
Mee Noodle Shop 192
Meet the Tastemakers . . 298
Mekka 65
Melampo Imported
    Foods 197
Menchanko-Tei 197
MENU SAVVY 274
Mercer Kitchen 33
Merchant's NY 158
Merlot 293
Merlot Bar & Grill 161
Mesa Grill 79
Mesopotamia 60
Metisse 162
MEXICAN &
    LATIN AMERICAN . . 200
Mexicana Marna 202
Mezcal's 250
Mezzaluna 143
Mezzogiorno 33
Mi Cocina 60
Mi Colombia 261
Michael Jordan's The
    Steak House NYC . . 100
Michael's 121
Middle Eastern
    Cuisine 203, 252
MIDTOWN EAST 89
MIDTOWN WEST 111
Mie 61
Mike & Tony's 242
Mingala West 159
Minter's Ice Cream
    Kitchen 210
Miracle Grill 61
Mistral Terrace 158
Mitali East 194
Mitali West 194
Molyvos 121
Mom's Bagels
    & Catering 185
Mom's Bagels & Tables 200
Monkey Bar 100
Mono 61
Monsoon 207
Monte's Venetian Room 243
Montrachet 34
Monzù 34

Moomba. 62
Moreno Ristorante 80
Moroccan Cuisine. 204
Morton's of
    Chicago. 34, 100
Motown Café 216
Moustache—Brooklyn . 252
Mr. K's 101
Mrs. Stahl's Knishes . . . 248
Mugs Ale House. 247
Murray's Cheese Shop . 226
Myers of Keswick 224

N

Naples 45 101
Nathan's Famous 173
Navia's Diner 218
Negril Island Spice . . . 190
Neuchatel Chocolates . . 227
New City Café 243
New Prospect Café 243
New World Coffee
    & Bagels 175
New York Noodletown . 192
New York's Neighbors:
    Good & Getting
    Better 288
Next Door Nobu 35
Nha Trang 207
The Nice Restaurant 35
Nino's. 143
Ninth Avenue International
    Food Festival. 298
Nippon. 101
Nobu 35
Northside Café 251
Nougatine Café. 158
Novitá 80
Novocento 175
Nyonya. 252

O

O Lavrador. 261
Oceana 102
The Odéon. 36
Odessa 243
Oishi Noodle 198
Old Bermuda Inn 272
Old Devil Moon 205
Old Homestead
    Restaurant. 80
Old Town Bar. 170

Olive Vine 253
Ollie's Noodle Shop
    & Grille. 192
Omen. 36
ON MENUS 11
One If By Land, Two If
    By Sea 66
Oriental Pearl 36
THE ORIGINS OF THE
    COFFEE CRAZE. . . . 283
Orologio. 197
Orso 122
Osteria del Circo. 122
OUR RESTAURANT RATING
    SYSTEM 8
Oyster Bar &
    Restaurant. 102
Oznot's Dish 244

P

Paggio 36
Palio. 122
Palm Two 103
The Palm 102
Pamir 103, 144
PAN-ASIAN 204
Panchito's. 202
Panya 166
Paola's Restaurant. 144
Papaya King 173
Paper Moon 103
Paper Moon Express . . . 103
Paramount Hotel 178
Parioli Romanissimo . . . 144
Park Avalon 81
Park Avenue Café 145
Park Bistro 81
Park Slope Brewing
    Company. 247
Park View at the
    Boathouse 145
The Park. 103
Parlour Café 178
Pasqua 175
Passage to India 194
Pastabreak. 28
Patria 81
Patroon 104
Patsy's. 123
Patsy's Pizza 212
Payard Patisserie
    & Bistro 145, 226
Peacock Alley 104
Pearl Oyster Bar 37
Peligrinos 37

The Pembroke Room . . 153
Penang Cuisine
   Malaysia 262
Penang SoHo 45
Penang West 162
Peppermint Park 210
Periyali 81
Petaluma 146
Pete's Downtown 245
Peter Luger 244
Peter's Ice Cream Parlor
   & Coffee House . . . 255
Petite Abeille 188
Petrossian 123, 226
Piadina 62
Picholine 159
Picnic 183
Pier 25A 263
Pig Heaven 146
PINOT NOIR 293
Pitchoune 87
PIZZA . . 211, 236, 255, 267
Plan Eat Thai 254
Planet Hollywood 216
Pò 62
POLISH 205, 253
Polska 253
Pommes Frites 188
Portico 146
Post House 147
Pravda 37
Primavera 147
The Prime Burger 174
Primola 147
Promise of the
   Empire State 287
Provence 37

Q
Quatorze Bis 148
Queen 245
QUEENS 257
Quilty's 38

R
Radio Mexico Café 46
Raffetto's 227
Raga 63
Rain 162
The Rainbow Room . . . 123
Randazzo's Clam Bar . . 251

Rao's 148
Raoul's 38
Raphaël 123
Rasputin 246
The Ravioli Store 227
Ray's of Greenwich
   Village 212
The Red Rose 252
Red Wine Varietals . . . 292
The Redeye Grill 124
Remi 124
René Pujol 124
Republic 204
Restaurant 222 159
Restaurant 147 82
RESTAURANT CATEGORIES 8
Restaurant Daniel . . 12, 148
Restaurant Day,
   June 18 298
RESTAURANT EQ 63
RESTAURANT INDEXES 312
Restaurant Week,
   June 21-26 298
RESTAURANTS BY CUISINE. 312
RESTAURANTS BY NOTABLE
   FEATURES 323
RESTAURANTS BY AREA 328
Restivo Ristorante 82
Rialto 39
Richart Design
   et Chocolat 227
RIESLING 294
The River Café 245
Rizzo's 267
Rocco Pastry Shop 166
Rocking Horse Café
   Mexicano 82
Ronnybrook Farm
   Dairy 221
Rosa Mexicano 105
Rosemarie's 39
Rotunda 133
Russ and Daughters . . . 228
Russian Samovar 125
Ruth's Chris Steakhouse 105
Ruthy's Cheesecake 221

S
S.P.Q.R. 40
Sable's Smoked Fish . . . 185
Sakagura 110
Salam 203-204
Salient 39
Salumeria Biellese 197
Sam's 129

Sammy's Roumanian
    Steakhouse 39
Sample Review 12
San Domenico 125
San Gennaro Festival. . . 299
San Giusto 105
Sandy's Roti Shop. 264
Sant Ambroeus . . . 149, 210
Sarabeth's 167
Sardi's. 125
Sarge's 229
Sassy's Sliders 174
SAUVIGNON BLANC. . . 295
Savories. 179
Savoy 40
Scarabée 105
School Bus 235
The Screening Room . . . 46
Seafood. 236
The SeaGrill 125
Seasonal Food Tips 297
Second Avenue
    Kosher Deli . . . 186, 200
SECOND-HAND SMOKE . 11
Serafina Fabulous Grill . 154
Serafina Fabulous Pizza. 212
Serendipity 3. 210
Seryna. 106
Shaan 126
Shaffer City Oyster
    Bar & Grill 83
Shamiana Restaurant. . . 266
Shun Lee Palace 106
Siegel's Kosher Deli
    & Restaurant. 200
Siena. 83
Silver Spurs 174
Silver Star Restaurant . . 183
Sistina. 149
69 Mott Street 193
Sky Grille 160
The Slaughtered
    Lamb Pub 216
Smith & Wollensky 107
SO FRESH,
    IT'S STILL SWIMMING 12
Sobaya 198
SoHo Kitchen & Bar. . . . 46
Sonia Rose 83
Sorrento 40
Sorrento Coffee Shop . . 174
Sosa Borella 187
Souen 218
Soul Fixins'. 206
SOUL FOOD 254
SOUL FOOD/SOUTHERN . . 205
SOUP 213

Soup Kitchen
    International 213
SPANISH CUISINE 206
SPARKLING WINES 295
Sparks Steakhouse. 107
Speengar Shish
    Kebab House. 264
Spy 46
Squeeze Lounge 156
Stage Deli 186
Starbucks 175, 283
STATEN ISLAND 269
Steak Au Poivre. 154
Steak Frites 84
StepMama. 205
Sud. 66
SUMMER IN THE CITY . . 12
Surya 66
Sushi Bar 107
Sushisay 107
Sybil's 250
Sylvia's Restaurant. 150
Syrah 150, 293

T

Tabla 84
Taco Taco. 203
Tai Hong Lau 41
Takashimaya Teabox
    Café 214
Taliesin 41
Taormina 41
Tapika. 126
Taste of Times Square . . 298
Tatou 108
Tavern on the Green . . . 160
Tea & Sympathy 214
TEA ROOMS
    & PÂTISSERIES 213
Telephone Bar & Grill. . 188
Terrace 160
Teuscher Chocolates of
    Switzerland 228
THAI CUISINE . . . 206, 254
Thai Taste. 254
Thailand Restaurant . . . 41
THAT'S MY CAR! 11
THEME RESTAURANTS. 214
Tibet Shambala 207
Tibetan Cuisine. 207
Tierras Colombianas . . . 262
Timothy's 175
Tito Puente's 233
Tom's Restaurant 248

Tommaso's 246
The Tonic. 84
TOQUE TALLY 13
THE TOQUE, CIRCA 170013
Torre di Pisa 126
Totonno's 212, 256
Traditional Irish Bakery/
    The Snug Irish
    Restaurant 235
Trattoria Romana 271
Trattoria Venti Trè 42
Treehouse. 63
TriBakery 167
TriBeCa Grill 42
Trois Canards 85
Trois Jean 150
Tropica. 110
Trumpets Restaurant. . . . 92
Tsampa. 207
Tupelo Grill 85
Turkish Grill 203
Turkish Kitchen 85
20 Mott Street
    Restaurant. 42
"21" Club 127
27 Standard/The Jazz
    Standard 85
Two Boots 212, 256
Two Tom's 246
Typhoon Brewery 110

Uncle George's 265
Uncle Nick's. 193
Union Pacific 86
Union Square 229
Union Square Café 86
UPPER EAST SIDE 131
UPPER WEST SIDE 155
USING OUR RATING
    SYSTEM 8
Uzie & Marco's 154

Veggie/Organic 217
Veniero's. 167
Verbena 87
Veritas. 87
Veselka 183
Vietnam 208
VIETNAMESE CUISINE . 207
Vince and Eddie's 161

Vincent's Restaurant 43
Vinegar
    Factory . . 151, 179, 222
VINTAGE WINE CHART 296
Virgil's Real Barbecue . . 168
Vong. 108

Walid Demis Moustache
    Pitza 253
Water Savvy 304
Water's Edge. 262
Waterfront Crab House. 263
Waterloo. 64
Wells Restaurant 206
Westside Brewing
    Company. 171
White Horse Tavern . . . 170
WhiteWine Varietals . . . 294
Whole Wheat 'n'
    Wild Berrys 218
Wilkinson's Restaurant . 151
Windows on the World . . 43
Wine & Spirits Education
    Courses 297
WINE OF THE NORTHEAST
    REGION: BEYOND
    TRADITION. 287
WINE SAVVY. 287
WINE TOURING
    NEW YORK 290
Won Jo Korean-Japanese
    Restaurant 199
Wong Kee. 43
Woo Chon 87
THE WORLD OF
    COFFEE. 284

Ye Waverly Inn 64
Yonah Schimmel 229

Zabar's 222
Zarela 108
Zen Palate. 127
Zenon. 262
Zinfandel 293
Zoë. 43

GAYOT PUBLICATIONS

on the Internet

GAYOT PUBLICATIONS/GAULTMILLAU IS PROUD
TO FEATURE RESTAURANT, HOTEL AND
TRAVEL INFORMATION FROM OUR BOOKS AND
UPDATES ON MANY INTERNET WEB SITES.

We suggest you start surfing at:
http://www.gayot.com

*We welcome your questions and comments
at our e-mail address:*
gayots@aol.com

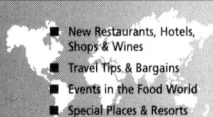

GAYOT PUBLICATIONS

**GAYOT PUBLICATIONS GUIDES ARE AVAILABLE
AT ALL FINE BOOKSTORES WORLDWIDE.**

**INTERNATIONAL DISTRIBUTION IS
COORDINATED BY THE FOLLOWING OFFICES:**

MAINLAND U.S.
Publishers Group West
1700 Fourth St.
Berkeley, CA 94710
(800) 788-3123
Fax (510) 528-3444

CANADA
Publishers Group West
543 Richmond St. West
Suite 223, Box 106
Toronto, Ontario
M5V 146 CANADA
(416) 504-3900
Fax (416) 504-3902

HAWAII
Island Heritage
99-880 Iwaena
Aiea, HI 96701
(800) 468-2800
Fax (808) 488-2279

AUSTRALIA
Little Hills Press Pty. Ltd.
Regent House,
37-43 Alexander St.
Crows Nest (Sydney)
NSW 2065 Australia
(02) 437-6995
Fax (02) 438-5762

TAIWAN
Central Book Publishing
2nd Floor, 141, Section 1
Chungking South Rd.
Taipei, Taiwan R.O.C.
(02) 331-5726
Fax (02) 331-1316

HONG KONG & CHINA
Pacific Century
Distribution Ltd.
G/F No. 2-4
Lower Kai Yuen Ln.
North Point, Hong Kong
(852) 2811-5505
Fax (852) 2565-8624

UK & EUROPE
World Leisure Marketing
Unit 11, Newmarket Court
Newmarket Drive
Derby DE24 8NW
(01332) 573737
Fax (01332) 573399

FRANCE
GaultMillau, Inc.
01.48.08.00.38
Fax 01.43.65.46.62

SOUTH AFRICA
Faradawn C.C.
P.O. Box 1903
Saxonwold 2132
Republic of South Africa
(11) 885-1787
Fax (11) 885-1829

TO ORDER THE GUIDES FOR GIFTS,
CUSTOM EDITIONS OR CORPORATE SALES
IN THE U.S., CALL OUR TOLL-FREE LINE.

**ORDER TOLL-FREE
1 (800) LE BEST 1**

NYCRESTAURANTS

We wish

to thank

our

generous

sponsors

for their

invaluable

contributions

which

made this

book

possible

- **Broadbent Selections**
  www.broadbent-wines.com
- **De Ladoucette**
- **Forbes**
  www.forbes.com
- **The James Beard Foundation**
  www.jamesbeard.org
- **L'Annuaire Francais de New York**
- **La Cucina Italiana**
  www.piacere.com
- **The Mark**
  www.themarkhotel.com
- **Masterplanner**
- **Meridian Vineyards**
  www.meridianvineyards.com
- **Perrier**
  www.perrier.com
- **Ramos-Pinto**
- **Roederer Champagne**
- **The Underground Wine Journal**
- **Vittel**
- **Windward Vineyards**
  www.windwardvineyard.com
- **Woltner Estates**
- **Zone Vodka**
  www.zonevodka.com